T0339838

Demand for Emerging Transportation Systems

Demand for Emerging Transportation Systems

Modeling Adoption, Satisfaction, and Mobility Patterns

Constantinos Antoniou
Chair of Transportation Systems Engineering,
Technical University of Munich, Munich, Germany

Dimitrios Efthymiou
Chair of Transportation Systems Engineering,
Technical University of Munich, Munich, Germany

Emmanouil Chaniotakis
Bartlett School of Environment, Energy and Resources,
University College London (UCL), London, United Kingdom

ELSEVIER

Elsevier
Radarweg 29, PO Box 211, 1000 AE Amsterdam, Netherlands
The Boulevard, Langford Lane, Kidlington, Oxford OX5 1GB, United Kingdom
50 Hampshire Street, 5th Floor, Cambridge, MA 02139, United States

Notices
Knowledge and best practice in this field are constantly changing. As new research and experience broaden our understanding, changes in research methods, professional practices, or medical treatment may become necessary.

Practitioners and researchers must always rely on their own experience and knowledge in evaluating and using any information, methods, compounds, or experiments described herein. In using such information or methods they should be mindful of their own safety and the safety of others, including parties for whom they have a professional responsibility.

To the fullest extent of the law, neither the Publisher nor the authors, contributors, or editors, assume any liability for any injury and/or damage to persons or property as a matter of products liability, negligence or otherwise, or from any use or operation of any methods, products, instructions, or ideas contained in the material herein.

Library of Congress Cataloging-in-Publication Data
A catalog record for this book is available from the Library of Congress

British Library Cataloguing-in-Publication Data
A catalogue record for this book is available from the British Library

ISBN: 978-0-12-815018-4

For information on all Elsevier publications visit our website at
https://www.elsevier.com/books-and-journals

Publisher: Joe Hayton
Acquisition Editor: Brian Romer
Editorial Project Manager: Andrae Akeh
Production Project Manager: Anitha Sivaraj
Cover Designer: Matthew Limbert

Typeset by TNQ Technologies

Dedication

Constantinos Antoniou:
To Mari-Elen, Maira, Harry and Cecilia

Dimitrios Efthymiou:
To Alexia and Vasilis

Emmanouil Chaniotakis:
To Irini and Zoi

Contents

Part C
Methods

Part D
Applications

11. Carsharing: An overview on what we know 211

Stefan Schmöller and Klaus Bogenberger

12. SMART mobility via prediction, optimization and personalization 227

Bilge Atasoy, Carlos Lima de Azevedo,
Arun Prakash Akkinepally, Ravi Seshadri, Fang Zhao,
Maya Abou-Zeid and Moshe Ben-Akiva

Part E
Outlook

Contributors

Maya Abou-Zeid, Department of Civil and Environmental Engineering, American University of Beirut, Lebanon

Arun Prakash Akkinepally, Department of Civil and Environmental Engineering, Massachusetts Institute of Technology, Cambridge, MA, United States

Christelle Al Haddad, Chair of Transportation Systems Engineering, Department of Civil, Geo and Environmental Engineering, Technical University of Munich, Munich, Germany

Constantinos Antoniou, Chair of Transportation Systems Engineering, Department of Civil, Geo and Environmental Engineering, Technical University of Munich, Munich, Germany

Bilge Atasoy, Department of Maritime and Transport Technology, Delft University of Technology, Delft, the Netherlands

Moshe Ben-Akiva, Department of Civil and Environmental Engineering, Massachusetts Institute of Technology, Cambridge, MA, United States

Klaus Bogenberger, Department of Civil Engineering and Environmental Sciences, Bundeswehr University Munich, Bavaria, Germany

Emmanouil Chaniotakis, Bartlett School of Environment, Energy and Resources, University College London (UCL), London, United Kingdom

Francesco Ciari, Polytechnique Montréal, Montréal, QC, Canada

Adam Cohen, Transportation Sustainability Research Center, University of California, Berkeley, CA, United States

Dimitrios Efthymiou, Chair of Transportation Systems Engineering, Department of Civil, Geo and Environmental Engineering, Technical University of Munich, Munich, Germany

Mengying Fu, Bauhaus Luftfahrt e.V., Taufkirchen, Germany

Maxim Janzen, IVT, ETH Zürich, Zürich, Switzerland

Haris N. Koutsopoulos, Department of Civil and Environmental Engineering, Northeastern University, Boston, MA, United States

Masahiro Kuwahara, Toyota Motor Corporation, Toyota, Japan

Carlos Lima de Azevedo, Department of Management Engineering, Technical University of Denmark, Lyngby, Denmark

Dimitris Milakis, Institute of Transport Research, German Aerospace Center (DLR), Berlin, Germany

Toshiyuki Nakamura, Institute of Innovation for Future Society, Nagoya University, Nagoya, Japan

Tomoki Nishigaki, Department of Urban Management, Kyoto University, Kyoto, Japan

Raoul Rothfeld, Bauhaus Luftfahrt e.V., Taufkirchen, Germany; Chair of Transportation Systems Engineering, Department of Civil, Geo and Environmental Engineering, Technical University of Munich, Munich, Germany

Jan-Dirk Schmöcker, Department of Urban Management, Kyoto University, Kyoto, Japan

Stefan Schmöller, Department of Civil Engineering and Environmental Sciences, Bundeswehr University Munich, Bavaria, Germany

Ravi Seshadri, Singapore-MIT Alliance for Research and Technology (SMART), Singapore

Susan Shaheen, Transportation Sustainability Research Center, University of California, Berkeley, CA, United States

Anna Straubinger, Bauhaus Luftfahrt e.V., Taufkirchen, Germany

Yannis Tyrinopoulos, University of West Attica, Department of Civil Engineering, Athens, Greece

Nobuhiro Uno, Department of Civil and Earth Resource Engineering, Kyoto University, Kyoto, Japan

Bert van Wee, Transport and Logistics Group, Faculty of Technology, Policy and Management, Delft University of Technology, Delft, The Netherlands

Akira Yoshioka, Toyota Motor Corporation, Toyota, Japan

Zhan Zhao, Department of Civil and Environmental Engineering, Massachusetts Institute of Technology, Cambridge, MA, United States

Jinhua Zhao, Department of Urban Studies and Planning, Massachusetts Institute of Technology, Cambridge, MA, United States

Fang Zhao, Singapore-MIT Alliance for Research and Technology (SMART), Singapore

Cezary Ziemlicki, SENSE, Orange Labs, Paris, France

About the editors

Constantinos Antoniou is a Full Professor and the Chair of Transportation Systems Engineering at the Technical University of Munich (TUM), Germany. He holds a Diploma in Civil Engineering from NTUA (1995), an MS in Transportation (1997) and a PhD in Transportation Systems (2004), both from MIT. His research focuses on big data analytics, modeling and simulation of transportation systems, intelligent transport systems (ITS), calibration and optimization applications, road safety, and sustainable transport system. In his 25 years of experience, he has held key positions in a number of research projects in Europe, the United States, and Asia, while he has also participated in a number of consulting projects. He has received numerous awards, including the 2011 IEEE ITS Outstanding Application Award. He has authored more than 350 scientific publications, including more than 110 papers in international, peer-reviewed journals (including in Transportation Research Parts A, B, and C, Transport Policy, Accident Analysis and Prevention, and Transport Geography), 240 in international conference proceedings, 3 books, and more than 20 book chapters. He is a member of several professional and scientific organizations, editorial boards (Member of the Editorial Board of Transportation Research—Parts A and C, Accident Analysis and Prevention, *Journal of Intelligent Transportation Systems*; Associate editor of *EURO Journal of Transportation and Logistics*, IET Intelligent Transportation Systems, and Transportation Letters), and committees (such as TRB committees AHB45—Traffic Flow Theory and Characteristics and ABJ70—Artificial Intelligence and Advanced Computing Applications, Steering Committee of hEART—The European Association for Research in Transportation, FGSV committee 3.10 "Theoretical fundamentals of road traffic"), and a frequent reviewer for a large number of scientific journals, scientific conferences, research proposals, and scholarships.

Dimitrios is Senior Program Manager at Amazon and Research Affiliate at TUM. Before joining Amazon, he was Postdoctoral Researcher in Transportation Systems Engineering at TUM and Senior Consultant in Data Science at Ernst & Young (EY). He holds a PhD in Transportation Systems NTUA (2014), an MSc and DIC in Transport and Business Management from Imperial College and UCL (2010), and a Diploma in Rural and Surveying Engineering from NTUA (2008). His research focuses on modeling transportation systems, demand forecasting, spatial econometric models, and machine learning in Transportation. He has been involved in consulting projects in the fields of Mobility, Banking, Telecommunications, CPG, and Shipping, and European and national research projects. He has authored more than 30 scientific publications including 19 papers in international peer-reviewed journals (including Elsevier's Transportation Research Part A: Policy and Practice, Transport Policy and Journal of Transport Geography), 29 in international conference proceedings, and 2 book chapters. He is member of several professional and scientific organizations.

Emmanouil (Manos) Chaniotakis is a Lecturer (Assistant Professor) at MaaSLab, UCL Energy Institute, University College London (UCL), United Kingdom. He holds a diploma in Rural and Surveying Engineering from Aristotle University of Thessaloniki (AUTh), an MSc degree in Transportation Infrastructure and Logistics from Delft University of Technology (TUDelft), and a PhD from Technical University of Munich (TUM). His research focuses on modeling and simulation of transportation systems, including conventional and emerging transportation systems, demand modeling, and machine learning in transportation. He has worked on numerous European and national projects in the area of transport modeling and machine learning and he has been involved in consulting projects for establishment of strategic and operational transport models, estimation of behavioral models as well as the investigation of impacts of new mobility services. He has authored more than 30 scientific publications in peer-reviewed journals, conferences, and books. He is a member of several professional and scientific organizations and a frequent reviewer for many scientific journals and conferences.

Part A

Introduction

Chapter 1

Introduction

Constantinos Antoniou[1], Emmanouil Chaniotakis[2],
Dimitrios Efthymiou[1]

[1]*Chair of Transportation Systems Engineering, Department of Civil, Geo and Environmental Engineering, Technical University of Munich, Munich, Germany;* [2]*Bartlett School of Environment, Energy and Resources, University College London (UCL), London, United Kingdom*

Chapter outline

1. Challenges of a fast-changing landscape

Mobility is one of the most important aspects of human activity, with direct and indirect implications on the life of every individual. It can be argued that mobility has been mostly stagnant for the second half of the 20th century, with cars/buses/rail and trucks/rail being the dominant modes for passenger and goods transport, respectively. Traditionally, in most places around the world, transportation have been centrally developed, coordinated, and operated primarily by local or regional authorities, reacting slowly to the changing needs. Existing data collection processes and modeling paradigms have thus been adequate in modeling and optimizing these modes, supporting policy-makers and planners in improving the quality of life and minimizing the societal impacts of mobility.

The changes we observe can be enclosed upon the "three revolutions": shared, electric, and automated. We are called to forecast the impact of these revolutions (e.g., highly automated vehicles), when the technology is not yet here, and the trajectories for transition (e.g., from a fully conventional vehicle fleet to a partly or fully automated one) to be unknown or expected to take many years, even decades. Similarly, other new modes appear (and disappear) at a blink of an eye, without prior information or notification, and—typically—with little or no regulation or coordination (at least initially). These uncertainties are not only related to the technological characteristics and the capacity of the vehicles but also to the business models that will become widespread (e.g., individually owned vs. shared). Even for specific modeling extensions (e.g., modeling autonomous vehicles' impacts), during this long transition period, the underlying conditions will be changing constantly, thus not leaving time for conventional models to "catch-up."

The situation is exacerbated when dealing with more volatile new modes. For example, Uber (a rather new phenomenon, founded 10 years ago) is currently generating 14 million trips daily,[1] while its Chinese counterpart DiDi is generating 30 million trips daily. Uber has extended its business model from single passenger trips to shared trips, while recently decided to also offer shared bicycles, scooters, and even helicopter rides (operation started in New York City in May 2019). Respectively, the oBike shared bike system flooded European cities (such as Munich and Zurich) in 2017, only to disappear in 2018, amid privacy and sidewalk-squatting complaints. Similarly, recently inaugurated shared electric bicycle systems in the northeastern US were shuttered, a few months after the start of operation, due to safety concerns. What complicates the situation even further is that, besides the nature of the modes, their funding, business model, and ownership status varies, as well, as these initiatives are typically not controlled by the authorities, but originate from private companies (ranging from start-ups to established entities like car and aircraft manufacturers). The uncertainty is also great, as many business models are tried at the same time; e.g., Airbus is developing a large number of different urban air mobility vehicles in parallel, in order to cover all possible outcomes, while Uber (and similar companies like Lyft and Grab) also explore different types of services.

Mobility of goods and people is becoming increasingly more intertwined and harder to distinguish. People and packets are increasingly considered as mixed demand patterns. Passenger and freight transport chains are getting increasingly more entangled, with the potential for synchronization and couse of infrastructure, and—thus—strong synergies and benefits. The idea is that as the same vehicles and services can serve them, an integrated transport system can emerge on both a demand and a supply side. Thus, instead of developing two parallel systems, each being underutilized for a majority of the day and/or space, we can develop systems that are complementing each other, bringing along benefits and efficiency.

Another big change that is emerging is the move from a primarily plane-based transportation system (surface, plus some underground and some elevated modes) into a really three-dimensional (3D) situation. Commercial air drones and urban air mobility (Fu et al., 2019), as well as urban aerial cableways, that see a revival of interest, e.g., in Munich, but also underground

---

1. https://www.uber.com/newsroom/company-info/.

tunnels (e.g., from Elon Musk's Boring Company) and hyperloop concepts above and below ground, respectively. This trend has the potential to increase the available capacity and foster the development of additional novel solutions, but of course makes the application of existing models very challenging.

As it is made understood, these new mobility modes are emerging (and sometimes disappearing) in a high pace. Transportation services provision is now considered a profitable business often attracting start-ups and other private companies who operate at rapid paces, with minimal warning. The aforementioned existing modeling paradigms are not sufficiently agile to respond to these rapidly changing conditions, which often propose and leverage fundamentally new concepts, such as autonomy, connectivity, sharing, and the gig-economy. These all constitute changes that require us to come up with methods that can function within an environment of radical transformation that completely changes the mobility landscape. This has immensely increased the complexity of transportation systems in terms of

1. **Design:** From a need-based design, we observe a change toward a creating needs process, where emerging modes competition and availability drives the creation of additional demand, which was not present the last few years. This has been facilitated by a number of technological drivers such as the widespread use of Information and Communication Technology (ICT). These drivers are essentially changing the potential of developing transport-related services and goods while in the same time creating new data sources to be explored.
2. **Coordination:** New actors change the traditionally followed processes of transportation system management and introduce new and possibly contradictory objectives (welfare vs. profit).
3. **Representation:** The activities of planners have been supported by a number of models, of varying characteristics, including resolution (microscopic and macroscopic, but also mesoscopic, i.e., models comprising micro- and macroscopic components), but also commercial versus open-source or general purpose versus custom. All these models shared one common attribute: rigid functional forms, making it extremely difficult to extend and adapt them to effectively incorporating the emerging modes and data. Lately, modeling of transportation systems must distinguish between different forms of private car use (e.g., carsharing, ridesharing, and ridehailing) and other emerging modes of transport (e.g., kick scooter and shared bicycles; autonomous vehicles). Additionally, the modeling paradigm changes, with dynamically defined supply, which is shaped upon the demand itself (e.g., availability of a shared vehicle in an area is defined by the demand of trips to that area).
4. **Data Availability:** "If you cannot measure it, you cannot improve it," as per the aphorism attributed to Lord Kelvin, and during this period we have been using a limited amount of data (mostly point data from loop detectors,

and more recently some limited travel time information). During the last decade, an avalanche of rich, ubiquitous data are becoming increasingly available, ranging from social media data to telecommunication data and from floating car to vehicle status data.

2. How can we respond to the challenges arising?

Transportation and mobility planning need to be completely rethought to leverage changes in a sustainable and flexible way forward. Conventional and newly emerging modeling techniques should be combined to better understand the situation and evaluate scenarios of what the future of transportation will be. Attempts toward this new transportation planning reality should not overlook emerging modeling tools, emerging data sources, multiactors environment, rapid innovation cycles, model and data transferability, as well as participatory planning.

Statistical learning techniques (such as machine or reinforcement learning) and flexible models has been found to yield more accurate results in some cases, such as short-term traffic prediction (Vlahogianni et al., 2005) and car following models (Papathanasopoulou and Antoniou, 2015). Data-driven methods extend the spectrum of variables included in an analysis potentially better representing the transportation system (Durán Rodas et al., 2019). However, all these new modeling techniques need to be compared to the conventionally used methods as in some cases, conventional methods are found to have better prediction performance (e.g., for discrete choice models, Hensher and Ton, 2000).

Central to this change of mobility planning for Emerging Transportation Systems is the data used to predict aspects of adoption, satisfaction, and use. Conventional data collection and modeling approaches are clearly insufficient in terms of capturing the rapidly changing mobility landscape and related changes of goods and passenger mobility. New data collection methods are becoming established, ranging from opportunistic sensors, such as Wi-Fi and Bluetooth detectors, to smartphone-based apps [e.g., Future Mobility Surveys: Danaf et al. (2019); meili: Prelipcean et al. (2018); nervousnet: Pournaras et al. (2015)] that provide rich insights into the mobility patterns, but also trajectory data and satellite images (e.g., Efthymiou et al., 2018) and, even, videos. The fact that emerging and future transportation systems are in many cases unrealized, and their exact characteristics are yet unknown, make the assumptions defined and the data used even more important. The recently available data sources have been found to produce an immense amount of data (Big Data—Buckley and Lightman, 2015; Chaniotakis et al., 2016; Reades et al., 2007) that could potentially be used to improve transportation systems, first in terms of identification and prediction and second of optimization. On the same time, pervasive systems have allowed for several supporting services to rapidly emerge and be widely used, such as the concepts of Mobility as a Service (MaaS—Matyas and Kamargianni, 2018) and vehicle sharing.

This book aims at serving as a medium for understanding demand for emerging transportation systems. It critically approaches the pertinent literature in order to establish the necessary background on the modes that are typically explored, the factors that affect use and satisfaction and the implications that emerging modes bring with regards to sustainability and human well-being. Aiming at the establishment of a spherical evaluation, aspects of the methods and data commonly deployed are explored and applications are discussed.

3. Structure of this book

This book is structured in three main parts:

Part I: Background and critical review of the state-of-the-art. This part comprises three chapters providing a critical review of the factors affecting the adoption of established and emerging modes in general (Chapter 2), an analysis of mobility on demand, with an emphasis on its interactions with public transport (Chapter 3) and a view on the implications of automation on accessibility and social inclusion (Chapter 4).

Part II: Methods. This part comprises four chapters, covering data aspects (Chapter 5) and methodological components for location planning for one-way carsharing systems (Chapter 6), as well as the analysis of spatiotemporal structures using smart card data (Chapter 7), and modelling requirements and concepts for shared autonomous vehicles (Chapter 8).

Part III: Applications. This part comprises five chapters, with key applications covering public transport (Chapter 9), vehicle sharing adoption (Chapter 10), carsharing (Chapter 11), smart mobility planning (Chapter 12), and Urban air mobility (Chapter 13).

Introductory and concluding chapters round the book up.

References

Buckley, S., Lightman, D., 2015. Ready or not, big data is coming to a city (transportation agency) near you. In: Transportation Research Board 94th Annual Meeting, number 15-5156 in TRB2015.

Chaniotakis, E., Antoniou, C., Pereira, F., 2016. Mapping social media for transportation studies. IEEE Intelligent Systems 31 (6), 64—70.

Danaf, M., Atasoy, B., de Azevedo, C.L., Ding-Mastera, J., Abou-Zeid, M., Cox, N., Zhao, F., Ben-Akiva, M., 2019. Context-aware stated preferences with smartphone-based travel surveys. Journal of Choice Modelling 31, 35—50.

Duran-Rodas, D., Chaniotakis, E., Antoniou, C., June 2019. Built Environment Factors Affecting Bike Sharing Ridership: Data-Driven Approach for Multiple Cities. https://doi.org/10.1177/0361198119849908. Transportation Research Record.

Efthymiou, D., Antoniou, C., Siora, E., Argialas, D., 2018. Modeling the impact of large-scale transportation infrastructure development on land cover. Transportation Letters 10 (1), 26–42.

Fu, M., Rothfeld, R., Antoniou, C., 2019. Exploring preferences for transportation modes in an urban air mobility environment: munich case study. Transportation Research Record.

Hensher, D.A., Ton, T.T., 2000. A comparison of the predictive potential of artificial neural networks and nested logit models for commuter mode choice. Transportation Research Part E: Logistics and Transportation Review 36 (3), 155–172.

Matyas, M., Kamargianni, M., 2018. The Potential of Mobility as a Service Bundles as a Mobility Management Tool. Transportation.

Papathanasopoulou, V., Antoniou, C., 2015. Towards data-driven car-following models. Transportation Research Part C: Emerging Technologies 55, 496–509. Engineering and Applied Sciences Optimization (OPT-i) - Professor Matthew G. Karlaftis Memorial Issue.

Pournaras, E., Moise, I., Helbing, D., 2015. Privacy-preserving ubiquitous social mining via modular and compositional virtual sensors. In: 2015 IEEE 29th International Conference on Advanced Information Networking and Applications, pp. 332–338.

Prelipcean, A.C., Gidofalvi, G., Susilo, Y.O., 2018. MEILI: a travel diary collection, annotation and automation system. Computers, Environment and Urban Systems 70, 24–34.

Reades, J., Calabrese, F., Sevtsuk, A., Ratti, C., 2007. Cellular census: explorations in urban data collection. Pervasive Computing, IEEE 6 (3), 30–38.

Vlahogianni, E.I., Karlaftis, M.G., Golias, J.C., 2005. Optimized and meta-optimized neural networks for short-term traffic flow prediction: a genetic approach. Transportation Research Part C: Emerging Technologies 13 (3), 211–234.

Part B

A critical review of (emerging?) transportation systems

Chapter 2

Review of factors affecting transportation systems adoption and satisfaction

Yannis Tyrinopoulos[1], Constantinos Antoniou[2]

[1]*University of West Attica, Department of Civil Engineering, Athens, Greece;* [2]*Chair of Transportation Systems Engineering, Department of Civil, Geo and Environmental Engineering, Technical University of Munich, Munich, Germany*

Chapter outline

1. Introduction

The factors that influence the use and adoption of transportation systems can be examined from different standpoints, such as organizational, financial, legislative, technological, and user acceptance. All these different factors play

Demand for Emerging Transportation Systems. https://doi.org/10.1016/B978-0-12-815018-4.00002-4

a minor or major role in the use of the large variety of transportation systems and modes. Their understanding is of vital importance for creating a sustainable transportation system. However, the variety of transportation modes and systems that currently exist and those that will emerge in the near future makes the review of these factors quite complicated. In addition, when analyzing two or more transportation systems that are closely related, as in the case of shared mobility, overlaps and conflicts between these factors often occur. Thus, the examination of each transportation system and mode separately helps to overcome those shortcomings.

The purpose of this chapter is to present and analyze the key determinants, factors, and eventually motivators that affect the use, adoption, and satisfaction of transportation systems from the point of view of the end users, i.e., commuters and travelers. The focus is placed on passenger transport for urban, suburban, and periurban contexts. The findings of this review, and more particularly the sound understanding of the determinants influencing their use, may be quite useful for transport operators and policy makers to better tackle commuters' and travelers' perception and to plan the appropriate mobility management actions and policies.

To assist the factors' review and discussion, the transportation systems and modes have been classified into three broad categories: established, emerging, and future. *Established* refers to the systems that already exist, such as public transport and taxi. *Emerging* refers to concepts that have been already implemented in some areas and continue to emerge, while *future* refers to concepts which have received attention from the transport community and industry, but they have not been implemented (yet). The systems and modes that fall into these three categories are briefly described below.

2. Transportation systems

2.1 Established transportation systems

Established transportation systems have been long examined upon the distinction of private and public transportation. Private transportation usually refers to modes owned by the user, such as car, bike, and walk. Public transport usually refers to the modes, which are operated by an authority or organization. The characteristics of public transport vary a lot depending on the mode (metro, bus, etc.), and it has been claimed to be the most viable solution to the negative effects of urban congestion. In most cases, public transport operates on predefined schedules and routes. However, flexible forms of public transport providing services more associated to demand are demand-responsive transit, also known as paratransit. It includes services where a transit vehicle does not operate on a fixed-route, but picks up and drops off passengers at locations in response to specific service requests.

Taxi is one of the most well-known traditional systems. A long standing debate exists on the categorization of taxis in terms public or private transport; thus it is referred here as a separate transportation system. There are four major market segments in the taxi industry: hail, taxi rank, prebook, and contract (Aarhaug, 2016). The hail and taxi rank segments are unique to the industry, while the prebook and contract segments overlap to some extent with nontaxi industries. Taxis are a vital link in public transport systems, functioning in accordance with public demand. They can be considered as a useful supplement to conventional public transport (Aarhaug, 2016). In most big cities around the world (Beijing, Paris, Chicago, London) taxis account for 1% of the modal share (StudyLib, 2019).

2.2 Emerging transportation systems

Emerging transportation systems refer to concepts and modes, which have been implemented in various areas, but are continuously expanded. It should be noted that emerging does not necessarily means new. Most of these concepts have been present for decades in some cities (e.g., bikesharing and carsharing); however, their widespread deployment has been intensified in the past few years with the assistance of some enabling factors, such as the development of information and communications technologies (ICT).

Shared mobility is a broad term that includes many forms of mobility, in which travelers share vehicles or rides. It is an innovative transportation strategy that enables users to gain short-term access to transportation modes on an "as-needed" basis (Shaheen et al., 2015). Carsharing, carpooling, vanpooling, bikesharing, ridehailing, ridesharing, and shared e-scooters are forms, practices, or models of shared mobility, and some of them are often confused. Although there are clear similarities and differences between these mobility practices, the factors affecting their use are not so different. This is considered in the next section (review of factors).

Carsharing is a practice or a model of car rental, where people rent cars for short distances and for short periods of time. Although carsharing has already a long history in the urban mobility contexts, it is continuously enhanced. Recently, more flexible carsharing alternatives have emerged, such as free-floating carsharing, where a car can be picked and parked on (usually) any public parking spot, and peer-to-peer (P2P) carsharing, where privately owned vehicles are available for use by other members.

Similar to carsharing is bikesharing for bicycles. The number of bikesharing programs has increased rapidly in recent years and there are over 700 programs in operation globally, as of 2015 (Fishman et al., 2015). Due to the mode used (bicycle), bikesharing offers significant benefits to the end users and the society. It is thus examined separately.

Ridehailing is another concept that has emerged, and it is being explored the last few years, affecting strongly the market share of taxis. In ridehailing, a rider hires a personal driver to take him/her exactly where he/she needs to go. In the initial practice of ridehailing, the transportation vehicle is not shared with other riders, nor does it make several stops along a route. Uber and Lyft now offer services where sharing the vehicle is possible (ridesharing). Although ridehailing exists for many years, its popularity continuously increases (Statista, 2018). Companies offering ridehailing services, such as Uber, Lyft, and Grab, increase their modal share. For example, almost 10 years after it was founded, Uber topped the list of the world leading ridehailing operators in May 2018. Uber is a transportation network company operating in 65 countries and serving 75 million customers (Statista, 2018). These new approaches are expected to become the mainstream.

Another form of mobility that exists for many years and that is continuously expanding is carpooling. Carpooling allows travelers to share a vehicle with others to a common destination. It is not personal transportation, as the space is shared, and it will make stops to pick up other riders. According to Shaheen et al. (2018), carpooling is the second most common travel mode to work in the United States after driving alone, although in the recent years its modal share declines (from 19.7% in 1980 to 9% in 2016). Carpooling can include several forms of sharing a ride. Based on this established form, others keep emerging, such as flexible carpooling, which is a form of ad hoc, informal carpooling among strangers, and dynamic carpooling, which allows people to arrange ad hoc rides on demand (or very short notice) using smartphone apps or a website.

Similar to carpooling, vanpooling serves more passengers (usually 7–15), who share the cost of a van. Indicative companies offering vanpooling services are Panda Bus (China), BerlKönig (Berlin), and Ally (Germany), Jetty (Mexico City).

Ridesharing is essentially the same as carpooling, but ridesharing tends to indicate a more on-demand mobility scheme and it does not require the rider to ever be a driver. In addition, carpooling is a bit more organized and preagreed, than ridesharing.

In addition to the above shared mobility practices, this chapter examines one more emerging mode: shared electric scooters (e-scooters in short). Although entered the mobility marketplace very recently, the electric scooter is one of the micromobility modes that have an increasing presence in many countries worldwide, such as United States, China, Paris, Madrid, London, and Vienna (Shaheen and Cohen, 2019). It consists of a modern trend in short distance urban mobility; it exploits advanced technologies; and it is environmentally friendly. Despite its benefits, its impact to traffic and road safety is questionable and there is usually no regulation applying to it; therefore, new regulation is required.

2.3 Future transportation systems

Future transportation systems can include any possible way that is believed it is possible to be present in the future. It becomes obvious that an effort to enumerate all possible variants would lead to an open-ended discussion and, for that reason, only two major innovations that are expected to influence urban mobility in the future: shared autonomous vehicles (SAVs) and urban air mobility (UAM), are extensively discussed. The reason behind this choice is that these two concepts both radically change the way that travel is perceived and are widely studied in the pertinent literature. There is currently a lot of debate and uncertainty regarding the exact timeframe that these will reach a critical mass. However, this is not the point here, but rather to explore their differentiation and possible added value in the urban transportation landscape of the future.

2.3.1 Autonomous vehicles

Automated vehicles are vehicles with some level of automation to assist or replace human control. The Society of Automotive Engineers (SAE) has defined different levels of automated functionality, ranging from no automated features (Level 0) to full automation (Level 5, commonly referred to as self-driving or autonomous vehicles). After an initial period of extended hype, we are currently reaching a point where the challenges and opportunities associated with autonomous vehicles (AV) are gradually becoming better appreciated. While the benefits and problems related to their introduction are being debated, practically all major technology companies and car manufacturers invest billions of dollars annually in a race to gain a competitive advantage in this field (Korosec, 2018; Trivedi, 2018). Although the precise solution characteristics are in general uncertain, the actions of the autonomous vehicle manufacturers and their other industrial partners point toward the initial deployment of autonomous vehicles as shared autonomous mobility services. For example, BMW Group, Intel and Mobileye aim to produce autonomous vehicles by 2021 for the purpose of ridesharing (BMW Group, 2016); General Motors plans to operate autonomous taxi services by 2019 (Hawkins, 2017); Ford also plans to introduce autonomous ridehailing or ridesharing services in 2021 (The Ford Company, 2016); Volkswagen Group and Hyundai in collaboration with Aurora Innovations plan to begin autonomous on-demand services by 2021 (O'Kane, 2018); Daimler and Toyota have partnered with Uber (Daimler AG, 2017; Monaghan, 2018); and, last but not least, Waymo has recently started commercial autonomous ridesharing service, available in Tempe, Mesa and Chandler, Arizona (LeBeau, 2018).

TABLE 2.1 Major strengths and weaknesses of transportation systems and modes.

System/mode	Major strengths	Major weaknesses
Established transportation systems/modes		
Public transport	Reduction of road congestion, economy savings for commuters, accessible to all population categories, reduction of pollutants (Tyrinopoulos and Antoniou, 2013)	Congestion onboard vehicles, lack of comfort, time uncertainty, need for transfers, lack of control (Anwar, 2009)
Demand-responsive transit	Cost-efficient connectivity for rural populations, supporting citizens with limited mobility (Hunkin and Krell, 2018)	Relatively high cost of provision, lack of flexibility in route planning, inability to manage high demand (Ambrosino et al., 2003); DRT not realistically costed or designed based on a full understanding of the market (Enoch et al., 2006)
Taxi	Prompt pick-up and drop facility, convenience, 24/7 service	Relatively expensive especially in peak hours/periods
Emerging transportation systems/modes		
Carsharing	Reduced vehicle ownership, less parking requirements, reduced vehicle travel, cost savings (TCRP Report 108, 2005)	Lack of one-way trip option (TCRP Report 108, 2005)
Bikesharing	Health benefits, reduced road congestion, reduced fuel consumption, financial savings, low carbon emissions (Shaheen et al., 2010; Qiu and He, 2018; Yang et al., 2010; Shaheen and Cohen, 2019)	Limited payment options (debit/credit cards) impose barriers for consumers who are underbanked or unbanked, requirement for a smartphone and high-speed data packages to access services (Shaheen and Cohen, 2019); limited use of helmets, limited capacity of docking stations in heavy traffic hours, unfamiliarity with cycling for first-time cyclists leading to accidents
Ridehailing	High-vehicle occupancy, increased convenience, reduced vehicle miles traveled (Lavieri and Bhat, 2018)	Reduced transit ridership and active travel (Lavieri and Bhat, 2018); increased motorized travel (Rayle et al., 2016)

TABLE 2.1 Major strengths and weaknesses of transportation systems and modes.—cont'd

System/ mode	Major strengths	Major weaknesses
Carpooling/ vanpooling	Reduced vehicle miles traveled, reduction in fuel consumption, reduction in greenhouse gas (GHG) emissions, cost savings for public agencies and employers, convenience (Shaheen et al., 2018)	Lack of trust leading to reduced safety and security ("stranger danger") (Olsson et al., 2019)
Ridesharing	Cost savings for riders, reduced vehicle miles traveled, reduction in fuel consumption, reduction in greenhouse gas (GHG) emissions	Lack of trust leading to reduced safety and security, reduced transit ridership and active travel, increased motorized travel
Shared e-scooters	Increased mobility, reduced GHG, decreased automobile use, health benefits (Shaheen and Cohen, 2019)	Limited payment options (debit/credit cards) impose barriers for consumers who are underbanked or unbanked, requirement for a smartphone and high-speed data packages to access services (Shaheen and Cohen, 2019); unfamiliarity with e-scooters for first-time users leading to accidents
Future transportation systems/modes		
Autonomous vehicles	Major cost reduction (due to elimination of driver costs) (Litman, 2018); increased accessibility, e.g., for segments of the population that cannot drive (e.g., young, old, disabled) (Meyer et al., 2017); possible reduction in emissions (Greenblatt and Saxena, 2015) and increase in capacity (Friedrich, 2015); safety improvements (Teoh and Kidd, 2017)	Might lead to extra vehicle miles traveled (VMT) e.g., due to extra trips and cruising instead of parking (Litman, 2018); increased cybersecurity danger (Petit and Shladover, 2014)

Continued

TABLE 2.1 Major strengths and weaknesses of transportation systems and modes.—cont'd

System/ mode	Major strengths	Major weaknesses
Urban air mobility	Drastic reduction of travel time in some cases (Antcliff et al., 2016); effectively adds a third dimension and additional capacity for urban mobility	Requires massive infrastructure investments (e.g., vertiports); not being on the ground raises safety/security/cost questions

2.3.2 Urban air mobility ("flying taxis")

As already discussed, shared mobility services are providing users with more efficient travel options, characterized by lower demand for parking spaces, lower vehicle ownership, but also reduced environmental impacts resulting from lower emissions (Baptista et al., 2014). Furthermore, autonomous vehicles may offer safer and more comfortable transportation options, which has led most automobile manufacturers to explore and invest in autonomous vehicles (Bimbraw, 2015). Besides this, there is currently a new third dimension that is actively explored for urban mobility, that of the sky.

While several services exist that use conventional aerial vehicles (such as helicopters) to offer urban services, e.g., Voom in Brazil (Airbus, 2018) and recently even Uber in New York, there is a massive recent movement that aims to use autonomous, "unmanned aerial vehicles" (UAVs) to provide systematic transportation services in cities. The US National Aeronautics and Space Administration (NASA) is developing a framework for the coordination of all actors and stakeholders into a functioning system (Tripphavong et al., 2018). Shamiyeh et al. (2017), indicating that the time is currently ripe for such services, due to a number of technological advances, e.g., in battery storage, electrical power transmission, and distributed propulsion systems. Companies often investigate multiple alternative ideas, such as Airbus (2018), which explores several different vehicle architectures, such as Vahana and CityAirbus aiming to serve one or multiple passengers, respectively.

The development of the business models is also a key aspect of such innovative services. Uber assumes a vehicle for four passengers (Uber Elevate, 2016), while Porsche Consulting (2018) defines the entire chain of such services, starting from the first mile (access to the vertiport), moving on to the vehicle boarding, then the core flight, and the corresponding stages at the destination (deboarding process and last mile transfer).

2.4 Strengths and weaknesses of the systems and modes examined

Table 2.1 presents the major strengths and weaknesses of the above transportation systems and modes. The table has been enriched with the appropriate references, while for some modes, the strengths and weaknesses are obvious and no references have been included. The latter are based on the personal opinion of the authors.

3. Factors affecting transportation systems adoption and satisfaction

The factors affecting the use, adoption, and satisfaction of the transportation systems presented above have been identified through a review of many research and scientific articles, but also reports and studies.

3.1 Established transportation systems

3.1.1 Public transport

The factors affecting the use of public transport by passengers (both current and future) depend on many aspects and elements, such as the mode (metro, bus, etc.), the type of user (male, female, young, elderly, disabled, students, etc.), the area covered (regional, urban, suburban, touristic), also the time (peak, off-peak). Thus, it is attempted below to find as much as possible a common ground of factors, combining many of these aspects.

De Oña et al. (2016) proposed a model for predicting the intentions of passengers to continue to use transit services, especially light rail transit (LRT). Their analysis concluded that service quality is mostly explained by aspects related to comfort, accessibility, and timeliness, followed by information and safety.

Tyrinopoulos and Antoniou (2008) conducted a research focusing on passengers' perception on transit performance with an emphasis on the variability between transport operators and the policy implications of such differences. They examined five transit systems in the two major urban conurbations in Greece, Athens and Thessaloniki. For the transit companies operating bus and trolley bus services in Athens, quality of service is primarily driven by quality attributes such as service frequency, information provision, waiting and in-vehicle conditions, accessibility, and transfer coordination. The metro service operating in Athens depends on the transfer coordination with other means and information provision because in Athens the high-quality services of metro are taken for granted. In Thessaloniki, the sole bus transit operator should include in its policy plans immediate corrective measures addressing the service frequency, waiting time, and vehicle cleanliness attributes.

Eboli and Mazzulla (2015) formulated a structural equation model to explore the impact of the relationship between global customer satisfaction and the quality of services offered by rail (regional and suburban) operators in Northern Italy. They found that information, cleanliness, and service characteristics like punctuality and frequency of runs have the highest positive effect on service quality.

Passenger car and its various forms (e.g., carsharing) are the major competitors of public transport in urban areas. In this respect, Tyrinopoulos and Antoniou (2013) estimated probit and structural equation models and performed additional statistical analysis to gain insight into the key factors affecting modal choices of commuters and the reasons that discourage them from using public transport services. According to their analysis, the main factor affecting the preference of commuters toward passenger car is the availability of parking space. The factor that discourages most commuters from using public transport is crowding followed by service unreliability. Another interesting finding was that high fare levels do not discourage commuters from using public transport.

Based on the above review, it seems that the main factors influencing most public transport use and satisfaction are accessibility, service reliability, crowding, and safety. The factors differ depending on the type of mode. In particular, waiting and in-vehicle conditions (like comfort) play a decisive role for bus transit, while for metro systems the key factors are punctuality and information provision.

3.1.2 Demand responsive transit

Demand-responsive transit (DRT) emerged in the 1970s to serve the niche market of people with mobility difficulties. Since the beginning of 1990s, it has grown in popularity for several reasons, one of which is the lack of the adaptability of conventional regular bus and taxi services. DRT typically serves the general population in low-density and/or rural communities, as well as the disabled population.

Ambrosino et al. (2003) prepared a report that concerned primarily with the potential contribution of advanced public transport systems to sustainable mobility, placing particular focus on DRT. In their user needs analysis, they reported that the main factors that drive DRT users' adoption include the wide range of destinations/coverage, easy access to services (walk, wait), accessibility to complete and reliable information, easiness and speed of booking, reliability of service and arrival times, and reasonable pricing structure.

An interesting research was conducted by Enoch et al. (2006). They examined mainstream DRT schemes from around the world that have failed with the aims to identify the reasons for failure and to draw lessons that can help to prevent similar outcomes occurring. Several reasons of failure were recognized, such as poor planning, insufficient stakeholder commitment, inflexible funding arrangements, low fares, and many others. From the point of view of the end users, a successful DRT system is simple, is of low cost, and provides low-volume schemes that succeeded in concentrating demand in time and geography—often with semischeduled core routes.

Concluding, DRT has important equity and accessibility benefits. In order to be successful and well adopted by the end users it needs to be well scheduled, of reasonable cost and targeted to a wider market and not only addressed to the mobility impaired population.

3.1.3 Taxi

Taxis (or cabs) provide a publicly available service and hold a favorable place in the urban mobility contexts. The lack of regular schedules, routes, and stations gives them a semiprivate character. Still a key characteristic of taxis is their close interaction with the customers. This characteristic makes the factors affecting the use of taxis by commuters even more significant.

Khan et al. (2016) conducted an empirical research to determine the factors affecting customer satisfaction in the taxi service industry in India. This industry has seen a very significant growth in the recent past in India and there are many players operating there. They found that driver professionalism and convenience of booking were found to have a significant impact on overall satisfaction. The condition of the car seems to have less impact on satisfaction.

Kumar and Kumar (2016) applied descriptive statistics and regression modeling in order to study the factors influencing the consumers while selecting taxi services. They concluded that price consciousness, coupon redemption behavior, and innovativeness are influencing the consumers in their selection of cab services. In their analysis, the consumers who are price conscious are likely to redeem coupons while booking cabs; the consumers are interested to adopt for new technology like the use of apps for booking taxis, while the redemption of coupons is a motivating factor for consumption of taxi services.

3.2 Emerging transportation systems

3.2.1 Carsharing, ridesharing, ridehailing, carpooling, and vanpooling

As stated above, these five shared mobility schemes and practices have similarities and differences in their operation; however, the factors that affect their use and satisfaction are quite common.

Ballús-Armet et al. (2014) examined the public perception and the potential market characteristics of P2P carsharing through an intercept survey conducted in the San Francisco Bay Area. Their study revealed that the top three reasons for using P2P carsharing include convenience and availability, monetary savings, and expanded mobility options. Another interesting finding is that many respondents cited liability and trust concerns as primary deterrents. Finally, the low awareness of P2P carsharing was evident among the respondents.

TCRP Report 108 (2005) provides a substantive resource with considerable information and useful tools for the development and implementation of carsharing services. There, a number of success factors were analyzed in detail. One of the most important findings in this report is the need to provide access to a car during the working day, since many employees drive to work because they need a car during the working day. The authors referred to a survey conducted in the San Francisco Bay Area, according to which 11% of commuters cite the need for a car for work as an impediment to commuting by transit, bicycle, or carpool (RIDES for Bay Area Commuters, 2003). Providing carsharing at workplaces may help to eliminate this barrier, and many employers have introduced carsharing as a part of their commute trip reduction program.

Lavieri and Bhat (2018) investigated ridehailing experience, frequency, and trip characteristics through two multidimensional models estimated using data from the Dallas-Fort Worth Metropolitan Area. Their results revealed that people's privacy concerns are a key deterrent to pooled ridehailing adoption. Furthermore, their literature review revealed interesting findings derived from other studies. Most notably, the ease of payment, the ease to call, the lower cost, and the shorter waiting times are frequently cited by individuals as reasons to use ridehailing relative to taxis. In addition, shorter travel times are identified as the primary reason to prefer ridehailing over public transit and active modes (bicycling and walking), while limited parking at the destination and avoiding driving while intoxicated are the typical reasons for preferring ridehailing over driving a private car (Rayle et al., 2016; Alemi et al., 2018a, 2018b; Zheng et al., 2018).

One study of casual carpooling in the San Francisco Bay Area found that convenience, time savings, and monetary savings were key motivators to carpool (Shaheen et al., 2016). This study cited also other studies that derived the same conclusions (Maltzman, 1987; Reno et al., 1989; Beroldo, 1990; Burris and Winn, 2006). Finally, one more study found that the top reason for someone choosing to be a rider was the desire to save on the cost of gasoline, followed by a preference to do other things during the drive (Oliphant, 2008).

Balachandran and Bin Hamzah (2017) conducted a study with the aim to identify the factors affecting service quality and customer satisfaction of ridesharing services in Malaysia. Their analysis derived that reliability, price, promotion and coupon redemption, and comfort have positive influence on customer satisfaction. From all the variables examined, comfort is the most influencing factor.

The employees of large firms are one of the most important target groups of ridesharing. Hwang and Giuliano (1990) performed a wide literature review and made a summary on the effectiveness of employee ridesharing programs.

One of their most important findings is that the most effective incentives of ridesharing are parking charges, parking restrictions, and transportation allowance. For example, imposing parking charges on employees who previously had free parking, or providing cash subsidies for transit or vanpools equivalent in value to the parking subsidy will have a significant impact to the adoption of ridesharing.

Due to the similarities between some shared mobility practices, the factors identified above for a particular practice may also apply to other(s). More specifically, the factors identified for ridesharing also apply to carpooling and vanpooling. These are cost savings, comfort, and convenience. These factors have also been identified as primary reasons for using ridehailing and carsharing. However, there are also other determinants, such as liability, privacy, and trust concerns, as well as accessibility to car and parking elements, which are associated with the satisfaction of using ridesharing and especially carsharing.

3.2.2 Bikesharing

Bikesharing systems encourage cycling, whose benefits to the user and to the society as a whole are well known. Cycling is a form of physical activity in which health authorities place great hope, because it can be easily incorporated into daily routines and yields cardiovascular benefits (Yang et al., 2010). It is also an environmentally friendly transportation mode that provides additional mobility at an affordable cost (Shaheen et al., 2010).

Bachand-Marleau et al. (2012) conducted a survey in Montreal, Quebec, Canada, to determine the factors that encouraged individuals to use bikesharing systems and the elements that influenced their frequency of use. Their survey found that the factor imposing the greatest effect on the likelihood for use of a shared bicycle system is the proximity of home to docking stations. Another factor of equal effect is the fear of bicycle theft, while transit users, people combining cycling and transit for their trips, and those who have a driver's license were more likely to use shared bicycle systems.

Fishman et al. (2015) conducted a study aiming to understand and quantify the factors influencing bikeshare membership in Australia's two bikeshare programs located in Melbourne and Brisbane. Convenience, ease accessibility, and distance to the closest docking station emerged as important influencing factors for increasing the membership of the programs.

3.2.3 Shared e-scooters

The electric scooter (e-scooter in short) is a convenient option for last-mile transportation. In 2018, this micromobility trend was reenergized with the emergence of the shared and dockless e-scooters, pioneered by Lime and Bird in the United States. Due to their short presence in the transportation landscape, the factors influencing the use and adoption of shared e-scooters are still unknown. A recent report (Shaheen and Cohen, 2019) is perhaps currently the only source looking deeper into micromobility including shared e-scooters, as it presents a toolkit which outlines policies and practices for cities integrating shared micromobility into the built environment. Still, the motivators of users toward e-scooters have not been identified. However, the cost savings and convenience are the two obvious factors that affect their popularity.

In response to their rapid recent growth, some backlash has started occurring, mostly related to their higher risk (especially when circulating in the street) and their negative interactions with pedestrians (when moving on the sidewalk, where many cities start prohibiting them). A current trend is to suggest that they share the cycling facilities; however, cyclists are also resisting this, especially in cities with high cycling penetration, arguing that the cycleways are already congested.

3.3 Future transportation systems

3.3.1 Shared autonomous vehicles

As discussed above, services such as carsharing, bikesharing, scooter-sharing, on-demand ride services, and ridesharing fall into the category of shared mobility. Shared mobility services enable cost savings, convenience, and reduction of vehicle usage, ownership, and vehicle miles/kilometers traveled (VMT/VKT) (Shaheen and Chan, 2015). Autonomous vehicle technology could accelerate the growth of shared services (Thomas and Deepti, 2018) and shared mobility can make the deployment of autonomous vehicles financially viable (Gurumurthy and Kockelman, 2018; Stocker and Shaheen, 2018), especially when combined with electrification (Sprei, 2018; Walker and Johnson, 2016; Weiss et al., 2017).

A number of factors have been identified as relevant in the future adoption of SAVs. For example, Nazari et al. (2018) remark that the adoption of SAVs could be limited, primarily due to personal safety concerns. Other factors include exact pickup time and drop-off times, while factors such as choice of route and efficiency of matching with other passengers had a much lesser importance (Philipsen et al., 2019). Amanatidis et al. (2018) found that users have different expectations for autonomous vehicle user interface, depending on whether the vehicle is owned or shared. This suggests that design and development should differ between personal and shared autonomous vehicles. Becker and Axhausen (2017) provide a summary of variables that affect acceptance of autonomous vehicles (both personal and shared). Narayanan et al. (2019) present a very recent, comprehensive review of relevant studies in the field of SAV, considering various aspects of SAV deployment, including, for example, identified impacts, estimated demand, and required policies, concentrating primarily on Level 5 automation (i.e., what is commonly referred to as autonomous, self-driving, or driverless vehicles).

3.3.2 Urban air mobility

Urban air mobility (UAM) is subject to several constraints, including stake-holders' regulations, availability of infrastructure, air traffic control, environmental impacts, and user/community acceptance (Vascik, 2017). Cohen (1996) examined infrastructure constraints and in particular examined vertiport prototypes with respect to land use, site selection, etc., while Fadhil (2018) focused on ground infrastructure selection for UAM. Straubinger and Verhoef (2018) evaluated implications on the urban space and the city inhabitants, while Rothfeld et al. (2018) used MATSIM, an agent-based microscopic simulator, to study the performance of different operational scenarios.

Considering that UAM is rather different than other modes, it is essential to explore, prior to its implementation, the factors that affect its community and user acceptance. Peeta et al. (2008) were probably the first ones who conducted a stated-preference experiment on this topic and found the importance of travel distance, service fare, and accessibility as key factors. Garrow et al. (2018) collected 2500 survey responses from high-income workers in the United States in an effort to understand demand for UAM. Fu et al. (2019) also used choice modeling and collected data from Munich, Germany. Assessing the characteristics that are expected to determine the use of UAM, Antcliff et al. (2016) suggest that Silicon Valley would be an ideal region for early deployment, as it combines good weather, high incomes, and housing prices, as well as high commute durations. Privacy and safety are anticipated as main concerns in the user perception and acceptance of such services (Wang et al., 2016; Chamata, 2017; MacSween, 2003; Lidynia et al., 2017; Clothier et al., 2015).

Al Haddad et al. (2019) developed a framework for UAM acceptance in general and its time adoption in particular, with a focus on intercity application. This is based on the development of a novel stated preference survey design with time adoption as a dependent variable, with the aim to reveal factors affecting adoption of this service. These are identified by exploring the factors found to be significant for technology acceptance in general, and acceptance of autonomous vehicles in particular. In addition, factors relevant to UAM are also included, based on a review of its related studies and properties. The analysis highlighted the importance of socio-demographic parameters and their attitudes in adoption, including the affinity to automation, data and safety concerns, the value of time savings, in addition to social attitudes, such as environmental awareness, the affinity to social media, online services, and sharing. Based on a number of developed econometric models, the influence of socio-demographics, cultural impact, and affinity to automation (including the enjoyment and trust of automation) were shown. Trust and safety were found as key components for UAM adoption; in particular, the presence of in-vehicle cameras and operators, as well as performance expectancy in terms of service reliability and on-time performance were noted. Data

TABLE 2.2 Key factors influencing transportation systems and modes use and satisfaction.

System/mode	Main influencing factors							
	Accessibility	Service reliability	Crowding	Safety	Time savings	Cost savings	Comfort/convenience	Other
Established								
Public transport	++ [1,2]	+++ [2]/ −− [4]	−−− [4]	++ [1]	+/− [*]	+++ [2]	++ [1,2]	Information provision punctuality, cleanliness [1,3]; waiting conditions and in-vehicle conditions, transfer coordination [2]
Demand-responsive transit	++ [5]	++ [5]				++ [6]		Range of destinations/coverage, information provision, pricing structure [5], simplicity, planning/scheduling [6]
Taxi				+	+	++ [7]		Technology aided booking [7]; driver professionalism, convenience of booking [8]
Emerging (shared mobility)								
Carsharing	+ [9]					+ [10]	++ [10]	Expanded mobility options, liability, and trust concerns [10]
Ridehailing		++	−−		++ [11]	++ [11]		Privacy concerns [12], ease of payment, ease to call, availability of parking [11]

Mode				Do other things during the drive [14]	Parking charges and restrictions [16]	Distance to the closest docking station [17]; proximity of home to docking stations; fear of bicycle theft [18]	Perception (lack) of safety; locus of control; privacy concerns
Carpooling/vanpooling	++	--	+ [13]	+ [13,14]	++ [13]		
Ridesharing	+ [15]		+ [15]	++ [15]	++ [15]		
Bikesharing	+ [17]	--	++	+ [17]		++ [17]	
Shared e-scooters		--	+	+		+	
Future							
(Shared) Autonomous vehicles	+ [19]	++ [20]	++ [21] (**)	+ [22]			+ [23]
Urban air mobility	++ [24]	-- [25]	+++ (**)	+ [26]			

[1] De Oña et al., 2016.
[2] Tyrinopoulos and Antoniou, 2008.
[3] Eboli and Mazzulla, 2015.
[4] Tyrinopoulos and Antoniou, 2013.
[5] Ambrosino et al., 2003.
[6] Enoch et al., 2006.
[7] Kumar and Kumar, 2016.
[8] Khan et al., 2016.
[9] TCRP Report 108, 2005
[10] Ballús-Armet et al., 2014.
[11] Rayle et al., 2016; Alemi et al., 2018a; Alemi et al., 2018b; Zheng et al., 2018.
[12] Lavieri and Bhat, 2018.

Continued

TABLE 2.2 Key factors influencing transportation systems and modes use and satisfaction.—cont'd

System/mode	Main influencing factors							
	Accessibility	Service reliability	Crowding	Safety	Time savings	Cost savings	Comfort/convenience	Other

(13)Shaheen et al., 2016; Maltzman, 1987; Reno et al., 1989; Beroldo, 1990; Burris and Winn, 2006.
(14)Oliphant, 2008.
(15)Balachandran and Bin Hamzah, 2017.
(16)Hwang and Giuliano, 1990.
(17)Fishman et al., 2015.
(18)Bachand-Marleau et al., 2012.
(19)Meyer et al., 2017.
(20)Keeney, 2017; Fagnant and Kockelman, 2015.
(21)Singleton, 2018.
(22)Keeney, 2017.
(23)Shaheen and Chan, 2015.
(24)Peeta et al., 2008.
(25)MacSween, 2003; Wang et al., 2016.
(26)Rychel, 2016.
(*)Depending on mode, e.g., + for fixed right of way, typically − for shared right of way.
(**)Including lower value of time, due to ability to multitask during trip.

concerns, the value of time savings and costs, social attitudes including a high affinity to social media were also found as highly influential for UAM adoption. Finally, public transportation as a commute mode was found to be rather related to late adoption.

4. Synthesis of factors

Table 2.2 presents an overview of the most important factors identified above. The influence of these factors may be positive or negative, while the degree of influence may be low, medium or high. This is depicted in the table as follows: "+++" = high influence, "++" = medium influence and "+" = low influence. The opposite applies to the negative influence using the indication "−."

It should be stressed that the degree of influence embeds the subjective opinion of the authors, while some additional factors have been included. In particular, where references are included next to the factors, these come from the review, while where there are no references, the factors have been derived by the authors taking into account their own extensive knowledge and long experience in the field of urban mobility.

5. Conclusions

The best indicators of a good mobility system or mode are customer satisfaction and frequency of use. In this respect, this chapter provides an overview of the key determinants that drive the use, adoption, and satisfaction of urban and periurban mobility systems and modes. Although the factors and determinants that influence the use and adoption of a mobility system or mode vary significantly (financial, technological, regulatory, etc.), this chapter analyzes those related to the users' acceptance and satisfaction.

For public transport, service reliability is the most influencing factor, especially for persons commuting for work. The cost savings are also a strong determinant. It has to be noted here that the perceived cost for the end users is more important in relation to the nonperceived cost. In public transport, the perceived cost corresponds directly to the ticket fare, while in personal vehicles, the perceived cost may include parking fee, fuel, tolls, etc. Other factors that attract users to public transport, as revealed by many surveys, are comfort and ease accessibility to transit infrastructures (vehicles and stations).

Taxis are an instantly recognizable transport mode found in almost every city around the world (Aarhaug, 2016). The review showed that driver professionalism, convenience of booking, and price are the factors that mostly influence the use and satisfaction of taxi services by their customers.

The authors of this chapter placed particular emphasis on the growing demand for shared mobility. The latter is part of the wider concept of "sharing economy," which is a developing phenomenon around renting and borrowing goods and services rather than owning them (Shaheen et al., 2015). Shared mobility takes different forms and models: carsharing, carpooling, vanpooling, bikesharing, ridehailing, ridesharing, and shared e-scooters. For these forms and models, the authors provided their definitions, similarities, and differences. However, the factors affecting their use are not so different. Table 2.2 clearly depicts that comfort and convenience, cost savings, and time savings are the primary common factors that have the highest positive effect on service quality, followed by other factors, such as easy of payment and others. Additional factors have been identified for the various shared mobility systems. For example, carsharing is also affected by liability and trust concerns, while ridehailing by the ease of payment and ease to call (book).

The chapter discussed also two major innovations that are expected to influence urban mobility in the future: SAVs and UAM. SAVs can further enhance the factors that encourage the use of shared mobility, as discussed above. On the other hand, the adoption of SAVs could be hindered due to personal safety concerns. Concerning UAM, time savings are expected to be the primary driving factor for attracting end users and to a lesser extent convenience and service reliability, while privacy concerns and lack of safety may be the main discouraging factors.

Concluding, the deep understanding of the key determinants that drive commuters' satisfaction may be quite useful for transport operators and policy makers in order to plan and take the appropriate mobility management actions and policies. A relevant example comes from the public transport analysis: the fact that high fare levels do not discourage commuters from using public transport, as revealed by some studies, may allow policy makers to slightly increase fares and redirect additional revenue to improve other public transport services, which are more essential according to commuters, such as crowding and service unreliability (Tyrinopoulos and Antoniou, 2013).

References

Aarhaug, J., 2016. Taxis as a Part of Public Transport. Sustainable Urban Transport Technical Document #16. GIZ, Germany.

Airbus, 2018. Urban Air Mobility-The Sky Is Yours. https://www.airbus.com/innovation/Urban-air-mobility-the-sky-is-yours.html.

Al Haddad, C., Chaniotakis, E., Straubinger, A., Plötner, K., Antoniou, C., 2019. User acceptance and adoption of urban air mobility. Under review in Transportation Research Part A: Policy and Practice.

Alemi, F., Circella, G., Handy, S., Mokhtarian, P., 2018a. What influences travelers to use Uber? Exploring the factors affecting the adoption of on-demand ride services in California. Travel Behaviour and Society 13, 88—104.

Alemi, F., Circella, G., Mokhtarian, P., Handy, S., 2018b. Exploring the latent constructs behind the use of ridehailing in California. Journal of Choice Modelling 29, 47—62.

Amanatidis, T., Langdon, P., Clarkson, P.J., 2018. Needs and expectations for fully autonomous vehicle interfaces. In: Companion of the 2018 ACM/IEEE International Conference on

Human-Robot Interaction HRI '18. ACM, New York, NY, USA, pp. 51–52. https://doi.org/ 10.1145/3173386.3177054. http://doi.acm.org/10.1145/3173386.3177054.

Ambrosino, G., Nelson, J.D., Romanazzo, M., 2003. Demand Responsive Transport Services: Towards the Flexible Mobility Agency. ENEA (Italian National Agency for New Technologies, Energy and the Environment), Italy.

Antcliff, K.R., Moore, M.D., Goodrich, K.H., 2016. Silicon valley as an early adopter for on-demand civil VTOL operations. In: 16th AIAA Aviation Technology, Integration, and Operations Conference, p. 3466.

Anwar, A.M., 2009. Paradox between public transport and private car as a modal choice in policy formulation. In: SMART Infrastructure Facility Papers. University of Wollongong, Australia.

Bachand-Marleau, J., Lee, B.H.Y., El-Geneidy, A.M., 2012. Better understanding of factors influencing likelihood of using shared bicycle systems and frequency of use. In: Transportation Research Record: Journal of the Transportation Research Board, No. 2314, Transportation Research Board of the National Academies, Washington, D.C., pp. 66–71.

Balachandran, I., Hamzah, I.B., 2017. The influence of customer satisfaction on Ride-Sharing services in Malaysia. International Journal of Accounting and Business Management 5 (No.2), 184–196 doi: 24924/ijabm/2017.11/v5.iss2/184.196.

Ballús-Armet, I., Shaheen, S.A., Kelly, C., Weinzimmer, D., 2014. Peer-to-peer (P2P) carsharing: exploring public perception and market characteristics in the san Francisco Bay area. Transportation Research Record 2416, 27–36.

Baptista, P., Melo, S., Rolim, C., 2014. Energy, environmental and mobility impacts of car-sharing systems. Empirical results from Lisbon, Portugal. Procedia-Social and Behavioral Sciences 111, 28–37.

Becker, F., Axhausen, K.W., 2017. Literature review on surveys investigating the acceptance of automated vehicles. Transportation 44, 1293–1306. https://doi.org/10.1007/s11116-017-9808-9.

Beroldo, S., 1990. Casual carpooling in the san Francisco Bay area. Transportation Quarterly 44 (1), 133–150.

Bimbraw, K., 2015. Autonomous cars: past, present and future a review of the developments in the last century, the present scenario and the expected future of autonomous vehicle technology. In: Informatics in Control, Automation and Robotics (ICINCO), 2015 12th International Conference on, vol. 1. IEEE, pp. 191–198.

BMW Group, 2016. BMW Group, Intel and Mobileye Team up to Bring Fully Autonomous Driving to Streets by 2021. https://www.press.bmwgroup.com/global/article/detail/ T0261586EN/bmw-group-intel-and-mobileye-team-up-to-bring-fully-autonomous-driving-to-streets-by-2021?language=en.

Burris, M., Winn, J., 2006. Slugging in Houston - casual carpool passenger characteristics. Journal of Public Transportation 9 (5), 23–40.

Chamata, J., 2017. Factors delaying the adoption of civil drones: a primitive framework. The International Technology Management Review 6, 125–132.

Clothier, R.A., Greer, D.A., Greer, D.G., Mehta, A.M., 2015. Risk perception and the public acceptance of drones. Risk Analysis 35, 1167–1183.

Cohen, M.M., 1996. The Vertiport as an Urban Design Problem (Technical Report SAE Technical Paper).

Daimler, A.G., 2017. Daimler and Uber join forces to bring more self-driving vehicles on the road. https://media.daimler.com/marsMediaSite/en/instance/ko/Daimler-and-Uber-join-forces-to-bring-more-self-driving-vehicles-on-the-road.xhtml?oid=15453638.

de Oña, J., de Oña, R., Eboli, L., Forciniti, C., Mazzulla, G., 2016. Transit passengers' behavioural intentions: the influence of service quality and customer satisfaction. Transportmetrica: Transport Science. https://doi.org/10.1080/23249935.2016.1146365.

Eboli, L., Mazzulla, G., 2015. Relationships between rail passengers' satisfaction and service quality. Public Transport 7, 185−201. https://doi.org/10.1007/s12469-014-0096-x.

Enoch, M., Stephen, P., Graham, P., Mark, S., 2006. Why Do Demand Responsive Transport Systems Fail? Transportation Research Board 85th Annual Meeting, Washington DC.

Fadhil, D.N., 2018. A GIS-Based Analysis for Selecting Ground Infrastructure Locations for Urban Air Mobility. Master's Thesis, Technical University of Munich.

Fagnant, D.J., Kockelman, K., 2015. Preparing a nation for autonomous vehicles: opportunities, barriers and policy recommendations. Transportation Research Part A: Policy and Practice 77, 167−181. https://doi.org/10.1016/j.tra.2015.04.003.

Fishman, E., Washington, S., Haworth, N., Watson, A., 2015. Factors influencing bike share membership: an analysis of Melbourne and Brisbane. Transportation Research Part A 71, 17−30.

Friedrich, B., 2015. Verkehrliche wirkung autonomer fahrzeuge. In: Maurer, M., Gerdes, J.C., Lenz, B., Winner, H. (Eds.), Autonomes Fahren: Technische, rechtliche und gesellschaftliche Aspekte. Springer Berlin Heidelberg, Berlin, Heidelberg, pp. 331−350. https://doi.org/10.1007/978-3-662-45854-916.

Fu, M., Rothfeld, R., Antoniou, C., 2019. Exploring preferences for transportation modes in an urban air mobility environment: a Munich case study. Transportation Research Record: Journal of the Transportation Research Board. https://doi.org/10.1177/0361198119843858 (Published online May 21, 2019).

Garrow, L.A., German, B., Mokhtarian, P., Daskilewicz, M., Douthat, T.H., Binder, R., 2018. If you fly it, will commuters come? A survey to model demand for e−VTOL urban air trips. In: Aviation Technology, Integration, and Operations Conference, p. 2882.

Greenblatt, J.B., Saxena, S., 2015. Autonomous taxis could greatly reduce greenhouse-gas emissions of US light-duty vehicles. Nature Climate Change 5, 860−863. https://doi.org/10.1038/nclimate2685.

Gurumurthy, K.M., Kockelman, K.M., 2018. Analyzing the dynamic ride-sharing potential for shared autonomous vehicle fleets using cellphone data from Orlando, Florida. Computers, Environment and Urban Systems 71, 177−185. https://doi.org/10.1016/j.compenvurbsys.2018.05.008.

Hunkin, S., Krell, K., 2018. Demand-responsive Transport: A Policy Brief from the Policy Learning Platform on Low-Carbon Economy. Interreg Europe.

Hawkins, A.J., 2017. GM says it will launch a robot taxi service in 2019. The Verge. https://www.theverge.com/2017/11/30/16720776/gm-cruise-self-driving-taxi-launch-2019.

Hwang, K., Giuliano, G., 1990. The Determinants of Ridesharing: Literature Review. The University of California Transportation Center, University of California. Working Paper, UCTC No. 38.

Keeney, T., 2017. Mobility-as-a-service: why self-driving cars could change everything.

Khan, A.W., Jangid, A., Bansal, A., Maruthappan, S., Chaudhary, S., Tyagi, V., Rao, P.H., 2016. Factors affecting customer satisfaction in the taxi service market in India. Journal of Entrepreneurship and Management 5 (3), 46−53.

Korosec, K., 2018. Ford Plans to Spend $4 Billion on Autonomous Vehicles by 2023. https://techcrunch.com/2018/07/24/ford-plans-to-spend-4-billion-on-autonomous-vehicles-by-2023.

Kumar, P.K., Kumar, N.R., 2016. A study on factors influencing the consumers in selection of cab services. International Journal of Social Science and Humanities Research 4 (3), 557−561.

Lavieri, P.S., Bhat, C.R., 2018. Investigating Objective and Subjective Factors Influencing the Adoption, Frequency, and Characteristics of Ride-Hailing Trips.

LeBeau, P., 2018. Waymo starts commercial ride-share service. https://www.cnbc.com/2018/12/05/waymo-starts-commercial-ride-share-service.html.

Lidynia, C., Philipsen, R., Ziefle, M., 2017. Droning on about drones acceptance of and perceived barriers to drones in civil usage contexts. In: Advances in Human Factors in Robots and Unmanned Systems. Springer, pp. 317–329.

Litman, T., 2018. Autonomous vehicle implementation predictions: implications for transport planning (Technical Report).

MacSween, S., 2003. A public opinion survey-unmanned aerial vehicles for cargo, commercial, and passenger transportation. In: 2nd AIAA "Unmanned Unlimited" Conf. And Workshop & Exhibit, p. 6519.

Maltzman, F., 1987. Casual Carpooling: An Update. RIDES for Bay Area Commuters, San Francisco, CA.

Meyer, J., Becker, H., Bösch, P.M., Axhausen, K.W., 2017. Autonomous vehicles: the next jump in accessibilities? Research in Transportation Economics 62, 80–91. https://doi.org/10.1016/j.retrec.2017.03.005.

Millard-Ball, A., Murray, G., Ter Schure, J., Fox, C., Burkhardt, J., 2005. Car-Sharing: Where and How it Succeeds. TCRP Report 108. Transportation Research Board, Washington, D.C.

Monaghan, A., 2018. Toyota to invest $500m in Uber for self-driving car programme. The Guardian. https://www.theguardian.com/business/2018/aug/28/toyota-to-invest-500m-in-uber-for-self-driving-car-programme.

Narayanan, S., Chaniotakis, E., Antoniou, C., 2019. Impacts of Shared Autonomous Vehicle Services: A Comprehensive Review (under review).

Nazari, F., Noruzoliaee, M., Mohammadian, A., 2018. Shared versus private mobility: modeling public interest in autonomous vehicles accounting for latent attitudes. Transportation Research Part C: Emerging Technologies 97, 456–477. https://doi.org/10.1016/j.trc.2018.11.005.

O'Kane, S., 2018. Former google self-driving wiz will help Volkswagen and Hyundai build fully autonomous cars. The Verge. https://www.theverge.com/2018/1/4/16846526/aurora-chris-urmson-volkswagen-hyundai-self-driving-cars.

Oliphant, M., 2008. The Native Slugs of Northern Virginia: A Profile of Slugging in the Washington DC. Region. Major Paper, Master of Sciences in Urban and Regional Planning, Urban Affairs and Planning, Virginia Tech. Available at: www.toolsofchange.com/userfiles/Slugging_Report_Oliphant(2).pdf.

Olsson, L.E., Maier, R., Friman, M., 2019. Why do they ride with others? Meta-analysis of factors influencing travelers to carpool. Sustainability 11, 2414. https://doi.org/10.3390/su11082414.

Peeta, S., Paz, A., DeLaurentis, D., 2008. Stated preference analysis of a new very light jet based on-demand air service. Transportation Research Part A: Policy and Practice 42, 629–645.

Petit, J., Shladover, S.E., 2014. Potential cyberattacks on automated vehicles. IEEE Transactions on Intelligent Transportation Systems 16 (2), 546–556.

Philipsen, R., Brell, T., Ziefle, M., 2019. Carriage without a driver – user requirements for intelligent autonomous mobility services. In: Stanton, N.A. (Ed.), Advances in Human Aspects of Transportation [electronic Resource]. Springer volume 786 of Advances in intelligent systems and computing, Cham, pp. 339–350. https://doi.org/10.1007/978-3-319-93885-1_31, 2194-5357.

Porsche Consulting, 2018. The Future of Vertical Mobility: Sizing the Market for Passenger, Inspection, and Good Services until 2035.

Qiu, L.-Y., He, L.-Y., 2018. Bike sharing and the economy, the environment, and health-related externalities. Sustainability 10, 1145, pp. 2−10.

Rayle, L., Dai, D., Chan, N., Cervero, R., Shaheen, S., 2016. Just a better taxi? A survey-based comparison of taxis, transit, and ridesourcing services in San Francisco. Transport Policy 45, 168−178.

Reno, A.T., Gellert, W.A., Verzosa, A., 1989. Evaluation of Springfield instant carpooling. Transportation Research Record 1212, 53−62.

RIDES for Bay Area Commuters, 2003. Commute Profile 2003 - A Survey of San Francisco Bay Area Commute Patterns. RIDES for Bay Area Commuters, Oakland.

Rothfeld, R.L., Balac, M., Ploetner, K.O., Antoniou, C., 2018. Initial analysis of urban air mobility's transport performance in Sioux falls. In: AIAA AVIATION, Modeling and Simulation for Unmanned and Personal Aerial Vehicle Operations. Atlanta.

Rychel, A., 2016. Cultural Divides: How Acceptance of Driverless Cars Varies Globally. https://www.2025ad.com/latest/driverless-cars-acceptance/.

Shaheen, S., Chan, N., 2015. Mobility and the Sharing Economy: Impacts Synopsis. http://innovativemobility.org/wp-content/uploads/Innovative-Mobility-Industry-Outlook_SM-Spring-2015.pdf.

Shaheen, S., Cohen, A., 2019. Shared Micromoblity Policy Toolkit: Docked and Dockless Bike and Scooter Sharing. https://doi.org/10.7922/G2TH8JW7. https://escholarship.org/uc/item/00k897b5.

Shaheen, S.A., Guzman, S., Zhang, H., 2010. Bikesharing in Europe, the Americas, and Asia: past, present and future. Transportation Research Record: Journal of the Transportation Research Board, No. 2143 159−167. Transportation Research Board of the National Academies, Washington, D.C.

Shaheen, S., Chan, N., Bansal, A., Cohen, A., 2015. Shared Mobility − A Sustainability and Technologies Workshop: Definitions, Industry Developments and Earky Understanding. TSRC, UC Berkeley.

Shaheen, S., Chan, N., Gaynor, T., 2016. Casual carpooling in the San Francisco Bay area: understanding characteristics, behaviors, and motivations. Transport Policy 51, 165−173.

Shaheen, S., Cohen, A., Bayen, A., 2018. The Benefits of Carpooling. https://doi.org/10.7922/G2DZ06GF. UC Berkeley, US.

Shamiyeh, M., Bijewitz, J., Hornung, M., 2017. A Review of Recent Personal Air Vehicle Concepts. Bucharest, Romania.

Singleton, P.A., 2018. Discussing the "positive utilities" of autonomous vehicles: will travellers really use their time productively? Transport Reviews 17, 1−16. https://doi.org/10.1080/01441647.2018.1470584.

Sprei, F., 2018. Disrupting mobility. Energy Research & Social Science 37, 238−242. https://doi.org/10.1016/j.erss.2017.10.029.

Statista, 2018. Ride-hailing market value worldwide as of May 2018, by key operator. https://www.statista.com/statistics/729049/ride-hailing-gross-revenue-by-key-operator-globally.

Stocker, A., Shaheen, S., 2018. Shared automated vehicle (sav) pilots and automated vehicle policy in the U.S.: Current and future developments. In: Meyer, G., Beiker, S. (Eds.), Road Vehicle Automation, 5. Cham: Springer volume 143 of Lecture Notes in Mobility, pp. 131−147. https://doi.org/10.1007/978-3-319-94896-6-12.

Straubinger, A., Verhoef, E.T., 2018. Working Paper) Options for a Welfare Analysis of Urban Air Mobility. Hong Kong.

StudyLib. Passenger Transport Mode Shares in World Cities. https://studylib.net/doc/7972629/passenger-transport-mode-shares-in-world-cities. Accessed May 8, 2019.

Teoh, E.R., Kidd, D.G., 2017. Rage against the machine? Google's self-driving cars versus human drivers. Journal of Safety Research 63, 57—60. https://doi.org/10.1016/j.jsr.2017.08.008.

The Ford Company, 2016. Ford targets fully autonomous vehicle for ride sharing in 2021; invests in new tech companies, doubles Silicon Valley team. https://media.ford.com/content/fordmedia/fna/us/en/news/2016/08/16/ford-targets-fully-autonomous-vehicle-for-ride-sharing-in-2021.html.

Thipphavong, D.P., Apaza, R., Barmore, B., Battiste, V., Burian, B., Dao, Q., Feary, M., Go, S., Goodrich, K.H., Homola, J., et al., 2018. Urban air mobility airspace integration concepts and considerations. In: 2018 Aviation Technology, Integration, and Operations Conference, p. 3676.

Thomas, M., Deepti, T., 2018. Reinventing Carsharing as a Modern and Profitable Service. https://ridecell.com/wp-content/uploads/White-Paper-Presentation_Reinventing-Carsharing-As-A-Modern-And-Profitable service.pdf.

Trivedi, A., 2018. Honda and Toyota Are Piling Billions of Dollars into Autonomous Cars. https://www.bloomberg.com/opinion/articles/2018-10-04/japan-s-carmakers-throw-money-at-the-future-of-driving.

Tyrinopoulos, Y., Antoniou, C., 2008. Public transit user satisfaction — variability and policy implications. Transport Policy 14 (Number 5), 260—272.

Tyrinopoulos, Y., Antoniou, C., 2013. Factors affecting modal choice in Urban Mobility. European Transport Research Review 5 (1), 27—39. https://doi.org/10.1007/s12544-012-0088-3.

Uber Elevate, 2016. Fast-forwarding to a Future of On-Demand Urban Air Transportation.

Vascik, P.D., 2017. Systems-level Analysis of on Demand Mobility for Aviation. Ph.D. thesis. Massachusetts Institute of Technology.

Walker, J., Johnson, C., 2016. Peak Car Ownership: The Market Opportunity of Electric Automated Mobility Services. https://rmi.org/insight/peak-car-ownership-report/.

Wang, Y., Xia, H., Yao, Y., Huang, Y., 2016. Flying eyes and hidden controllers: a qualitative study of people's privacy perceptions of civilian drones in the US. Proceedings on Privacy Enhancing Technologies 2016, 172—190.

Weiss, J., Hledik, R., Lueken, R., Lee, T., Gorman, W., 2017. The electrification accelerator: understanding the implications of autonomous vehicles for electric utilities. The Electricity Journal 30, 50—57. https://doi.org/10.1016/j.tej.2017.11.009.

Yang, L., Sahlqvist, S., McMinn, A., Griffin, S., Ogilvie, D., 2010. Interventions to promote cycling: systematic review. British Medical Journal 341, C5293.

Zheng, H., Chen, X., Chen, X.M., 2018. How does on-demand ridesplitting influence vehicle use and ownership? A case study in Hangzhou, China. In: Presented at the 97th Annual Meeting of the Transportation Research Board, Washington, D.C., January, Paper No. 18-04327.

Further Reading

Airbus, 2017. Rethinking Urban Air Mobility. https://www.airbus.com/newsroom/stories/rethinking-urban-air-mobility.html.

Brown, T., 2018. The Impact of Driverless Technology on Independent Driving Jobs. https://www.itchronicles.com/artificial-intelligence/the-impact-of-driverless-technology-on-independent-driving-jobs/.

Dowling, R., Maalsen, S., Kent, J.L., 2018. Sharing as sociomaterial practice: car sharing and the material reconstitution of automobility. Geoforum 88, 10—16. https://doi.org/10.1016/j.geoforum.2017.11.004.

Fagnant, D.J., Kockelman, K.M., 2014. The travel and environmental implications of shared autonomous vehicles, using agent-based model scenarios. Transportation Research Part C: Emerging Technologies 40, 1−13.

Hansman, J., Vascik, P., 2016. Operational Aspects of Aircraft-Based On-Demand Mobility. https://research.ark-invest.com/hubfs/1_Download_Files_ARK-Invest/White_Papers/Self-Driving- Cars_ARK- Invest- WP.pdf.

Chapter 3

Mobility on demand (MOD) and mobility as a service (MaaS): early understanding of shared mobility impacts and public transit partnerships

Susan Shaheen, Adam Cohen
Transportation Sustainability Research Center, University of California, Berkeley, CA, United States

Chapter outline

1. Introduction

For as long as there have been cities, urban mobility has been at its core. As cities and technologies have evolved, societies have moved from wheeled carts and horses to horseless carriages and modern cars. Today, this evolution continues. Technology is changing the way we move, which is in turn reshaping cities and society. Shared and on-demand mobility represent one of the notable shifts in transportation in the 21st century. Some suggest revolutionary changes could lead to the end of the automobile due to a number of

Demand for Emerging Transportation Systems. https://doi.org/10.1016/B978-0-12-815018-4.00003-6

forces, including automated vehicle technology and innovative service models; however, this seems unlikely. Rather, these advances, coupled with public policy, suggest we could reimagine how we use and interact with vehicles, including private-vehicle ownership. The integration of transportation modes, real-time information, and instant communication and dispatch—all possible with the click of a mouse or a smartphone app—is redefining "auto mobility." Rather than rendering cars obsolete, the convergence of on-demand shared travel, automation, and electric-drive technology could change our relationship with the automobile, making vehicles more cost-effective, efficient, and convenient.

Demographic shifts, advancements in technology, congestion, the commodification of transportation services, and heightened awareness about the environment and climate change are contributing to the growth of shared on-demand mobility. In recent years, mobility on demand (MOD)—where consumers access mobility, goods, and services on-demand—has grown due to advancements in technology; changing consumer preferences (mobility and retail consumption); and a myriad of economic, environmental, and social factors. Key industry benchmarks exemplify developments in this emerging sector:

- **Carsharing**—As of January 2017, there were 21 active carsharing programs in the United States (U.S.) with over 1.4 million members sharing more than 17,000 vehicles (Shaheen et al., 2018).
- **Bikesharing**—As of the end of 2017, the U.S. had more than 200 bikesharing operators with more than 100,000 bicycles (Russell Meddin, unpublished data). More than 84 million trips were taken on micromobility (bikesharing and scooter sharing) in the U.S. in 2018 (NACTO, 2018).
- **Transportation network companies (TNCs, also known as ridesourcing and ridehailing)**—As of the end of 2018, Lyft reported 18.6 million active riders and more than 1.1 million drivers operating in more than 300 markets throughout the U.S. and Canada (based on SEC filings). Uber operated in 63 countries serving an estimated 82 million users as of December 2018 (based on SEC filings).
- **Pooling**—As of December 2017, uberPOOL and Lyft Shared rides, a pooled version of for-hire TNCs, were available in 14 and 16 U.S. markets, respectively (Paige Tsai, personal communication; Peter Gigante, personal communication). Innovative carpool apps, such as Scoop and Waze Carpool, also are enabling on-demand higher occupancy commuting.

The growth of on-demand mobility and courier services is contributing to private-sector interest. Acquisitions, investments, partnerships, internal development of technologies, and mobility services are contributing to a growing interest in MOD by automakers (Shaheen et al., 2017). In the logistics sector, companies are testing a variety of automated vehicle and drone delivery innovations. For example, FedEx and UPS are developing delivery vans that are paired with drone systems, which can make short-range aerial deliveries while a parcel van makes another delivery (Shaheen and Cohen, 2017; Yvkoff, 2017; Franco, 2016). Automated parcel stations, lockers, and delivery drones are being tested by Amazon and DHL (Shaheen and Cohen, 2017; Yvkoff, 2017; Franco, 2016). Startups, such as Starship, are developing automated delivery robots for restaurants, retailers, and e-commerce companies (McFarland, 2017; Starship n.d.).

A growing array of on-demand mobility options are raising awareness of innovative mobility options that may complement and/or compete with public transportation. These trends are leading to fundamental changes requiring policymakers and public transit agencies to consider the individual and collective impacts of these services on public transportation, ridership, system design, and first-mile/last-mile connections (Shaheen and Cohen, 2018). In the future, automation could be the most transformative change impacting travel behavior and public transport since the automobile. Shared automated vehicles (SAVs) could create new opportunities for public transportation such as: (1) enabling infill development and increased density that support public transportation and (2) reducing the operational costs of public transit, making it more or less competitive with other modes depending on the context.

There are six sections in this chapter. First, we briefly explain the methodology we employed to research MOD and other innovative transportation services. We then define distinguishing characteristics of MOD, mobility as a service (MaaS), and current and emerging shared modes. We also explore a range of public transit and MOD service models and enabling partnerships (e.g., trip planning, fare integration, guaranteed ride home, and data sharing). In the next section, we review emerging trends impacting public transportation and the literature documenting the impacts of shared modes on public transit. In the section that follows, we review the potential impacts of automation on public transportation. We conclude the chapter with a summary of the potential trends that could impact the future of public transportation.

2. Methodology

For this research, we used a multi-method qualitative approach for researching MOD, MaaS, and shared mobility. First, we conducted a literature review of on-demand and shared mobility systems including: definitions, concepts, and impact studies. We supplemented the published literature with an Internet-based review and conducted targeted interviews and webinars with approximately 30 experts to identify emerging trends in mobility. Many of these sources filled gaps in the literature where existing publications have not kept pace with innovative transportation services. Additionally, we hosted two, one-day workshops comprised of plenary and breakout sessions and moderated discussions to engage MOD stakeholders at two Transportation Research Board Annual Meetings (2017 and 2018). These workshops included breakout sessions on opportunities and challenges in four areas: (1) understanding and managing pilot data; (2) accessibility and equity; (3) innovative business models; and (4) planning for MOD (e.g., the built environment, rights-of-way management, land use, and zoning). Over 150 transportation practitioners and researchers representing the public and private sectors participated in each workshop (Shaheen et al., 2018; Shaheen et al., 2017). We also coauthored the U.S. Department of Transportation's (USDOT) Mobility on Demand (MOD) Operational Concept Report, a multimodal effort initiated by the Intelligent Transportation Systems (ITS) Joint Programs Office (JPO) and the Federal Transit Administration (FTA) to help guide MOD concept development, pilots, testing, demonstration projects, research, and public policy (Shaheen et al., 2017).

Additionally, we sponsored the SAE International standard J3163 to develop definitions for terminology related to shared mobility and enabling technologies. As part of this process, we facilitated stakeholder engagements with 12 experts as part of four expert panel meetings. We also engaged 30 experts as part of five task force meetings and solicited feedback from 30 voting members and approximately 100 participants on the Shared and Digital Mobility Committee through SAE's ballot and comment process. Participants included academic researchers, transportation professionals, policymakers, automakers, and mobility-service providers. Participants were selected by SAE based on their experience and knowledge with shared and on-demand mobility services. Each engagement averaged approximately one hour in length.

In addition, we have collectively researched approximately 15 studies on the social, environmental, and travel behavior impacts of shared mobility. These studies are typically comprised of focus groups, expert interviews, self-report surveys, and activity data. More information on the study methodologies can be obtained by reviewing the cited material (e.g., (Lazarus et al., 2018; Lazarus et al., 2018; Martin and Shaheen, 2016; Martin and Shaheen, 2011; Rayle et al., 2016; Shaheen, Chan and Gaynor, 2016; Shaheen et al., 2014)).

Finally, we are members of the independent evaluation team for FTA's MOD Sandbox demonstration of 12 pilot projects focused on MOD partnerships with public transit operators. This helped inform the chapter's development. While the methods we employed to document MOD definitions, developments, and concepts were extensive, it is important to note that this sector is evolving rapidly. Thus, it is possible that potential literature, experts, and developments may not have been included in our review.

3. Definitions of MOD, MaaS, and shared modes

MOD is an innovative transportation concept where consumers can access mobility, goods, and services on-demand by dispatching or using shared mobility, courier services, unmanned aerial vehicles, and public transportation strategies (Shaheen et al., 2017). MOD is an emerging concept based on three core principles:

1. *Commodification of transportation* where modes have economic values that are distinguishable in terms of cost, travel time, wait time, number of connections, convenience, vehicle occupancy, and other attributes (Shaheen et al., 2017);
2. *Embracing the needs of all users* including travelers, couriers, consumers, public and private market participants, active and motorized transportation modes, and users with special needs (e.g., older adults, low-income, people with disabilities) (Shaheen et al., 2017); and
3. *Improving the efficiency of the transportation network* through multimodal travel, supply-and-demand management, and active transportation demand management by allowing market participants to predict, monitor, and influence conditions across the entire transportation ecosystem.

MOD differs from the emerging European concept of MaaS. MOD focuses on the commodification of passenger mobility and goods delivery and transportation systems management, whereas MaaS primarily focuses on passenger mobility aggregation and subscription services. Brokering travel with suppliers, repackaging, and reselling it as a bundled package is a distinguishing characteristic of MaaS (Sochor et al., 2015). See Fig. 3.1 below for a comparison of MOD and MaaS.

MOD passenger services can include: bikesharing; carsharing; microtransit; ridesharing (i.e., carpooling and vanpooling); TNCs; scooter sharing; shuttle services; urban air mobility (UAM); and public transportation. MOD

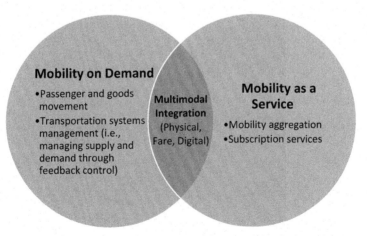

FIGURE 3.1 Comparison of mobility on demand (MOD) and mobility as a service (MaaS).

courier services can include app-based delivery (also known as courier network services or CNS); robotic delivery; and aerial delivery (e.g., drones). Definitions of current and emerging MOD services are included in Table 3.1 below.

TABLE 3.1 Definitions of existing and emerging MOD/MaaS services.

Mode	Definition
Bikesharing (also known as micromobility)	Offers users on-demand access to bicycles at a variety of pick-up and drop-off locations for one-way (point-to-point) or roundtrip travel. Bikesharing fleets are commonly deployed in a network within a metropolitan region, city, neighborhood, employment center, and/or university campus (Shaheen, Cohen and Zohdy, 2016) (SAE International, 2018).
Carsharing	Provides users vehicle access through membership in an organization that maintains a fleet of cars and/or light trucks. These vehicles may be located within neighborhoods, public transit stations, employment centers, universities, etc. Carsharing organizations typically provide insurance, gasoline, parking, and maintenance. Members who join a carsharing organization typically pay a fee each time they use a vehicle (also known as pay-as-you-go pricing) (Shaheen, Cohen and Zohdy, 2016).
Courier network services (CNS)	Facilitate for-hire delivery services for monetary compensation using an online application or platform (such as a website or smartphone app) to connect couriers using their personal vehicles, bicycles, or scooters with packages, food, etc. (Shaheen, Cohen, et al., 2016).
Delivery drones	Use unmanned aerial vehicles to transport packages, food, or other goods.
Microtransit	Uses multi-passenger/pooled shuttles or vans to provide technology-enabled, on-demand or fixed-schedule services with either dynamic or fixed routing (SAE International, 2018).

TABLE 3.1 Definitions of existing and emerging MOD/MaaS services.—cont'd

Mode	Definition
Ridesharing (carpooling and vanpooling)	The formal or informal sharing of rides between drivers and passengers with similar origin-destination pairings. Ridesharing includes carpooling and vanpooling, which consists of 7 to 15 passengers who share the cost of a van and operating expenses and may share driving responsibility (Shaheen, Cohen and Zohdy, 2016).
TNCs (also known as ridesourcing and ridehailing)	Prearranged and on-demand transportation services for compensation in which drivers and passengers connect via digital applications. Digital applications are typically used for booking, electronic payment, and ratings (Shaheen, Cohen and Zohdy, 2016) (SAE International, 2018).
Robotic delivery (automated delivery vehicles)	Transport of food, groceries, and small packages using an automated robot that operates at low speeds on sidewalks, bicycle lanes, or other concrete or paved surface.
Scooter sharing (also known as micromobility)	Offers individuals access to scooters by joining an organization that maintains a fleet of scooters at various locations. Scooter-sharing models can include a variety of motorized and nonmotorized scooter types. The scooter service provider typically provides gasoline or power (in the case of motorized scooters), maintenance, and may include parking as part of the service. Users typically pay a fee each time they use a scooter (Shaheen, Cohen and Zohdy, 2016). Scooter sharing includes two types of services: 1) Standing electric scooter sharing using shared scooters with a stand design, including a handlebar, deck, and wheels, that is propelled by an electric motor. The most common scooters today are made of aluminum, titanium, and steel. 2) Moped-style scooter sharing with a seated design, either electric or gas powered, which generally have a less stringent licensing requirement than motorcycles designed to travel on public roads.

Continued

TABLE 3.1 Definitions of existing and emerging MOD/MaaS services.—cont'd

Mode	Definition
Shuttles	Shared vehicles (frequently vans or buses) that connect passengers from a common origin or destination to public transit, retail, hospitality, or employment centers. Shuttles are typically operated by professional drivers, and many provide complimentary services to the passengers (Cohen and Shaheen, 2016) (SAE International, 2018).
Taxis	Prearranged and on-demand transportation services for compensation through a negotiated price, zone pricing, or taximeter (either traditional or GPS-based). Passengers can schedule trips in advance (booked through a phone dispatch, website, or smartphone app); street hail (by raising a hand on the street, standing at a taxi stand, or specified loading zone); or e-Hail (by dispatching a driver on-demand using a smartphone app) (Cohen and Shaheen, 2016) (SAE International, 2018).
Urban air mobility	A system for air passenger and cargo transportation within an urban area, including small package delivery and other urban unmanned aerial services, that supports a mix of onboard/ground-piloted and autonomous operations (NASA, 2017).

TNCs, transportation network companies.
Source: Adapted from Cohen, A., and S. Shaheen., 2016. Planning for Shared Mobility. Chicago: American Planning Association; Shaheen, S., Cohen, A., Zohdy, I., and Kock, B., 2016. Smartphone Applications to Influence Traveler Choices Practices and Policies. Washington D.C.: U.S. Department of Transportation; SAE International. 2018. Axonomy and Definitions for Terms Related to Shared. Detroit: SAE International.

4. Common public transit and MOD service models and enabling partnerships

With a growing number of on-demand mobility options, public agencies are increasingly faced with opportunities to partner with private-sector mobility providers. For example, the FTA has developed the MOD Sandbox, an ongoing research initiative to study the potential impacts of MOD and assess how existing FTA policies and regulations may support or impede these innovative transportation services. Based on our literature review and targeted expert interviews, we identified four common MOD service models and four enabling MOD public transit partnership approaches, described in the following sections.

4.1 Common MOD service models

1. *First- and last-mile connections to public transit services* involve a public agency providing a subsidy (monetary, in-kind support, or rights-of-way access) to encourage private operators to make trips beginning or ending at a public transit stop. In Summit, New Jersey, the city has partnered with Lyft and Uber to provide free rides to and from their station during weekday commute hours in an effort to increase station passenger throughput without having to build additional parking.
2. *Gap filling services*:
   a. *Low-density service* involves a public agency providing a subsidy to initiate or expand service in suburban or rural areas. For example, in Pinellas County, Florida, the Pinellas Suncoast Transit Authority (PSTA) partners with TNCs (Lyft and Uber) and taxi providers to offer subsidized first- and last-mile rides to bus stops in low-density service areas. The public transit agency provides a US$5 discount per trip under the program, lowering the rider cost to US$1 per trip to travel to the nearest bus stop for most users (New York Public Transit Association, 2018).
   b. *Off-peak services* offer limited time-of-day subsidies during late-night or other public transit off-peak times. In particular, off-peak service subsidies can help public transit agencies reduce costs associated with providing high-capacity fixed routes during lower-demand times. For example, in Florida, the PSTA funded US$300,000 to subsidize up to 23 free, late-night rides for low-income residents and workers between 9 p.m. and 6 a.m. for travelers departing from or going to a residence or workplace (Pinellas Suncoast Transit Authority n.d.).
3. *Public transit replacement services* subsidize MOD providers that offer service in areas with insufficient public transit ridership. These types of partnerships can allow transit agencies to replace low-ridership routes or low-level services (e.g., long headways) with a lower-cost alternative or more frequent service alternative. In Arlington, Texas, the city has replaced local bus services with Via, a microtransit service. Via operates a fleet of 10 commuter vans in downtown Arlington and charges a fare of US$3 per ride (Etherington, 2018).
4. *Paratransit services* employ MOD to supplement or replace an existing paratransit service. Typically, many public transit agencies subcontract to

third-party paratransit vendors to provide service, which in some cases can cost more than US$50 per trip (Penny Grellier, unpublished data, 2018). In Boston, the Massachusetts Bay Transportation Authority (MBTA) has partnered with Lyft and Uber to provide MBTA's existing paratransit riders with US$1 uberPOOL rides and US$2 uberX or Lyft rides. MBTA also pays any trip costs over US$15. The program has reduced MBTA paratransit costs approximately 20%, while riders increased use by approximately 28%, saving an average of 6% on a per-trip basis (Massachusetts Governor's Office, 2016).

4.2 Enabling MOD public transit partnership approaches

1. *Trip planning partnerships* often focus on developing and/or integrating multimodal trip planning into a single platform. Common goals of trip planning partnerships include: (1) increasing consumer trip planning convenience, (2) encouraging multimodal transportation, and (3) reducing barriers to public and active transportation use. In Los Angeles, Conduent Inc's Go-LA app allows Angelinos to plan a trip using many MOD modes in conjunction with public transportation (e.g., Lyft, taxis, and Zipcar) (Conduent Inc. n.d.).
2. *Fare integration partnerships* allow riders to easily pay for trips that span across public and private transportation modes and allow riders to either: (1) pay for each trip leg using the same fare medium or (2) pay for trip legs employing a single fare (that is apportioned to each mobility provider that serves each trip leg on the backend). In Chicago, Divvy bikesharing and the Chicago Transit Authority are testing an integrated fare card concept as part of FTA's MOD Sandbox demonstration (William Trumbull, unpublished data, 2018).
3. *Guaranteed ride home (GRH) partnerships* consist of a private-sector provider subsidizing this public-sector service. In San Diego, the San Diego Association of Governments (SANDAG) has partnered with Uber to provide a guaranteed ride home for commuters. Uber subsidizes this program up to US$20,000 annually (SANDAG, unpublished data, March 2018).
4. *Data sharing partnerships* involve the private-sector sharing mobility data to enhance local transportation planning and operations. For example, during the 2014 World Cup in Rio de Janeiro, the government obtained driver navigation data from Google's Waze app and combined it with information from pedestrians who use the public transportation app Moovit, which provides local authorities with valuable real-time information about the transportation network. Together, these services could jointly aggregate and identify thousands of operational issues ranging from congestion to roadway hazards (Olson, 2014).

5. Emerging trends and potential impacts of MOD/MaaS on public transportation

After peaking in 2014, average U.S. public transit ridership declined approximately 5% between 2014 and 2017 (American Public Transit Association, 2017). Technological, mobility, and societal trends are contributing to declining public ridership and the evolving nature of how Americans are traveling (Shaheen and Cohen, 2018; Shaheen et al., 2018). Changing attitudes toward sharing and MOD, as well as an increasing number of on-demand, flexible-route options, are impacting the nature of public transportation (Shaheen and Cohen, 2018). Emerging transportation services can both facilitate first- and last-mile connections and compete with public transit. In this evolving transportation marketplace, public transportation faces an increasingly competitive environment where mobility consumers select modes based on a range of factors including: price, wait time, travel time, number of connections, convenience, and traveler experience (Shaheen et al., 2017).

In North America, shared mobility began with the launch of roundtrip carsharing in 1994, where a vehicle had to be returned to its origin (Shaheen et al., 2005). However, over the years IT-based technologies have enabled the growth of one-way and flexible-route, shared services. In 2007, Tulsa Townies, a station-based IT-enabled bikesharing program, was launched in Oklahoma (Shaheen et al., 2014). This was followed by the launch of the TNC services Lyft, Sidecar, and uberX between 2012 to 2013 (Shaheen, Cohen and Zohdy, 2016). In North America, dockless "smartbike" concepts began to emerge in 2012, although Deutsch Bahn "Call a Bike" (incorporating text message delivery of access codes to lock and unlock dockless bikesharing) had been in existence in Germany since 2000 (Call a Bike, 2018). As of May 2018, the U.S. had 261 bikesharing operators with more than 48,000 bicycles (Russell Meddin, unpublished data). Dockless bikesharing accounted for approximately 44% of bikesharing equipment and approximately 4% of bikesharing trips in 2017 in the U.S. (National Association of City Transportation Officials (NACTO), 2018). In some cases, programs are employing hybrid or flexible models that blend aspects of station-based and dockless systems that can provide users with some predictability that equipment will be available at specific locations. In 2014, microtransit services that offered a combination of fixed and flexible route, scheduled and dispatch services began to emerge in San Francisco (Berrebi, 2017). Over time, however, many of these services began to leverage IT-enabled hardware and advanced algorithms to offer a variety of demand-responsive services. More recently, the growth of micromobility, such as standing scooter sharing has continued this trend toward on-demand mobility. As of September 2018, two U.S. scooter-sharing providers were operating in 100 cities worldwide and had logged 21.5 million rides (Dickey, 2018). As of September 2018, there were an estimated 65,000 scooters available across the U.S. (Dobush, 2018). According to NACTO, an estimated 84 million shared micromobility trips were taken using bikesharing and scooter sharing in the U.S. in 2018 (NACTO, 2018).

MOD growth has created new opportunities and challenges for public transportation. For example, dockless systems may have less visibility at public transit hubs as users may have less predictable drop-off or pick-up points requiring a user to walk a few blocks to pick up a scooter or dockless bike rather than accessing one from an on-site kiosk. However, public transit agencies may be able to overcome these challenges by implementing incentives to encourage riders to return dockless bikes and scooters close to public transportation and working with service providers to develop pricing and marketing strategies that target transit riders. Other potential concerns for public transit agencies can include worries about bicycles or scooters piling up at public transit facilities and blocking sidewalk and curb access. Public transit agencies can help mitigate these and other concerns through proactive policies that regulate: equipment standards; insurance; indemnification of liability; requirements for equipment rebalancing; dedicated rights-of-way and equipment parking guidance; and processes for parking enforcement, such as fines and equipment impounding (Cohen and Shaheen, 2016).

While a number of studies have examined the social, environmental, and behavioral impacts of MOD, more research is needed to understand the precise impacts of these services on public transportation. Several studies indicate that MOD can both complement and compete with public transit depending upon a variety of factors such as: accessibility, frequency of service, walkability of the community, density and land use, sociodemographics, cultural norms, and other factors.

As noted in the methodological discussion, we have collectively researched approximately 15 studies on the social, environmental, and travel behavior impacts of shared mobility. These studies are typically comprised of focus groups, expert interviews, and self-report surveys. A summary of results from these studies and the associated impacts on public transportation are provided in Table 3.2 below. More information on each of these study methodologies can be obtained by reviewing the original cited material.

A number of carsharing studies have examined the impact of roundtrip and one-way carsharing on public transit and nonmotorized travel (Martin and Shaheen, 2016; Martin and Shaheen, 2011; Cervero, 2003; Cervero and Yuhsin, 2004; Cervero et al., 2007; Firnkorn and Müller, 2012; Lane, 2005). Martin and Shaheen (2011) found that roundtrip carsharing in North America had a neutral to negative impact on public transit ridership. For every five members that used rail less, four used rail more, and for every ten members that took the bus less, almost nine took it more. Martin and Shaheen (2016) also studied free-floating carsharing in five North American cities. They found that in four of the five cities surveyed, a majority of respondents stated that one-way carsharing had no impact on their public transit use. For those respondents who used public transit less, the primary reason was that one-way

TABLE 3.2 Summary of shared mobility impacts on public transit.

Mode (study locations)	Decrease/Increase	Public transit impacts
Roundtrip carsharing (North America)	Net decrease	Across the entire sample, the results showed an overall decline in public transit use that was statistically significant, as 589 carsharing members reduced rail use and 828 reduced bus use, while 494 increased rail use and 732 increased bus use. Thus, for every five members that use rail less, four ride it more. For every 10 members that use the bus less, 9 ride it more (Martin and Shaheen, 2011).
Roundtrip and station-based one-way carsharing (France)	-Slight increase (roundtrip) -Net decrease (station-based one-way)	A French national survey comparing roundtrip and station-based carsharing found that roundtrip carsharing slightly increased public transit use, whereas station-based one-way carsharing reduced it (6t 2014).
One-way carsharing (North America)	Net decrease (although an exception in Seattle)	In Seattle, a small percent of respondents increased their use, which exceeded the smaller percent of respondents that decreased their rail use. Across the other four cities, more people reported a decrease in their frequency of urban rail and bus use than an increase (Martin and Shaheen, 2016).
P2P carsharing (North America)	Not a notable net increase or decrease	There was not a notable net increase or decrease in public transit use. Those increasing and decreasing their bus and rail use were closely balanced in number, with 9% increasing bus use and 10% decreasing use. Similar effects were found with rail, as 7% reported increasing rail use, while 8% reported decreasing it (Shaheen et al., 2018).
Station-based bikesharing (North America)	-Net increases in bus/rail in small- and medium-sized cities -Small net decreases in bus/rail in larger cities	-Small net increases in bus and rail use in small- and medium-size cities (e.g., Minneapolis). -Small net decreases in bus and rail use in larger cities (e.g., Mexico city) (Shaheen and Martin, 2015)

Continued

TABLE 3.2 Summary of shared mobility impacts on public transit.—cont'd

Mode (study locations)	Decrease/Increase	Public transit impacts
		(Shaheen, Martin, et al. public bikesharing in North America during A Period of rapid Expansion: Understanding business models, industry trends and user impacts, 2014) (Shaheen et al., 2013).
Station-based bikesharing (New York City)	Net decrease in bus/rail riders	Electric bikesharing is more likely to attract regular users of subway, personal car, taxi, and bus riders (in particular) (Campbell et al., 2016). Seventy percent of bikesharing members may come from previous bus riders.
Casual carpooling (San Francisco Bay Area)	Net decrease	The majority of casual carpoolers were public transit users. In the Bay Area, 75% of casual carpoolers shifted from public transit (Shaheen, Chan and Gaynor, 2016).
TNCs (San Francisco Bay Area)	Net decrease	TNCs drew 30% of passengers from public transit. Forty percent employed TNCs as a first-mile and last-mile option (destination or origin is a public transit stop) (Rayle et al., 2016).
TNCs (Denver, Colorado)	Net decrease	This study found that 22% of respondents would have used public transportation, if TNCs were not available.
TNCs (Boston, Massachusetts)	Net decrease	Study participants were asked how they would have traveled, if TNCs were unavailable. Forty-two percent of respondents said they would have taken public transit. The study concluded that 15% of TNC trips were added during the morning and evening commute hours (Gehrke et al., 2018).
TNCs (seven US cities)	Net decrease in bus and light rail use; slight increase in commuter rail use	This study found that TNCs compete with bus services and light rail (a net reduction of 6% and 3%, respectively), but they complement commuter rail services (3% increase). However, the

TABLE 3.2 Summary of shared mobility impacts on public transit.—cont'd

Mode (study locations)	Decrease/Increase	Public transit impacts
		aggregation of the results makes it challenging to discern the respective impacts on public transit in each city (Clewlow and Mishra, 2017).
TNCs (seven US cities)	Net increase	This study found that 43% of shared mobility users rode public transit more compared to 28% who took public transit less. The self-selection of shared mobility users may have contributed to a response bias in this survey (Feigon and Murphy, 2016).

TNCs, transportation network companies.

carsharing is more time efficient. Those respondents using public transit more reported the primary reason was the first- and last-mile connectivity that carsharing provides. A French national survey comparing the impacts of roundtrip and station-based carsharing on modal shift found that roundtrip carsharing slightly increased public transit use, whereas station-based, one-way carsharing reduced it (6t 2014).

Studies on the impacts of carpooling on public transit ridership are limited. However, a study of casual carpooling in the San Francisco Bay Area found that 75% of casual carpool respondents were previous public transit users compared to approximately 10% that previously drove alone (Shaheen, Chan and Gaynor, 2016).

Research has also shown that public bikesharing has mixed impacts on public transit ridership. Campbell et al. (2016) found that electric bikesharing is more likely to attract regular users of subway, personal car, taxi, and bus riders (in particular) (Campbell et al., 2016). Campbell and Brakewood (2017) found that for every 1,000 station-based bikesharing docks within a quarter mile distance from a bus route, there is a 2.42% decrease in the number of passengers who board New York City Transit buses in Manhattan and Brooklyn per day, which is equivalent to a total daily decrease in ridership of approximately 18,100 (Campbell and Brakewood, 2017). The authors concluded that bikesharing may be drawing approximately 70% of its members from previous bus riders. In a study of station-based bikesharing in Minneapolis—Saint Paul, more people shifted toward rail (15%) than away from it (3%) in response to bikesharing. The study also found a slight decline in bus ridership: 15% of respondents increased their use of buses compared to 17% that decreased it. The study also found in Washington, DC more people shifted away from rail (47%) than to it (7%), and more respondents shifted away from riding the bus with just 5% of respondents increasing bus ridership compared to 39% that decreased it (Shaheen et al., 2014; Shaheen et al., 2013). Shaheen and Martin conducted a geospatial analysis and found that shifts away from public transportation due to station-based bikesharing were most prominent in urban environments within high-density urban cores. Shifts toward public transportation in response to station-based bikesharing tended to be more prevalent in lower-density regions on the urban periphery, suggesting that public bikesharing may serve as a first- and last-mile connector in smaller metropolitan regions with lower densities and less robust public transit networks. In larger metropolitan regions with higher densities and more robust transit networks, public bikesharing may offer faster, cheaper, and more direct connections compared to short-distance transit trips (Shaheen and Martin, 2015). A study comparing the impacts of station-based and dockless bikesharing in the San Francisco Bay Area by Lazarus et al., (2018) found that station-based trips tended to be short, flat commute trips, mostly connecting to/from major public transit transfer stations, while dockless trips tended to be longer, more spatially distributed, and serviced more lower-density neighborhoods (Lazarus et al., 2018). However, more research is needed to understand the modal impacts of dockless bikesharing and other dockless modes across a large sample of cities.

There have also been approximately half a dozen studies that have assessed the impact of TNC services on modal shift. Generally, TNC users are either replacing a trip they formerly made with another transportation mode (public transit, driving, walking, biking, etc.) or they are making a new trip they otherwise would not have made without the availability of TNC services (i.e., induced demand). While a few studies have found that TNCs are substituting less for public transit trips (Feigon and Murphy, 2016; Hampshire et al., 2017; Clewlow and Mishra, 2017), with shifts of 15% or less, several others have found that TNCs compete more intensively, creating modal shifts between 22% and 42% away from public transit (Rayle et al., 2016; Henao, 2017; Henao and Marshall, 2018; Gehrke et al., 2018). Typically, studies measure modal shift by employing surveys that ask respondents about the transportation modes they would have used, had TNCs not been available. Table 3.3 below shows results from six surveys regarding mode replacement of TNC trips. It is important to note that different methodologies for measuring modal shift can have a large impact on findings, and the asterisks denote variations in survey question design and analysis methodologies.

Modal shift can vary depending on the location, type of survey, and the analysis methods chosen. These studies indicate that in cities with greater population density and higher public transit use, TNCs may draw more heavily from public transit than in less dense cities with higher proportions of trips

TABLE 3.3 TNC Mode replacement impacts.

Study authors location survey year	Rayle et al.[a] San Francisco, CA 2014	Henao and Marshall Denver and Boulder, CO 2016	Gehrke et al.[a] Boston, MA 2017	Clewlow and Mishra[b] Seven US Cities[e] two phases, 2014–16	Feigon and Murphy[f] Seven US Cities[e] 2016	Hampshire et al.[d] Austin, TX 2016	Alemi et al.[f] California 2015
Drive (%)	7	33	18	39	34	45	66
Public transit (%)	30	22	42	15	14	3	22
Taxi (%)	36	10	23	1	8	2	49
Bike or walk (%)	9	12	12	23	17	2	20
Would not have made trip (%)	8	12	5	22	1	–	8
Carsharing/car rental (%)	–	4	–	–	24	4	–
Other/other TNCs (%)	10	7	–	–	–	42 (another TNC) 2 (other)	6 (van/ shuttle)

[a]Survey question: "How would you have made your last trip, if TNC services were not available?"

[b]Survey question: "If TNC services were unavailable, which transportation alternatives would you use for the trips that you make using TNC services?"

[c]Survey crosstab and question: For respondents that use TNCs most often compared to other shared modes: "How would you make your most frequent (TNC) trip if TNCs were not available?"

[d]Survey question: "How do you currently make the last trip you took with Uber or Lyft, now that these companies no longer operate in Austin?"

[e]The impacts in both of these studies were aggregated across: Austin, Boston, Chicago, Los Angeles, San Francisco, Seattle, and Washington, DC.

[f]Survey question: "How would you have made your most recent TNC trip (if at all) if these services had not been available?" This study allowed multiple responses to the question: "How would you have made your most recent TNC trip (if at all) if these services had not been available?" This is why the percentages add up to more than 100%, making it challenging to directly compare the results to the other studies.

made with personal vehicles. The studies in the denser cities of San Francisco (Rayle et al., 2016) and Boston (Gehrke et al., 2018) both found that a higher proportion of respondents would have used public transit (30% and 42%, respectively) than would have driven (7% and 18%, respectively), if TNC services were unavailable. Conversely, in the studies in Denver and Austin, Henao and Marshall (2018) and Hampshire et al., (2017) found driving to be the most common replacement mode if TNCs not been available (33% and 45%, respectively). The two seven-city studies and the Alemi et al. study in California also found personal driving to be the most common mode replaced, although city-specific impacts are obscured in these studies due to aggregation of survey results across all of the cities.

6. Potential impacts of automation on public transportation

In the future, vehicle automation will likely change the nature of conventional public–private relationships in transportation (Shaheen and Cohen, 2018). Automation has the potential to reduce vehicle ownership costs due to SAVs (a fleet of for-hire AVs akin to automated taxis) that could change urban parking needs. A reduction in the need for urban parking has the potential to create new opportunities for infill development and increased densities. While SAVs could compete with public transit, infill development could also create higher densities to support additional public transit service and allow for the conversion of bus transit to rail transit in urban centers (Shaheen and Cohen, 2018). However, the growth of telecommuting and AVs could make longer commutes less burdensome and encourage suburban and exurban lifestyles in an automated vehicle future. While vehicle automation pose a number of risks to public transportation, AVs also have the potential to reduce labor and operating costs that could be passed on to riders in the form of lower fares. SAVs could also make flexible-route, on-demand services more feasible, making public transit more convenient or competitive with other modes, resulting in increased ridership (Shaheen and Cohen, 2018). For all of these reasons, the potential impacts of vehicle automation on public transit are difficult to model and forecast.

Studies that employ travel models to simulate the possible future modal shift impacts of private AVs generally find that they lead to a reduction in public transit use and active modes, such as cycling and walking, leading to a higher overall share of personal vehicle travel in many cases (Kim et al., 2015). Similarly, studies that include SAVs also indicate reductions in existing public transit use and active transportation modes (Bösch et al., 2018; Chen and Kockelman, 2016). In contrast, some SAV studies forecast a decrease in private-vehicle trips, with one such study predicting a private-vehicle use decrease of 48% to 36% in Switzerland, which is attributed to the introduction of SAV services (Bösch et al., 2018).

While the impacts of vehicle automation on public transportation are uncertain, vehicle automation has the potential of changing long-standing costs of public and private services. The nature of public—private partnerships will also likely evolve over time based on differences in geographies, densities, existing infrastructure, and other factors over time (Lazarus et al., 2018). In the future, vehicle automation may enable some public transit agencies to provide more flexible, demand-responsive services in smaller vehicles, while others may pursue these systems through public—private partnerships. The types of public—private partnerships that evolve in an automated vehicle future will likely vary locally depending on the context (Lazarus et al., 2018). By leveraging automated, flexible route, on-demand services, public transportation has an opportunity to reinvent itself as a more competitive alternative to private automated vehicle ownership, increase its market share, and reduce transport inefficiencies in the future (Shaheen and Cohen, 2018).

7. Conclusion

In recent years, the commodification of transportation services where consumers make modal choices based on factors such as: cost, travel and wait time, number of connections, convenience, vehicle occupancy, and other attributes is contributing to MOD/MaaS growth. MOD passenger services can include: bikesharing; carsharing; microtransit; ridesharing (i.e., carpooling and vanpooling); TNCs; scooter sharing; shuttle services; UAM; and public transportation. MOD courier services may include app-based delivery services (known as courier network services or CNS); robotic delivery; and aerial delivery (e.g., drones). Although closely related to MaaS, MOD includes passenger and goods movement and incorporates principles of transportation systems management (e.g., feedback control to better manage supply and demand), whereas MaaS emphasizes mobility aggregation and subscription services that bundle multiple services into a pricing package.

In this emerging mobility ecosystem, public agencies are increasingly being confronted with opportunities to partner with private-sector mobility providers. Current MOD services in the U.S. include: (1) first- and last-mile connections to public transit; (2) gap filling services, such as low-density and off-peak services; (3) public transit replacement; and (4) paratransit services. Some approaches that support MOD public-transit partnerships include: (1) trip planning; (2) fare integration; (3) guaranteed ride home initiatives; and (4) data sharing.

Technology, mobility, and societal trends are contributing to declining public transit ridership and starting to change how Americans are traveling. New attitudes toward sharing, MOD, MaaS, and an increasing number of on-demand, flexible-route transportation options are creating new opportunities and challenges for public transportation. While a number of studies have examined the impacts of MOD services on public transportation, more research is needed to better understand how geospatial and temporal dimensions impact this relationship. In some cases, MOD can complement existing services by filling gaps and providing first- and last-mile connections. In other cases, MOD may compete with public transit. Better understanding of the impacts of MOD and MaaS on public transportation in a range of land use and built environments is needed. Several studies already indicate that MOD can complement and compete with public transportation in the U.S., depending on a variety of factors such as: public transit accessibility, frequency of transit service, walkability of the community, density and land use, and sociodemographics. Research to advance this understanding can help to inform the policy-making process to better leverage positive impacts and reduce unintended consequences.

While the impacts of vehicle automation on public transportation are difficult to model and forecast, AVs will likely change long-standing public- and private-sector relationships that have characterized the transportation network. Automation has the potential to foster competition with public transportation through SAVs, but it also has a chance to create new opportunities (e.g., microtransit services, first- and last-mile connections). For instance, SAVs could reduce some public transit labor and operating costs. These savings could be passed on to riders in the form of lower fares or enable more flexible route, on-demand services. In the future, vehicle automation could make public transit more convenient and competitive with other modes, resulting in increased ridership in a range of policy scenarios. MOD/MaaS partnerships offer an opportunity for public transit to reinvent itself, fostering a more a convenient, customer-focused, and on-demand alternative to private- vehicle use.

Acknowledgments

We would like to acknowledge the numerous MOD service providers, public agencies, and other experts and practitioners that provided valuable data and input to support our research. We would also like to express our gratitude to the American Planning Association, Caltrans, the Mineta Transportation Institute, and the U.S. Department of Transportation for supporting this research. We would also like to thank Richard Davis, Emily Farrar, Elliot Martin, Adam Stocker, and Michael Randolph for their involvement in our MOD research at the Transportation Sustainability Research Center at the University of California, Berkeley.

References

6t, 2014. One-Way Carsharing: Which Alternative to Private Cars? 6t, Paris.

American Public Transit Association, 2017. Transit Ridership Report. http://www.apta.com/resources/statistics/Documents/Ridership/2017-q2-ridership-APTA.pdf.

Berrebi, S., 2017. Don't Believe the Microtransit Hype. https://www.citylab.com/transportation/2017/11/dont-believe-the-microtransit-hype/545033/.

Bösch, P., Ciari, F., Kay, A., 2018. Transport Policy Optimization with Autonomous Vehicles. Transportation Research Record.

Call a Bike, 2018. Call a Bike. https://www.callabike-interaktiv.de/de.

Campbell, K., Brakewood, C., 2017. Sharing riders: how bikesharing impacts bus ridership in New York City. Transportation Research Part A: Policy and Practice 100, 264−282.

Campbell, A., Cherry, C., Ryerson, M., Yang, X., 2016. Factors influencing the choice of shared bicycles and shared electric bikes in Beijing. Transportation Research Part C: Emerging Technologies 67, 399−414.

Cervero, R., 2003. City CarShare: first-year travel demand impacts. Transportation Research Record 1839, 159−166.

Cervero, R., Yuhsin, T., 2004. City CarShare in san Francisco, California: second-year travel demand and car ownership impacts. Transportation Research Record 1887, 117−127.

Cervero, R., Golub, A., Nee, B., 2007. City carshare: longer-term travel demand and car ownership impact. Transportation Research Record 1992, 70−80.

Chen, D., Kockelman, K., 2016. Management of shared, autonomous, electric vehicle fleet: implications of pricing schemes. Transportation Research Record 2572, 37−46.

Clewlow, R., Mishra, G.S., 2017. Disruptive Transportation: The Adoption, Utilization, and Impacts of Ride-Hailing in the United States. University of California, Davis.

Cohen, A., Shaheen, S., 2016. Planning for Shared Mobility. American Planning Association, Chicago.

Conduent Inc. n.d. Go-LA App. https://itunes.apple.com/us/app/go-la/id1069725538?mt=8.

Dickey, M.R., 2018. Bird Hits 10 Million Scooter Rides. https://techcrunch.com/2018/09/20/bird-hits-10-million-scooter-rides/.

Dobush, G., 2018. The Booming E-Scooter Market Just Reported its First Fatality. http://fortune.com/2018/09/21/escooter-share-first-fatality-lime-helmet/.

Etherington, D., 2018. Arlington, Texas Replaces Local Bus Service with via On-Demand Ride-Sharing. https://techcrunch.com/2018/03/12/arlington-texas-replaces-local-bus-service-with-via-on-demand-ride-sharing/.

Feigon, S., Murphy, C., 2016. Shared Mobility and the Transformation of Public Transit. TCRP 188. Transportation Cooperative Research Program, Washington DC.

Firnkorn, J., Müller, M., 2012. Selling mobility instead of cars: new business strategies for automakers and the impact of private vehicle holdings. Business Strategy and the Environment (4), 264−280.

Franco, M., 2016. DHL Uses Completely Autonomous System to Deliver Consumer Goods by Drone. New Atlas. http://newatlas.com/dhl-drone-delivery/43248/.

Gehrke, S., Felix, A., Reardon, T., 2018. A Survey of Ride-Hailing Passengers in Metro Boston. Metropolitan Area Planning Council, Boston.

Hampshire, R., Simek, C., Fabusuyi, T., Di, X., Chen, X., 2017. Measuring the Impact of an Unanticipated Disruption of Uber/Lyft in Austin. University of Michigan, TX, Ann Arbor.

Henao, A., 2017. Impacts of Ridesourcing-Lyft and Uber-On Transportation Including VMT, Mode Replacement, Parking, and Travel Behavior. University of Colorado, Boulder.

Henao, A., Marshall, W., 2018. The impact of ride-hailing on vehicle miles traveled. Transportation 1−22.

Kim, K., Rousseau, G., Freedman, J., Nicholson, J., 2015. The travel impact of autonomous vehicles in metro atlanta through activity-based modeling. In: 15th TRB National Transportation Planning Applications Conference. Transportation Research Board, Washington D.C.

Lane, C., 2005. PhillyCarShare: first-year social and mobility impacts of carsharing in Philadelphia, Pennsylvania. Transportation Research Record 1927, 158−166.

Lazarus, J., Carpentier Pourquier, J., Frank, F., Henry, H., Shaheen, S., 2018. Bikesharing Evolution and Expansion: Understanding How Docked and Dockless Models Complement and Compete — A Case Study of San Francisco. Submission to the Transportation Research Board, Washington D.C.

Lazarus, J., Shaheen, S., Young, S., Fagnant, D., Tom, V., Baumgardner, W., James, F., Sam Lott, J., 2018a. Shared automated mobility and public transport. In: Meyer, G., Beiker, S. (Eds.), Road Vehicle Automation, vol. 4. Springer International Publishing, New York City, pp. 141–161.

Martin, E., Shaheen, S., 2011. The impact of carsharing on public transit and non-motorized travel: an exploration of North American carsharing survey data. Energies 2094–2114.

Martin, E., Shaheen, S., 2016. Impacts of Car2go on Vehicle Ownership, Modal Shift, Vehicle Miles Traveled, and Greenhouse Gas Emissions: An Analysis of Five North American Cities. Transportation Sustainability Research Center, Berkeley.

Massachusetts Governor's Office, 2016. Governor Baker, MBTA Launch Innovative Program to Enlist Uber, Lyft to Better Serve Paratransit Customers. September 16. Accessed August 31, 2018. https://blog.mass.gov/governor/transportation/governor-baker-mbta-launch-innovative-program-to-enlist-uber-lyft-to-better-serve-paratransit-customers/.

McFarland, M., 2017. Robot Deliveries Are about to Hit U.S. Streets. January 18. Accessed August 21, 2018. https://money.cnn.com/2017/01/18/technology/postmates-doordash-delivery-robots/index.html.

NASA, 2017. NASA Embraces Urban Air Mobility, Calls for Market Study. November 7. Accessed August 21, 2018. https://www.nasa.gov/aero/nasa-embraces-urban-air-mobility.

National Association of City Transportation Officials, 2018. Shared Micromobility in the U.S.: 2018. National Association of City Transportation Officials, New York City.

New York Public Transit Association. 2018. October 31. https://nytransit.org/index.php/8-legislative/209-president-s-proposed-ffy-14-budget-ananlysis.

Olson, P., 2014. Why Google's Waze Is Trading User Data with Local Governments. Forbes. July 7.

Pinellas Suncoast Transit Authority. n.d. PSTA, Uber Offer Free, Late-Night Rides for Low-Income Residents. https://www.psta.net/about-psta/press-releases/2016/psta-uber-offer-free-late-night-rides-for-low-income-residents/.

Rayle, L., Dai, D., Chan, N., Cervero, R., Shaheen, S., 2016. Just a better taxi? A survey-based comparison of taxis, transit, and ridesourcing services in San Francisco. Transport Policy 168–178.

SAE International, 2018. Axonomy and Definitions for Terms Related to Shared. SAE International, Detroit.

Shaheen, S., Cohen, A., 2017. Mobility Innovations Take Flight: Flying Cars Are on Their Way. InMotion. March 31. https://www.inmotionventures.com/mobility-innovations-flying-cars/.

Shaheen, S., Cohen, A., 2018. Is it time for a public transit renaissance? Navigating travel behavior, technology, and business model shifts in a brave new world. Journal of Public Transportation 67–81.

Shaheen, S., Martin, E., 2015. Unraveling the Modal Impacts of Bikesharing. Access 8-15.

Shaheen, S., Cohen, A., Roberts, D., 2005. Carsharing in North America: market growth, current developments, and future potential. Transportation Research Record 1986, 106–115.

Shaheen, S., Martin, E., Cohen, A., 2013. Public bikesharing and modal shift behavior: a comparative study of early bikesharing systems in North America. International Journal of Transportation 35–54.

Shaheen, S., Martin, E., Chan, N., Cohen, A., Pogodzinski, M., 2014. Public Bikesharing in North America during A Period of Rapid Expansion: Understanding Business Models, Industry Trends and User Impacts. Mineta Transportation Institute, San Jose.

Shaheen, S., Chan, N., Gaynor, T., 2016a. Casual carpooling in the San Francisco Bay area: understanding characteristics, behaviors, and motivations. Transport Policy 51. https://doi.org/10.1016/j.tranpol.2016.01.003.

Shaheen, S., Cohen, A., Zohdy, I., 2016. Shared Mobility Current Practices and Guiding Principles. U.S. Department of Transportation, Washington D.C.

Shaheen, S., Cohen, A., Zohdy, I., Kock, B., 2016. Smartphone Applications to Influence Traveler Choices Practices and Policies. U.S. Department of Transportation, Washington D.C.

Shaheen, S., Cohen, A., Yelchuru, B., Sarkhili, S., 2017. Mobility on Demand Operational Concept Report. U.S. Department of Transportation, Washington D.C.

Shaheen, S., Bell, C., Cohen, A., Yelchuru, B., 2017. Travel Behavior: Shared Mobility and Transportation Equity. U.S. Department of Transportation, Washington D.C.

Shaheen, S., Cohen, A., Martin, E., 2017. The U.S. Department of Transportation's Smart City Challenge and the Federal Transit Administration's Mobility on Demand Sandbox. E-Circular. Transportation Research Board, Washington D.C.

Shaheen, S., Cohen, A., Bayen, A., 2018. The Benefits of Carpooling. https://doi.org/10.7922/G2DZ06GF.

Shaheen, S., Cohen, A., Jaffee, M., 2018. Innovative Mobility Carsharing Outlook. University of California, Berkeley.

Shaheen, S., Cohen, A., Martin, E., 2018. US DOT's Mobility on Demand (MOD) Initiative: Moving the Economy with Innovation and Understanding. E-circular, Washington D.C. (Transportation Research Board).

Shaheen, S., Martin, E., Bansal, A., 2018. Peer-To-Peer (P2P) Carsharing: Understanding Early Markets, Social Dynamics, and Behavioral Impacts. Transportation Sustainability Research Center, Berkeley.

Sochor, J., Stromberg, H., Karisson, M.A., 2015. Implementing mobility as a service: challenges in integrating user, commercial, and societal Perspectives. Transportation Research Record: Journal of the Transportation Research Board 1—9.

Starship. n.d. Starship. https://www.starship.xyz/ (accessed 21.08.18.).

Yvkoff, L., 2017. FedEx Sees Robots, Not Drones, as the Next Big Thing in Logistics. The Drive. February 7. http://www.thedrive.com/tech/7430/fedex-sees-robots-not-drones-as-the-next-big-thing-in-logistics.

Chapter 4

Implications of vehicle automation for accessibility and social inclusion of people on low income, people with physical and sensory disabilities, and older people

Dimitris Milakis[1], Bert van Wee[2]

[1]*Institute of Transport Research, German Aerospace Center (DLR), Berlin, Germany;* [2]*Transport and Logistics Group, Faculty of Technology, Policy and Management, Delft University of Technology, Delft, The Netherlands*

Chapter outline

1. Introduction

Transport can have significant effects on a critical aspect of social sustainability: social inclusion (Lucas, 2012). Limited accessibility to economic, social, cultural, and political opportunities by lack of adequate transport can affect both the quality of life of individuals and the equity and cohesion of society as a whole (Levitas et al., 2007).

Depending on the level of automation (Society of Automobile Engineers-SAE levels 1–5; SAE International, 2016), the introduction of automated vehicles could influence accessibility levels of certain social groups who

Demand for Emerging Transportation Systems. https://doi.org/10.1016/B978-0-12-815018-4.00004-8

currently do not have access to cars, such as people on low income, people with physical and sensory disabilities, and older people facing accessibility constraints, and consequently levels of social exclusion (Shaheen et al., 2017). Below we will address the importance of SAE levels where needed. For example, people not owning a car or not being able to drive (younger, older, and people with disabilities) could reach activities via shared on-demand automated vehicles overcoming current accessibility limitations. (Shared) on-demand mobility services for older people, children, and people with disabilities are already in place both in the United States (see e.g., UberWAV, UberASSIST, Lift Hero, HopSkipDrive) and Europe (see e.g., Taxistop, Wheeliz).

Thus far, research on possible long-term implications of automated vehicles for social inclusion is scarce (see Milakis et al., 2017). Few studies have focused on possible positive effects of in-vehicle technologies on driving conditions of older people (see Eby et al., 2016) and on potential travel demand changes of social groups such as nondriving, older people, and people with travel-restrictive medical conditions (see Harper et al., 2016). Cohn et al. (2019) explored potential transport-related changes (e.g., job accessibility) in the case of the introduction of automated vehicles in low-income areas and in areas with higher levels of minority populations in Washington DC. Milakis et al. (2018) identified differences in distribution of automated vehicles—related benefits between social groups, while Mladenovic and McPherson (2016) analyzed traffic control systems in an automated vehicles context focusing on social justice design principles.

Both policy and research interests in possible implications of vehicle automation for social inclusion has increased lately. This chapter aims to contribute to this topic by analyzing the implications of vehicle automation for the accessibility of vulnerable social groups (i.e., people on low income, people with physical and sensory disabilities, older people) and consequently for their transport-related social exclusion.

Our chapter is structured as follows. Section 2 describes the conceptual model on long-term implications of automated vehicles for social inclusion that our analysis is based on. The implications of automated vehicles for the accessibility and transport-related social exclusion of people on low income, people with physical and sensory disabilities, and older people are analyzed in Sections 2.1−2.3, respectively. Section 3 provides the conclusions of this chapter.

2. Implications of vehicle automation for social inclusion

Automated vehicles could influence accessibility of vulnerable social groups in urban and rural areas and consequently have implications for transport-related social exclusion. The magnitude and direction of such implications for different social groups is a function of the accessibility component affected by automated vehicles, the level of vehicle automation as well as the mobility service model (i.e., private or shared vehicles). In this chapter, we focus on the implications of vehicle automation for the accessibility and transport-related social exclusion of people on low income, people with physical and sensory disabilities, and older people.

Our analysis departs from the conceptual model of Milakis (2019) on long-term implication of automated vehicles for social inclusion and public health (Fig. 4.1) The conceptual model builds on Geurs and van Wee's (2004) conceptual framework for accessibility which identify four accessibility components (i.e., land use system, temporal constraints, individuals' abilities and opportunities, and the transport system). In the conceptual model, the impact paths through which automated vehicles could influence various accessibility components and finally accessibility of certain social groups are presented. In the following subsections, we analyze these paths for people on low income, people with physical and sensory disabilities and older people. We first describe which component of accessibility is relevant for each social group, to what extent this component can be influenced by vehicle automation and at

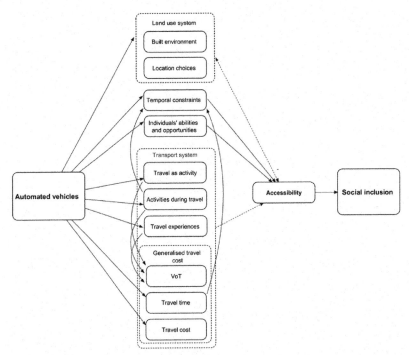

FIGURE 4.1 The conceptual model of the long-term implications of automated vehicles for social inclusion. *Source: Adapted from Milakis, D., 2019. The societal dimension of the emerging mobility technologies transition: towards a research agenda. The Case of Automated Vehicles (Working paper).*

which level of automation. We also explore whether having shared instead of private automated vehicles could enhance or reduce this impact. We summarize the accessibility changes for each group in Table 4.1.

2.1 People on low income

People on low income experience constraints in accessing opportunities because of the fixed (capital) cost of owning a vehicle (Fig. 4.1: individuals' abilities and opportunities), the financial cost of travel (Fig. 4.1: travel cost), as well as the spatial allocation of activities (Fig. 4.1: land use system).

The first generation of SAE level 4 and 5 automated vehicles is expected to be much more expensive than comparable conventional vehicles because of the advanced hardware and software technologies involved. Mass deployment of automated vehicles could reduce the cost of owning such a vehicle, but in any case this will not be as low as the cost of a conventional vehicle (Fagnant and Kockelman, 2015). The financial cost of travel could be reduced through lower fuel consumption. Studies report fuels savings for automated vehicles up to 31%, with higher savings found in simulations involving increased penetration rates of automated and connected vehicles (Milakis et al., 2017). Regarding long-term changes in the land use system, automated vehicles are expected to trigger a dual urban process involving both further dispersion and concentration of activities in urban centers (see Gelauff et al., 2017; Milakis et al., 2018; Zakharenko, 2016; Zhang and Guhathakurta, 2018). Further suburbanization of urban activities would lead to higher travel time and cost and therefore reduced accessibility for poorer social groups. On the other hand, concentration of urban activities in urban areas could enhance accessibility to those areas. Yet, increased demand for land in central areas (e.g., substituting former parking garages with commercial or residential uses) might drive land prices higher reducing housing affordability and thus displacing people on low income from those areas (see Hochstenbach and Musterd, 2018) (Table 4.1).

For shared (electric) automated vehicles, the fixed (capital) cost of owning a car will not exist. The financial travel cost is expected to be significantly lower than the current cost of accessing taxi services, mainly because of lower operating costs. For example, in Zurich the cost of a taxi driver represents 88% of the taxi operating costs (Bösch et al., 2018). Yet, access to shared automated vehicle services would require owning a smartphone, internet connectivity and/or mobile data package as well as a banking account and a credit card, which could constitute an important barrier for people on low income. In Western Europe and the United States that represent two of the largest smartphone markets, about 30% of the population do not own a smartphone (Statista, 2018, 2017). Moreover, 37% of the adults (mainly women, poorer, and lower educated) in developing economies (mainly Bangladesh, China, India, Indonesia, Mexico, Nigeria, and Pakistan) still are unbanked

TABLE 4.1 Overview of possible accessibility changes for vulnerable social groups because of automated vehicles (↔: no change, ↑: increase, ↓: decrease).

Accessibility component affected	Changes in accessibility because of automated vehicles		
	Private automated vehicles (up to SAE level 3)	Private automated vehicles (SAE level 4–5)	Shared automated vehicles (SAE level 4–5)
People on low income			
Individuals' abilities and opportunities	↔	↔/↓	↔/↓
	Capital cost will be higher than conventional vehicles.	Capital cost will be higher than conventional vehicles.	The increased cost (e.g., owning a smartphone) for digitally accessing shared automated vehicles services can limit access to such services.
Travel cost	Fuel consumption could be reduced.	Fuel consumption could be reduced.	Lower operating costs, will reduce the cost of hailing a shared automated vehicle, but could compromise conventional public transport services.
Land use system		Suburbanization or concentration of activities triggered by private automated vehicles in the city center would negatively impact poorer social groups	Suburbanization or concentration of activities triggered by shared automated vehicles in the city center would negatively impact poorer social groups by reducing accessibility and housing affordability respectively.

Continued

TABLE 4.1 Overview of possible accessibility changes for vulnerable social groups because of automated vehicles (↔: no change, ↑: increase, ↓: decrease).—cont'd

	Accessibility component affected	Changes in accessibility because of automated vehicles		
		Private automated vehicles (up to SAE level 3)	Private automated vehicles (SAE level 4—5)	Shared automated vehicles (SAE level 4—5)
People with physical and sensory disabilities	Individuals' abilities and opportunities	↔ A fully capable driver will still be needed to take over control of the vehicle.	by reducing accessibility and housing affordability respectively. ↑/↔ Accessibility to opportunities can increase through use of private automated vehicles. Custom-designed vehicles will be needed. Purchase price will be higher.	↑/↔ Accessibility to opportunities can increase through use of shared automated vehicles. Custom-designed vehicles and operating complexities can lead to higher cost for using such services.
Older people	Individuals' abilities and opportunities	↑/↔ Private automated vehicles could be used for more years by older people. Operation and learning difficulties, uncertainty, insecurity, and distrust	↑/↔ Private automated vehicles could be used for more years by older people.	↑/↔ Accessibility to opportunities can increase through use of shared automated vehicles. Uncomfortability with digital access

	might prevent adoption of such new vehicle technologies.	and anxiety with online payment could prevent older people from using such services.
Travel cost	Operation and learning difficulties, uncertainty, insecurity, distrust, and higher price due to custom-design might prevent adoption of such new vehicle technologies.	Lower operating costs, will reduce the cost of hailing a shared automated vehicle.
Land use system	Urban dispersion because of private automated vehicles would reduce accessibility of older people because of increased travel cost, time, and effort to reach opportunities.	Urban dispersion because of shared automated vehicles would reduce accessibility of older people because of increased travel cost, time, and effort to reach opportunities.

(Demirgüç-Kunt et al., 2018) (Table 4.1). However, we need to consider that these figures might be different when full vehicle automation becomes available in the future.

For automated public transport, a reduction in financial travel cost is also expected given that the cost of bus drivers represents a significant part of the operating costs (e.g., 55% of bus operating costs in Zurich). If automated public transport offers access by physical means (e.g., waiting at the station instead of digitally calling public transport service, payment in cash), then no additional financial costs will occur for public transport users. On the other hand, a modal shift from conventional public transport to shared automated vehicles is possible (Clewlow and Mishra, 2017). Such modal shift could be gradually enhanced if public transport services would be cut due to limited viability in a more suburbanized urban context after introduction of automated vehicles unless those two systems are complementary (Ohnemus and Perl, 2016). Reduction of conventional public transport services could lead to further increase of travel cost and time for public transport users and subsequently a reduction in their public transport–based accessibility levels and it is not clear if this reduction in accessibility will be compensated by the increase accessibility due to the availability of shared automated vehicles.

2.2 People with physical and sensory disabilities

People with physical and sensory disabilities experience constraints in accessing opportunities because they are typically not able to drive or having difficulties to access other travel modes (e.g., public transport, bicycle) (see Fig. 4.1: individuals' abilities and opportunities).

Lower levels of vehicle automation (up to SAE level 3) are not expected to remove the constraints related to driving. A fully capable driver will still be needed to take over control of the vehicle whenever is required by the automated system. People with physical and sensory disabilities are expected to be able to use a private automated vehicle of SAE level 4 or 5 and therefore significantly improve accessibility to opportunities. Yet, custom-design of those vehicles, complying with specific needs of people with different types of disabilities will be necessary which would result in higher purchase price. For example, for people with physical disabilities, vehicles would need to be wheelchair accessible (e.g., having a ramp), while for people with sensory disabilities in-vehicle audible and braille information systems about refueling and maintenance would be necessary (Table 4.1).

Shared automated vehicles, could also increase accessibility levels for people with physical and sensory disabilities. Yet, several technical issues need to be solved (e.g., identification of appropriate boarding spot avoiding access obstacles), while the price of such services is expected to be higher than the typical for-hire services cost because of the custom-designed vehicles needed (i.e., wheelchair accessible; multiple wheelchair seating arrangements)

(Table 4.1). Complementary public transport services (i.e., paratransit) for people with disabilities have been proven to be both expensive and difficult to coordinate and operate (Fei and Chen, 2015). For people with sensory disabilities, vehicle sharing software/apps need to be custom-designed (building on existing smartphones' accessibility features like on-screen magnifier, large text option, VoiceOver) offering seamless access to ride-hailing/sharing services.

2.3 Older people

Older people combine characteristics and thus constraints facing both people on low income and people with physical and sensory disabilities (see Sections 2.1 and 2.2, respectively). For example, older people experience constraints in accessing opportunities because of reduced ability (or even inability) to drive due to health reasons (e.g., reduced vision and reflexes, fatigue) and to own a car or afford travel costs after retirement due to less income (see Fig. 4.1: individuals' abilities and opportunities). In addition, older people could experience constraints because of reduced (perception of) safety (Adler and Rottunda, 2006). Below, we focus on constraints and subsequently accessibility implications specific for older people.

Both lower levels (up to SAE level 3, e.g., lane departure warning, forward collision warning, blindspot warning, parking assistance, adaptive cruise control) and especially higher levels of vehicle automation (i.e., SAE levels 4 and 5) could enhance the ability of older people to drive or use a vehicle for more years despite possible problems with their health (Eby et al., 2016). Vehicle automation might also improve their perception of safety that constitutes another barrier for this social group in using a vehicle. Hartwich et al. (2018) reported that older drivers in a driving simulation experiment of automated driving preferred driving styles unfamiliar to them (e.g., higher speed). Moreover, automated vehicles could be used by older people to accomplish shopping activities (e.g., grocery shopping) and deliver them to their home without the need to move. The price of private automated vehicles will be higher than conventional vehicles. Moreover, several adaptations to automated vehicles design will likely be needed to serve particular needs of this social group (e.g., panic button, medication box, small kitchen, large windows, seats facing each other, table for lunch or playing card games: see Obst et al., 2017) that will probably result in even higher purchase price. Thus, older people facing also income constraints would probably be difficult to acquire vehicles equipped with automated driving features. Possible further dispersion of urban activities because of automated vehicles would also cause a reduction in accessibility levels of older people both for financial reasons (i.e., increased travel cost) but also because of the extra effort and time needed to reach activities.

The extent to which older people will adopt such advanced technologies in their daily mobility routines is still an open question. Several studies have shown that technology acceptance by older people is influenced by the ease of use and learning the new system, trust, social norms, earlier experience with technology and perceived behavioral control (i.e., self-efficacy and capacity to use the new technology) (Morris and Venkatesh, 2000; Reimer, 2014; Renaud and van Biljon, 2008). For acceptance of (owned) automated vehicles by older people, initial studies confirm that effort and especially operation and learning difficulties (Ingeveld, 2017) as well as uncertainty, insecurity and distrust (Obst et al., 2017) have a strong negative effect (Table 4.1). Such constraints might change over time as new technologies are introduced into daily life and new generations of older people become more familiar with them. For example, the results of a focus group with older drivers aged between 70 and 81 years, most of them owning a navigation aid system in the car, showed that this group was on average very positive regarding advanced navigation aid systems (e.g., based on augmented reality) (Bellet et al., 2018).

Shared automated vehicles, could enhance accessibility of older people by removing constraints related to driving as well as by reducing the cost of such services. Yet, older people might face constraints accessing those services because of the requirements for owning and using a smartphone or other internet access devices as well as to perform online transactions. Shirgaokar (2018) reported that senior citizens in Edmonton, Canada stated that they feel anxious with online transactions because of possible fraud and uncomfortable with using taxi-hailing smartphone apps. Moreover, part of the sample in this survey reported that they only had basic cell phones for cost reasons. Ingeveld (2017) found that the intention of older people to use shared automated vehicles in the Netherlands is mainly influenced by the operation and learning difficulty of the system and to a lesser extent by social and peer pressure (Table 4.1). Also, custom-designed apps for older people might be necessary to overcome health-related constraints in using those apps such as reduced visibility and hearing acuity. Finally, possible cuts of conventional or automated public transport services because of competition with shared automated vehicles and suburbanization of urban activities could also negatively influence accessibility levels of older people.

3. Conclusions

Automated vehicles could influence long-term social sustainability by affecting levels of social inclusion. Such effect has attracted little attention in the literature, thus far. In this chapter, we contribute to this topic by analyzing the implications of vehicle automation for the accessibility of vulnerable social groups (i.e., people on low income, people with physical and sensory disabilities, older people) and consequently for their transport-related social exclusion. Below we present our conclusions.

The conceptual model that we based our analysis on shows that changes in accessibility because of automated vehicles constitute a key path through which certain social groups (e.g., people on low income, people with physical and sensory disabilities, older people) could possibly experience changes in levels of social inclusion. The component of accessibility affected by automated vehicles, the vehicle automation level, and the mobility service model (i.e., private or shared vehicles) are expected to define the magnitude and direction of implications for different social groups.

According to our analysis, accessibility to opportunities for people on low income could either remain unchanged (lower levels of vehicle automation) or negatively influenced (higher levels of vehicle automation) in a context of private automated vehicles, despite the fact that such vehicles can be more fuel efficient already from lower levels of automation (Table 4.1). Shared automated vehicles could lead to lower financial travel cost but increased cost for digitally accessing those services could compromise possible gains. Moreover, further suburbanization or concentration of activities in the city center would negatively impacts poorer social groups by reducing accessibility and housing affordability respectively. Finally, automated public transport will likely enhance accessibility of low-income group through reduced financial travel cost. Competition between shared automated vehicles and automated public transport might compromise accessibility benefits for public transport users.

Accessibility to opportunities for people with physical and sensory disabilities is not expected to change in lower levels of vehicle automation (up to SAE level 3) (Table 4.1). Both private and shared automated vehicles of SAE level 4 and 5 could enhance accessibility for this social group. Yet, custom-design of the vehicle as well as operating complexities could result in higher prices for owning or hailing such vehicles compared to conventional automated vehicles. Thus, for people facing both income constraints as well as physical or sensory disabilities the introduction of automated vehicles is not expected to alter the level of their accessibility to opportunities.

Accessibility to opportunities for older people could be increased by both lower and higher levels of (private) automated vehicles because they could enhance the ability of this social group to use a vehicle for more years (Table 4.1). Yet, it is unclear to what extent older people would overcome operation and learning difficulties, uncertainty, insecurity, and distrust to adopt such new vehicle technologies. Moreover, adaptation of automated vehicle design to older people's needs would drive purchase price even higher, making difficult for this social group to own such a vehicle. Further urban dispersion because of automated vehicles could compromise accessibility to opportunities for older people. Shared automated vehicles could enhance accessibility of older people but the requirement of digital access and online payment for this service could prevent them from using such services both for psychological and financial reasons.

Acknowledgments

The authors would like to thank two referees for their constructive comments on an earlier version of this chapter.

References

Adler, G., Rottunda, S., 2006. Older adults' perspectives on driving cessation. Journal of Aging Studies 20 (3), 227−235.

Bellet, T., Paris, J.-C., Marin-Lamellet, C., 2018. Difficulties experienced by older drivers during their regular driving and their expectations towards advanced driving aid systems and vehicle automation. Transportation Research Part F: Traffic Psychology and Behaviour 52, 138−163.

Bösch, P.M., Becker, F., Becker, H., Axhausen, K.W., 2018. Cost-based analysis of autonomous mobility services. Transport Policy 64, 76−91.

Clewlow, R.R., Mishra, G.S., 2017. Disruptive Transportation: The Adoption , Utilization , and Impacts of Ride-Hailing in the United States. Institute of Transportation, UC Davis, Davis, California.

Cohn, J., Ezike, R., Martin, J., Donkor, K., Ridgway, M., Balding, M., 2019. Examining the equity impacts of autonomous vehicles: a travel demand model approach. Transportation Research Record: Journal of the Transportation Research Board 2673 (5), 23−35.

Demirgüç-Kunt, A., Klapper, L., Singer, D., Ansar, S., Hess, J., 2018. The Global Findex Database 2017: Measuring Financial Inclusion and the Fintech Revolution. World Bank, Washington DC.

Eby, D.W., Molnar, L.J., Zhang, L., Louis, R.M.S., Zanier, N., Kostyniuk, L.P., Stanciu, S., 2016. Use, perceptions, and benefits of automotive technologies among aging drivers. Injury Epidemiology 3, 1−20.

Fagnant, D.J., Kockelman, K.M., 2015. Preparing a nation for autonomous vehicles: opportunities, barriers and policy recommendations for capitalizing on self-driven vehicles. Transportation Research Part A: Policy and Practice 77, 167−181.

Fei, D., Chen, X., 2015. The Americans with Disabilities Act of 1990 (ADA) paratransit cost issues and solutions: case of Greater Richmond Transit Company (GRTC). Case Studies on Transport Policy 3 (4), 402−414.

Gelauff, G., Ossokina, I., Teulings, C., 2019. Spatial and welfare effects of automated driving: Will cities grow, decline or both? Transportation Research Part A: Policy and Practice 121, 277−294.

Geurs, K.T., van Wee, B., 2004. Accessibility evaluation of land-use and transport strategies: review and research directions. Journal of Transport Geography 12 (2), 127−140.

Harper, C., Hendrickson, C.T., Mangones, S., Samaras, C., 2016. Estimating potential increases in travel with autonomous vehicles for the non-driving , elderly and people with travel-restrictive medical conditions. Transportation Research Part C: Emerging Technologies 72, 1−9.

Hartwich, F., Beggiato, M., Krems, J.F., 2018. Driving comfort, enjoyment and acceptance of automated driving − effects of drivers' age and driving style familiarity. Ergonomics 61 (8), 1017−1032.

Hochstenbach, C., Musterd, S., 2018. Gentrification and the suburbanization of poverty: changing urban geographies through boom and bust periods. Urban Geography 39 (1), 26−53.

Ingeveld, M., 2017. Usage Intention of Automated Vehicles Amongst Elderly in the Netherland (Master's Thesis). Delft University of Technology, Delft, The Netherlands.

Levitas, R., Pantazis, C., Fahmy, E., Gordon, D., Lloyd, E., Patsios, D., 2007. The Multi-Dimensional Analysis of Social Exclusion. University of Bristol, Bristol.

Lucas, K., 2012. Transport and social exclusion: where are we now? Transport Policy 20, 105−113.

Milakis, D., 2019. The societal dimension of the emerging mobility technologies transition: towards a research agenda (Manuscript submitted for publication). The case of automated vehicles.

Milakis, D., van Arem, B., van Wee, B., 2017. Policy and society related implications of automated driving: a review of literature and directions for future research. Journal of Intelligent Transportation Systems: Technology, Planning, and Operations 21 (4), 324−348.

Milakis, D., Kroesen, M., van Wee, B., 2018. Implications of automated vehicles for accessibility and location choices: evidence from an expert-based experiment. Journal of Transport Geography 68, 142−148.

Mladenovic, M.N., McPherson, T., 2016. Engineering social justice into traffic control for self-driving vehicles? Science and Engineering Ethics 22, 1131−1149.

Morris, M., Venkatesh, V., 2000. Age differences in technology adoption decisions: implications for changing workforce. Personnel Psychology 53 (2), 375−403.

Obst, M., Marjovi, A., Vasic, M., Navarro, I., Martinoli, A., Amditis, A., Pantazopoulos, P., Llatser, I., LaFortelle, A.D., Qian, X., 2017. Automated driving: acceptance and chances for elderly people. In: Proceedings of the 9th International ACM Conference on Automotive User Interfaces and Interactive Vehicular Applications. AutomotiveUI, Oldenburg, Germany, pp. 561−570.

Ohnemus, M., Perl, A., 2016. Shared autonomous vehicles: catalyst of new mobility for the last mile? Built Environment 42 (4), 589−602.

Reimer, B., 2014. Driver assistance systems and the transition to automated vehicles: a path to increase older adult safety and mobility? Public Policy & Aging Report 24 (1), 27−31.

Renaud, K., van Biljon, J., 2008. Predicting technology acceptance and adoption by the elderly. In: Proceedings of the 2008 Annual Research Conference of the South African Institute of Computer Scientists and Information Technologists on IT Research in Developing Countries Riding the Wave of Technology - SAICSIT '08 210−219.

SAE International, 2016. Taxonomy and Definitions for Terms Related to Driving Automation Systems for On-Road Motor Vehicles. SAE International, Warrendale, PA.

Shaheen, S., Bell, C., Cohen, A., Yelchuru, B., 2017. Travel Behavior: Shared Mobility and Transportation Equity. US Department of Transportation, Washington DC.

Shirgaokar, M., 2018. Expanding seniors' mobility through phone apps: potential responses from the private and public sectors. Journal of Planning Education and Research.

Statista, 2017. Smartphones in the U.S. - Statistics & Facts. The. Statista, Hamburg, Germany.

Statista, 2018. Smartphone User Penetration as Percentage of Total Population in Western Europe from 2011 to 2018. Statista, Hamburg, Germany.

Zakharenko, R., 2016. Self-driving cars will change cities. Regional Science and Urban Economics 61, 26−37.

Zhang, W., Guhathakurta, S., 2018. Residential location choice in the era of shared autonomous vehicles. Journal of Planning Education and Research. https://doi.org/10.1177/0739456X18776062.

Part C

Methods

Chapter 5

Data aspects of the evaluation of demand for emerging transportation systems

Emmanouil Chaniotakis[1], Dimitrios Efthymiou[2],
Constantinos Antoniou[2]
[1]*Bartlett School of Environment, Energy and Resources, University College London (UCL), London, United Kingdom;* [2]*Chair of Transportation Systems Engineering, Department of Civil, Geo and Environmental Engineering, Technical University of Munich, Munich, Germany*

Chapter outline

1. Introduction

Central to the estimation of the demand for emerging transportation systems is the data used to predict aspects of adoption, satisfaction, and use. The fact that emerging and future transportation systems are in many cases unrealized and their exact characteristics are yet unknown makes the assumptions defined and the data used very important. In transportation, data collection conventionally relied upon the use of surveys and the use of some actively collecting data tools (Handy, 1996; Leduc, 2008; Calabrese et al., 2013). However, transportation surveys have limitations, mainly due to their high cost and questioned validity of the results (Handy, 1996; Audirac, 1999), and traffic counts offer limited potential of representing the transportation demand and illustrate limited spatial coverage (Leduc, 2008).

Lately, the widespread use of information and communication technology (ICT) is changing data availability in a broad spectrum of applications creating new data sources to be explored. The size of datasets changes, as is the diversity of those available. These changes in data availability can be attributed to the evolution of pervasive systems (i.e., GPS handsets, cellular networks) and especially the connectivity that has been available to a growing number of individuals with the evolution of the Internet. The deployment of these systems has received wide attention from the transport scientific community toward the utilization of the increasingly available data (Big Data) (Buckley and Lightman, 2015; Reades et al., 2007). The lately available data sources have been found to produce an immense amount of data (thus named Big Data) that could potentially be used to improve transportation systems, first in terms of identification and prediction and second of optimization. On the same time, pervasive systems have allowed for several supporting services to rapidly emerge and be widely used (such as the concepts of Mobility as a Service [MaaS] and Vehicle Sharing).

The explosion of the data collected and the existence of diverse datasets collected have imposed the shift of the discussion from data availability to data quality (Cai and Zhu, 2015) and in some cases to data usability (e.g., referring to spatial data, Hunter et al., 2003). Data quality is commonly described as "fitness of use" implying a relative evaluation, based on the application and the context (Tayi and Ballou, 1998). Adjacent to the discussion of data usability and quality is the exploration of aspects of transferability of methods with regards to both spatial and data (in terms of type or source) transferability.

The above-discussed data aspects all originate from decisions taken during the data collection process. Thus it is clear that the preliminary investigation of the data collection methods and an exploration of the data characteristics are vital for the proper use of data. In this chapter, an overview of the data sources commonly used or lately emerging is presented, followed by a classification, based on the component of the transportation system that they refer to. The evolution of the different data sources through time is pursued using Scopus queries and the different benefits and shortcomings of datasets commonly used are discussed. A meta-analysis is also performed for the exploration of data quality aspects concerning transport-related datasets.

2. Evolution of data collection methods

As the transportation system is rather complex, the diversity of the collected data is vast. A wide categorization of the various data sources can be viewed from the perspective of the examined component of the transportation system on which the data collection is oriented, for example user-oriented or network-oriented (Fig. 5.1). Efforts in working with this yet growing amount of data have been directed toward all aspects of the Big Data Life Cycle (data acquisition, information extraction and cleaning, data integration, aggregation and representation, modeling analysis and interpretation; see Jagadish et al., 2014) constituting a rather multidisciplinary research topic. In the same time, choosing the data to base the analysis required needs to be a cautious decision based on some key aspects that define the requirements of this analysis. The overall task of data collection is to provide responses to a research question. Thus the goals of performing such an endeavor have to be clear from the very beginning.

Historically, collecting data for transportation studies has been a rather difficult endeavor, with the most widely used method to be travel surveys, dating back in the 1950s. The first approach has been face-to-face interviews, followed by the exploration of mail surveys and telephone surveys (Shen and Stopher, 2014). In addition, the prevailing method to collect network-oriented data has been the use of observers or traffic counts. Concerns of data quality

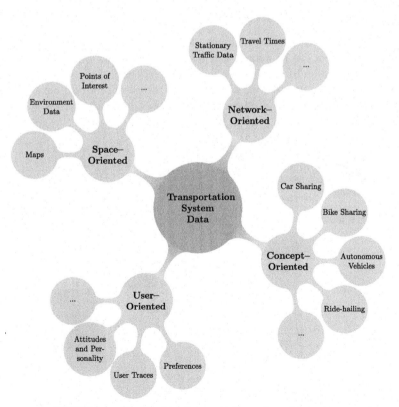

FIGURE 5.1 Classification of transportation systems data sources.

and cost have fueled the exploration of other data sources. This exploration of different data sources for transportation research has intensified recently. Content analysis for exploring the evolution of data sources used in transportation research is rather informative: In April 2019, the search "TITLE (data AND transport) AND (LIMIT-TO [SUBJAREA, "ENGI"])" was performed using the Scopus search engine. This resulted in 830 documents. After a manual relevance filtering (two observers), 158 were found to be relevant. The documents were reviewed and the data sources used where extracted. As it is observed in Fig. 5.2 for the five most frequently explored data sources, exploration of different data sources emerged the last 2 decades with the exploration of smart card, GPS, and mobile phone data. Combination of different data source is being increasingly more pervasive. Another interesting finding is the emergence of the discussion on open-source (such as Open-StreetMaps and in general open network data) data. Apart from the top five data sources that are presented in Fig. 5.2, researchers commonly study data related to connected and/or autonomous vehicles, accident data, and video data.

3. Conventional data collection methods

Much ambiguity exists in the literature on what is defined as conventional data sources and what can be defined as emerging. The distinction can be defined upon their duration of existence of the characterization of the way they have been collected (centralized vs. decentralized; using conventional data collection tools vs. using mobile phone apps), however, this still remains an open

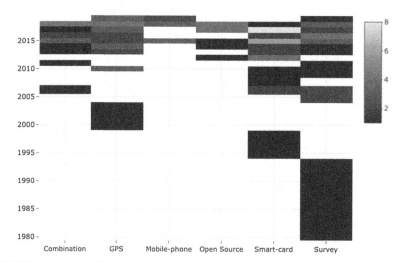

FIGURE 5.2 Historical evolution of data sources. Legend refers to intensity of number of references per item. Y-axis is year. Dark blue referring to less studies and yellow to more.

question. In this chapter, conventional data are characterized as data collected following a hypothesis-based approach. The categorization of the data takes place upon the categorization presented in Fig. 5.1. Given the prevalence of user-oriented data observed in the literature, with regards to conventional data, such methods are extensively discussed (Section 3.1) and a discussion on the remaining data sources is included in Section 3.2.

3.1 User data

Conventionally the collection of user data has been performed primarily using travel surveys (Efthymiou et al., 2013). This in some cases includes experiments created based on experts opinion about the factors that are relevant to the research question examined, utilizing also state-of-the-art results. The following paragraphs provide a short overview of the various components that comprise running experiments for evaluating the demand for emerging transportation systems and the some key sources of error that should be taken into account in their design and execution.

3.1.1 Experimental settings

The main categorization of experiments for demand is on the basis of **stated** preference (SP) or **revealed** preference (RP) survey research. This distinction has been established in the pertinent literature (Louviere et al., 2000; Ben-Akiva and Lerman, 1985). As Train (2009) states, revealed preference data are related to people's actual choices in real-world situations, while SP presents hypothetical choice situations. For both types of data collection, a long debate took place about the ability to acquire valid data and on to what extent they can reproduce actual people's behavior and be used to draw conclusions for further planning (Audirac, 1999; Hensher, 1994).

SP methods receive criticism due to their reference to a nonexperienced situation and as a consequence possibly not well defined by the researcher. Since the information is not directly observed, they are susceptible to various sorts of biases. On the other hand, there is the advantage that researchers control the situation presented including subjects that they want to be analyzed (Louviere et al., 2000). Also SP allows trading-off for attributes of different alternatives which allow for the estimation of important for transportation constructs, such as the willingness to pay and allow for multiple observations from each individual (Hess et al., 2010). With all the advantages and disadvantages, SP is widely used in transport research (Hensher, 1994). Finally, for situations that happen rarely, it is doubtful if people act as they answer and it has been argued that choices taken, recorded on revealed preference survey do not imply the same behavior to conditions other than the one exposed (Audirac, 1999; Train, 2009).

For both methods, the construction of the experiment requires the selection of the preferences to be recorded. For example, when interested in investigating the factors that affect mode of choice using RP, the question would be "how many times did you use the indicated service" (e.g., in Martin et al., 2010), while for the case of SP, the question would be structured as a choice experiment, where participants would be asked to select what they "would choose," given a description of the researcher's situation (e.g., in Fu et al.). Given this flexibility in defining the experiment scenarios and the ability to ask more than one question in SP experiment, research focuses on the determination of the methods to create the experiment. However, the number of scenarios increases with the number of attributes/alternatives (Louviere et al., 2000), making the evaluation of all combinations (full factorial design) in most cases impossible. To overcome this issue, several methods have been proposed. The simplest selection method, given a large sample size, is the random selection of scenarios (from the full factorial design). In most cases, however, the creation of orthogonal designs is pursued (Ben-Akiva and Lerman, 1985). In order to make data collection more efficient, several contributions in the direction of optimally selecting the scenarios have been proposed (e.g., Bliemer et al., 2009; Rose et al., 2008). Although debatable (see Walker et al., 2018; Kladeftiras and Antoniou, 2015), efficient designs attempt to maximize the information obtained from an experiment design (in the form of maximizing a metric of the information matrix). As with most optimal experiment design cases (Pronzato and Zhigljavsky, 2010), this is performed on the basis of prior information about individual choice (thus the parameters of a previously defined model for the factors examined). Finally, researchers have tried to evaluate alternative ways to represent the situation examined, by presenting videos or pictures of the scenarios (e.g., Bafatakis et al., 2015) or even introducing games, where choices of individuals are recorded (Doirado et al., 2012).

Conventional surveys also introduce characteristics of the individuals, in the form of sociodemographic characteristics, personality traits, as well as attitudinal characteristics with regards to the transportation system. This is commonly performed in the form of indirect questions, which aim at evaluating the impact that they have, using usually latent class models and factor analysis. For example, in an evaluation of Urban Air Mobility, five-point scaled answers were used to understand attitudes autonomous to driving and sharing (Fu et al.). These questions are formed as statements, where respondents would have to indicate on a rating scale (e.g., five-point scale from strongly agree to strongly disagree), commonly referred to as Likert scale (Likert, 1932).

The definition of the settings of such experiments involves trade-offs between quantity of responses, quality of the results, and information volumes (Richardson et al., 1995). This might lead to situations where hypotheses and related work might dictate many more factors affecting demand than what can be included in a survey. For example in Durán Rodas et al. (2019), there were on average approximately 17 built environment parameters that were found to be significant, when estimating models for demand for bike sharing using a data-driven approach. Such a high number is in many cases prohibiting to evaluate in a survey. Respondents can process only a limited survey load before fatigue kicks-in (Porter et al., 2004). Additionally, if much effort is required to understand the questions, respondents tend to either abandon the survey or answer in an inconsistent/nonattendance or other way, introducing biases in their responses (Hess et al., 2010).

3.1.2 Collection instrument

The instruments to perform data collection for transportation have also been found to affect the data collection process. For many years, the collection of data was performed on the premises of paper-based surveys and focus groups, which were later extended to telephone surveys. Lately, online surveys have been widely used, however not without issues; with the main to be the representativeness of the internet users, given the ease of using online social networks for distribution. As it is rather clear, each of these methods bear the risk of not being representative as access to the instruments might be limited.

All collection instruments deployed impose constraints to the data collection process. For instance, telephone surveys are restrictive in terms of describing scenarios with different attributes for alternatives, while distributing surveys over post does not allow for the explanation of the situation by an interviewer. They also bear the risk of introducing additional errors and biases in the data collection process. For example, an interviewer can contribute to biases related to acquaintance; presentation of scenarios misusing colors might create conditions for prompt choice; fatigue of an interview over the phone could result in different reporting than paper survey.

A special case of data collection is that of the focus group (Morgan, 1997). The idea is that a group of people is formed to discuss a topic, with the main goal is to have a guided (by a moderator) discussion, on the subject to be investigated. Focus groups are set to answer questions in a usually open-ended way. In focus groups, the moderator plays a sensitive role and should exhibit specific skills that would allow the extraction of proper information (Krueger and Casey, 2002). In transportation, the use of focus groups has been pursued for a wide variety of topics. In most of the reported cases of using focus groups, this has been done in conjunction with performing surveys and other data collection methods; while the focus has primarily been placed on the collection of qualitative aspects of the examined topic. To name but a few, Preston and Rajé (2007) studied social exclusion in terms of accessibility using a combination of surveys and focus groups; Akyelken et al. (2018) studied aspects of shared mobility for London; Daziano et al. (2017) studied willingness to pay for automation, using a combination of survey data and qualitative indicators from focus groups; while Politis et al. (2018) studied driving habits, in relation to handovers of control in autonomous cars.

3.1.3 Sampling

The sampling procedure plays a significant role in the data collection. Most of the models used assume data from random respondents (strata are commonly specified to ensure representativeness, but within strata, data collection is assumed to be random) Ben-Akiva and Lerman (1985). However, this is a prerequisite which is difficult to comply with.

An ill-defined sample could lead to what is commonly referred to in the literature as sampling bias. Sampling biases affect the quality of the data and refer to situations where some categories of the examined population are less likely to be represented. One widely discussed bias is the nonresponse bias (or also discussed as the counterpart self-selection bias). Apart from the obvious issues related to spatial distribution and representativeness, researchers have to deal with nonresponse bias, which refers to individuals who choose to not respond or responds late to such surveys (Richardson, 2003). Nonrespondents or late respondents might have a completely different behavior from those who respond (on time), as well as with people who deliberately choose to respond to a survey. Brog and Meyburg (1980) analyzed data from different cities in Germany and found that there is a strong correlation between trip-making characteristics reported and time taken to respond to the survey. The impact of sampling has become more apparent with the widespread of web-based data collection instruments and distribution methods, as they reach specific population groups, who have access to these instruments and can be reached from the distribution method. Some additional categories include undercoverage bias; survivorship bias; exclusion bias; overmatching bias; prescreening, or advertising bias.

Aiming at correcting some of the potential sources of bias and being able to have enough data to have the essential degrees of freedom to perform model estimation and capture heterogeneity in responses, research focuses on the estimation of the sample sizes. Again here, controversy arises. The proper statistical way of estimating sample sizes usually requires some prior knowledge of the system studied. This leads to the use of rule of thumb for coming up with an adequate sample size, which as it is understandable, suffers from the danger to introduce bias in the estimation (Washington et al., 2010; Johnson and Wichern, 2002).

3.1.4 Response

Measurement errors in surveys refer generally to the situation where responses provide other-than-true results (Biemer et al., 2011). This could be attributed broadly to any type of error source which results in difference between the true response and the recorded one. For example, respondents could not understand the question or do not want to answer in a true way or a mistake takes place when the interviewee records the answers or there is a GPS positioning error when using data loggers. Biemer et al. (2011) identify measurement errors sources: (1) Survey design, (2) Data collection method, (3) Interviewer, and (4) Respondent.

Measurement errors could be of random nature (nonsampling errors), or they could be systematic ones. When the later relates to the way that participants respond, it refers to a category of errors commonly known as response bias. Response bias is generally referring to the situation when respondents illustrate a tendency to answer questions in a different way that what the context defined suggests (Paulhus, 1991). For example, a respondent would like to have a particular service offered to them, so they report overuse of this service (if it would have been available), or a respondent wants to be liked by the interviewer. Response biases can widely affect the validity of the data collected (Furnham, 1986; Orne, 1962). Response biases are related to response styles, which describe the tendency of individuals to follow a specific response policy. Some widely discussed response biases pertain social desirability and its opposite, acquiescence or yea-saying and its opposite and extremity response or midpoint response. In their seminal work, Furnham (1986); Nederhof (1985) describe the techniques used to try and control for these types of biases, by measures of prevention, measurement, and correction.

Another family of systematic bias relates to halo effects and leniency or severity biases. In the former, respondents tend to be positive or negative with the evaluation subject (e.g., car sharing) by aspects not observed or included in the survey such as own expectations and preferences (Kahneman, 2011). Leniency bias may occur when an observer has the tendency to be lenient in all of his/her assessments while severity bias may occur when the respondent has the opposite tendency to be harsh/severe.

Stated preference experiments bear also a significant amount of other biases. The main reason is that the scenarios collected from the same participant could provide more information on how an individual chooses. In that sense, the effect of nontrading, lexicographic, and inconsistent choice has received attention (Hess et al., 2010). In nontrading behavior, it is clearly observed that individuals do not change their choices even if other alternatives are more attractive, while in lexicographic behavior, individuals choose always the alternative that has a specific property (for example, the cheapest in every case). Finally, inconsistent choices refer to the situation where choices between alternatives are not consistent, in terms of how participants value each attribute. Additionally, other biases discussed include the anchoring bias (McFadden, 2001), inertia bias (Thaler and Sunstein, 2009), hypothetical bias (Murphy et al., 2005), and aggregation bias (Morrison, 2000), as well as attribute nonattendance bias (Hensher et al., 2012).

3.2 Concept-, spatial, and network-oriented data

Other possible sources of data are categorized in terms of concept-, spatial, and network-oriented data. With regards to concept-oriented data, the collection of data has mainly relied on aggregated data to characterize demand (Bagchi and White, 2005). For instance, data collection for public transport demand was either performed on the basis of ticket counting or with observers who monitored the demand in the vehicles themselves. However, as different types of tickets existed and transfers are in many cases allowed using one ticket, the actual demand is very difficult to be observed. Additionally, data related to the routes and schedules as well as delays were scarcely available and, in many cases (even today), collected on a report basis, where the driver or the operator has to report an incident and the corresponding delay.

Spatial data are relevant for identifying demand for transportation systems, as the information that they describe essentially drives demand (Efthymiou and Antoniou, 2014). Spatial data have been originally collected in the form of land use and built environment characteristics. This has been usually available from registries available by the relevant public authorities, following in most cases troublesome acquisition processes and being scarcely updated. The granularity of the spatial data collected in a centralized way did not allow for evaluation in a spatial scale smaller than the one defined by traffic analysis zones, constituting a dataset of low resolution.

Network-oriented data on the other hand have been collected to monitor demand, primarily for car transport. The instruments in most cases have been the use of loop detectors, cameras, and radar or lidars. In some cases, plate recognition was used for the extraction of travel time, however, as these efforts were taking place following a centralized deployment approach, data collection takes place on some parts of the network, and inference techniques are deployed for the estimation of network performance metrics (e.g., in Tamin and Willumsen, 1989). As conventional network data do not offer disaggregated insights for the majority of emerging transport mode, the further exploration of them is considered to be out of scope.

4. Emerging data collection methods

Lately, the widespread use of ICT is changing data availability in a broad spectrum of applications creating new data sources to be explored. The size of dataset has changed, as has the diversity of the available datasets. These changes in data availability can be attributed to the evolution of pervasive systems (i.e., GPS handsets, cellular networks) and especially the connectivity that has been available to a growing number of individuals with the evolution of the Internet. In many cases, the data typology is the same, however, the data collection instruments introduced enable the collection of richer datasets. In other cases, however (such as the case of social media), this type of data typology has been completely new, enabling data-oriented research on data quality aspects. In addition, users are much more willing to share their data, usually in exchange of services, while the concept of open sharing of data is in some cases viewed as a mean to empower citizens and build the so-called digital democracy (Helbing and Pournaras, 2015). These changes observed and the sources of data available have received wide attention from the transport scientific community toward the utilization of the increasingly available data (Big Data) (Buckley and Lightman, 2015; Reades et al., 2007).

4.1 User-oriented collection methods

For performing surveys, the use of GPS-based data loggers for supplementing the traditional surveys was initially pursued (Doherty et al., 2001). However, the high investment cost and the unease that carrying an additional device imposes made them obsolescent against the use of smartphones (Cottrill et al., 2013). With their widespread (Pew Research Center, 2019) and very high penetration rates, research has been performed on the benefits of using smartphone apps for performing collection of data that comprise both travel survey as well as performance of RP and SP experiments. The benefits of smartphone are rather clear: users carry them charged everywhere, they comprise an increasing number of sensors, and they offer the opportunity to communicate with the user. Prelipcean et al. (2018) provide a recent overview of the development of such smartphone apps. Most of these apps are usually closed-source or provided by external developers and used specifically as an experiment tool that collects specific data types. The process followed in most of the cases is the collection of GPS traces, automatic or manual data annotation, and user validation (Cottrill et al., 2013). In most of these cases, incentives provided are monetary, in the form of eitherdirectly earning money while using the app or participating in a draw to win a prize.

These apps were mainly designed for passively collecting travel date and are scarcely used to conduct preference experiments that relate to the trips performed by individuals (e.g., asking mode alternatives for a trip performed.) To the best of our knowledge, in the transportation community, the only exception is the recently published paper from Danaf et al. (2019), where they create context-aware experiments for better mode choice prediction. Within the Internet of Things, the development of apps for social data is also growing. Griego et al. (2017) have used an app for collecting spatially aware urban qualities for smart cities. In an innovative data collection concept, users entering a geo-fenced area are asked questions and simultaneously collect environmental and mobility data.

Another interesting source of data that have emerged the last few years is that one of social media. From their rise, they have received attention from the scientific community, forming a potentially new stream of research. The reasons behind this attention can be summarized upon the unprecedented amount of information that can be extracted and the opportunities that social media platform use can provide on direct communication with users. The additional information collected from social media can complement conventional data collection methods and ultimately provide a better understanding of daily urban rhythms. The use of social media across the world is astonishing: Facebook and Twitter are ranked as third and eleventh most visited websites globally (www.Alexa.com). In 2018, there are 100 million daily active users on Twitter sending 500 million tweets every day (www.omnicoreagency.com); while there are around 1.47 billion daily active users on Facebook, 88% of them access the site via mobile phones (blog.hootsuite.com). From a research perspective, a growing amount of related work has been published in the last few years, showcasing the potential of using social media in transportation. Chaniotakis et al. (2016) have provided a comprehensive review of the directions that transportation-related social media research is positioned. Social media are explored as a source of data which could potentially increase the accuracy of transportation modeling, understanding travel behavior, allowing for event prediction and detection, extracting mobility-related patterns and spatial characteristics, as well as interacting with users.

Apart from the general merits of exploring user-generating content, interesting to the exploration of emerging mobility concepts is the extraction of sentiment with regards to transportation (Collins et al., 2013). However, the use of social media data introduces also a variety of issues. One of the first issues is the data ownership which actually differs from conventionally used data on the basis that social media data might be open but is not public. Researchers and practitioners should practice carefulness and always consider terms of data use (which might be updated without notice). In addition, issues related to intentionally fake information or high information noise (such as nonsense posts) degrade data quality. Finally, posts on social media might originate from a misrepresentative sample where differences between real life and online life need the proper normalization of the information extracted (Chaniotakis et al., 2016).

The user-oriented data collection extends apart from the above to a variety of seemingly unrelated to transportation data sources that have been used in various applications. To name but a few, Sobolevsky et al. (2014) investigated bank card transactions for extracting mobility patterns of individuals in Spain, while many researchers have focused on the exploration of the use of mobile phone data for estimation of travel demand (Alexander et al., 2015; Caceres et al., 2007; Calabrese et al., 2011).

4.2 Concept-oriented collection methods

One of the key aspects of ICT advancement is that they enabled the collection of data for all transport concepts. An example for public transport is the introduction of smart-card data, where users of public transport are required to tap-in (and in some systems, tap-out) whenever using them. This has lead to the definition of a spectrum of methods varying from data mining (Ma et al., 2013), and demand estimation (Jun and Dongyuan, 2013) to individual pattern extraction (Zhao et al., 2018) and metrics of user satisfaction (Ingvardson et al., 2018).

Similar use data can be extracted for many of the emerging mobility systems. With regards to bike-sharing, there are more than 800 programs around the world with a fleet of more than 900,000 bicycles with trip proposes to be commute to work on weekdays and leisure and/or social purposes (Fishman et al., 2013). Many of these programs publish their data as open data allowing for data analytics concepts where data from different cities are compared. For instance, Chardon et al. (2017) studied the trips per day per bicycle in a city level in 75 station-based bike-sharing systems in Europe, Israel, United States, Canada, Brazil, and Australia, with the independent variables being the operator's attributes, the compactness, the weather, the transportation infrastructure, and the geography; Zhao et al. (2014) correlated the logarithm of ridership and turn-over rate using data of 69 SSBS systems in China with urban features and system characteristics, and Durán Rodas et al. (2019) developed a data-driven method for estimation of demand models of station-based bike sharing using built environment factors where data of multiple cities are pooled in one dataset.

Car-sharing is the short-term rental of a car. Subscribed customers are charged to use vehicles based on various pricing schemes (based on vehicle type, kilometer driven, location, time of use) and in some cases, a subscription fee. The recent wide implementations of car sharing (in July 2019 Share Now operates more than 20,000 vehicles in more than 30 cities worldwide——https://www.your-now.com/) have led to the availability of datasets for some of the cities operated. Acquiring the data is on a request to the providers' basis (e.g., Share–now, ZipCar); (Schmöller et al., 2015); however, attempts have been made on extracting data from the application programming interface (API) (Trentini and Losacco, 2017). This latter method is subject to the general data use policy of the provider and bears issues such as inability to define relocation, false/canceled reservations, and routes. The exploration of these datasets has yielded interesting results with regards to their use.

4.3 Network-oriented data

Advances in ICT have also brought new data on a network level. Departing from the conventional traffic count data, efforts have been put through to use different types of sensors for capturing the network-based data. This has been directed toward the deployment of networks of Bluetooth or WiFi sensors aiming at capturing the users of smartphones or cars who bear these features. In most of these cases, the deployment of sensors is a rather cheap solution (from a report in Greece the cost for one sensor including installation and 3 years warranty was 2300 Euros (Mitsakis and Iordanopoulos, 2014)). Reliability of such systems relies on the penetration rate of devices which broadcast such signals (Friesen and McLeod, 2015). In addition, placing the sensors and data cleaning are very important to ensure representativeness and reliability. For the former, optimization techniques have been used using different optimization criteria such as observability or flow estimation and origin destination (OD) pair separation Gentili and Mirchandani (2012); Zhou and List (2010); Fei and Mahmassani (2011). On the latter, aspects of mode detection and scaling of the Bluetooth/WiFi flows to actual traffic flows have been explored (Barcelö et al., 2010; Bhaskar and Chung, 2013).

5. Data quality assessment

The emergence of diverse data sources implies the investigation and assessment of data quality. The discussion however is not new: metrics for data quality have long been present in statistical analyses and methods to quantify data quality have long been discussed (e.g., statistical tests). Research has extensively focused on the impacts of data quality to the information systems. For example, Ballou and Pazer (1985) presented a model for the propagation of errors in information systems, following the extensive work that had been done in accounting literature for evaluating the impact of errors and controls on financial balances (e.g., in Cushing, 1974). Later, the idea of assessing data quality on the basis of propagation of errors has been extended, to cater for the multidimensional concept of data quality. Batini et al. (2009) provided a review of 13 prevailing methodologies for data quality assessment and reported the used quality dimensions. From a meta-analysis of the Batini et al. (2009) work, the prevailing criteria of data quality (with regards to data) are presented in Fig. 5.3. As it is clearly obvious, the prevailing factors are included in most

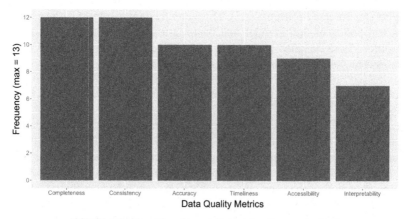

FIGURE 5.3 Prevailing data quality metrics (Frequency ≥ 5).

of the studies examined. A striking difference is that in most cases the evaluation of data in transport takes place on either the accuracy or in some cases for emerging data on interpretability and accessibility, without however a clear and consistent use of metrics that would allow their comparison.

Going in detail with each data quality criterion, Batini et al. (2009) provides a comprehensive overview of the definitions that the difference studies examined use. Here, we are consolidating the information and providing some definitions and notes related to transportation. Starting with **completeness**, it is generally used to refer to the ability of the data to describe the system for the application at hand. Essentially completeness related to extent that the dataset examined has all the required elements (or variables) to achieve observability and to be used to do analysis and perform modeling. Some researchers have used completeness to describe how much data are available with regards to the maximum possible data (or information) that can be achieved (Biswas et al., 2006) or to evaluate to what extend reports have been completed (Tin et al., 2013) or define the magnitude of missing values (Naumann, 2002). Clearly, there are differences in the above definition and also the reference system (Batini et al., 2009). Based on the above, for the case of evaluating data, completeness for emerging transport systems and their demand completeness should be examined on the basis of exploring the extend to which data can actually describe the system and the interconnections to the remaining transportation system. An example could be bike-sharing data. Assuming that only a sample of 10% of all bookings per day is provided, completeness could be as high as 10% (but in many cases much lower) of the information needed to describe the bike-sharing system and even less for describing the transportation system of an area. This could be easily been understood when taking into account that bike sharing could be as low as, for example, 5% of the modal split.

Consistency usually refers to compliance with some data-related rules. Several subcategories of data consistency exist such as interrelation and intrarelation (Batini et al., 2009) or internal and external consistency. The former categorization refers mainly to the relationships between data (and can be viewed as the examination of internal consistency), while the latter could be viewed as a metric of consistency in terms of data being consistent with data and data being consistent with the real system observed. One example of internal consistency could be that all age data for a particular study refer to individuals of age 20–30 years old, while external consistency could be viewed from the perspective that people of the 20–30 age group are the only people that interact with the system.

Accuracy is one of the data quality measures that has been long discussed; with different definitions to be found in the literature. As described in Batini et al. (2009), Wang and Strong (1996) define accuracy based on "the extent to which data are correct, reliable and certified" and Ballou and Pazer (1985) refer to the data correspondence to real values, Redman (1997) and the proximity of a data value, to some other value that is considered correct. In transportation and particularly with regards to the emerging mobility concepts, measuring accuracy of the data is a rather complicated task, with the main reason to be nonexistence of reference data on the base of which we could compare. For example, many studies explore acceptance and adoption of shared autonomous vehicles. The only way of evaluating the accuracy of these can be based on the comparison of the results of different studies, in many cases performed in different places around the world. For the evaluation of data accuracy, there are various statistical tests that can be deployed, for example, examining if the results belong to the distribution. For more information, the reader is referred to the comprehensive overview of statistical methods for transportation provided by Washington et al. (2010).

Timeliness is found in the literature to be used to describe the time that it takes (delay) so that changes of the real system are reflected to the data (Batini et al., 2009). Timeliness needs in transport differ on the basis of the commonly followed distinction between off-line and online use of transport data. Also, depending on the type of the data, timeliness of transport data can vary from years to a few seconds. To give some examples, travel diary surveys happen in a range of 2–10 years, traffic counts provide aggregated results every 1–15 min; while smart-card reads and trajectory data can be available almost instantly to the database used.

Finally, **accessibility** is defined upon the possibility of getting access to the data and in some cases as the time to get the request, based on the delivery time, request time, and deadline time (essentially more referring to the timeliness). Accessibility is particularly important for transportation studies, as several datasets exist for a case study, but only very few can become available to researchers or municipalities. This is particularly evidenced in the case of emerging data sources (e.g., data collected through mobile-phone apps): although there exist companies which collect data from large numbers of individuals, such datasets are usually not utilized for improvements of the transportation system or for the evaluation of new forms of mobility. Finally, **interpretability** refers to the extent to which data are interpretable, as a measure of being meaningful.

6. Transferability

Patterns of time use and travel can be significantly different among individuals at different stages in their life cycle living in places that offer different opportunities for activity participation. It is very important to understand the underlying behavior that governs the choices made in different contexts (i.e., different countries and different cities) for policy definition, and this has attracted the interest of research as a potential tool for understanding the outcome of adopting policies and transferring models (Lleras et al., 2002; Timmermans et al., 2003). This need has become imperative lately with the introduction of new disruptive forms of mobility (i.e., car sharing, autonomous vehicles) as well as new types of data (Cramer and Krueger, 2016; Belk, 2014). Comparisons of different travel characteristics and activity patterns are not new in the pertinent literature. Schafer (2000) presented a comparison of around 30 travel surveys in different countries for regularities in time and travel budgets. Lleras et al. (2002) presented an international comparison using travel survey data, using structural equation modeling and latent variables to explain mobility changes, number of trips, and total travel time. Simma and Axhausen (2001) performed a comparison of mode choices commitment in a joint relation of car ownership and ticket availability. These studies have shown that transferability of average indicators is in most cases not an adequate solution and should be avoided. de Abreu e Silva and Goulias (2009) performed a comparison between Seattle, WA, USA, and Lisbon, Portugal, including residential location choice, car ownership, and travel characteristics, and Kühne et al. (2018) investigated the car ownership characteristics in Germany and California. Pendyala (14) studied time allocation in different countries finding differences and similarities and this is the only study that examines aspects of daily rhythms across different countries.

Examination of the underlying behavioral characteristics related to activities performed and daily rhythms (such as daily time allocation, activity timing and scheduling, activity frequency) has been found to govern decision-making for travel-related behaviors and should be included in transportation models (de Abreu e Silva and Goulias, 2009). In other words, if people behave the same within clusters of individuals behaviors, there is a good basis that they would behave the same when it comes to aspects such as new forms of mobility, response to changes in life, and new infrastructure. Therefore, studies examining daily summaries in different countries or different cities within countries need to expand their repertory to time of day dynamics.

Emerging data sources have the benefit of, in many cases, being centrally collected, which allows for the comparison of patterns in such a way and makes this evaluation possible. Such an example is found in Chaniotakis et al. (2017) where the comparison of the differences in terms of data collected from social media for 10 cities around the world is pursued.

7. Conclusions and discussion

This chapter presented an overview of the prevailing data sources used in transportation for the evaluation of emerging transportation systems. This has been performed on the basis of a broad classification of data sources both in terms of their reference to transportation system component, as well as in terms of conventional and emerging data sources. Additionally, the important aspect of data quality is presented and discussed with regards to transportation research. Throughout this chapter, data-related issues have been highlighted, with the goal of accentuating the importance of using data quality measures for the evaluation of transportation data. Although efforts on data quality in different fields of research can serve as a starting point, the specifics of transportation pose the need of revisiting, adapting, and defining new, more relevant, measures. Finally, the potential of exploring transferability has been discussed, as a mean to reduce the transportation data collection cost, and help better understand the difference and similarities between people living in different places around the world.

References

Akyelken, N., Banister, D., Givoni, M., 2018. The sustainability of shared mobility in London: the dilemma for governance. Sustainability 10 (2), 420.

Alexander, L., Jiang, S., Murga, M., Gonzlez, M.C., 2015. Origin–destination trips by purpose and time of day inferred from mobile phone data. Transportation Research Part C: Emerging Technologies 58, 240–250. http://www.sciencedirect.com/science/article/pii/S0968090X1500073X. https://doi.org/10.1016/j.trc.2015.02.018.

Audirac, I., 1999. Stated preference for pedestrian proximity: an assessment of new urbanist sense of community. Journal of Planning Education and Research 19 (1), 53–66. http://jpe.sagepub.com/content/19/1/53.abstract.

Bafatakis, C., Duives, D., Daamen, W., 2015. Determining a pedestrian route choice model through a photo survey. In: Transportation Research Board 94th Annual Meeting, Washington DC. Number 15-4859 in TRB2015.

Bagchi, M., White, P., 2005. The potential of public transport smart card data. Transport Policy 12 (5), 464–474. http://www.sciencedirect.com/science/article/pii/S0967070X05000855. https://doi.org/10.1016/j.tranpol.2005.06.008 (road User Charging: Theory and Practices).

Ballou, D.P., Pazer, H.L., 1985. Modeling data and process quality in multi-input, multi-output information systems. Management Science 31 (2), 150–162.

Barceló, J., Montero, L., Marqués, L., Carmona, C., 2010. Travel time forecasting and dynamic origin-destination estimation for freeways based on bluetooth traffic monitoring. Transportation Research Record 2175 (1), 19–27.

Batini, C., Cappiello, C., Francalanci, C., Maurino, A., 2009. Methodologies for data quality assessment and improvement. ACM Computing Surveys (CSUR) 41 (3), 16.

Belk, R., 2014. You are what you can access: sharing and collaborative consumption online. Journal of Business Research 67 (8), 1595–1600.

Ben-Akiva, M.E., Lerman, S.R., 1985. Discrete Choice Analysis: Theory and Application to Travel Demand, vol. 9. MIT press.

Bhaskar, A., Chung, E., 2013. Fundamental understanding on the use of bluetooth scanner as a complementary transport data. Transportation Research Part C: Emerging Technologies 37, 42–72.

Biemer, P.P., Groves, R.M., Lyberg, L.E., Mathiowetz, N.A., Sudman, S., 2011. Measurement Errors in Surveys, vol. 173. John Wiley & Sons.

Biswas, J., Naumann, F., Qiu, Q., 2006. Assessing the completeness of sensor data. In: International Conference on Database Systems for Advanced Applications. Springer, pp. 717–732.

Bliemer, M.C., Rose, J.M., Hensher, D.A., 2009. Efficient stated choice experiments for estimating nested logit models. Transportation Research Part B: Methodological 43 (1), 19–35.

Brog, W., Meyburg, A.H., 1980. Nonresponse problem in travel surveys: an empirical investigation. Transportation Research Record (775), 34–38.

Buckley, S., Lightman, D., 2015. Ready or not, big data is coming to a city (transportation agency) near you. In: Transportation Research Board 94th Annual Meeting. Number 15-5156 in TRB2015.

Caceres, N., Wideberg, J., Benitez, F., 2007. Deriving origin—destination data from a mobile phone network. IET Intelligent Transport Systems 1 (1), 15—26.

Cai, L., Zhu, Y., 2015. The challenges of data quality and data quality assessment in the big data era. Data Science Journal 14.

Calabrese, F., Di Lorenzo, G., Liu, L., Ratti, C., 2011. Estimating origin-destination flows using mobile phone location data. IEEE Pervasive Computing 10 (4), 36—44. https://doi.org/10.1109/MPRV.2011.41.

Calabrese, F., Diao, M., Di Lorenzo, G., Ferreira Jr., J., Ratti, C., 2013. Understanding individual mobility patterns from urban sensing data: a mobile phone trace example. Transportation Research Part C: Emerging Technologies 26 (0), 301—313. http://www.sciencedirect.com/science/article/pii/S0968090X12001192. https://doi.org/10.1016/j.trc.2012.09.009.

Chaniotakis, E., Antoniou, C., Pereira, F., 2016. Mapping social media for transportation studies. IEEE Intelligent Systems 31 (6), 64—70. https://doi.org/10.1109/MIS.2016.98.

Chaniotakis, E., Antoniou, C., Goulias, K., 2017. Transferability and sample specification for social media data: a comparative analysis. In: Proceedings of the mobil. TUM 2017 Conference. Munich, Munich Germany.

Chardon, C.M.D., Caruso, G., Thomas, I., 2017. Bicycle sharing system success determinants. Transportation Research Part A: Policy and Practice 100, 202—214. https://doi.org/10.1016/j.tra.2017.04.020.

Collins, C., Hasan, S., Ukkusuri, S.V., 2013. A novel transit rider satisfaction metric: rider sentiments measured from online social media data. Journal of Public Transportation 16 (2), 2.

Cottrill, C., Pereira, F., Zhao, F., Ferreira Dias, I., Beng Lim, H., Ben-Akiva, M., Zegras, C., 2013. Future mobility survey. Transportation research record. Journal of the Transportation Research Board 2354, 59—67. https://doi.org/10.3141/2354-07.

Cramer, J., Krueger, A.B., 2016. Disruptive change in the taxi business: the case of uber. The American Economic Review 106 (5), 177—182.

Cushing, B.E., 1974. A mathematical approach to the analysis and design of internal control systems. The Accounting Review 49 (1), 24—41. http://www.jstor.org/stable/244795.

Danaf, M., Atasoy, B., de Azevedo, C.L., Ding-Mastera, J., Abou-Zeid, M., Cox, N., Zhao, F., Ben-Akiva, M., 2019. Context-aware stated preferences with smartphone-based travel surveys. Journal of Choice Modeling 31, 35—50. http://www.sciencedirect.com/science/article/pii/S1755534518300381. https://doi.org/10.1016/j.jocm.2019.03.001.

Daziano, R.A., Sarrias, M., Leard, B., 2017. Are consumers willing to pay to let cars drive for them? analyzing response to autonomous vehicles. Transportation Research Part C: Emerging Technologies 78, 150—164. http://www.sciencedirect.com/science/article/pii/S0968090X17300682. https://doi.org/10.1016/j.trc.2017.03.003.

de Abreu e Silva, J., Goulias, K.G., 2009. Structural equations model of land use patterns, location choice, and travel behavior: Seattle, Washington, compared with lisbon, Portugal. Transportation Research Record 2135 (1), 106—113. https://doi.org/10.3141/2135-13. https://doi.org/10.3141/2135-13. https://doi.org/10.3141/2135-13.

Doherty, S.T., Noël, N., Gosselin, M.L., Sirois, C., Ueno, M., 2001. Moving beyond observed outcomes: integrating global positioning systems and interactive computer-based travel behavior surveys. Technical Report; Transportation Research Board 449—466. https://trid.trb.org/view/686721.

Doirado, E., van den Berg, M., van Lint, H., Hoogendoorn, S., Prendinger, H., 2012. Everscape: the making of a disaster evacuation experience. In: CHI'12 Extended Abstracts on Human Factors in Computing Systems. ACM, pp. 2285−2290.

Durán Rodas, D., Chaniotakis, E., Antoniou, C., 2019. Built environment factors affecting bike sharing ridership: a data-driven approach for multiple cities. Transportation Research Record. https://doi.org/10.1177/0361198119849908.

Efthymiou, D., Antoniou, C., 2014. Measuring the effects of transportation infrastructure location on real estate prices and rents: investigating the current impact of a planned metro line. EURO Journal on Transportation and Logistics 3 (3−4), 179−204.

Efthymiou, D., Antoniou, C., Waddell, P., 2013. Factors affecting the adoption of vehicle sharing systems by young drivers. Transport Policy 29, 64−73. http://www.sciencedirect.com/science/article/pii/S0967070X13000607. https://doi.org/10.1016/j.tranpol.2013.04.009.

Fei, X., Mahmassani, H.S., 2011. Structural analysis of near-optimal sensor locations for a stochastic large-scale network. Transportation Research Part C: Emerging Technologies 19 (3), 440−453. http://www.sciencedirect.com/science/article/pii/S0968090X10001105. https://doi.org/10.1016/j.trc.2010.07.001.

Fishman, E., Washington, S., Haworth, N., 2013. Bike share: a synthesis of the literature. Transport Reviews 33 (2), 148−165. https://doi.org/10.1080/01441647.2013.775612 cited By 98.

Friesen, M.R., McLeod, R.D., 2015. Bluetooth in intelligent transportation systems: a survey. International Journal of Intelligent Transportation Systems Research 13 (3), 143−153. https://doi.org/10.1007/s13177-014-0092-1. https://doi.org/10.1007/s13177-014-0092-1.

Fu, M., Rothfeld, R., Antoniou, C. Exploring preferences for transportation modes in an urban air mobility environment: Munich case study. Transportation Research Record 0(0):0361198119843858. doi:10.1177/0361198119843858.

Furnham, A., 1986. Response bias, social desirability and dissimulation. Personality and Individual Differences 7 (3), 385−400. http://www.sciencedirect.com/science/article/pii/0191886986900140. https://doi.org/10.1016/0191-8869(86)90014-0.

Gentili, M., Mirchandani, P., 2012. Locating sensors on traffic networks: models, challenges and research opportunities. Transportation Research Part C: Emerging Technologies 24, 227−255. http://www.sciencedirect.com/science/article/pii/S0968090X1200006X. https://doi.org/10.1016/j.trc.2012.01.004.

Griego, D., Buff, V., Hayoz, E., Moise, I., Pournaras, E., 2017. Sensing and mining urban qualities in smart cities. In: 2017 IEEE 31st International Conference on Advanced Information Networking and Applications (AINA). IEEE, pp. 1004−1011.

Handy, S., 1996. Methodologies for exploring the link between urban form and travel behavior. Transportation Research Part D: Transport and Environment 1 (2), 151−165. https://doi.org/10.1016/S1361-9209(96)00010-7. http://www.sciencedirect.com/science/article/pii/S1361920996000107.

Helbing, D., Pournaras, E.S., 2015. Build digital democracy. Nature News 527 (7576), 33.

Hensher, D.A., 1994. Stated preference analysis of travel choices: the state of practice. Transportation 21 (2), 107−133.

Hensher, D.A., Rose, J.M., Greene, W.H., 2012. Inferring attribute non-attendance from stated choice data: implications for willingness to pay estimates and a warning for stated choice experiment design. Transportation 39 (2), 235−245.

Hess, S., Rose, J.M., Polak, J., 2010. Non-trading, lexicographic and inconsistent behaviour in stated choice data. Transportation Research Part D: Transport and Environment 15 (7), 405−417.

Hunter, G.J., Wachowicz, M., Bregt, A.K., 2003. Understanding spatial data usability. Data Science Journal 2, 79−89.

Ingvardson, J.B., Nielsen, O.A., Raveau, S., Nielsen, B.F., 2018. Passenger arrival and waiting time distributions dependent on train service frequency and station characteristics: a smart card data analysis. Transportation Research Part C: Emerging Technologies 90, 292–306.

Jagadish, H., Gehrke, J., Labrinidis, A., Papakonstantinou, Y., Patel, J.M., Ramakrishnan, R., Shahabi, C., 2014. Big data and its technical challenges. Communications of the ACM 57 (7), 86–94.

Johnson, R.A., Wichern, D.W. (Eds.), 2002. Applied Multivariate Statistical Analysis. Prentice-Hall, Inc., Upper Saddle River, NJ, USA.

Jun, C., Dongyuan, Y., 2013. Estimating smart card commuters origin–destination distribution based on APTS data. Journal of Transportation Systems Engineering and Information Technology 13 (4), 47–53. http://www.sciencedirect.com/science/article/pii/S1570667213601166. https://doi.org/10.1016/S1570-6672(13)60116-6.

Kahneman, D., 2011. Thinking, Fast and Slow. Macmillan.

Kladeftiras, G., Antoniou, C., 2015. Social networks impact on carpooling systems performance: privacy vs. efficiency. In: Transportation Research Board 94th Annual Meeting. DC, Washington. Number 15-1540 in TRB2015.

Krueger, R.A., Casey, M.A., 2002. Designing and Conducting Focus Group Interviews.

Kühne, K., Mitra, S.K., Saphores, J.D.M., 2018. Without a Ride in Car Country A Comparison of Carless Households in Germany and California. Transportation Research Part A: Policy and Practice 109, 24–40. http://www.sciencedirect.com/science/article/pii/S0965856417305621. https://doi.org/10.1016/j.tra.2018.01.021.

Leduc, G., 2008. Road traffic data: collection methods and applications. Working Papers on Energy, Transport and Climate Change 1, 55.

Likert, R., 1932. A technique for the measurement of attitudes. Archives of psychology 22 (140, 55).

Lleras, G.C., Simma, A., Ben-Akiva, M., Schafer, A., Axhausen, K.W., Furutani, T., 2002. Fundamental relationships specifying travel behavior an international travel survey comparison. In: Proceedings of 82nd Annual Meeting of the Transportation Research Board. DC, Washington,.

Louviere, J.J., Hensher, D.A., Swait, J.D., 2000. Stated Choice Methods: Analysis and Applications. Cambridge university press.

Ma, X., Wu, Y.J., Wang, Y., Chen, F., Liu, J., 2013. Mining smart card data for transit riders travel patterns. Transportation Research Part C: Emerging Technologies 36, 1–12. http://www.sciencedirect.com/science/article/pii/S0968090X13001630. https://doi.org/10.1016/j.trc.2013.07.010.

Martin, E., Shaheen, S.A., Lidicker, J., 2010. Impact of carsharing on household vehicle holdings: results from North American shared-use vehicle survey. Transportation Research Record 2143 (1), 150–158. https://doi.org/10.3141/2143-19. https://doi.org/10.3141/2143-19. https://doi.org/10.3141/2143-19.

McFadden, D., 2001. Economic choices. The American Economic Review 91 (3), 351–378. https://doi.org/10.1257/aer.91.3.351. http://www.aeaweb.org/articles?id=10.1257/aer.91.3.351.

Mitsakis, E., Iordanopoulos, P., 2014. SEEITS: Deliverable D7.1.1: Cost-Benefit Analysis Report for the Deployment of ITS in Greece. Technical Report.

Morgan, D.L., 1997. The Focus Group Guidebook, vol. 1. Sage publications.

Morrison, M., 2000. Aggregation biases in stated preference studies. Australian Economic Papers 39 (2), 215–230.

Murphy, J.J., Allen, P.G., Stevens, T.H., Weatherhead, D., 2005. A meta-analysis of hypothetical bias in stated preference valuation. Environmental and Resource Economics 30 (3), 313–325. https://doi.org/10.1007/s10640-004-3332-z. https://doi.org/10.1007/s10640-004-3332-z.

Naumann, F. (Ed.), 2002. Information Quality Criteria. Springer Berlin Heidelberg, Berlin, Heidelberg, pp. 29–50. https://doi.org/10.1007/3-540-45921-9_3. https://doi.org/10.1007/3-540-45921-9_3.

Nederhof, A.J., 1985. Methods of coping with social desirability bias: a review. European Journal of Social Psychology 15 (3), 263–280. https://doi.org/10.1002/ejsp.2420150303. https://onlinelibrary.wiley.com/doi/abs/10.1002/ejsp.2420150303. https://onlinelibrary.wiley.com/doi/pdf/10.1002/ejsp.2420150303.

Orne, M.T., 1962. On the social psychology of the psychological experiment: with particular reference to demand characteristics and their implications. American Psychologist 17 (11), 776.

Paulhus, D.L., 1991. Chapter 2 - measurement and control of response bias. In: Robinson, J.P., Shaver, P.R., Wrightsman, L.S. (Eds.), Measures of Personality and Social Psychological Attitudes. Academic Press, pp. 17–59. http://www.sciencedirect.com/science/article/pii/B978012590241050006X. https://doi.org/10.1016/B978-0-12-590241-0.50006-X.

Pew Research Center, 2019. Smartphone Ownership is Growing Rapidly Around the World, but Not Always Equally. Technical Report.

Politis, I., Langdon, P., Bradley, M., Skrypchuk, L., Mouzakitis, A., Clarkson, P.J., 2018. Designing autonomy in cars: a survey and two focus groups on driving habits of an inclusive user group, and group attitudes towards autonomous cars. In: Di Bucchianico, G., Kercher, P.F. (Eds.), Advances in Design for Inclusion. Springer International Publishing, Cham, pp. 161–173.

Porter, S.R., Whitcomb, M.E., Weitzer, W.H., 2004. Multiple surveys of students and survey fatigue. New Directions for Institutional Research 2004 (121), 63–73. https://doi.org/10.1002/ir.101. https://doi.org/10.1002/ir.101.

Prelipcean, A.C., Gidfalvi, G., Susilo, Y.O., 2018. MEILI: a travel diary collection, annotation and automation system. Computers, Environment and Urban Systems 70, 24–34. http://www.sciencedirect.com/science/article/pii/S0198971517305240. https://doi.org/10.1016/j.compenvurbsys.2018.01.011.

Preston, J., Rajé, F., 2007. Accessibility, mobility and transport-related social exclusion. Journal of Transport Geography 15 (3), 151–160.

Pronzato, L., Zhigljavsky, A., 2010. Optimal Design and Related Areas in Optimization and Statistics, vol. 28. Springer Science & Business Media.

Reades, J., Calabrese, F., Sevtsuk, A., Ratti, C., 2007. Cellular census: explorations in urban data collection. Pervasive Computing, IEEE 6 (3), 30–38.

Redman, T.C., 1997. Data Quality for the Information Age, first ed. Artech House, Inc., Norwood, MA, USA.

Richardson, A.J., 2003. Behavioral mechanisms of nonresponse in mail-back travel surveys. Transportation Research Record 1855 (1), 191–199. https://doi.org/10.3141/1855-24.

Richardson, A.J., Ampt, E.S., Meyburg, A.H., 1995. Survey Methods for Transport Planning. Eucalyptus Press Melbourne.

Rose, J.M., Bliemer, M.C., Hensher, D.A., Collins, A.T., 2008. Designing efficient stated choice experiments in the presence of reference alternatives. Transportation Research Part B: Methodological 42 (4), 395–406.

Schafer, A., 2000. Regularities in Travel Demand: An International Perspective.

Shen, L., Stopher, P.R., 2014. Review of gps travel survey and gps data-processing methods. Transport Reviews 34 (3), 316–334.

Simma, A., Axhausen, K., 2001. Structures of commitment in mode use: a comparison of Switzerland, Germany and great Britain. Transport Policy 8 (4), 279–288. http://www.

sciencedirect.com/science/article/pii/S0967070X01000233. https://doi.org/10.1016/S0967-070X(01)00023-3.

Sobolevsky, S., Sitko, I., Combes, R.T.D., Hawelka, B., Arias, J.M., Ratti, C., 2014. Money on the move: big data of bank card transactions as the new proxy for human mobility patterns and regional delineation. The case of residents and foreign visitors in Spain. In: 2014 IEEE International Congress on Big Data, pp. 136—143. https://doi.org/10.1109/BigData.Congress.2014.28.

Schmöller, S., Weikl, S., Müller, J., Bogenberger, K., 2015. Empirical analysis of free-floating carsharing usage: the Munich and Berlin case. Transportation Research Part C: Emerging Technologies 56, 34—51. http://www.sciencedirect.com/science/article/pii/S0968090X1500087X. https://doi.org/10.1016/j.trc.2015.03.008.

Tamin, O.Z., Willumsen, L.G., 1989. Transport demand model estimation from traffic counts. Transportation 16 (1), 3—26. https://doi.org/10.1007/BF00223044. https://doi.org/10.1007/BF00223044.

Tayi, G.K., Ballou, D.P., 1998. Examining data quality. Communications of the ACM 41 (2), 54—57.

Thaler, R.H., Sunstein, C.R., 2009. Nudge: Improving Decisions about Health, Wealth, and Happiness. Penguin.

Timmermans, H., van der Waerden, P., Alves, M., Polak, J., Ellis, S., Harvey, A.S., Kurose, S., Zandee, R., 2003. Spatial context and the complexity of daily travel patterns: an international comparison. Journal of Transport Geography 11 (1), 37—46.

Tin, S.T., Woodward, A., Ameratunga, S., 2013. Completeness and accuracy of crash outcome data in a cohort of cyclists: a validation study. BMC Public Health 13 (1), 420.

Train, K.E., 2009. Discrete Choice Methods with Simulation. Cambridge university press.

Trentini, A., Losacco, F., 2017. Analyzing carsharing public (scraped) data to study urban traffic patterns. Procedia Environmental Sciences 37, 594—603. http://www.sciencedirect.com/science/article/pii/S1878029617300464. https://doi.org/10.1016/j.proenv.2017.03.046. green Urbanism (GU).

Walker, J.L., Wang, Y., Thorhauge, M., Ben-Akiva, M., 2018. D-efficient or deficient? a robustness analysis of stated choice experimental designs. Theory and Decision 84 (2), 215—238.

Wang, R.Y., Strong, D.M., 1996. Beyond accuracy: what data quality means to data consumers. Journal of Management Information Systems 12 (4), 5—33.

Washington, S.P., Karlaftis, M.G., Mannering, F., 2010. Statistical and Econometric Methods for Transportation Data Analysis, second ed. Chapman and Hall/CRC.

Zhao, J., Deng, W., Song, Y., 2014. Ridership and effectiveness of bikesharing: the effects of urban features and system characteristics on daily use and turnover rate of public bikes in China. Transport Policy 35, 253—264. https://doi.org/10.1016/j.tranpol.2014.06.008.

Zhao, Z., Koutsopoulos, H.N., Zhao, J., 2018. Individual mobility prediction using transit smart card data. Transportation Research Part C: Emerging Technologies 89, 19—34. http://www.sciencedirect.com/science/article/pii/S0968090X18300676. https://doi.org/10.1016/j.trc.2018.01.022.

Zhou, X., List, G.F., 2010. An information-theoretic sensor location model for traffic origin-destination demand estimation applications. Transportation Science 44 (2), 254—273. https://doi.org/10.1287/trsc.1100.0319. https://doi.org/10.1287/trsc.1100.0319. https://doi.org/10.1287/trsc.1100.0319.

Chapter 6

Location planning for one-way carsharing systems considering accessibility improvements: the case of super-compact electric cars

Tomoki Nishigaki[1], Jan-Dirk Schmöcker[1], Toshiyuki Nakamura[2], Nobuhiro Uno[3], Masahiro Kuwahara[4], Akira Yoshioka[4]

[1]*Department of Urban Management, Kyoto University, Kyoto, Japan;* [2]*Institute of Innovation for Future Society, Nagoya University, Nagoya, Japan;* [3]*Department of Civil and Earth Resource Engineering, Kyoto University, Kyoto, Japan;* [4]*Toyota Motor Corporation, Toyota, Japan*

Chapter outline

1. Introduction

Carsharing schemes have been rapidly increasing all over the world in recent years. They have evolved from long-term and short-term rentals where customers had to return the vehicle to the same location as the pick-up point (or pay an additional service charge) to one-way carsharing schemes, to free-floating carsharing schemes without any predefined locations. A good example for this development is Montreal, Canada, where first carsharing clubs, then one-way carsharing schemes have evolved fairly early. Since 2015, the one-way or "station-based" carsharing operator has then added

Demand for Emerging Transportation Systems. https://doi.org/10.1016/B978-0-12-815018-4.00006-1

free-floating vehicles to the fleet, which has rapidly increased in popularity (Wielinski et al., 2019).

Free-floating schemes require the availability of on-street parking. In Japan, as this is nearly nonexisting, free-floating carsharing schemes are not in operation. Also, one-way carsharing schemes in Japan have been growing slowly. Aside from some early experiments reported in Shaheen et al. (2015), it has only been since 2014 that the Japanese Ministry of Land, Infrastructure, Transportation and Tourism (MLIT) has changed the legislation to permit commercial operation of such schemes (MLIT, 2014). There are a few schemes operated for demonstration purposes since then, but most are operated on very limited area and are not profitable. One of these is "Times car sharing" which has been in operation from 2015 around Japan in collaboration with Toyota and which will be discussed in this contribution. The scheme is called "Ha:mo" as abbreviation for "Harmonious Mobility." Round-trip city carsharing has been in operation since around 2005 with again "Times" as the largest operator, and "Orix car share" as another example. Since 2017, "ChoiMobi Yokohama" is also in operation which operates with small electric vehicles, similar to Ha:mo (but in collaboration with Nissan).

There are a number of reasons why carsharing is used less is Japan. Arguably, the concept of "my car" and more generally a stricter distinction between private goods and public goods is still stronger embedded in Japanese culture. Also other sharing industries are still less developed in Japan compared to Western countries. Furthermore, the Traffic Ecology and Mobility Foundation points out three features of carsharing management in Japan compared to other countries that provide additional reasoning for its slow development. Firstly, in general, the cooperation of carsharing operators with public authorities is poor. Secondly, also the cooperation with other transport providers, in particular public transport operators, is limited. And thirdly, a main reason is that, in public, there is relatively poor recognition of carsharing as a form of public transport (MLIT, 2006). To the last point, one might add that in general public transport provision is of high quality in most Japanese metropolitan areas, which arguably reduces the need for introducing carsharing.

Based on this background, in this research, we aim to quantify the impact of carsharing on mobility in a city. If one can show that the city at large is able to benefit from carsharing, then also it will be easier for carsharing operators to discuss with authorities the suitable role of carsharing and to obtain support to establish their business as part of a multimodal transport framework. We consider the gain in accessibility as a suitable index for this discussion. We suggest that the network-wide accessibility improvement in terms of travel costs between different areas of the network will indicate how the city benefits through the (occasional) usage of carsharing in case of inconvenient public transport connections. We conduct a case study based on the public transport network of Toyota City, Japan, where the Ha:mo carsharing scheme is operating. We illustrate the change in accessibility in terms of path costs through the introduction of carsharing. A specific contribution of the study is that the nonlinearity in walking costs is considered explicitly in the search for shortest paths.

The remainder of this chapter is organized as follows: Section 2 reviews related literature on carsharing and accessibility. Section 3 describes the Ha:mo carsharing scheme in Toyota as an example of the most-used one-way carsharing scheme in Japan. Section 4 provides the methodology and parameter settings for the results presented in Section 5. Section 6 then advances the study by optimizing the arrangement of parking places within the city before Section 7 concludes this chapter.

2. Literature review and positioning of this chapter

There is a fairly rich body of literature on the impact of carsharing schemes on travel patterns. Based on the estimate of travel behavioral impacts, environmental impacts are also assessed. A number of, mostly US-based, studies documented that carsharing reduces the number of vehicles on the road, vehicle miles traveled (VMT), greenhouse gas (GHG) emissions, and transportation costs for individuals (Shaheen and Cohen, 2013). For example, Cervero and Tsai (2004) report that 30% of city carsharing members significantly reduced their own personal cars' usage and that two-thirds chose to postpone the purchase of vehicles after 2 years usage of the service. The potential reduction of private vehicles through carsharing is also reported in Martin and Shaheen (2011) who suggest that one carsharing vehicle can replace 9 to 13 private vehicles.

Another notable impact of carsharing is modal shift. The same study of Martin and Shaheen (2011) studied also the impact of carsharing on public transit and nonmotorized travel. While there was a slight overall decline in public transit usage, significant increases in walking, bicycling, and carpooling were observed. Partly because of reduced car ownership costs and partly due to better usage of the full set of available transport modes, carsharing can therefore reduce overall transportation costs (Duncan, 2011). We highlight that most of these studies are based on a US context with, in general, much lower public transport share than Japanese cities.

Clearly, whether carsharing achieves its desired behavioral impacts or not is to a large degree depending on its attractiveness compared to alternative modes. Therefore, system configuration and operational strategies are key factors. For one-way carsharing, in particular, the network layout has received attention in the literature. Wakabayashi et al. (2013) formulated the station location design problem as profit maximization problem. They considered the carsharing choice probability based on time, fare, and the probability of a person being able to participate in the scheme. This was done by considering the probability as to whether a vehicle is available at a station as well as the probability that there might be no free parking space at the destination point. Boyaci et al. (2015) formulate a multiobjective problem considering both station design and relocation strategies for one-way carsharing schemes with electric vehicles. The model is applied to data from Nice, France, illustrating demand sensitivity as well as the trade-off between operator revenue and citizens benefits. They had to make a number of assumptions in their approach to estimate the carsharing demand, and in general it appears to be a fair conclusion that estimating the demand sensitivity of one-way carsharing with respect to parking station layout remains difficult.

Further on station layout optimization, Kumar and Bierlaire (2012) consider the arrangement of public transport, the demand attraction through hotels and commercial facilities, as well as the actual usage of carsharing in their approach. First, they formulated the performance of carsharing stations by a linear regression model, where performance is measured in terms of average number of picked-up cars at a station. Second, based on this performance, they optimized the station locations to maximize the total system performance. In their approach, they predefined the number of stations. Similar to the aforementioned study of Boyaci et al. (2015), their case study is an application to "Auto Bleue" in Nice.

Moving on to research on operational characteristics, several papers have discussed the design of the reservation system and price setting. Hara and Hato (2014) propose a reservation system that maximizes the utility of users by introducing a tradable permit mechanism. In their approach, users buy the right to use carsharing for one trip at an auction. They aim to maximize the sum of the prices paid by users for their rights and suggest this is equivalent to maximizing the total utility of users and operators. Wakabayashi et al. (2014) study pricing for the "ChoiMobi" system in Yokohama advancing their work reviewed above. They evaluate a pricing system considering an innovative policy in which prices are doubled if the usage disturbs the system in the sense that cars accumulate in a place where they are not likely to be needed. Contrary, if one uses a car from a parking place with few demand and returns it to a parking place of high demand, the usage price is halved. With this setting, they show that they can maximize the operator income. To note is that they assumed the usage pattern to be known.

For one-way carsharing as well as free-floating carsharing, furthermore vehicle redistribution is an important issue. The problem arises due to asymmetric demand patterns within a day as well as between different days. Several solution approaches have been proposed as in Fan et al. (2008) and Weikl and Bogenberger (2013). The latter work divided the area where carsharing is operating into several sections, categorized the demand by subarea, day of the week, and time of day using actual data and then classified the usage patterns. By observing the transition of demand patterns, real-time demand forecasting is possible. Based on this, a method is developed to plan redistribution with the objective to minimize operational costs. In Kek et al. (2009)

further the time when there is no vehicle in the parking lot, the time when there is no space in the parking space, the number of redistributions is explicitly considered for the design of a redistribution plan.

We conclude that various approaches have been proposed to optimize the design and operation of carsharing systems. The objective functions in resulting optimization problems have been mostly focusing on operational costs and profit maximization from an operator perspective. A few studies have also considered user cost minimization. Instead, in this research, we aim to set the objective wider and to evaluate carsharing from a city-wide accessibility perspective, which is the potential to travel to destinations inside the city. To the best of our knowledge, carsharing and accessibility have not been the specific focus of attention in previous research even though clearly (multimodal) accessibility has been defined and evaluated in a range of studies as reviewed in Páez et al. (2012). As Boisjoly and El-Geneidy (2017) point out, in practical transport planning, however, accessibility has still been often marginalized, and in particular with the presence of carsharing and other new mobility forms, the distinction between mobility and accessibility requires additional attention. We suggest that one of the main effects of carsharing is not its impact on "mobility", as the modal share of carsharing is in many cases low, but in terms of enabling persons to reach diverse destinations when needed. This "safety net" function of carsharing is potentially important to avoid transport exclusion and to support reliable transport in case of unexpected disruptions.

3. General transport situation and Ha:mo in Toyota City, Japan

Toyota City is located about 30 km outside Nagoya in central Japan and best known for the headquarter of Toyota Motor cooperation who gave the city its name. It is a medium-sized city with a population of about 0.4 million people. The local economy and the population's commuting patterns are dominated by its vicinity to Nagoya and Toyota manufacturing. There is a direct rail connection to Nagoya, but transport inside the city is dominated by private cars as there is limited local rail. In contrast to the major Japanese metropolitan areas where public transport reaches a much higher modal share, in Toyota, car traffic accounts for 72.9% according to person trip survey data from 2011 (Toyota City, 2019), with an upward tendency (in 2001 the share of cars was 1.7% lower). Rail only accounts for 7.6% of the trips in the region. Furthermore, within the city, there is a local bus system, which, however, only accounts for 0.4% of trips in the region. Fig. 6.5 in Section 4 shows the local public transport with its two rail lines and seven major bus lines. As one can clearly see, the periphery of the city is not served well by public transport.

In order to improve the local transport situation as well as to test the demand for shared transport, Toyota cooperation introduced Ha:mo in 2012. In

Japan, the scheme operates in one part of Tokyo, Toyota and Okinawa. Ha:mo is further currently operated in Bangkok, Thailand. In recent years, there were also trials in the Japanese cities Okayama and Hagi as well as in Grenoble, France. The three currently operated cases within Japan allow for a comparison of usage in very different settings, that is, in a dense and large metropolitan situation with good public transport (Tokyo), in a midsize city context (Toyota) as well as on a touristic island where Ha:mo vehicles are used mainly between the airport and the local city (Okinawa). Details of Ha:mo can also be seen from their webpage: http://www.toyota.co.jp/jpn/tech/its/hamo/.

Besides a brief experiment with shared bicycles from 2012 to 2013, Ha:mo RIDE in Toyota City and the other sites in Japan has been operating with small electric vehicles. These "Coms" and "i-Road" vehicles seat one or two persons only and their trunk is large enough to fit one small suitcase. Their simple and light design is an attractive point as well as demerit of these vehicles. On the one hand, operating these vehicles is simple, does not require complex introductions, and provides a different driving experience than operating a standard vehicle. On the other hand, the limited space clearly limits the type of trips that can be made by these vehicles. The vehicles also do not have heating or air conditioning, reducing their attractiveness in hot Japanese summers and cold winters. Fig. 6.1 illustrates the Toyota City and Tokyo scheme logos, the types of vehicles used, and the pricing. Users need to plug and unplug the vehicles from their power source every time before/after usage. In Tokyo, the scheme is operated in collaboration with a local parking place company, where at selected parking places, the vehicles can be parked and charged. In Toyota City also, public parking places are used for the vehicles, but the parking place operator is not an official project partner. Reservations for vehicles can be

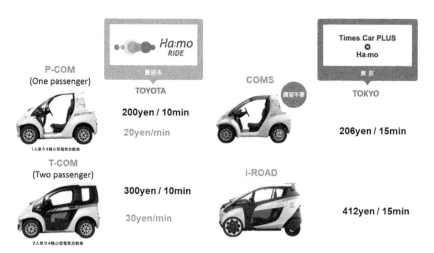

FIGURE 6.1 The Ha:mo carsharing vehicles.

made via a mobile phone application up to 30 min before intended usage. There are 60 dedicated stations, 250 parking slots and 100 cars as of April of 2019. It is noteworthy that the parking places are not evenly distributed over the city. Whereas some parts of Toyota City are not well covered by stations, especially around the central station as well as near Toyota Company a few stations are located close to each other.

Fig. 6.2 shows the idea of Ha:mo in Toyota City as promoted by the operator. Ha:mo enables users to travel to dedicated parking places near the public transportation stations and provides a means of access, egress, and direct trips between Ha:mo's stations which are far from public transportation stations. Precisely this aspect as to whether carsharing is used rather as replacement of public transport or in fact promotes further public transportation usage in Toyota has been a key research question that also motivates this research.

Fig. 6.3 shows trip patterns by time of day. The usage peaks on weekdays concur with typical morning and evening commute times. A main trip pattern for Ha:mo usage during weekdays is for commuters from other Japanese cities traveling to Toyota's headquarter. They reach Toyota station by rail and then use Ha:mo to one of the several parking lots near Toyota headquarter. On weekends, the peak usage is during midday as on those days it is mainly used

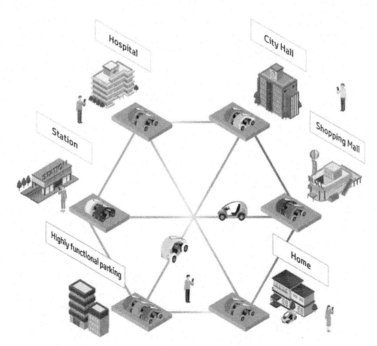

FIGURE 6.2 The idea of the Ha:mo mobility network in Toyota.

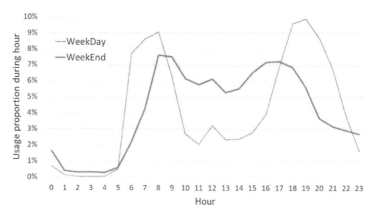

FIGURE 6.3 Trip pattern by hour of day (Apr. 2014–Mar. 2017).

for private trips. It is to be noted that 90% of all Ha:mo trips occur on weekdays and only 10% on weekends. Therefore, though such trips exist, the usage of Ha:mo for shopping and other leisure activities as proposed in Fig. 6.2 is in fact still fairly minor. In the majority of cases, Ha:mo is used for commuting or for business-related trips.

Fig. 6.4 shows the classification results in terms of trip types by using the approach of Kuwahara et al. (2018). "Intermodal transport" is the major mode, which is defined here as usage by members residing outside the city, who are using both public transport and one-way carsharing for their travel to destinations in Toyota City. It is not known how many of these users would have come all the way by private car if Ha:mo would not have existed or how many would have remained public transport users and would have taken a taxi or a bus for the last leg of their trip. Additionally, 13% of the Ha:mo trips are for access or egress purposes to public transportation stations by local members. Again, it is not clear which mode the travelers used before Ha:mo, but we suggest that nevertheless it is encouraging to see that, for the majority of trips, Ha:mo was used in cooperation with public transportation (share of intermodal trips and access/egress trips). Only 5% of trips are made between Ha:mo parking locations where both origin and destination are close to public transport stations where it is likely that Ha:mo has taken some market share from the public transport provider. "Complementary transport" is defined as trips, where neither origin nor destination is close to a public transport station, so these trips might either be replacement of trips otherwise made by taxi or private car or a possibly induced demand. Finally, we find that 13% of trips are round trips, where the user parks the car at the same location where s/he picked it up and likely completed some nearby errands in between as the Ha:mo rental period is mostly short.

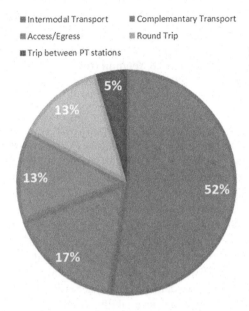

FIGURE 6.4 Ha:mo trip types (Apr. 2014–Mar. 2015).

4. Definition of availability index and case study specification

With this background, we return to our main objective to evaluate the improvement in the local transport situation through carsharing. We divide our analysis area into spatial meshes and define their accessibility index considering travel time, expected waiting time, access time, and fares. For access time, we consider the time it takes to reach a carsharing station as well as other means of transportation.

Eq. (6.1) defines the costs in scenario s when traveling from mesh i to mesh j on path p where the first term indicates travel time, the second indicates waiting time, and the third term the expected cost. $\delta_{l,p}^{S}$ is one if path P includes link l and 0 otherwise. For the first term, we note that we obtain the distance costs for walking links in a different way. We create walking links between all meshes and consider that long walking is nonlinearly more onerous than short walks. This is considered with the distance cost function shown in Eq. (6.2) where the parameters are taken from Nguyen and Yoshikawa (2016). Nguyen and Yoshikawa measured the energy consumption of walking and assumed physical resistance to walking per minute corresponds to walking distance. Considering that one gets more tired the further one is walking, this leads to the second order term in the equation. We consider a constant travel speed for each of the different modes k denoted by v^k.

The second term describes the waiting time for public transport with a link frequency f_l^k. The parameter α denotes the cost travelers attach to waiting compared to traveling on-board. We take a value of two, following for example Goodwin (1976) and subsequent literature. Finally, in the third term, the parameter β describes the value of time in order to transfer the fare also into time. Here, we take a value of 29.8 Yen/min (roughly equivalent to US$20/h), which Kato and Hashimoto (2008) calculated as a result of meta-analysis from various studies conducted in Japan.

The path costs are then obtained by summing up the costs over all links included in the path. Our scenario superscript denotes here whether or not car-sharing is included in the choice set. That is, for $C_{ij,p}^{+}$, we consider the set {walk, bus, train, carsharing} and, for $C_{ij,p}^{-}$, we omit carsharing. We applied Dijkstra's shortest path algorithm to obtain the shortest cost path (including the "walking link paths"). We note that for the public transport path, we also experimented with finding the shortest hyperpath instead of shortest path, but found this not to be of significance for this network, due to its low level of complexity.

We further take the simplifying assumption that all travelers use the shortest path and that congestion on public transport and on the roads can be ignored. In the case of Toyota City, this is again a fairly reasonable assumption. With this assumption we define (inverse) accessibility A_{ij}^{s} as the minimum path cost as in Eq. (6.3). The accessibility improvement AI_{ij}^{s}, due to the presence of carsharing, is then obtained as in (6.4) and in (6.5) as ratio. Eqs. (6.6) and (6.7) denote the averaging of (6.4) to firstly denote accessibility for a certain mesh and then for the network as a whole.

$$C_{ij,p}^{S} = \sum_{l} \sum_{k \in S} \delta_{l,p}^{S} \left(f_k \left(d_l^k \right) / v^k + \alpha \frac{60}{2f_l^k} + \frac{1}{\beta} F_l^k \right) \tag{6.1}$$

with

$$f_k \left(d_l^k \right) = \begin{cases} 0.00489 \left(d_l^k \right)^2 + 1.0462 \left(d_l^k \right), (k = walk) \\ d_l^k, (k = bus, train, CS) \end{cases} \tag{6.2}$$

$$A_{ij}^{s} = \min_{p} \left[C_{ij,p}^{s} \right] \tag{6.3}$$

$$AI_{ij} = A_{ij}^{-} - A_{ij}^{+}, \tag{6.4}$$

$$AR_{ij} = \left(A_{ij}^{-} - A_{ij}^{+} \right) / A_{ij}^{-} \tag{6.5}$$

$$AI_j = \overline{AI_{ij}} \tag{6.6}$$

$$AI = \overline{AI_j} \tag{6.7}$$

We demonstrate our approach with a network that can be considered an abstraction of the Toyota city network and is shown in Fig. 6.5. The city has a size of 20 × 20 meshes and each quadratic mesh has a side length of 500 m (and hence an area of 250,000 m^2). The figure illustrates the bus stops, train stations, and carsharing parking stations. The red and blue squares indicate the rail stations of two different lines and light green meshes indicate the presence of carsharing. This arrangement roughly corresponds to the real arrangement in Toyota. We note that our mesh discretization of space also significantly reduces the number of carsharing parking places, since, as noted before, there are often multiple stations close together, i.e., in the same mesh. Inside a mesh we locate public transport stations and carsharing parking facilities at the center of the mesh, which means that usually walking between carsharing and public transport is not far, which again, appears to be close to reality.

We set the speed and waiting time of public transport as well as the walking speed as given in Table 6.1. The public transport fare is set according to distance as common in Japan with a fare of 100 Yen per 1.5 km. The railway fare is set at 200 Yen for the first ride and increases by 50 Yen each time the travel distance increases by 3 km. For waiting time, the line frequencies are shown in the table below. If several lines serve a mesh, we aggregate frequencies; therefore, implicitly assuming that services arrive with equal headways.

5. Resulting accessibility indices

Given the arrangement of carsharing parking places as in Fig. 6.5, we now illustrate the improvement in accessibility. Fig. 6.6 shows values for the

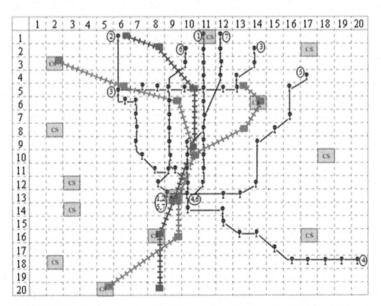

FIGURE 6.5 The mesh network with example allocation of carsharing stations.

TABLE 6.1 Parameter settings.

d_{lm}	Distance to a neighbor mesh: 500m	f_{ij}^{CS}	Frequency of CS per hour: ∞ (no waiting time)
v^{walk}	Walking speed: 70 m/min (4.2 km/h)	F_{ij}^{walk}	Fare for walking: 0JPY
v^{bus}	Bus journey speed: 300 m/min (18 km/h)	F_{ij}^{bus}	Fare for buses: 100 JPY/1.5 km
v^{train}	Train speed: 1500 m/min (90 km/h)	F_{ij}^{train}	Fare for trains:
v^{CS}	Carsharing speed: 500 m/min(30 km/h)		$\sim$3 km: 200 JPY, 3$\sim$6 km: 250 JPY, 6$\sim$9 km: 300 JPY, 9 km$\sim$:350 JPY
f_{ij}^{walk}	Frequency of walking per hour: ∞ (no waiting time)	F_{ij}^{CS}	Fare for CS: 206 JPY/15min (206 JPY/7.5 km)
f_{ij}^{bus}	Frequency of buses per hour Line1: 1, Line2: 1, Line3: 1, Line4: 1, Line5: 0.5, Line6: 0.5, Line7: 1	α	Time value for waiting time compared to moving time: 2
		β	Value of time: 29.8 JPY/min
f_{ij}^{train}	Frequency of trains per hour Red line: 2, Blue line: 2		

network-wide accessibility in the scenarios without (left) and with carsharing (middle) as well as the mesh-specific accessibility. To better illustrate the differences, the right figure is added. We note the difference in scale for the three figures; the generally larger values in scenario A^- indicate the lower accessibility without carsharing.

Looking at the results before the introduction of carsharing, Fig. 6.6 shows that, in general, accessibility along the rail line is much better. In contrast the areas only served by bus routes (or those far from any public transport) have relatively poor accessibility. This is explainable given the, in general, lower service quality of the buses. Looking at this in more detail in the left figure of Fig. 6.6, one can see more clearly the "influence range" of the rail lines and to a lower degree of the bus lines. More generally, we suggest that the accessibility focused analysis illustrates that it is distance to the stop/station and its interaction with service quality that determine the influence range.

Considering now the results with carsharing, it can be seen that the range of good accessibility has expanded around the locations where the carsharing parking lots have been introduced. The good accessibility around these meshes is clearly visible. Further, it is noteworthy that accessibility improved a lot in meshes at the periphery compared to meshes that are close to public transport stations.

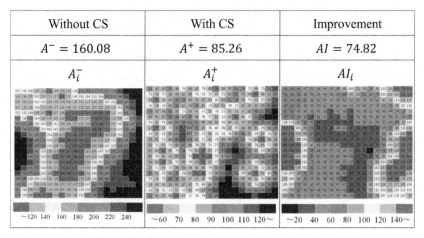

Without CS	With CS	Improvement
$A^- = 160.08$	$A^+ = 85.26$	$AI = 74.82$
A_i^-	A_i^+	AI_i

FIGURE 6.6 Resulting accessibility indices A, AI, and AI_i.

Fig. 6.7 illustrates the "modal share" in terms of which modes are used when traveling on the shortest paths between Origin-Destination (hereafter OD) pairs. The pie chart on the left indicates the means of transportation before the introduction of carsharing. As shown, 20% of all OD pairs are traveled best by walking whereas the remaining 80% of OD pairs involve at least one leg with public transportation. The central and right graph show the

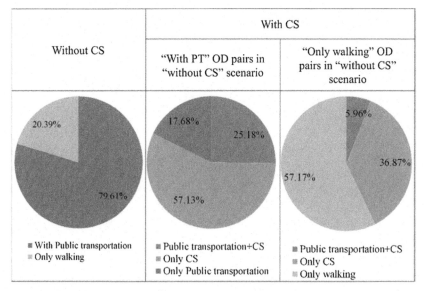

FIGURE 6.7 Percentage of OD pairs for which a mode is used on the shortest path before and after carsharing introduction (overall).

means of transportation after carsharing introduction, split by OD pairs for which public transport (central) and for which only walking was the preferred mode (right).

The results illustrate that using carsharing for the whole trip becomes the best choice for a large number of OD pairs. Among the previously public transport OD pairs, this occurs even for the majority and among the previously walking OD pairs still for around 30% of OD pairs. This illustrates that carsharing has the potential to replace the inconvenient public transport connections. Furthermore, even in this relatively small city, there is a significant scope of carsharing to be used in collaboration with public transport.

Inducing travelers to use carsharing instead of public transport creates more traffic and might not be desired from a social welfare point of view. In order to provide some further information regarding this trade-off, we add Fig. 6.8. We plot here the cost reduction for the "converted" OD pairs. We observe that there are many OD relations where the cost reduction is significant, arguably justifying the presence of carsharing.

Finally, for further illustration of how carsharing and public transport might collaborate, we discuss the results for a specific area in the network. For this purpose, we take Mesh 193, which is the area in the network with the largest number of persons starting to use public transport as a result of carsharing introduction.

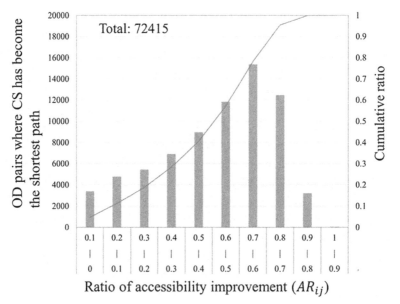

FIGURE 6.8 Accessibility improvement by OD pairs where carsharing has become the shortest path.

Fig. 6.9 illustrates the results in the same way as Fig. 6.6 with the areal plot now showing $AI_{193,j}$, i.e., the accessibility improvement to all other meshes in the network. The figure illustrates that even before carsharing introduction, the city center and areas along the railroad have been well accessible for travelers originating from this mesh. Accordingly, also the impact of carsharing on city center accessibility is minimal. Instead, one can observe that travel to the peripheral regions has significantly improved. Fig. 6.10 shows that for the OD pairs where the shortest path mode changed, there are in fact no OD pairs where carsharing by itself becomes the most attractive mode. Due to its vicinity to public transport, if walking is not the best option, the best option is always to take public transport first and then swap to carsharing if needed. We suggest this is a prime example how carsharing and public transport can collaborate instead of competing.

We further conduct a range of sensitivity analyses with respect to value of waiting time (parameters α) and value of time (parameter β). If α is reduced, then only public transport becomes more attractive; with the change of β, one can understand the impact on different population segments with different values of time. Further, a point relatively few discussed in the literature is the inclusion of the nonlinear walking costs. Therefore, we also test the effect of dropping this factor. If walking costs are reduced, one can consider the network to be denser as both carsharing and public transport are better accessible.

Fig. 6.11 shows that the influence of the waiting time value is significantly different depending on the presence or absence of physical resistance to walking. Furthermore, the correlation between time value and accessibility improvement is reversed. Investigating this further with Fig. 6.12, we observe

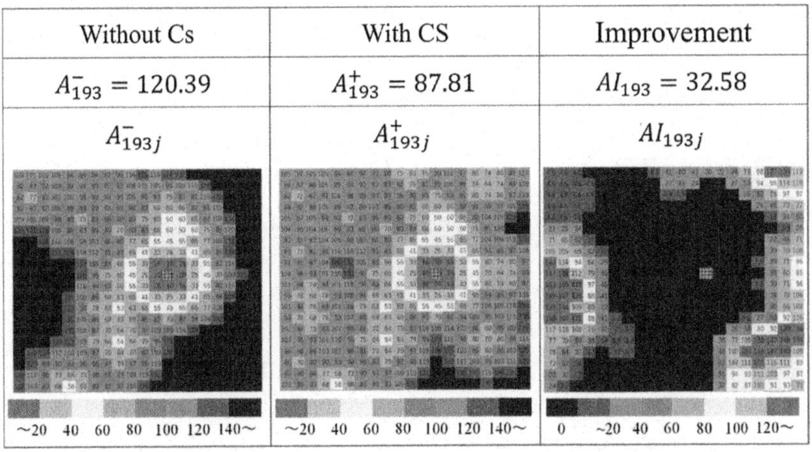

Without Cs	With CS	Improvement
$A^{-}_{193} = 120.39$	$A^{+}_{193} = 87.81$	$AI_{193} = 32.58$
A^{-}_{193j}	A^{+}_{193j}	AI_{193j}

FIGURE 6.9 Accessibility improvement for OD pair 193.

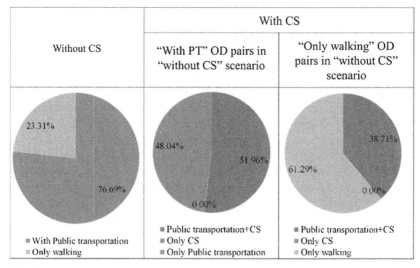

FIGURE 6.10 Percentage of OD pairs using each mode of transport before and after carsharing introduction (Mesh 193).

that if walking costs are reduced, there are far less cases of joined public transport and carsharing usage. This is reasonable, as carsharing will not be required as access or egress mode. Further, in case of low walking costs, clearly more OD pairs are traveled walking all the way so that, if carsharing is added, relatively more converted OD pairs stem from the pool of prior walking only relations.

We further observe that with reduced values of waiting time, the cases of multimodal travel using both public transport and carsharing increase. Also in case the value of time increases, as expected, walking will decrease and

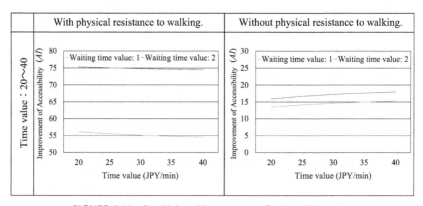

FIGURE 6.11 Sensitivity with respect to α, β and walking costs.

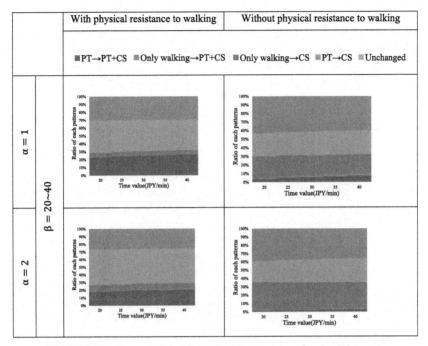

FIGURE 6.12 Change in "modal share" with respect to α, β and walking costs.

carsharing as well as multimodal travel will increase as travelers care less about the fares.

6. Optimal parking place layout and parking place numbers

We continue our study by deriving parking lot locations that maximize the improvement of regional accessibility. We further aim to understand how many parking places are useful considering installation and operational costs associated with parking places. We therefore derive a heuristic that solves Eq. (6.9) under the condition of Eq. (6.10) where δ_i^{CS} indicates whether there is a parking station in mesh i and ns denotes the total number of parking stations in the city.

$$\max[AI] \tag{6.9}$$

$$\sum_i \delta_i^{CS} = ns \tag{6.10}$$

As this combinatorial problem is known to be NP-hard, we solve the problem with a genetic algorithm (GA). For brevity we omit the details of the GA, except noting, that we find a two-step approach to work best. In Step 1, we obtain five near optimal solutions from a range of random starting points, and in Step 2, we use these five solutions to obtain our final solution. Each GA "chromosome" consists of a series of 400 binary "genes" denoting whether a mesh has a carsharing station or not. In Step 1, we create new genes by mutation only (keeping the total number of one's constant). In Step 2, we utilize mainly crossover between the five solutions obtained from Step 1 to further improve the solutions.

Firstly, to allow comparability to our case study, we show the optimal results with 13 parking stations as in the base case. Fig. 6.13 compares the solution presented in Fig. 6.5 with the optimal solution found through the GA application. We can observe that the main effect of the optimization is that areas of bad accessibility (dark blue) are eliminated whereas there is little change in the areas where accessibility was fairly good even before optimization. Fig. 6.14 shows the parking lot arrangement for the results of the five best GA solutions found after Step 1 of our GA and the final solution after Step 2 which is in fact identical to solution 3, meaning that the second GA step did not further improve the results. One can observe that similar layouts leading to largely similar accessibility values exist. In all cases, the layout is a mix of Ha:mo stations in peripheral areas as well as near the public transport stations as this allows for multimodal trips. Looking more closely at the results, we observe that at least one parking lot adjacent to two railway stations exists in all solutions.

We now vary the number of parking lots in the optimization problem to observe the marginal effect of additional parking places on accessibility. Obviously for very few parking places, the accessibility improvement is small, but as shown in Fig. 6.15, for a range of 5−25 each additional parking lot significantly increases the accessibility. If the number of parking places exceeds this number, the marginal improvement decreases due to saturation effects as well as due to the fact that making multimodal trips becomes less interesting.

7. Conclusions

In this study, we firstly discussed the role of carsharing in Japan, which is still in its beginning stages, due to operational as well as possibly cultural reasons. One of the few schemes in operation is Ha:mo, which operates with one- and two-seater electric vehicles. A key question for the advancement and support of urban carsharing in Japan is the role it might have within cities that are generally well served by public transport. We therefore analyze its impact based on generalized cost between OD relations. We consciously do not consider demand patterns to illustrate its areal accessibility impact and to avoid questions as to how far the existence of carsharing will change the demand patterns itself. However, if one wants to understand potential ridership and profit for the carsharing operator, this step clearly is also required and is

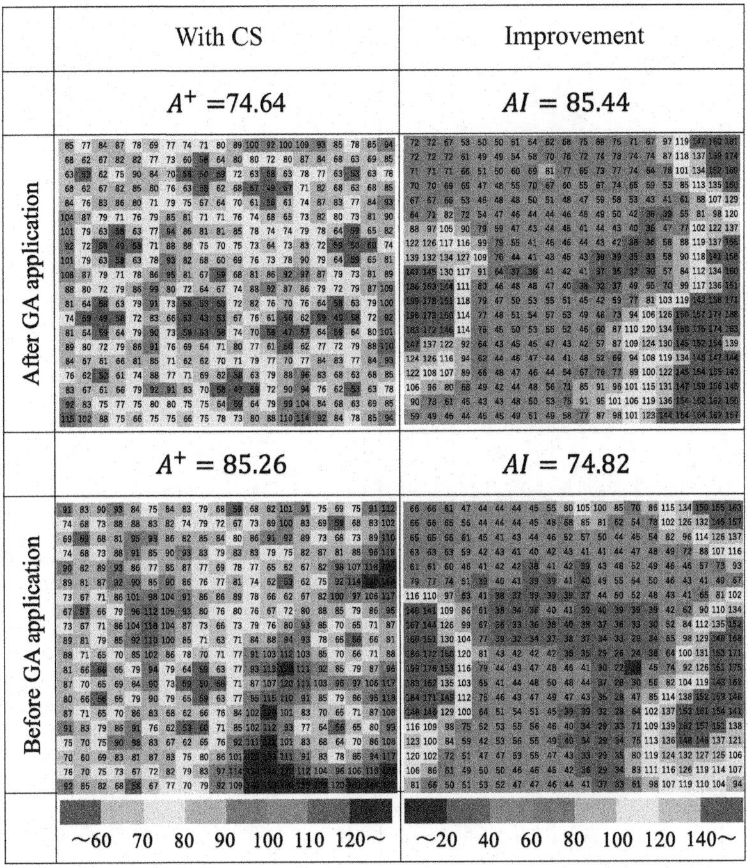

FIGURE 6.13 Comparison of accessibility before and after GA application.

one direction of further work. If demand patterns are known, the number of available vehicles at a particular station also has to be considered. One could then advance the current work by not only considering the number of parking lots but also the distribution of a given fleet over these parking places.

Our analysis emphasizes the role carsharing plays in connection with public transport. We show that carsharing can be considered a competitor but also a collaborator for an existing public transport network. On the one hand, carsharing has the potential to replace trips that are inconvenient by public transport; one the other hand, we show that a large number of OD relations are best served with multimodal trips combining carsharing and public transport. We note that this is the case even without a fare policy that further encourages such trips by, for example, integrated pricing concepts. Therefore a well-designed carsharing scheme has the potential to reduce public costs for an excessive public transport network, though obviously one needs to consider,

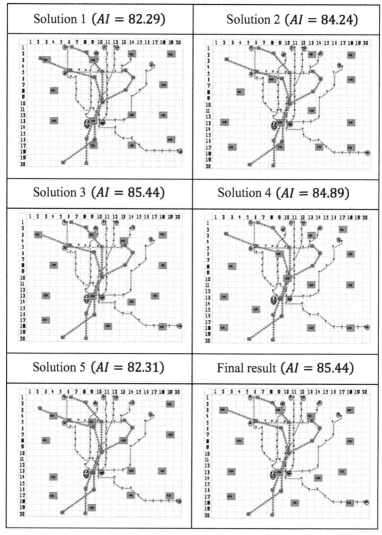

FIGURE 6.14 Five best GA results for 13 parking lots, after Step 1 optimization, and final result after running the GA once more.

that carsharing can be only used by the driving part of the population. We might add that our analysis could similarly be applied to bicycle sharing, where the methodology can remain largely unchanged except for parameter settings.

One specific point we paid attention to in our analysis is the access and egress costs to public transport and carsharing stations by considering the nonlinearly increasing walking costs with distance. Our analysis demonstrated

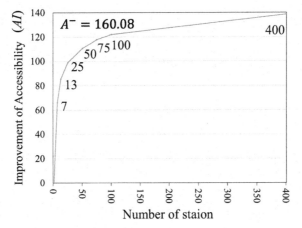

FIGURE 6.15 Accessibility improvement for optimal GA solution with varying number of parking lots.

that this point is indeed important, as neglecting this issue would result in far more walking cases as well as overestimation of multimodal shortest paths. We also obtained and discussed the optimal layout of the parking place arrangement in the network which showed the importance of having a mixed periphery/central distribution of parking lots. This might be obvious but should be a clear message to public transport operators that providing carsharing around the rail stations is important for end-to-end journey quality. We further showed that accessibility focused analysis allows to model the influence sphere of each public transport and carsharing station. Therefore, another direction of further work is to classify the carsharing spots according to their importance for the whole carsharing network.

References

Boisjoly, G., El-Geneidy, A., 2017. How to get there? A critical assessment of accessibility objectives and indicators in metropolitan transportation plans. Transport Policy 55, 38–50.

Boyaci, B., Zografos, K., Geroliminis, N., 2015. An optimization framework for the development of efficient one-way car-sharing systems. European Journal of Operational Research 240 (3), 718–733.

Cervero, R., Tsai, Y., 2004. City CarShare in San Francisco, California: second-year travel demand and car ownership impacts. Transportation Research Record 1887 (1), 117–127.

Duncan, M., 2011. The cost saving potential of carsharing in a US context. Transportation 38 (2), 363–382.

Fan, W.D., Randy, B.M., Lownes, N.E., 2008. Carsharing: dynamic decisionmaking problem for vehicle allocation. Transportation Research Record: Journal of the Transportation Research Board 2063, 97–104.

Goodwin, P.B., 1976. Human effort and the value of travel time. Journal of Transport Economics and Policy 10 (1), 3−15.

Hara, Y., Hato, E., 2014. Design of tradeable permit mechanism for mobility-sharing and its solution algorithm. Proceedings of the Japan Society for Comparative Endocrinology (4), 198−210.

Kato, H., Hashimoto, T., 2008. Mata-Analysis on Value of Travel Time Savings in Japan, vol. 38. Japan Society of Civil Engineers (In Japanese).

Kek, A.G.H., Cheu, R.L., Meng, Q., Fung, C.H., 2009. A decision support system for vehicle relocation operations in carsharing systems. Transportation Research Part E: Logistics and Transportation Review 45 (1), 149−158.

Kumar, V.P., Bierlaire, M., 2012. Optimizing locations for a vehicle sharing system. In: Swiss Transport Research Conference. Available from No. EPFL-CONF-195890, https://transp-or. epfl.ch/documents/proceedings/Kumar_ STRC_2012.pdf. [Accessed June 2019].

Kuwahara, M., Yoshioka, A., Honma, Y., Uno, N., Nakamura, T., Schmöcker, J.-D., 2018. Analysis of trip types when one-way car sharing is used within a trip chain. Japanese society for civil engineering. Journal D3 74 (5), I_1187−I_1195. https://doi.org/10.2208/jscejipm.74.I_1187 (In Japanese).

Martin, E.W., Shaheen, S.A., 2011. Greenhouse gas emission impacts of carsharing in North America. IEEE Transactions on Intelligent Transportation Systems 12 (4), 1074−1086.

MLIT, 2006. About The Spread of Carsharing (カーシェアリングの普及について). Available from: http://www.mlit.go.jp/singikai/koutusin/koutu/kankyou/9/shiryou3-3.pdf (In Japanese).

MLIT, 2014. About the Handling Pertaining to the Implementation of So-Called One-Way Car Rental Car Sharing. Available from: http://www.mlit.go.jp/report/press/jidosha03_hh_000176. html (In Japanese).

Nguyen, L., Yoshikawa, T., 2016. A method for quantitative evaluation of urban pedestrians accessibility by public transport. The Architectural Institute of Japan's Journal of Architecture and Planning 81, 1579−1588, 725.

Páez, A., Scott, D.A., Morency, C., 2012. Measuring accessibility: positive and normative implementations of various accessibility indicators. Journal of Transport Geography 25, 141−153.

Shaheen, S.A., Cohen, A.P., 2013. Carsharing and personal vehicle services: worldwide market developments and emerging trends. International Journal of Sustainable Transportation 7 (1), 5−34.

Shaheen, S., Chan, N.D., Micheaux, H., 2015. One-way carsharing's evolution and operator perspectives from the Americas. Transportation 42 (4), 519−536.

Toyota City, 2019. Report of Person Trip Survey Data. Available from. http://www.city.toyota. aichi.jp/_res/projects/default_project/_page_/001/005/143/01pdf (in Japanese).

Wakabayashi, Y., Hato, E., Saito, I., 2013. A port location problem in one-way car-sharing systems focused on demand distribution. Papers of Research Meeting on Civil Engineering Planning 48 (In Japanese).

Wakabayashi, Y., Hato, E., Saito, I., 2014. Optimization pricing of one-way car sharing systems with demand and supply uncertainty. Papers of Research Meeting on Civil Engineering Planning 49.

Weikl, S., Bogenberger, K., 2013. Relocation strategies and algorithms for free-floating car sharing systems. IEEE Intelligent Transportation Systems Magazine 5 (4), 100−111.

Wielinski, G., Trépanier, M., Morency, C., 2019. Exploring service usage and activity space evolution in a free-floating carsharing service. Transportation Research Record: Journal of the Transportation Research Board 2673 (8), 36−49.

Chapter 7

Uncovering spatiotemporal structures from transit smart card data for individual mobility modeling

Zhan Zhao[1], Haris N. Koutsopoulos[2], Jinhua Zhao[3]

[1]*Department of Civil and Environmental Engineering, Massachusetts Institute of Technology, Cambridge, MA, United States;* [2]*Department of Civil and Environmental Engineering, Northeastern University, Boston, MA, United States;* [3]*Department of Urban Studies and Planning, Massachusetts Institute of Technology, Cambridge, MA, United States*

Chapter outline

1. Introduction

With increasing concern over urban problems such as traffic congestion and vehicle emissions, the ability to manage urban mobility has become more and more important for the everyday functioning of cities and people's quality of life. While collective analysis of spatiotemporal patterns (i.e., focusing on aggregate statistics of large populations) reveal valuable properties of urban travel demand, we should also focus on the individual scale. Collective

Demand for Emerging Transportation Systems. https://doi.org/10.1016/B978-0-12-815018-4.00007-3
123

properties emerge from the behavior of individuals. Urban mobility is essentially the result of spatiotemporal choices (e.g., decisions to go somewhere at some time) made by individuals with diverse and dynamic preferences and lifestyles. A better understanding of the behavioral mechanisms underlying individual mobility can support the design of efficient measures to monitor, predict, and ultimately influence travel behavior. However, analysis at the individual scale is more challenging as the data are more sparse and the effects of behavioral variability are more prominent. This calls for the development of robust statistical models that can uncover individual mobility patterns and explain behavioral variability using available mobility data sources.

There are two research fields that study human travel at the individual level. Travel behavior research, largely based on microeconomic theories, focuses on the individual travel decision process. Survey data are typically necessary to collect the key decision variables, such as personal socioeconomic characteristics including age, gender, occupation, and income. However, it is well known that travel behavior is dynamic and varies across individuals but also for the same person over time (Huff and Hanson, 1986; Pas and Koppelman, 1987; Schönfelder and Axhausen, 2010). While conventional cross-sectional data, travel diary surveys, for example, can capture the heterogeneous travel patterns across individuals, they typically do not have large enough sample sizes and sampling frequency to capture the longitudinal variability in the spatiotemporal choices of a large number of individuals.

Recent advances in urban sensing technologies afford the opportunity to collect traces of individual mobility on a large scale and over extended periods of time. New mobility data sources, such as cellular network data and transit smart card records, enable detailed and reliable measurement of the behavioral dynamics in individual mobility. Enabled by the increasing availability of new mobility data, individual mobility becomes an emerging field focusing on discovering the properties that govern human movements. A primary goal of individual mobility research is to generate models that can capture the spatiotemporal patterns and regularity in individual trajectories, which has important applications in areas such as urban planning, traffic forecasting, location-based services, and the spread of biological and mobile viruses (Barbosa-Filho et al., 2017).

Although the two research fields share some mutual interests, they have different foci, and use different terminologies and approaches. While the new mobility data become increasingly popular, the behavioral framework is still useful in user-oriented applications (e.g., customized travel information and travel demand management). A key to bringing the two fields together is to combine the behavioral concepts in travel behavior research with the analytical approaches in individual mobility modeling. This requires new statistical approaches that are able to uncover behavioral structures from spatiotemporal observations over time.

Travel behavior exhibits some level of regularity, which describes the extent to which individual spatiotemporal choices repeat over time. According to activity-based travel theory, travel behavior is dictated by preferences, constraints, and needs which recur over time, at least to some degree (Kitamura and Hoorn, 1987). Although such detailed behavioral explanation, e.g., why someone goes to somewhere at some time, is typically not directly observable, longitudinal spatiotemporal data itself generally contains a significant amount of structure (Eagle and Pentland, 2009). The ability to track individual mobility over time makes it possible to extract recurrent spatiotemporal structures from the data and gain a better understanding of the underlying behavioral mechanisms, i.e., how people's spatiotemporal choices are generated.

To model individual mobility, the key is to capture the behavioral mechanisms that generate the spatiotemporal choices. This chapter presents recent developments in advanced individual mobility models that can extract meaningful structures that govern the spatiotemporal choices in individual travel-activity behavior from longitudinal mobility data. It begins by presenting a general conceptual framework of individual modeling in Section 2, followed by discussing different types of emerging mobility data sources and their characteristics in Section 3, before describing three specific case studies based on Zhao et al. (2018a, b, c) in Section 4. The chapter is concluded with discussion of methodological choices in Section 5 and potential future work in Section 6.

2. A conceptual framework of individual mobility modeling

The spatiotemporal aspects of our lives can be segmented into episodes of travel and activity participation. A travel episode, or *trip*, is defined as "the travel required from an origin location to access a destination for the purpose of performing some activity" (McNally, 2007), and an *activity episode* refers to a discrete activity participation (time allocated to activities) at a location (Bhat and Koppelman, 1999). By definition, each trip is immediately followed by an activity episode. Both trips and activity episodes are basic components of spatiotemporal behavior, characterized by a number of attributes chosen by individuals. Activities have long been recognized as the fundamental driver for travel demand; trips are usually derived from the need to participate in a certain activity at a certain time and location. Therefore, the ability to capture activity episodes is critical for understanding individual mobility patterns. Given the increasing abundance of mobility data, it is relatively straightforward to directly observe the time and location of each activity episode. What remains to be inferred is the type of activity, such as work, home, or recreation. Based on the activity-based travel behavior framework, the choice of activity affects the spatiotemporal choices not only for the activity episode (e.g., duration) but also for the preceding trip (e.g., destination).

There is a constant tension between dynamism and stability of travel behavior. Such tension can be examined at different levels. The specific trips or activity episodes vary from day to day but the underlying behavior pattern is more consistent. At a higher level, a *travel/activity pattern* describes the structure of travel/activity instances over a period of time; each pattern corresponds to a set of preferences and constraints that dictate the specific choices. Although stable in the short term, these patterns are also subject to change over months or years, contributing to the long-term behavioral dynamics. Individual travel-activity patterns may change when people move, change jobs, shift work schedules, purchase a new car/bike, or any other life event (e.g., a child starts school) that may alter their travel and activity routines. In the long term, a *dynamic travel/activity pattern* refers to travel/activity patterns that change over time.

The overall conceptual framework is shown in Fig. 7.1. Travel and activity instances, or at least their spatiotemporal attributes, may be directly observable in data. Most existing work on individual mobility modeling focuses on extracting short-term travel patterns from these observations. For example, studies using dollar bill tracking (Brockmann et al., 2006) and mobile phone data (González et al., 2008) have found that both the travel distances and activity episode durations can be characterized by fat-tailed distributions. On the other hand, research on travel demand modeling, and in particular activity-based

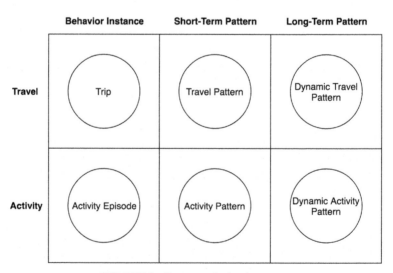

FIGURE 7.1 Summary of related concepts.

modeling, has studied the decision processes behind activity scheduling behavior and its impact on spatiotemporal choices (Axhausen and Gärling, 1992; Bowman and Ben-Akiva, 2001; Rasouli and Timmermans, 2014). However, these studies rely on travel and activity survey data to provide labeled daily travel-activity itineraries, and thus cannot be directly applied to human mobility data sources with only spatiotemporal observations (i.e., no information regarding the specific activity types). This chapter aims to demonstrate how we can extend the capabilities of individual mobility models by exploring the latent activity patterns and long-term behavioral dynamics.

3. Emerging mobility data

3.1 Overview of mobility data

Over many years, empirical models and technical tools have been developed based on the data available at the time. The classical travel behavior models, from the traditional four-step model (McNally, 2007) to the more recent activity-based models (Axhausen and Gärling, 1992; Rasouli and Timmermans, 2014), are developed based on data which are actively solicited, including travel surveys, travel surveys coupled with GPS loggers, and pure GPS-based surveys (Chen et al., 2016). All these surveys depend on active recruitment of subjects and information on their travel. As a result, such data contain richer behavioral and personal information beyond travel, e.g., daily activities and socioeconomic characteristics, but are limited in sample size, observation period, and precision of spatiotemporal information, making it difficult to capture the diverse behavior patterns across individuals and especially the longitudinal variability of the individual.

More recently, the emergence of individual mobility as a research field has been enabled by the increasing availability of large-scale datasets on individual movement. Unlike travel behavior research, mobility studies typically focus on the physical and mathematical properties of individual trajectories, with target applications beyond transportation. The most commonly used data source is mobile phone network data (Pappalardo et al., 2015; Schneider et al., 2013; Song et al., 2010; Eagle and Pentland, 2009; González et al., 2008). Other data sources, such as GPS (Zhao et al., 2015), Wi-Fi (Sapiezynski et al., 2015), and social media data (Colombo et al., 2012; Hasan et al., 2013), can also be collected through mobile phones using various sensors and applications. One common trait of these data sources is that they are generated by nontransportation activities and cannot be directly interpreted as travel behavior. For example, mobile phone network data are generated from cellular network activities including voice calls, text messages, cellular data activities, and cell tower handovers. Thus, there is a critical mapping required to bridge between telecommunications and travel behavior. This is not straightforward because both types of behavior are driven by correlated but distinct personal preferences that vary across individuals (Zhao et al., 2016). In this chapter, we refer to this type of data as *extrinsic mobility data*. Extrinsic mobility data capture individual mobility by sampling a person's location over time. The specific sampling process of a given data source is determined by its data-generating events. Under this data collection mechanism, individual mobility is represented as a series of sightings, each associated with a certain location and timestamp. A sighting does not have any obvious travel-related meaning. It may take place during a trip (i.e., pass-by point) or an activity episode (i.e., stay point). Many studies have been done to infer activities/trips from these sightings (Ahas et al., 2010; Candia et al., 2008; Calabrese et al., 2011; Iqbal et al., 2014; Alexander et al., 2015). However, unless the sampling frequency is high (e.g., GPS data), it is challenging to recover the full aspects of a trip (or an activity episode), especially its start and end time.

On the other hand, *intrinsic mobility data*, such as transit smart card data (Goulet-Langlois et al., 2016; Zhong et al., 2015; Hasan et al., 2012) and bikesharing data (Purnama et al., 2015), are directly collected from urban transportation systems. Unlike extrinsic mobility data, intrinsic mobility data are generated by travel events with each record typically indicating the start, or end, of a trip (or trip segment). Therefore, intrinsic mobility data provide direct information about individual mobility as a collection of trips (or trip segments), a representation that is more compatible with that used in travel behavior research. This raises the possibility of integrating the concepts and problems from the field of travel behavior analysis, with the terminology and methodology from the field of individual mobility, into a single framework. The result would be valuable for both fields. For travel behavior research, the characteristics of the intrinsic mobility data makes it possible to study the diversity and dynamics of travel behavior at a large scale over the long term. For individual mobility research, the integrated framework can potentially provide deeper behavioral insights to explain the physical movements observed over time and space. Furthermore, with high-quality extrinsic mobility data (e.g., GPS data) typically not available to them (at least not in real-time), transportation service providers have to rely on available intrinsic mobility data, especially for real-time applications.

3.2 Transit smart card data in London's passenger rail network

In this chapter, we focus on one class of intrinsic mobility data, transit smart card, which has been widely used in both research and practice for understanding how passengers use the public transit systems to move around a city. As each transit system is somewhat different, we provide an in-depth look at the pseudonymized data collected from London's passenger rail network as an example. The transit smart card, called the *Oyster card*, is a form of electronic ticket used on public transport in Greater London. It is issued and managed by Transport for London (TfL) and is valid on public transport modes across

London. Note that an individual may possess multiple cards and a card may be shared by multiple individuals. However, it is difficult to identify these instances. It is often assumed that each smart card corresponds to a single individual. The public transport system in London consists of several modes. Because of the difference in fare structures, our focus is limited to the rail systems, including the London Underground, Overground, Docklands Light Railway (DLR), and the part of the National Rail within Greater London. The fare structure for rail services in London is integrated, and priced on a zonal basis. The price of a journey depends on the starting and ending zones. As a result, travelers generate a transaction when they enter the network and another when they exit.

Such data directly capture, for each trip, its origin (rail) station, time of departure, destination (rail) station, and time of arrival. Fig. 7.2 shows an individual's travel itinerary in a week captured by the data. Each colored rectangle represents a unique station and the arrow between them indicates a trip. Note that in some cases, the origin of a trip may be different from the destination of the previous trip, such as the first trip on Friday.

As the origins and destinations are recorded at the station level, the location variables can only take discrete values, e.g., station IDs. In contrast, the time variable may be treated as continuous, as it is measured in seconds. However, depending on the problem and model assumptions, treating time as a discrete variable may be flexible and computationally convenient. By discretizing time into a series of intervals (e.g., 24 hourly intervals), it is possible to approximate distributions of any arbitrary shapes. Alternatively, we may consider using a mixture of multiple normal distributions to model temporal distributions. Depending on the problem, people's temporal behavior may be represented in different ways.

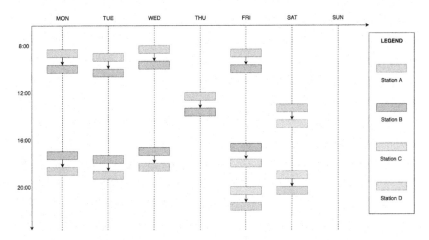

FIGURE 7.2 Travel itinerary of an individual in a week.

Still, the transit smart card data can only capture a part of individual mobility within the rail network. Trips, or trip segments, based on other modes (including buses) are not directly observable. This is a fundamental limitation of this specific dataset, and highlights a general problem shared by many other intrinsic mobility data sources. Intrinsic mobility data are usually mode-specific or network-specific, and thus can only capture a subset of an individual's total mobility pattern. However, as long as the subset is consistent, it can still provide a window through which portions of an individual's overall mobility patterns can be consistently observed over time.

4. New research opportunities

While passively collected human mobility data, such as transit smart card data, are readily available nowadays, we still need a new generation of statistical models or data mining tools to fully utilize the potential of such data for uncovering dynamic and interpretable behavior patterns underlying the physical spatiotemporal observations. The key is to reflect the characteristics of the data in the models, which includes highlighting their strengths (e.g., long observation periods) as well as managing their limitations (e.g., lack of activity information).

In this section, we show recent efforts in developing statistical approaches to extract meaningful travel-activity patterns and behavioral insights from individual-level longitudinal travel records. Specifically, we focus on three problems related to the spatiotemporal behavioral structures in individual mobility—next trip prediction, latent activity inference, and pattern change detection. They are intended to provide a better understanding to the following questions:

- **Next trip prediction.** Can we predict an individual's future spatiotemporal choices?
- **Latent activity inference.** What can we learn about individual activity patterns (e.g., home, work, or other) from observations of individual movements?
- **Pattern change detection.** How do individual mobility patterns change over time? How can we detect such changes?

The three research questions map directly to the conceptual framework shown in Fig. 7.1. Trips are directly observed from the data. Activity episodes, although not directly captured in the data, may be constructed from trips. The goal of next trip prediction is to extract travel patterns that capture the sequential dependency between trips. Latent activity inference intends to discover latent activity patterns from observed trips or activity episodes. Assuming that a dynamic travel pattern is a chain of short-term travel patterns with a series of changepoints, pattern change detection aims to find these changepoints.

4.1 Next trip prediction

Trips usually do not occur in isolation; instead, each trip is part of a larger sequence of trips. This is the basis of work on trip-chaining behavior, e.g., Primerano et al. (2008), and activity-based models, e.g., Bowman and Ben-Akiva (2001). It has been shown that much of the variability in travel choices (such as location choices) can be accounted for by considering the order of these choices (Goulet-Langlois et al., 2017). Sequential dependency between trips can be used for predicting the next trip of an individual based on the previous trip, and the prediction performance is an indicator of the strength of sequential dependency.

The ability to predict individual mobility is a critical enabler for various applications that support intelligent urban transportation systems, such as personalized traveler information, targeted demand management, and dynamic system operations. Although a number of algorithms have been proposed in the literature for next location prediction (Hawelka et al., 2017; Alhasoun et al., 2015; Lu et al., 2013; Gambs et al., 2012; Mathew et al., 2012; Noulas et al., 2012; Calabrese et al., 2010), there is no existing model for next trip prediction. Unlike timestamped locations, trips reflect critical travel decisions, and thus match the actual behavior process of individuals. However, to predict a trip, we need to predict its multiple spatiotemporal attributes, including, but not limited to, the origin, destination, and start time.

First proposed in Zhao et al. (2018c), a potential prediction mechanism for next trip prediction is shown in Fig. 7.3. We split the next trip prediction problem into two subproblems—*trip-making prediction* and *trip attribute prediction*. Trip-making prediction asks whether the user will travel within the day. Under the condition that the user will travel, we then predict the attributes of the next trip in the task of trip attribute prediction. Both subproblems can be

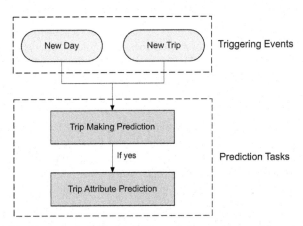

FIGURE 7.3 Alternative individual mobility prediction mechanism. (Zhao et al., 2018c)

triggered by either a new day or an observation of a new trip for the user. Thus, at the start of each day, the system predicts whether the user will travel within the day. If yes, it then predicts when and where the next trip will be. The prediction is updated every time we observe a new trip, until the end of that day. On the next day, the process is repeated.

In this approach, an individual's daily mobility is represented as a chain of trips, each defined as a combination of three attributes—start time t (aggregated to hourly intervals), origin o, and destination d. We assume these variables capture the most fundamental decisions users make when traveling. The need to consider the origin o is because intrinsic mobility data usually only capture a subset of trips pertaining to a certain mode. If complete information of all trips is available, o will always be the same as the d of the last trip.

Because of the data, o and d are discrete variables. The variable t is also assumed to be discrete, so that we may conveniently compute the joint probability of these variables. Specifically, t is aggregated to some prespecified intervals, and the interval length needs to be chosen based on the problem and application context. A shorter interval (e.g., 15 min) leads to higher precision, and is preferable for highly dynamic and time-sensitive applications (e.g., real-time information). However, it will likely result in low prediction accuracies, as the effect of data sparsity and behavior variability become more prominent.

The trip-making prediction is modeled as a binary classification problem (i.e., travel or not). Based on our test results, we find that individual-level regularized logistic regression models can achieve a median prediction accuracy of greater than 80%. For trip attribute prediction, a new model is developed, based on the hierarchical Dirichlet n-gram model used in language modeling, to estimate the attributes of the next trip. Overall, the prediction accuracy for an average individual is around 40% for t, 70%−80% for o, 60% −70% for d, and 20%−30% for the combination of (t,o,d). In addition, the results reveal several important behavioral findings:

- t is less predictable than o and d. One possible reason is the "boundary effect" caused by time discretization (i.e., 24 hourly intervals). However, even when the predicted time interval is extended to 2 h, its prediction accuracy (55%−60%) is still lower than that of o and d. This implies that people's temporal choices are inherently more variable than spatial choices.
- The first trip of the day is generally challenging to predict. However, once we have observed a trip, the predictability of the following trips within the day increases. This demonstrates the strong sequential dependency between consecutive trips within a day.
- The prediction accuracies vary significantly across individuals, implying a high degree of individual heterogeneity. Some individuals are more predictable than others. Furthermore, positive correlation across trip attributes

suggests individuals with higher predictability in one attribute tend to show higher predictability in other attributes.

Given the large variation in prediction accuracies across individuals, it is useful to develop some insights regarding what types of individuals are more predictable than others. Fig. 7.4 shows the spatiotemporal profiles of two anonymous individuals with very different predictabilities. In Fig. 7.4A, the individual origin-destination matrix is visualized as a chord diagram. Each station is represented by an arc and the trips between stations as a chord. The angle of each arc is proportional to the total number of trips starting from a station and the color of the arc matches the unique color assigned to the station. The number next to each arc indicates the ranking of the station based on frequency of usage. Each chord shows the flows between two stations, in both directions. During the observation period, the two individuals shown in the figure made a similar number of trips over a similar number of days. However, the origin-destination prediction accuracies for Individual 1 who visited 137 stations is significantly lower (30%−50%) than Individual 2 who only visited 15 stations (close to 100%). Note that most of the trips by Individual 2 are between two stations. Fig. 7.4B shows the distribution of trip start time for the same two individuals. While Individual 1's time of travel follows a bell-shaped distribution, Individual 2's trip start time concentrates on 2 hours, one in the morning and the other in the afternoon. As a result, the time prediction accuracy is around 30% for Individual 1, and close to 100% for Individual 2. Overall, the spatiotemporal choices of Individual 1 exhibit a much higher level of longitudinal variability than those Individual 2. It seems that Individual 2 is probably a regular commuter who uses rail transit in London almost exclusively for commuting. This implies that higher variability typically leads to lower predictability and people with regular commuting patterns are generally more predictable.

Because the full attributes of the next trip of an individual constitute a multidimensional distribution, the prediction of the combination of (t, o, d) is challenging. Nevertheless, certain individuals and certain aspects of travel behavior are more predictable than others. In practice, policies and strategies can be designed targeting the predictable individuals and behavior aspects. The proposed method provides a probability distribution over all possible outcomes of a trip. For some applications, we may need to account for a range of possibilities, based on the entire probability distribution. For example, a traveler information system may be developed to inform individuals about service delays in certain areas during certain time periods. This will allow people to make informed travel choices that potentially help rebalance the mismatch between travel demand and supply. Next trip prediction can be used to dynamically match individuals with relevant information based on the estimated probability that the individual will travel to the affected areas during the affected time periods.

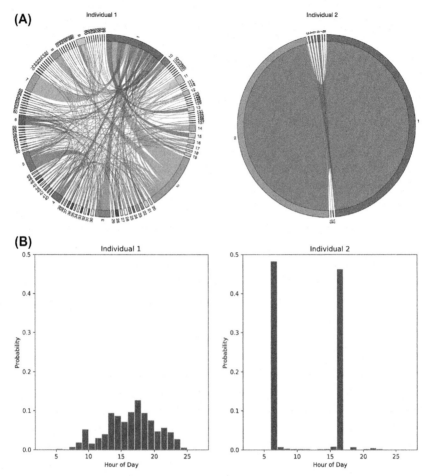

FIGURE 7.4 Spatiotemporal profiles of two anonymous individuals. (A) origin-destination distributions, (B) trip start time distributions.

4.2 Latent activity inference

Individual mobility is closely intertwined with activity participation. In activity-based analysis of travel demand, travel is typically treated as being derived from the need to pursue activities distributed in space (Axhausen and Gärling, 1992; Bhat and Koppelman, 1999; Bowman and Ben-Akiva, 2001). Understanding activity patterns has important applications in urban and transportation planning, location-based services, public health and safety, and emergency response.

Although automated data sources, such as transit smart card data, can capture the time and location of some human mobility with precision and at a fine level of detail, they do not explicitly provide any behavioral explanation, e.g., why people visit a certain place at a certain time. Traditionally, the most common way to collect such information is through manual surveys of individual activity participation, which are costly and do not scale well. Because of the limited sample size and observation period, such data may not capture the diversity and dynamics of activity patterns. Also, in these surveys, activities are typically treated as predefined (e.g., home, work, school, recreation). It is questionable whether such categorization is complete or detailed enough to represent the richness and diversity of human activities. Nevertheless, even without explicit activity information from other data sources, longitudinal spatiotemporal data itself generally contains a significant amount of structure (Eagle and Pentland, 2009). Assuming that people's spatiotemporal choices for each activity episode are generated based on the specific activity they intend to participate in, it is possible to infer the latent activity patterns that underlie human mobility. This calls for a new methodology that can uncover the latent activity patterns from large-scale human mobility datasets.

Automatic activity discovery is a challenging task, as people's spatiotemporal choices vary from day to day and from individual to individual. A suitable approach should be able to sift through large amounts of noisy data and find meaningful underlying activities. Similar to activity-based models, a supervised learning approach requires prior knowledge in the form of predefined activity categories and labeled data (Liao et al., 2005; Allahviranloo and Recker, 2013). In contrast, an unsupervised learning approach does not require training data and has the potential of automatic discovery of emerging activity patterns (Farrahi and Gatica-Perez, 2011; Hasan and Ukkusuri, 2014). One such approach can be developed by extending Latent Dirichlet Allocation (LDA), a well-known probabilistic topic model first introduced by Blei et al. (2003).

Topic models are generative models that represent documents as mixtures of topics and assign a topic to each word in a document. As this representation shares some similarities with individual mobility, it can be adapted for latent activity discovery. In a model first proposed in Zhao et al. (2018b), we treat the travel-activity history of each individual as a document, and each activity episode as a *multidimensional* word. The model incorporates multiple heterogeneous behavioral dimensions, and infers the latent activity associated with each activity episode and the activity mixture with each individual. The inferred activity patterns can then be used to understand time allocation behavior, predict human mobility, and characterize urban land uses.

Let us assume that for each individual m ($m=1,...,M$), we observe a collection of N_m trips, each followed by an activity episode, and the n-th trip (or activity episode) of individual m is associated with a latent activity z_{mn}. Only the spatiotemporal attributes of the activity episodes are observable. The goal is to find z_{mn} that can best explain the data.

To reflect individual heterogeneity, z_{mn} is assumed to follow an individual-specific categorical distribution parameterized by π_m. In other words, different individuals may have different composition of activities. For example, some individuals tend to travel mainly for commuting, while others travel mainly for recreation. π_m may be used to characterize the activity patterns of individual m.

Each activity episode is characterized by a set of spatiotemporal attributes, which should be chosen based on the problem and the available data source. For illustration, we consider four attributes: the location x_{mn}, arrival time t_{mn}, day of week d_{mn}, and duration r_{mn} (i.e., how long the activity episode lasts). Both d_{mn} and x_{mn} are discrete, but t_{mn} and r_{mn} are continuous variables. Based on the activity-based analysis framework, the distributions of these variables depend on z_{mn}. For this problem, x_{mn} and d_{mn} conditional on z_{mn} are assumed to follow a categorical distribution parameterized by θ_z and ϕ_z, respectively. t_{mn} is assumed to follow a normal distribution parameterized by mean μ_z and precision τ_z. Unlike arrival time, the distribution of duration is bounded on the left (i.e., nonnegative) and heavy-tailed on the right. Therefore, r_{mn} is assumed to follow a log-normal distribution parameterized by η_z and λ_z.

Bayesian inference and conjugate priors are commonly used for estimating distribution parameters from data. Based on Bayesian inference, we can update our knowledge of a parameter by incorporating new observations. The use of conjugate priors allow all the results to be derived in closed form. In this model, the prior distribution of π_m, θ_z, and ϕ_z is assumed to be a Dirichlet, which is the conjugate prior distribution of the categorical distribution. Both (μ_z, τ_z) and (η_z, λ_z) are assumed to be sampled from a NormalGamma distribution, which is the conjugate prior of the normal distribution with unknown mean and precision. These prior distributions have hyperparameters that need to be chosen by researchers.

Specifically, the proposed model assumes the data are generated according to the following process:

1. For each activity $z=1,2,...,Z$,
   (a) Sample a location distribution $\theta_z \sim \text{Dirichlet}(\beta)$
   (b) Sample a day of week distribution $\phi_z \sim \text{Dirichlet}(\gamma)$
   (c) Sample a time of day distribution $\mu_z, \tau_z \sim \text{NormalGamma}(\mu_0, \kappa_0, \varepsilon_0, \tau_0)$
   (d) Sample a duration distribution $\eta_z, \lambda_z \sim \text{NormalGamma}(\eta_0, \nu_0, \omega_0, \lambda_0)$
2. For each individual $m=1,2,...,M$,
   (a) Sample an activity distribution: $\pi_m \sim \text{Dirichlet}(\alpha)$
   (b) For each activity episode of the individual, $n=1,2,...,N_m$,
      i. Sample an activity $z_{mn} \sim \text{Categorical}(\pi_m)$
      ii. Sample a location $x_{mn} \sim \text{Categorical}(\theta_{z_{mn}})$
      iii. Sample a day of week $d_{mn} \sim \text{Categorical}(\phi_{z_{mn}})$
      iv. Sample a time of day $t_{mn} \sim \text{Normal}(\mu_{z_{mn}}, \tau_{z_{mn}})$
      v. Sample a duration $r_{mn} \sim \text{LogNormal}(\eta_{z_{mn}}, \lambda_{z_{mn}})$

In the literature, two types of approximate techniques have been adopted to estimate the LDA model—variational inference (Blei et al., 2003) and Gibbs sampling (Griffiths and Steyvers, 2004). The latter is used in this work, because it is more flexible and easier to implement. Gibbs sampling is a special case of the Markov Chain Monte Carlo (MCMC) methods, which can emulate the target posterior distribution by the stationary behavior of a Markov chain. In high-dimension cases, Gibbs sampling works by sampling each dimension iteratively, conditioned on the values of all other dimensions.

The application of the model requires the number of activities Z to be selected. The model is tested with different choices of the number of activities Z. The test results demonstrate that new patterns may emerge as Z increases. When Z is small, the temporal pattern plays a more important role in differentiating activities. As Z increases, the location becomes more important. The discovered activities reveal diverse spatiotemporal patterns and are mostly interpretable. Positive correlation is found between activities related to work, and activities related to staying home overnight between workdays. These findings make it possible to enrich human mobility data with activity information, and provide new ways to characterize an individual's spatiotemporal behavior and measure similarity between individuals.

4.3 Pattern change detection

At the most basic level, travel behavior is described by a series of travel choices associated with individuals, e.g., a trip starting at 8 a.m. going from point A to point B by car. Travel choices vary from day to day, but the underlying behavior pattern is more consistent. At a higher level, a travel pattern describes the organization of travel choices over a period of time; each pattern corresponds to a set of preferences and constraints that govern the specific choices. Although not directly observable, travel patterns may be statistically represented as the distribution of observed travel choices. Existing work on travel behavior modeling often makes the implicit assumption that a person's travel pattern is stable, i.e., the distribution of the travel choices observed in the past will not change in the future. While true in the short term, this assumption is less likely to hold over longer time periods. In the short term (e.g., days or weeks) within the same pattern, the dynamics of travel behavior are solely reflected through variations of travel choices. This is the focus of numerous studies on intrapersonal variability (Hanson and Huff, 1988; Pas and Koppelman, 1987), and regularity (Williams et al., 2012; Goulet-Langlois et al., 2017). In the long term (e.g., months or years), however, the travel patterns are also subject to change, contributing to the long-term behavioral dynamics. For example, when people move from a suburb to the central city, they may systematically increase overall travel frequency, shorten travel distances, shift commuting hours, increase the number of locations visited, and reduce car usage. The mechanism underlying such changes has been less studied.

Prior research on travel pattern changes has been centered around the effect of social, economic, environmental, and attitudinal factors (Arentze and Timmermans, 2008; Albert and Mahalel, 2006; Cao et al., 2007; Verplanken et al., 2008), as well as how to utilize these factors to induce travel pattern changes (Meyer, 1999; Bamberg, 2006). In the literature, panel survey data were often used to model the change of individual travel behavior over time (Goulias, 1999). However, Kitamura et al. (2003) showed that discrete time panels were not a dependable tool for observing dynamic behavior processes, pointing to the need for continuous data. With the increasing prevalence of urban sensing technologies in transportation and other urban systems, individual travel choices can be continuously captured by various data sources at a large scale and over the long term. A fundamental question is how to identify pattern changes from such data. Travel patterns and their changes are not directly observable; they are latent and must be inferred. Travel choices often exhibit substantial variability regardless of changes in travel patterns, making it a nontrivial task to infer pattern changes from the noisy stream of individual travel records. Furthermore, the multiple behavioral dimensions have to be taken into account since one may change travel pattern in certain dimensions but not in others. The ability to automatically detect travel pattern changes from individual-level longitudinal travel records can provide important insights into the dynamic nature of personal travel demand, and is critical for developing behavior models that are adaptive over time.

In order to detect changes in individual travel patterns, a potential solution, proposed by Zhao et al. (2018a), is to formulate it as a change detection problem in time series analysis, in which we aim to identify the time when the probability distribution of an individual's spatiotemporal choices changes. The problem concerns both detecting whether or not a pattern change has occurred, and, if yes, identifying the time point of such a change, referred to as a *changepoint*. The overall methodology consists of two steps. In the first step, a distribution of travel choices is specified for three distinct dimensions of travel behavior—the frequency of travel, time of travel, and origin/destinations. The model assumes that the parameters of the distribution change whenever a pattern change occurs. In the second step, a previously proposed online Bayesian change detection framework (Adams and MacKay, 2007) is adapted to compute the probability that a pattern change occurs at any timestep, e.g., a week.

For a behavior dimension, the travel incidences of an individual over time can be measured with a sequence of observations $X = \{x_1, x_2, \ldots\}$, where x_t represents the travel instances of an individual during time interval t observed from data. The time unit of t determines the timestep considered in the time series analysis, and it depends on the available data sources and the objective.

Both a day and a week are natural choices because they are natural periods of behavior cyclicality for human mobility (Kim and Kotz, 2007). Choosing a week is more convenient for modeling purposes because travel patterns in weekdays may be different from weekends. A larger time unit (e.g., a month) may be used with a trade-off; it can increase the robustness of detection results, at the cost of longer detection delay and worse detectable granularity for changepoints. Without the loss of generality, the time unit is assumed to be Q days; it is recommended to set Q as a multiple of a week, i.e., $Q=7,14,21,...$, so that every timestep contains a constant mixture of weekdays and weekends. As a demonstration, we set $Q=7$, but it can be easily adjusted depending on the specific use cases.

Over time, when a change occurs in the travel pattern, we assume the structure of the distribution $P(x_t|\theta)$ stays the same but the value of distribution parameter θ changes. Let us use a binary variable y_u to denote whether or not a change occurs at u. Then the problem is to compute the probability distribution of y_u, given the data seen so far $x_{1:t}$, or $P(y_u=1|x_{1:t})$ ($u \leq t$). To do this, we first estimate c_t, the time since the last changepoint at time t, based on the online Bayesian framework.

As the proposed change detection method operates at the individual level, it is useful to examine the results for a few individuals. Fig. 7.5 shows the change detection results for an anonymous individual. To visualize the individual-level results, we display nine subplots for each individual, organized in a 3-by-3 grid. All the subplots share the same x-axis, representing the active sequence of weeks for the individual. Let us assume that there are a total of T weeks in the sequence. The first row shows the input data, or $x_{1:T}$, in the three dimensions. For the frequency dimension, it is one-dimensional frequency array of length T, shown as a bar plot. For the temporal and spatial dimensions, it is an M-by-T sparse matrix, where each cell represents the

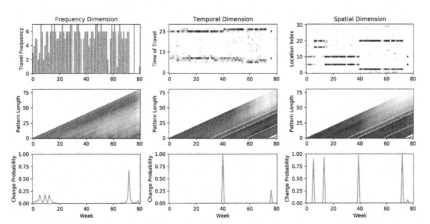

FIGURE 7.5 Change detection results for an anonymous individual. (Zhao et al., 2018a)

frequency of the m-th outcome at week t, or $x_t^{(m)}$. For the temporal dimension, the y-axis indicates the hour of day; for the spatial dimension, it is simply the indices of stations (with no meaningful order). The matrix is shown as a heat map, and the darkness of a cell is proportional to the frequency value. The second row of the grid plots shows the estimation of $P(c_t|x_{1:t})$ over time as a T-by-T matrix for each dimension. Each cell represents a combination of c_t and t. As c_t cannot be greater than t, only half of the cells have meaningful probability values. Again, we use the heat map to visualize the matrix. Because probability values tend to be small in most cases, the logarithm of the probabilities are used. Thus the darkness of a cell in the matrix is proportional to $\log(P(c_t|x_{1:t}))$. It is not straightforward to identify a changepoint from the heat maps. Note that the white strips in the temporal and spatial dimensions indicate $\log(P(c_t|x_{1:t})) \to -\infty$, or $P(c_t|x_{1:t}) \to 0$, which occurs when there is no travel observed during the corresponding week at the x-axis. Basically, without new observations, we assume no pattern change. The third row of the grid plots shows the estimation of $P(y_u=1|x_{1:T})$, where $u \leq T$. As $P(y_u=1|x_{1:t})$ is updated as new observation arrives, we only show the estimation results at the last timestep, or $t=T$. From these plots, one can pinpoint the exact weeks when travel pattern changes may occur, if any. The individual depicted in the figure appears to change his/her travel patterns in all three dimensions. Interestingly, there seems to be simultaneous changes in the temporal and the spatial dimensions.

Although the output of the model is probabilistic, we may obtain a maximum a posteriori probability (MAP) estimate by using a probability threshold of 0.5. Out of the 3210 individuals analyzed, the proposed Bayesian method detected 293 travel pattern changes in the frequency dimension affecting 279 individuals (8.7%), 1309 changes in the temporal dimension affecting 923 individuals (28.8%), and 2133 changes in the spatial dimension affecting 1435 individuals (44.7%). Overall, travel pattern changes are rare events; the average change probability for any individual in any week is 0.11%, 0.49%, and 0.80% in the frequency, temporal, and spatial dimensions, respectively. The improvement is especially pronounced in the spatial dimension. Modest positive correlation is found between the change probability in the temporal and spatial dimensions.

The proposed model offers a data-driven approach to detect statistical changes in individual travel patterns, but it does not attribute such changes to specific causes. A future research direction is to identify the causes of travel pattern changes. For example, some pattern changes are caused by home relocation and others by job change. The ability to find the causes of behavior change can provide a better understanding of the relationship between urban mobility and land use patterns. Future research should explore ways to infer the causes of the detected pattern changes.

5. Discussion

5.1 Application to other data sources

The approaches described in this chapter are generalizable and can be adapted for other data sources and contexts. While the London Underground was used as the example in this study, the approaches are agnostic to particular modes. The only information required is the longitudinal observations of individual travel history, including the start/end time, origin, destination, and individual identifier of each trip. Such travel information is generally available in most of the intrinsic mobility data sources. New mobility service providers, such as ride sharing, e-hailing services, bikesharing programs, carsharing services as well as on-demand "pop-up" bus services, also collect individual-level travel records similar to the transit smart card data. An important feature of the proposed approach is that the data sequence does not need to be complete. Although complete observations of travel-activity behavior of a person would help provide a holistic picture of individual mobility, the methods can work with any *consistent* subset of the travel sequences of a person, such as all the bicycle trips, all the taxi trips, and all the rail trips, etc.

Further distinction may be made between two types of transportation systems from which the data are collected. Some transportation systems are station-based, such as subway, buses, and docked bikesharing, while others are not constrained by stations and can provide "door-to-door" services, such as taxis, transportation network companies (TNCs), and dockless bikesharing. Data collected from the latter provide more accurate, and granular, measurement of spatial patterns. For example, the actual origin-destination of a trip is observable from taxi GPS data in longitude and latitude. In such cases, the spatial coordinates need to be aggregated to zones because people's location choices are assumed to be discrete. The spatial aggregation may be done based on census tracts, postal codes, transportation analysis zones (TAZs), or customized spatial grids. As with time discretization, the choice of the spatial discretization unit can have a significant influence on the analysis results.

For extrinsic mobility data, the application of the proposed approaches depends on specific data characteristics. Overall, extrinsic mobility data are advantageous in capturing individual mobility patterns across modes. In the temporal dimension, however, extrinsic mobility data are limited in capturing the key decision points in travel-activity behavior, i.e., the start and end time of a trip (or an activity episode). It is easier to extract trip start/end time from data with high sampling frequency, such as smartphone GPS data. Call detail record (CDR) data, on the other hands, are generated by telecommunication activities (e.g., phone calls) and thus exhibit a higher level of sparsity. As a result, the proposed approaches can only be applied to nonsparse data sources. With the increasing popularity of wearable devices, and location-aware applications, these data sources should become more prevalent in the future. However, these types of data are sensitive and need to be handled carefully, recognizing privacy concerns.

5.2 Unit of analysis

For all the approaches presented in this chapter, a unit of analysis needs to be chosen. The unit of analysis is a design parameter that needs to be specified based on the application, data, and model assumptions. Generally, the unit of analysis should be no smaller than the unit of data and no larger than the unit of behavior. The unit of data is given, but the unit of behavior is often unknown. It is straightforward in some cases, e.g., mode choices, but ambiguous in other cases, especially for spatiotemporal behavior. For example, for next trip prediction and pattern change detection, the unit of analysis for temporal behavior is specified as 1 h, but this may be adjusted, even though the unit of data is 1 s. The underlying assumption is that the unit of temporal behavior is at least 1 h. A smaller unit (e.g., 1 min) increases the granularity of the analysis, but may lead to a higher level of data sparsity and thus reduce the reliability of the analysis. This relationship is illustrated in Fig. 7.6.

The same discussion can be applied to latent activity inference. While the traditional activity surveys are based on a predetermined level of granularity for activities (e.g., home, work, and other), the proposed model may be used to explore different levels of granularity. Essentially, Z controls the level of granularity for activities. As Z increases, the granularity of discovered activities increases and more specific activity patterns emerge. Based on the target application, the desired granularity can be adjusted. For activity understanding, a smaller Z (and lower granularity) is sufficient; for mobility prediction, a much larger Z (and higher granularity) is needed.

5.3 Representation of continuous space

Like time, space can be regarded as either discrete or continuous. In this chapter, space is represented as a set of discrete locations (or rail stations) primarily because of the nature of transit smart card data. A discrete representation of space is computationally convenient and commonly used in existing mobility models. However, it ignores the geographical proximity between locations. As travel distance and time are important factors

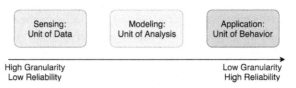

FIGURE 7.6 Granularity of behavior analysis.

influencing people's travel decisions, future individual mobility models should capture spatial proximity between locations. The underlying assumption is that, typically, locations that are closer to each other tend to be more similar. However, this may limit our ability to identify patterns that are shared by far away locations, e.g., two airports in the opposite sides of the same city.

One simple way to model continuous space is to assume that each location choice follows a bivariate normal distribution. If we combine it with the corresponding time choice, a spatiotemporal observation can be represented as a three-dimensional point (x,y,t) sampled from a trivariate normal distribution, where x and y are coordinates of the location and t is the timestamp. A trip can be represented as a directed line segment in this three-dimensional space, with a start point and an end point. Again, an appropriate measurement scale needs to be chosen so that the spatial and temporal attributes are relatively balanced.

In addition to geographical distance, network distance should also be incorporated. The presence of transportation networks, such as subway, may distort the actual geographical proximity between locations. For example, traveling between two locations that are connected via a subway line may take less time that what the physical distance suggests. The two types of distances are used in different scenarios. Specifically for next trip prediction, geographical distance may be used for origin prediction, while network distance is better suited for destination prediction. Future studies are needed to explore the effect of different representations of space in individual mobility modeling.

6. Future work

The three research problems discussed in this chapter are interconnected. Activity-based trip prediction may achieve better performance. The detected pattern changes may be incorporated in the next trip prediction model to enable model adaptivity over time. A similar pattern change detection approach can be applied to detect activity pattern changes. For example, Fig. 7.7 shows a possible framework for activity-based modeling of individual mobility, in which the spatiotemporal choices depend on the latent activities that are sequentially dependent. After a trip of an individual is observed, the location and arrival time of the current activity are known, but the duration needs to be estimated, which is equivalent to predicting the start time of the next trip. This can be done by summing over all the possible latent activities. As the duration variable is assumed to follow some continuous distribution conditional on the activity, e.g., log-normal, it makes it possible to predict the trip start time much more precisely, and, potentially, achieve better prediction performance.

Beyond the scope of this chapter, some other important research directions should be explored in future research. In particular, further studies are needed to address several technical challenges in individual mobility modeling. First,

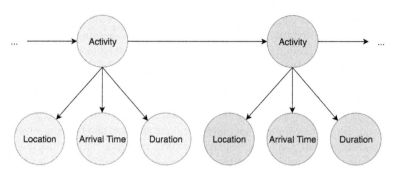

FIGURE 7.7 A framework of activity-based mobility prediction.

estimating the probability distribution of mobility patterns is a nontrivial task, primarily because of the high dimensionality of spatiotemporal choices. To address this issue, future research should experiment with new similarity metrics, dimension reduction techniques, and hierarchical models. Second, individual mobility concerns multiple heterogeneous dimensions, most notably the spatial and temporal dimensions. The mechanism that governs the dynamics of different dimensions over time is not yet well understood. New methods need to be developed to mine, and ultimately predict, coevolving time series data across behavioral dimensions. Finally, the inference of latent human activity patterns from spatiotemporal data is challenging due to the lack of ground truth observations. Unsupervised learning methods such as topic models are useful to decompose the data into latent components (i.e., activities). Future work should also explore the possibility of data fusion, by cross-referencing other data sources such as land use, points of interests (POIs), events, and social media posts. This will allow us to develop a probabilistic model to infer the activity type given a certain individual appearing at a certain location during a certain time period.

Another interesting research direction emerges if we move the focus from disaggregate-level mobility patterns of individuals to aggregate-level mobility patterns at a city scale. By aggregating the individual spatiotemporal choices at the city level, we can gain a deeper understanding of the mechanism of urban dynamics—the regularity of urban travel flows, the relationship between human mobility and economic activity distributions, the interplay across different areas/neighborhoods within a city, etc. Another important reason for studying human mobility at a city scale is related to the observation that cities typically have high levels of socioeconomic inequality and segregation among their residents. By linking people's mobility characteristics with their socioeconomic profiles, we may quantify the severity of, and perhaps, eventually, develop solutions to, social issues such as inequality and segregation.

Humans are social animals; as a result, human mobility is interconnected with social networks. People often travel for social reasons and their spatiotemporal behaviors are likely influenced by their friends' spatiotemporal behaviors. Future research may investigate the interaction between social relationships and mobility patterns. The primary goal is to understand the role that social relationships play in human mobility, and, ultimately, use social networks to influence people's travel choices for the purpose of promoting a sustainable mobility culture. For this problem, the mobile phone network data is advantageous because it reveals the telecommunication frequency between individuals, a proxy for the strength of social relationships (Xu et al., 2017). Without knowing the actual social networks between individuals, we can also study social phenomena such as familiar strangers, i.e., individuals who temporarily colocate in the same space but may not know each other (Sun et al., 2013). This may be useful for encouraging social mixing and mitigate segregation.

Acknowledgments

The authors would like to thank Transport for London for providing the financial and data support that made this research possible.

References

Adams, R.P., MacKay, D.J.C., 2007. Bayesian Online Changepoint Detection arXiv:0710.3742 [stat]. http://arxiv.org/abs/0710.3742.

Ahas, R., Silm, S., Järv, O., Saluveer, E., Tiru, M., 2010. Using mobile positioning data to model locations meaningful to users of mobile phones. Journal of Urban Technology 17, 3−27. https://doi.org/10.1080/10630731003597306.

Albert, G., Mahalel, D., 2006. Congestion tolls and parking fees: a comparison of the potential effect on travel behavior. Transport Policy 13, 496−502. https://doi.org/10.1016/j.tranpol.2006.05.007. http://www.sciencedirect.com/science/article/pii/S0967070X06000461.

Alexander, L., Jiang, S., Murga, M., González, M.C., 2015. Origin−destination trips by purpose and time of day inferred from mobile phone data. Transportation Research Part C: Emerging Technologies 58, 240−250. https://doi.org/10.1016/j.trc.2015.02.018. http://www.sciencedirect.com/science/article/pii/S0968090X1500073X.

Alhasoun, F., Alhazzani, M., Aleissa, F., Alnasser, R., González, M.C., August 14, 2017. City scale next place prediction from sparse data through similar strangers. In: Proceedings of ACM KDD Workshop, Halifax, Canada, pp. 1−8 (UrbComp'17).

Allahviranloo, M., Recker, W., 2013. Daily activity pattern recognition by using support vector machines with multiple classes. Transportation Research Part B: Methodological 58, 16−43. https://doi.org/10.1016/j.trb.2013.09.008.

Arentze, T., Timmermans, H., 2008. Social networks, social interactions, and activity-travel behavior: a framework for microsimulation. Environment and Planning B: Planning and Design 35, 1012−1027. https://doi.org/10.1068/b3319t. doi:10.1068/b3319t.

Axhausen, K.W., Gärling, T., 1992. Activity-based approaches to travel analysis: conceptual frameworks, models, and research problems. Transport Reviews 12, 323−341. https://doi.org/10.1080/01441649208716826.

Bamberg, S., 2006. Is a residential relocation a good opportunity to change people's travel behavior? Results from a theory-driven intervention study. Environment and Behavior 38, 820−840. https://doi.org/10.1177/0013916505285091.

Barbosa-Filho, H., Barthelemy, M., Ghoshal, G., James, C.R., Lenormand, M., Louail, T., Menezes, R., Ramasco, J.J., Simini, F., Tomasini, M., 2017. Human Mobility: Models and Applications arXiv:1710.00004 [physics]. http://arxiv.org/abs/1710.00004.

Bhat, C.R., Koppelman, F.S., 1999. Activity-based modeling of travel demand. In: Handbook of Transportation Science International Series in Operations Research & Management Science. Springer, Boston, MA, pp. 35−61. https://doi.org/10.1007/978-1-4615-5203-1-3. https://link.springer.com/chapter/10.1007/978-1-4615-5203-1_3.

Blei, D.M., Ng, A.Y., Jordan, M.I., 2003. Latent dirichlet allocation. Journal of Machine Learning Research 3, 993−1022. http:www.jmlr.org/papers/v3/blei03a.html.

Bowman, J.L., Ben-Akiva, M.E., 2001. Activity-based disaggregate travel demand model system with activity schedules. Transportation Research Part A: Policy and Practice 35, 1−28. https://doi.org/10.1016/S0965-8564(99)00043-9. http:www.sciencedirect.com/science/article/pii/S0965856499000439.

Brockmann, D., Hufnagel, L., Geisel, T., 2006. The scaling laws of human travel. Nature 439, 462−465. https://doi.org/10.1038/nature04292. http:www.nature.com/nature/journal/v439/n7075/full/nature04292.html.

Calabrese, F., Di Lorenzo, G., Liu, L., Ratti, C., 2011. Estimating origin-destination flows using mobile phone location data. IEEE Pervasive Computing 10, 36−44. https://doi.org/10.1109/MPRV.2011.41. http://ieeexplore.ieee.org/lpdocs/epic03/wrapper.htm?arnumber=5871578.

Calabrese, F., Lorenzo, G.D., Ratti, C., 2010. Human mobility prediction based on individual and collective geographical preferences. In: 2010 13th International IEEE Conference on Intelligent Transportation Systems (ITSC), pp. 312−317. https://doi.org/10.1109/ITSC.2010.5625119.

Candia, J., González, M.C., Wang, P., Schoenharl, T., Madey, G., Barabási, A.-L., 2008. Uncovering individual and collective human dynamics from mobile phone records. Journal of Physics A: Mathematical and Theoretical 41, 224015. https://doi.org/10.1088/1751-8113/41/22/224015. http://arxiv.org/abs/0710.2939.

Cao, X., Mokhtarian, P.L., Handy, S.L., 2007. Do changes in neighborhood characteristics lead to changes in travel behavior? A structural equations modeling approach. Transportation 34, 535−556. https://doi.org/10.1007/s11116-007-9132-x. https://link.springer.com/article/10.1007/s11116-007-9132-x.

Chen, C., Ma, J., Susilo, Y., Liu, Y., Wang, M., 2016. The promises of big data and small data for travel behavior (aka human mobility) analysis. Transportation Research Part C: Emerging Technologies 68, 285−299. https://doi.org/10.1016/j.trc.2016.04.005. http://www.sciencedirect.com/science/article/pii/S0968090X16300092.

Colombo, G.B., Chorley, M.J., Williams, M.J., Allen, S.M., Whitaker, R.M., 2012. You are where you eat: foursquare checkins as indicators of human mobility and behaviour. In: 2012 IEEE International Conference on Pervasive Computing and Communications Workshops, pp. 217−222. https://doi.org/10.1109/PerComW.2012.6197483.

Eagle, N., Pentland, A.S., 2009. Eigenbehaviors: identifying structure in routine. Behavioral Ecology and Sociobiology 63, 1057−1066. https://doi.org/10.1007/s00265-009-0739-0. http://link.springer.com/article/10.1007/s00265-009-0739-0.

Farrahi, K., Gatica-Perez, D., 2011. Discovering routines from large-scale human locations using probabilistic topic models. ACM Transactions on Intelligent Systems and Technology 2 (3), 1−3. https://doi.org/10.1145/1889681.1889684. http://doi.acm.org/10.1145/1889681.1889684.

Gambs, S., Killijian, M.-O., del Prado Cortez, M.N., 2012. Next place prediction using mobility Markov chains. In: Proceedings of the First Workshop on Measurement, Privacy, and Mobility MPM '12. ACM, New York, NY, USA, pp. 3:1−3:6. https://doi.org/10.1145/2181196.2181199. http://doi.acm.org/10.1145/2181196.2181199.

González, M.C., Hidalgo, C.A., Barabási, A.-L., 2008. Understanding individual human mobility patterns. Nature 453, 779–782. https://doi.org/10.1038/nature06958. http://www.nature.com/doifinder/10.1038/nature06958e.

Goulet-Langlois, G., Koutsopoulos, H.N., Zhao, J., 2016. Inferring patterns in the multi-week activity sequences of public transport users. Transportation Research Part C: Emerging Technologies 64, 1–16. https://doi.org/10.1016/j.trc.2015.12.012. http://www.sciencedirect.com/science/article/pii/S0968090X15004283.

Goulet-Langlois, G., Koutsopoulos, H.N., Zhao, Z., Zhao, Z., 2017. Measuring regularity of individual travel patterns. IEEE Transactions on Intelligent Transportation Systems 19 (5), 1583–1592. https://doi.org/10.1109/TITS.2017.2728704.

Goulias, K.G., 1999. Longitudinal analysis of activity and travel pattern dynamics using generalized mixed Markov latent class models. Transportation Research Part B: Methodological 33, 535–558. https://doi.org/10.1016/S0191-2615(99)00005-3. http://www.sciencedirect.com/science/article/pii/S0191261599000053.

Griffiths, T.L., Steyvers, M., 2004. Finding scientific topics. Proceedings of the National Academy of Sciences 101, 5228–5235. https://doi.org/10.1073/pnas.0307752101. http://www.pnas.org/content/101/suppl_1/5228.

Hanson, S., Huff, O.J., 1988. Systematic variability in repetitious travel. Transportation 15, 111–135. https://doi.org/10.1007/BF00167983. https://link.springer.com/article/10.1007/BF00167983.

Hasan, S., Schneider, C.M., Ukkusuri, S.V., González, M.C., 2012. Spatiotemporal patterns of urban human mobility. Journal of Statistical Physics 151, 304–318. https://doi.org/10.1007/s10955-012-0645-0. http://link.springer.com/article/10.1007/s10955-012-0645-0.

Hasan, S., Ukkusuri, S.V., 2014. Urban activity pattern classification using topic models from online geo-location data. Transportation Research Part C: Emerging Technologies 44, 363–381. https://doi.org/10.1016/j.trc.2014.04.003. http://www.sciencedirect.com/science/article/pii/S0968090X14000928.

Hasan, S., Zhan, X., Ukkusuri, S.V., 2013. Understanding urban human activity and mobility patterns using large-scale location-based data from online social media. In: Proceedings of the 2nd ACM SIGKDD International Workshop on Urban Computing UrbComp '13. ACM, New York, NY, USA, pp. 6:1–6:8. https://doi.org/10.1145/2505821.2505823. http://doi.acm.org/10.1145/2505821.2505823.

Hawelka, B., Sitko, I., Kazakopoulos, P., Beinat, E., 2017. Collective prediction of individual mobility traces for users with short data history. PLoS One 12, e0170907. https://doi.org/10.1371/journal.pone.0170907. http://journals.plos.org/plosone/article?id=10.1371/journal.pone.0170907.

Huff, J.O., Hanson, S., 1986. Repetition and variability in urban travel. Geographical Analysis 18, 97–114. https://doi.org/10.1111/j.1538-4632.1986.tb00085.x. http://onlinelibrary.wiley.com/doi/10.1111/j.1538-4632.1986.tb00085.x/abstract.

Iqbal, M.S., Choudhury, C.F., Wang, P., González, M.C., 2014. Development of origin–destination matrices using mobile phone call data. Transportation Research Part C: Emerging Technologies 40, 63–74. https://doi.org/10.1016/j.trc.2014.01.002. http://www.sciencedirect.com/science/article/pii/S0968090X14000059.

Kim, M., Kotz, D., 2007. Periodic properties of user mobility and access-point popularity. Personal and Ubiquitous Computing 11, 465–479. https://doi.org/10.1007/s00779-006-0093-4. https://link.springer.com/article/10.1007/s00779-006-0093-4.

Kitamura, R., Hoorn, T.V.D., 1987. Regularity and irreversibility of weekly travel behavior. Transportation 14, 227–251. https://doi.org/10.1007/BF00837531. https://link.springer.com/article/10.1007/BF00837531.

Kitamura, R., Yamamoto, T., Fujii, S., 2003. The effectiveness of panels in detecting changes in discrete travel behavior. Transportation Research Part B: Methodological 37, 191–206. https://doi.org/10.1016/S0965-8564(01)00036-2. http://www.sciencedirect.com/science/article/pii/S0965856401000362.

Liao, L., Fox, D., Kautz, H., 2005. Location-based activity recognition using relational Markov networks. In: Proceedings of the 19th International Joint Conference on Artificial Intelligence IJCAI'05. Morgan Kaufmann Publishers Inc, San Francisco, CA, USA, pp. 773–778. http://dl.acm.org/citation.cfm?id=1642293.1642417.

Lu, X., Wetter, E., Bharti, N., Tatem, A.J., Bengtsson, L., 2013. Approaching the limit of predictability in human mobility. Scientific Reports 3. https://doi.org/10.1038/srep02923. http://www.nature.com/articles/srep02923.

Mathew, W., Raposo, R., Martins, B., 2012. Predicting future locations with hidden Markov models. In: Proceedings of the 2012 ACM Conference on Ubiquitous Computing UbiComp '12. ACM, New York, NY, USA, pp. 911–918. https://doi.org/10.1145/2370216.2370421. http://doi.acm.org/10.1145/2370216.2370421.

McNally, M.G., 2007. The four-step model. In: Handbook of Transport Modelling. Emerald Group Publishing Limited volume 1 of Handbooks in Transport, pp. 35–53. https://doi.org/10.1108/9780857245670-003. http://www.emeraldinsight.com/doi/abs/10.1108/9780857245670-003.

Meyer, M.D., 1999. Demand management as an element of transportation policy: using carrots and sticks to influence travel behavior. Transportation Research Part A: Policy and Practice 33, 575–599. https://doi.org/10.1016/S0965-8564(99)00008-7. http://www.sciencedirect.com/science/article/pii/S0965856499000087.

Noulas, A., Scellato, S., Lathia, N., Mascolo, C., 2012. Mining user mobility features for next place prediction in location-based services. In: International Conference on Data Mining. IEEE.

Pappalardo, L., Simini, F., Rinzivillo, S., Pedreschi, D., Giannotti, F., Barabási, A.-L., 2015. Returners and explorers dichotomy in human mobility. Nature Communications 6, 8166. https://doi.org/10.1038/ncomms9166. http://www.nature.com/ncomms/2015/150908/ncomms9166/full/ncomms9166.html.

Pas, E.I., Koppelman, F.S., 1987. An examination of the determinants of day-to-day variability in individuals' urban travel behavior. Transportation 14, 3–20. https://doi.org/10.1007/BF00172463. https://link.springer.com/article/10.1007/BF00172463.

Primerano, F., Taylor, M.A.P., Pitaksringkarn, L., Tisato, P., 2008. Defining and understanding trip chaining behaviour. Transportation 35. https://doi.org/10.1007/s11116-007-9134-8.

Purnama, I.B.I., Bergmann, N., Jurdak, R., Zhao, K., 2015. Characterising and predicting urban mobility dynamics by mining bike sharing system data. In: 2015 IEEE 12th Intl Conf on Ubiquitous Intelligence and Computing and 2015 IEEE 12th Intl Conf on Autonomic and Trusted Computing and 2015 IEEE 15th Intl Conf on Scalable Computing and Communications and its Associated Workshops (UIC-ATC-ScalCom), pp. 159–167.

Rasouli, S., Timmermans, H., 2014. Activity-based models of travel demand: promises, progress and prospects. International Journal of Urban Sciences 18, 31–60. https://doi.org/10.1080/12265934.2013.835118.

Sapiezynski, P., Stopczynski, A., Gatej, R., Lehmann, S., 2015. Tracking human mobility using WiFi signals. PLoS One 10. https://doi.org/10.1371/journal.pone.0130824. http://www.ncbi.nlm.nih.gov/pmc/articles/PMC4489206/.

Schneider, C.M., Belik, V., Couronne, T., Smoreda, Z., Gonzalez, M.C., 2013. Unravelling daily human mobility motifs. Journal of the Royal Society Interface 10, 20130246. https://doi.org/10.1098/rsif.2013.0246. http://rsif.royalsocietypublishing.org/cgi/doi/10.1098/rsif.2013.0246.

Schönfelder, D.S., Axhausen, P.D.K.W., 2010. Urban Rhythms and Travel Behaviour: Spatial and Temporal Phenomena of Daily Travel. Ashgate Publishing, Ltd.. Google-Books-ID: W8SsCc0cReEC.

Song, C., Qu, Z., Blumm, N., Barabási, A.-L., 2010. Limits of predictability in human mobility. Science 327, 1018−1021. https://doi.org/10.1126/science.1177170. http://www.sciencemag. org/content/327/5968/1018.

Sun, L., Axhausen, K.W., Lee, D.-H., Huang, X., 2013. Understanding metropolitan patterns of daily encounters. Proceedings of the National Academy of Sciences 110, 13774−13779. https://doi.org/10.1073/pnas.1306440110. http://www.pnas.org/content/110/34/13774.

Verplanken, B., Walker, I., Davis, A., Jurasek, M., 2008. Context change and travel mode choice: combining the habit discontinuity and self-activation hypotheses. Journal of Environmental Psychology 28, 121−127. https://doi.org/10.1016/j.jenvp.2007.10.005. http://www.sciencedirect. com/science/article/pii/S0272494407000898.

Williams, M., Whitaker, R., Allen, S., 2012. Measuring individual regularity in human visiting patterns. In: Privacy, Security, Risk and Trust (PASSAT), 2012 International Conference on and 2012 International Confernece on Social Computing (SocialCom), pp. 117−122. https:// doi.org/10.1109/SocialCom-PASSAT.2012.93.

Xu, Y., Belyi, A., Bojic, I., Ratti, C., 2017. How friends share urban space: an exploratory spatiotemporal analysis using mobile phone data. Transactions in GIS 21, 468−487. https:// doi.org/10.1111/tgis.12285. https://onlinelibrary.wiley.com/doi/abs/10.1111/tgis.12285.

Zhao, K., Musolesi, M., Hui, P., Rao, W., Tarkoma, S., 2015. Explaining the power-law distribution of human mobility through transportation modality decomposition. Scientific Reports 5, 9136. https://doi.org/10.1038/srep09136. http://www.nature.com/srep/2015/150316/srep09136/full/ srep09136.html.

Zhao, Z., Koutsopoulos, H.N., Zhao, J., 2018a. Detecting pattern changes in individual travel behavior: a Bayesian approach. Transportation Research Part B: Methodological 112, 73−88. https://doi.org/10.1016/j.trb.2018.03.017. http://www.sciencedirect.com/science/article/pii/ S0191261518300651.

Zhao, Z., Koutsopoulos, H.N., Zhao, J., 2018b. Discovering latent activity patterns from human mobility. In: Proceedings of the 7th ACM SIGKDD International Workshop on Urban Computing (UrbComp'18). London, UK.

Zhao, Z., Koutsopoulos, H.N., Zhao, J., 2018c. Individual mobility prediction using transit smart card data. Transportation Research Part C: Emerging Technologies 89, 19−34. https://doi.org/10.1016/ j.trc.2018.01.022. http://www.sciencedirect.com/science/article/pii/S0968090X18300676.

Zhao, Z., Zhao, J., Koutsopoulos, H.N., 2016. Individual-level Trip Detection Using Sparse Call Detail Record Data Based on Supervised Statistical Learning. https://trid.trb.org/view.aspx? id=1393647.

Zhong, C., Manley, E., Müller Arisona, S., Batty, M., Schmitt, G., 2015. Measuring variability of mobility patterns from multiday smart-card data. Journal of Computational Science 9, 125−130. https://doi.org/10.1016/j.jocs.2015.04.021. http:www.sciencedirect.com/science/ article/pii/S1877750315000599.

Chapter 8

Planning shared automated vehicle fleets: specific modeling requirements and concepts to address them

Francesco Ciari[1], Maxim Janzen[2], Cezary Ziemlicki[3]
[1]*Polytechnique Montréal, Montréal, QC, Canada;* [2]*IVT, ETH Zürich, Zürich, Switzerland;* [3]*SENSE, Orange Labs, Paris, France*

Chapter outline

1. Introduction

Fully automated vehicles (AVs) are not yet on the road, except for experimental batches in some countries and a few commercial programs (SAE International, 2014). Despite this undeniable fact, researchers of several disciplines (transportation, economics, sociology, operation research) have dedicated a substantial effort in recent years trying to understand how an "AV world" could look like, and what would be the implications for individuals, the economy, society and the environment. Transportation scientists had, and currently have, a prominent role in this process. Many of them started dedicating less time to other research topics with more immediate application

Demand for Emerging Transportation Systems. https://doi.org/10.1016/B978-0-12-815018-4.00008-5
151

potential to fully embrace this new one. Such thematic shift happened in virtually no time, as researchers realized the enormous disruptive potential of the ongoing technological advances. A high level of attention is certainly good news, especially if one considers that at the dusk of automobility, transportation planning did not exist in the form we know it today and only a handful of utopian scientists reflected on future implications of the general diffusion of personal motorized vehicles. One could even argue that lack of planning, or a form of planning, which did not consider negative impacts of travel (externalities), paved the way for many of the problems we are fighting against today in transportation science. Only in the last few decades, the paradigm of transportation planning shifted from "predict and provide" toward a more comprehensive perspective, where the awareness of transportation externalities and the necessity to limit them is one of the central points.

There is this kind of awareness in AV research: the potential of AVs to become the backbone of the transportation system and reduce transportation externalities in the future is already a prominent research topic. A common assumption in this stream of research is that to maximize the benefits of automation, AVs should be shared (SAV), and any other application would possibly produce a significant backlash. The modeling techniques applied, basically covering the whole spectrum of strategic planning tools from aggregated models to agent-based simulations, were sometimes modified in order to characterize AV travel, for example, to represent automated relocation of vehicles. To the best knowledge of the authors, however, none of the existing studies focused on the modeling implications of a transportation system largely based SAVs.

The hypothesis behind this paper is that a generalized use of shared mobility warrants modifications to the current modeling approaches and perhaps even radically new ones. To confirm the validity of the hypothesis, the paper illustrates issues related to the modeling of large shared SAV systems, not considered in previous studies, discusses their modeling implications, and proposes ways to implement the requirements which stem from them. At this point, it is worth to stress that such issues are not directly related to AVs per se, but mainly with the fact that AV technology is suitable to enable shared systems at extremely large scale. This is probably also one of the reasons why they have been overlooked until now. Another important note is that the notion of modeling requirements in this paper is, first and foremost, conceptual rather than referring to the technicalities of modeling. Nevertheless, technical innovation might emerge in the future in order to accommodate such requirements.

The chapter is organized as follows: in section two, a short review of the relevant literature is provided, focusing on modeling large SAV fleets and in particular on the fleet size problem as example of a planning problem. Section three, based on assumptions and results of some of the most prominent papers on the topic, focuses on the implications of SAV ubiquity on the temporal scope of current modeling approaches. It argues that multiday models would be necessary and provides a concrete example of the issue through a simple analysis of longitudinal data for a set of large French cities (Paris, Marseille, Lyon, Nice, and Toulouse). Section four discusses other modeling issues related to a large SAV system, including another empirical example referring to Switzerland. Section five summarizes the modeling challenges described in the previous sections and proposes possible approaches to address them within an existing multiagent simulation framework. The sixth and last section summarizes the paper and delineates how this work will be further developed in the future.

2. SAV modeling

As mentioned above, although the implications that we want to single out here are related to large-scale shared vehicle systems, the focus on SAV is justified because there is virtually no modeling literature regarding large-scale shared systems of nonautomated vehicles. This issue will not be mentioned again in the remainder of the paper.

It is also important to note that we are addressing strategic planning intended as the elaboration of visions for the future and their quantitative assessment through different modeling tools. We also assume that the tools used should quantify dimensions beyond sheer transportation ones (i.e., travel time) and should at least provide a basis for the calculation of cost and benefits in the more general sense of these terms (i.e., not exclusively monetary ones).

Several modeling efforts on AVs can already be found in scientific literature. In this section, largely based on a previous unpublished literature review (Hörl et al., 2016), such approaches, are briefly discussed.

The list of modeling approaches include qualitative network-based analysis (Gruel and Stanford, 2016), systemic optimization techniques (Kang et al., 2015), and agent-based models of transportation (Fagnant and Kockelman, 2014, Hörl, 2016, Bischoff and Maciejewski, 2016, Boesch et al., 2016, 2018). In those studies, a recurrent assumption is that a large part of the existing travel demand, if not all of it, is served by AVs. There is an expectation that autonomous vehicles will become highly attractive compared to established travel modes and that they will disrupt the transport market (Maunsell et al., 2014) thanks to highly competitive prices (Chen, 2015), increased comfort, and the possibility to pursue useful activities while traveling (Litman, 2014) are mentioned as important factors for this fundamental change. Indeed, most research envisions that different forms of autonomous traveling will converge toward a universal travel mode of on-demand autonomous vehicle services (Enoch, 2015), which can be seen as a completely new mode of transport (Skinner and Bidwell, 2016).

A specific stream of research has been looking at the number of vehicles needed to cover today's demand with large shared AVs fleets. Although, they are generally not taking into account the rebound effect that reduced (generalized) costs and increased accessibility for some categories of people (impaired, kids, elderly) would probably cause (Litman, 2016), they aim at providing an order of magnitude of the number of cars that will populate the roads in the future. A study by the OECD (OECD/ITF, 2015) concluded that 10% of today's car fleet is needed to cover the existing demand in Lisbon, Portugal. A more recent one (OECD/ITF, 2017), found similar results for Helsinki, Finland, and applying ridesharing extensively would even further reduce this number.

Likewise, Bischoff and Maciejewski (2016) estimate that 10 cars in Berlin can be replaced by one SAV and Fagnant et al. (2015) estimate a ratio of 9:1 for Austin, Texas. A more recent study in the same city, which considers that AVs would be powered electrically and takes into account the necessary recharging infrastructure, estimates that 6.8 private cars can be replaced by one AV (Chen, 2015). Boesch et al. (2016) found that mobility needs currently fulfilled by privately owned cars, could be covered by a fleet of AVs of around 10% the current fleet size. Another study, focusing on Singapore, is probably the only one coming to substantially different figures, as 30% of the current fleet size would be needed to satisfy the existing demand (Spieser et al., 2014). A possible reason is the high modal share of taxis, which are in a way already shared vehicles, which implies a lower reduction potential as compared to other regions.

In summary, the following can be observed:

1) AVs are expected to enable shared systems prevalence and the emergence of a transportation system supplanting the current one, which is largely based on private car ownership.

2) Although the assumptions of the studies differ somewhat, and the characteristics of the case studies areas do too (sociodemographics, development style, etc.), a substitution rate of around 1 AV per 10 cars in urban areas is a recurrent outcome.

3) Long-distance travel is generally not explicitly considered in these studies.

These observations, based on the short literature review proposed, will give the direction to the rest of the chapter.

3. Planning large SAV fleets: beyond the one-day perspective?

Transportation planning experienced significant changes over the last few decades. For a long time, planners focused on infrastructural needs and on traffic flow's speed. The main task was to size road infrastructure, and for that planners looked at "peak hour" traffic. Nowadays, dealing with daily patterns is generally considered necessary for both a deeper insight on the transportation system and the consideration of externalities. Accordingly, current transportation models usually focus on a full day. This means, also, that we deem possible to answer most of the planning questions at hand looking at a single (average) day. In some cases, it can be necessary to look at different days (for instance, a working day and a weekend day), but it is unusual to look at multiple consecutive days. A key implicit assumption underlying such approach is that days can be considered as independent from each other. For example, demand patterns on 1 day will not impact the ability of the system to accommodate demand the next day. In a transportation system, as we know it today, the assumption seems reasonable. Privately owned vehicles are managed by individual owners, or at most within a household. Therefore, individuals generally have access to the vehicle of their choice, among those they own.

For carsharing, existing literature (Weikl and Bogenberger, 2015) shows that vehicle relocation in free-floating systems is affected by demand on the previous day. But given the low modal share of carsharing overall, this can be tackled with ad hoc models and does not fundamentally challenge the validity of the one-day model for the transportation system as a whole. We argue here that things may change for SAV-based transportation systems but, to the best knowledge of the authors, none of the existing modeling efforts in the AV domain ever questioned the temporal scope of the models used. One day approaches were used "per default", although it is one of the main critical points of those studies.

3.1 Holiday time: what if the fleet flees away?

Let us focus on a given urban area. If privately owned cars are prevalent, most of the cars in the system on a given day will start and end from/at the same location, be that the home of the owner, any facility related to a work activity or else. If somebody is staying overnight outside the region considered on a particular day it does impact the system only to a very limited extent. One less car in the system might mean a marginally lower competition for road space in the area considered. If many individuals are gone on a certain day, for example, during holidays, those remaining might experience a substantially better level of service (i.e., reduced travel time). From a modeling perspective, this simply means that such day is probably not the most representative one to use as a basis for planning. A commonly accepted notion is that the situation to plan against should be challenging for the system without being too extreme (in order to plan efficiently it should be a situation which recurs often enough and not a very rare event).

If we assume that the transportation system is based on ubiquitous SAVs, the same circumstances take a completely different angle. One shared vehicle is supposed to serve, over 1 day, the demand of several more people than a privately owned one would. We recall here that based on the existing literature, we assume that the vehicle substitution rate is 1:10. It means that one less vehicle in the system has way greater consequences. The marginal positive impact on traffic may still be there, but every vehicle removed from the system means also a negative impact on the level of service the SAV fleet can deliver. If many individuals are gone by SAV, a situation in that no more SAVs are available in a certain urban area would be possible. Obviously, SAV use could be limited to a certain area to avoid such a situation, or the problem could be mitigated through vehicles relocation. We will shortly deal with these points later in the discussion section. However, for the moment it is useful to bring the argumentation further without taking such possible actions into account. Is such a day, in which many cars are "removed" from the system, a logical choice to be taken as a reference day for planning in the case of SAV? At least, different than in the private ownership case, such a day cannot simply be ignored. The level of service of the system would be very low to inexistent, and it would likely not be accepted by the users, not for 1 day and probably not even for a few hours.

To avoid that kind of situation, one should size the system so that a certain minimum level of service is always available, even in days where it is expected that a substantial amount of people from the area would be gone. Considering such observation, it seems safe to assume that substitution rates of previous studies were in general optimistic. If all current uses of privately owned vehicles are considered (i.e., including long distance, multiday travel), lower rates appear more realistic.

To tackle the issue, one should look at all days over a period (say for instance 1 year) in which it is expected that a large (as compared to the SAV fleet size) part of the population of the area studied would be gone by car. A more precise definition (for example, which percentage of the population, how often should such situation occur, etc.) is beyond the scope of this paper but two observations can be made here:

- Free-floating shared systems are naturally instable in terms of vehicle locations and the availability in space and time of vehicles is path dependent (i.e., depends on previous demand).
- It seems unlikely that days with low SAV availability, due to long-distance trips outside the area in which the system is deployed, would never come consecutively (i.e., during summer holidays but also weekends)

These observations have the following implications:

- If we have consecutive days of low SAV availability, the modeling of longer-than-one-day periods seems unavoidable for SAV systems planning.
- Even if we assume that such days never come consecutively, modeling a longer period would be desirable as it would allow to explicitly address path dependent supply. Trying to define what day we should base the

planning on, it would be therefore well advised to look at a longer span of time.

Therefore, it seems logical that the planning of a transportation system based on SAVs should be executed using planning tools which have a longer temporal scope than one single day.

3.2 An empirical example: a summer in France

It is important to remember that the previous argumentation for multiday treatment of AV fleets planning is based on the assumptions that one shared AV would substitute 10 privately owned cars, and that during holidays and other days (weekend) more than 10% of the current fleet is gone from the urban area we were focusing on. Although it might sound reasonable, this was not based on empirical observations. To reinforce that reasoning, we provide a simple example.

For this purpose, we used a data set of mobile phone data recorded by Orange France. It consists of Call Detail Records (CDRs) covering mobile phone usage of around 23 million users of the Orange TM network in France during a period of 154 consecutive days (May 13, 2007 to October 14, 2007). In a first step, the home locations of the persons were inferred. This was done by identifying locations where persons had regular overnight stays. Afterward, we selected all persons with a home location in the five biggest French cities (Paris, Marseille, Lyon, Nice, Toulouse). The share of persons that did not travel further than 50 km from their home locations within the observation period was calculated for these five cities. These are 58.4% in Paris, 50.8% in Marseille, 67.8% in Lyon, 43.2% in Nice, and 70.9% in Toulouse. For further analysis, a sample of 5000 persons from Paris and 2000 persons from the other four cities were chosen. This sample includes just persons which traveled at least once more than 50 km away from their home location, so called (long distance) mobile persons. For each day of the observed period, the number of persons, which were not within the 50 km radius of their home location for the whole day, was calculated. The results are shown in Fig. 8.1 incorporating the share of mobile persons.

For example, the highest number of persons that are further away than 50 km can be found in Lyon on 13th August (namely 23%), because 67.8% of the Lyon population is mobile and 686 out 2000 persons in the sample traveled at this day.

Fig. 8.1 clearly shows the peaks during the weekends indicating that the inhabitants of big cities leave during weekends. Nevertheless, peaks blur away in the main school holiday period, when an overall peak is reached. It is interesting to note, however, that residents of the Cote d'Azur (Nice and Marseille) prefer to stay in their surrounding during the summer. Nevertheless, the other three cities loose around one-fifth of their population in the peak

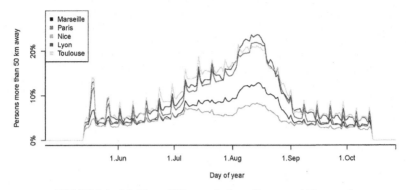

FIGURE 8.1 Inhabitants [%] away for long-distance multiday travel.

holiday period. To further validate the discussion above, it was necessary to show that a large part of the shared vehicles would be gone at some point for at least 1 day. What we found for some of these cities is that up to more of 20% of the inhabitants are away for several days in the month of August and more than 10% are away for several 1−2 days periods over the whole summer (weekends). Given the fact that in France around 80% of holiday travelers are moving by car and that average household size is around 2.2 (www. observationsociete.fr, 2017; https://fr.statista.com, 2017), it seems that the general validity of the previous discussion is confirmed. In fact, days in which an AV system sized based on a one-day model would be inadequate, are quite common in certain periods of the year.

4. Other modeling issues related to shared AV fleets ubiquity

New requirements regarding the temporal scope of transportation models seem to the authors of this paper the most important modeling issue that SAV fleets ubiquity would imply. Two other issues, perhaps less far reaching but also important, are discussed in this section.

4.1 Public servants, craftsmen, and other unsharable vehicles

If one looks at the overall fleet in a certain region (say, for example, a city, or even a whole country), there will be, in general, many vehicles which are not easy to share, or even inherently "unsharable". Specific statistic about this is hard to find, but as a first indicator we can use the number of cars owned by a legal entity. In Sweden, in 2016, for example, around 20% of passenger cars were owned by a company or a different kind of legal person (www.trafa.se, 2017). Most public service vehicles (i.e., police, post, ambulances, etc.) are unsharable because of their peculiar form and contents and, in some cases, also because of specific regulations. Other vehicles, for example, those of crafts-men are, at best, hard to share because many of them typically contain the tools of the profession. It is less clear how sharable corporate fleets would be, as they are generally more like regular vehicles and would therefore not boast physical impediments. A better indicator, albeit not perfect either, is to look at travel diaries.

In the Swiss microcensus (Are and BFS, 2017), there are two categories of trips, "work-related trips" and "services", which correspond to those which may be carried out with unsharable vehicles as described above. Although we have no information about which of them are effectively carried out with unsharable vehicles, the data can provide a further hint regarding the order of magnitude of such phenomena. In Fig. 8.2, we can see that for working days (Mo-Fr) during the morning (except for a low point around noon, supposedly lunch break time) and the afternoon until 5 p.m., 8%−14% of totals trips are trips of these two types. It is also important to note that between 7 a.m. and 4 p.m., many trips in general are carried out (as indicated by the cyan line) meaning that this corresponds to times of the day when an AV fleet would be quite busy, and therefore the existence of unshareble vehicles in this order of magnitude, which studies until now implicitly assumed being shareble, is likely relevant.

To the authors, no transportation models are known which are explicitly dealing with all such trips and vehicles. In fact, if the main goal of a model is reproducing traffic flows, this is not a particularly relevant issue. If one wants to get insight into mobility patterns (i.e., activity-based models), this is more of an issue, but not of a magnitude which would make the explicit modeling of such trips/vehicles strictly necessary. Apparently, this is at least what

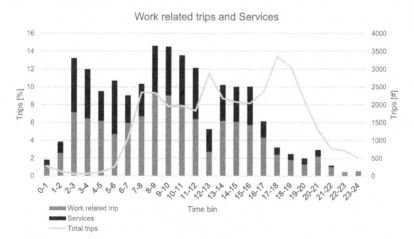

FIGURE 8.2 Work-related and service trips [in % of the total amount of trip] at a certain time of the day (Individuals surveyed on Monday to Friday).

researchers and planners have assumed so far. The presented data though suggests that in the modeling of a transportation system based on SAVs, and in the context of predicted substitution rates (AV/CV) of around 1/10, this needs to get a different kind of attention. If the fleet size of the AVs-based system turns out being of the same order of magnitude of that of all unsharable vehicles, the latter cannot be neglected anymore.

4.2 Fleet size and externalities

In a system based on private vehicle ownership, fleet size is, at least partly, a consequence of transportation infrastructure and transportation policies. Cultural and other situational factors are also playing an important role. But thinking at externalities related to transportation, vehicles footprint is a second order impact, since the fleet is not a planning dimension, and depends on individual choices. In a system based on large SAV fleets, the fleet size itself is part of the planning, for example, according to expected demand and the desired level of service. The perspective on transportation externalities is, therefore, changed. Fleet size impacts the level of service, where a larger fleet will generally provide a better level of service, which will likely lead to more traveled distance in turn. Fleet size impacts also relocation, where a smaller fleet will imply more relocation needed given a targeted level of service, and therefore more traveled distance (in particular more empty travel). Some of these trade-offs are specific of such a service and involve the whole life cycle of vehicles. Some researchers (Chen and Kockelman, 2016) have already explored this notion. Analyses, however, should go beyond showing the trade-off and the models should at least support, if not directly provide, instruments to quantitatively assess the trade-off.

Please note that, in this account, it should not be neglected that fleet turn-around will probably become quicker, as cars would be more intensively used.

5. Discussion

Specific model requirements for each of the issues discussed in the previous sections have been shortly suggested. In this section, we try to create a coherent picture on models for the planning of large shared AV systems. Requirements and possible solutions are not necessarily modeling requirements in a strict technical meaning. The discussion is more conceptual and addresses how the models should be applied and eventually combined with other modeling tools.

5.1 Modeling requirements

A general requirement not directly discussed earlier in this paper, but commonly considered necessary to model shared mobility is:

a The model should have high temporal and spatial resolution to meaningfully represent shared mobility operations (since availability at precise points in time and space is crucial) and represent both users and vehicles individually (Ciari et al., 2014).

The main requirements inherent to the modeling of large SAV systems are:

b The temporal scope of the models needs to go beyond 1 day. Even though it might not be strictly necessary to use a transportation model which represents traffic flows in detail over several days, it will be necessary to understand what sequences of days would need to be considered as basis for the planning.

c Several types of vehicles are unsharable for their own nature. They are: currently not explicitly represented in most transportation models, or at best they tend to get "confused in the crowd". This is acceptable, and accepted, because they are only a small part of the overall fleet. If the overall fleet is reduced to a size the same order of magnitude of the number of such special vehicles, a deeper insight on them becomes necessary, their explicit modeling may become necessary too.

d A model which is used to plan a system but also to assess cost and benefits including possible externalities—which is more and more what transportation models do—should be able to capture first order impacts. As vehicles become part of the planning, the model should at least support an assessment of the externalities related to the introduction in the system of an additional vehicles.

5.2 Addressing the requirements: an example based on MATSim

In the following paragraph, we propose some ideas to address the modeling requirements listed above. For a more concrete discussion, we base it on an existing simulation tool, MATSim (Horni et al., 2016) which has been already widely used to model shared mobility systems, including AV-based ones (Ciari et al., 2016; Bischoff and Maciejewski, 2016; Hörl, 2016, Liu et al., 2017). The ideas discussed though are not only applicable to MATSim and are valid for any model complying to requirement a) above.

The temporal scope of the model is probably the most far-reaching issue. Three different aspects need to be addressed. The traffic simulation needs to be technically capable of simulating multiple days. In the case of MATSim, experiments exist which extended the simulation beyond 1 day of simulated time. In Ordóñez Medina (2016), for example, one full week was simulated. In general, the technical capability should not be a major problem even in other modeling frameworks, as usually simulating multiple days does not require any fundamental change in the model per se, but computation time might become an issue. The second aspect is the data. Longitudinal data is needed to get insight on the day sequences which we need to base the planning on. The one analyzed in the previous section, is a good example. However, it should be remembered that the general availability of mobile phone data is not always guaranteed. In several countries, data protection laws may prevent, or limit, the use of this kind of data even for research purposes, especially if sociodemographic information is attached to it. To get a deeper insight on the mechanisms behind decision-making, one could also think at specific surveys using tracking apps (Becker et al., 2017). Ultimately, national travel diaries surveys might need to evolve into multiday tracking surveys complemented by sociodemographic information.

If both, a model which can deal with multiple days and longitudinal travel demand data are available, it is in principle already possible to deal with the issue at hand. In that case, the day sequences, on which the planning would be based, are exogenous to the model, as they would come from empirical data.

Another possibility, even more radical, would be to make the long-term behavior of the agents endogenous to the model. That is, make the agents capable of organizing their plans in complete freedom according to their needs. This mechanism has not been created yet in MATSim and this is probably beyond the scope of what can be expected in the near future especially in a multiday version. One should also consider that such an approach would imply running a computationally costly traffic simulation over several days (if not months) of simulated time, which is an unpractical option. Making such kind of planning endogenous though is desirable because it allows representing directly the mutual influences between the actual implementation of an AV system and individual travel behavior. It would allow, for example, getting insight on the system's resilience, which is expected to become a much more important topic if the system is based on AV fleets. Multiday activity-based models have been implemented sparsely in the past, and examples of multimonths treatments of the problem have been extremely rare. This kind of tools, however, would be the ideal complement to a model like MATSim, or any other of similar nature, to get a much deeper insight into the issues mentioned above. It would be used to generate plans over some months and get hints on which multiday sequences would be suitable to plan the system on. The proper planning exercise would then be executed with MATSim. An example of such tools is provided in Janzen and Axhausen (2017).

At this point, it is worth addressing service area restrictions and vehicles relocation as potential demand and fleet management strategies. The first would potentially limit travel outside the area analyzed, while the second could reduce the impact on SAV level of service of such travel. These could be arguments against extending the temporal scope of the models. One should consider, though, that if travel with the SAV fleet is prohibited outside a certain service area, then other solutions to fulfill that travel demand should be proposed. If no such solutions are explicitly considered, any comparison involving a transportation system based on SAV fleets and the current transportation system (or any future one which would be based on private car ownership) would be invalid. We would compare the current transportation system with one which is not capable of satisfying the entirety of travel demand which the current one does satisfy. This has implications for all travel dimensions but probably more prominently for how externalities would be (not) accounted for. For example, vehicles fleet size reduction due to SAV fleets would come at the (possibly very high) cost of creating additional capacity for long-distance travel. We have seen that a correct evaluation of the trade-offs implied can be done if a multiday approach is taken. Similarly, if (automated) relocation would be used to bring back vehicles within the original area, the additional vehicle miles traveled (VMT) generated should be considered and traded-off with other possible negatives (i.e., fleet size) and an evaluation over a multi-day span is necessary since the realization of such trade-offs is tied to the temporal pattern of in and out flows of people from the area's boundaries. More in general, considering the mere existence of such operational solutions as a reason to stay with a one-day approach, means explicitly avoiding looking at all externalities implied by a certain solution. Implicitly, it means moving away from the strategic perspective which inspires the concepts presented in this chapter.

The problem of unsharable vehicles seem simple to deal with in modeling terms, as far as the behavior of the agent does not need to mimic the one of individuals using those vehicles at high detail level. In fact, if the relevant data is captured in the datasets on which the agent-based population is built upon, typically travel diaries surveys; it should not be a problem to offer a reasonable picture of how such vehicles are traveling. This would allow planning the SAV system without mistakenly assuming (at least implicitly) that those vehicles would be part of it and available to other users. In travel diary surveys, the profession of the interviewees is not necessarily always captured at a high level of detail, but datasets provide hints on who would possibly drive unsharable vehicles. In terms of activity type, which is usually captured as the purpose of the trip, it is often reported that this is not a regular work activity but rather a service (as it is the case for the Swiss microcensus, as showed in Fig. 8.2). If this is not explicitly reported, it may help detecting such activities that chains of this type will also tend to have many such trips during a one-day span and the work activities (or services) in between will be carried out at different locations. From a modeling perspective, the issue could be solved treating the agents corresponding to these individuals in a slightly different way than the regular ones. For them, one should adjust the criteria for the location choice of the activities, as it would not be fixed, but also not driven by considerations of convenience or attractiveness. A more detailed representation, for example, one where the need that the agents are supposed to fulfill is explicitly represented would not add, in the view of the authors, enough valuable insight to be worth the considerable additional effort. It should be also mentioned, that the reasoning above, does not consider a possible further growth of e-shopping. On the one hand, this would increase the impact on overall traffic flows of unsharable vehicles. On the other hand, the impact of such cultural change on individual mobility patterns (i.e., substitution effects) is still uncertain. The current research on the topic could not yet find a final answer on its impact. This subject has been therefore left out of the discussion on purpose.

In transportation planning, the discourse on externalities is usually limited to those related to vehicle use. VMT is the key value for a whole array of externalities calculations. If also externalities related to vehicle production need to be taken into account, as it was argued earlier in this chapter, life cycle assessment (LCA) is among the most well established techniques. The idea of LCA is to analyze all environmental effects generated by products and services by quantifying all inputs and outputs of material flows and assessing how these material flows affect the environment. The specific application of LCA to vehicles and fuel is known as Well-to-Wheel assessment. However, applications in the transportation planning are limited, and LCA is more commonly applied to compare single products (i.e., the impact of new vehicle technology). To the best knowledge of the authors, applications of LCAs as part of the assessment of AVs systems do not exist yet. We mentioned that some authors (Chen and Kockelman, 2016) already pointed at the trade-off between VMT and number of vehicles in SAV systems but in the future, this should be done systematically and assessed quantitatively. LCA is a useful basis for this kind of assessment as it is typically divided in stages corresponding to a phase of the life cycle of the product and could complement the externalities assessment made directly through the model. This should be true for any model where single vehicles, and possibly also vehicle types, would be explicitly represented. In the case of MATSim, applications where the output of the software was used as input for LCA exist already (Bauer et al., 2016).

6. Summary and outlook

This chapter dealt with the issue of strategic planning for large SAV systems and argued that a transportation system which would be based on such fleets would create new modeling requirements. In fact, the whole discussion is based on rather simple observations. Yet, one of its main contributions is recognizing that such observations possibly have far-reaching implications in terms of planning tools requirements to be used for planning SAV systems.

The importance of such aspects was not recognized so far in the existing literature on AVs. At best, certain AV characteristics were considered but the planning implications of a transportation system largely relying on shared mobility was not (Bischoff and Maciejewski, 2016; Boesch et al., 2016; Spieser et al., 2014; Fagnant and Kockelman, 2015). We showed that the results of previous studies, which had a sort of convergence on a value of around 10 conventional vehicles substituted by one AV, would probably be incompatible with situations which normally occur. The most important ones are all those situations where a large part of the AV fleet would head out of the study area and reduce the level of service to very low levels. We noted that in order to suitably tackle this planning problem, the temporal scope of the model should be extended beyond 1 day. An example based on empirical data for five French cities confirmed that a system based on SAV fleets would indeed experience criticalities if planned considering one single day. In fact, what we found out is not only that a one-day perspective is not enough, but for the nature of shared systems, the days, or series of days, against which an AV fleet should be planned are not necessarily the same as those which would be considered for a planning exercises assuming private ownership.

We showed that relocation, which would come cheap compared to today's free-floating systems, as no drivers would be needed, would be a possible strategy but it would not change the fact that a multiday perspective would be needed for planning. The same applies also for possible restrictions in the use of the vehicles outside a certain area. Additionally, the latter, does not seem in tune with the current developments, as transportation seems directed toward multimodal solutions and integrated systems and virtually unlimited flexibility. Introducing artificial barriers to such evolution appears, at least with today's eyes, an unlikely turn of things. On the contrary, if shared mobility is indeed the new paradigm, it should be acknowledged that also bounding our modeling efforts to specific regions will be more and more difficult to do.

Other issues, related to the mobility paradigm's shift toward shared systems, have been shortly discussed too, namely what we called unsharable vehicles and the need to consider life cycle impact. Their modeling implications have also been discussed.

The chapter also proposed solutions to deal with such issues. Solutions were not technical but were much more about how available modeling tools should be applied and combined for large SAV fleets planning. In this sense, the discussion rather provided guidelines on how to set up this kind of planning exercise than introducing a specific new methodology. Nevertheless, to give to the discussion a more practical cut, it was referred to MATSim as the basis for a hypothetical modeling system which would address all the mentioned issues. The most important integration in the framework would be a model that would deal with long-term travel demand and would be able to provide insight on the series of days that should be considered for planning of AV fleets (Janzen and Axhausen, 2017).

We also observed that datasets, different than the ones currently prevalent in transportation research, would be needed to understand on which sequence of days the planning of the AV system should be based on (together with or instead of the kind of model mentioned above). This also raises a different question, as not only the models but also the data collection will be impacted by AVs. Longitudinal data will become not only attractive, but necessary to deal properly with such planning questions. It might be necessary to rethink nationwide travel diary surveys, rely more heavily on innovative tracking solution, but also rediscover the panel nature of some datasets which are not commonly used as such (for example, traffic counts).

It is important to stress that the requirements above are not relevant only if one assumes that SAV systems will likely become the new backbone of transportation. In fact, one could argue that the only case in which they are not relevant is if there are strong reasons to believe that SAV systems cannot become prevalent in future transportation systems and we don't need to plan for them. As technological progress makes such systems possible, it seems reasonable that such scenarios are considered in planning exercises and should be compared to others were AV would not have such a prominent role. This would also help bringing the discussion on the future of transportation and the impact of AVs beyond "heaven or hell" views, which are certainly catching the attention but are not sufficiently substantiated.

A paradigm shift toward shared mobility probably means that more complexity needs to be captured by models. For sure a different kind of complexity. It is shared mobility's nature providing a "stochastic" supply. Supply is path dependent and complex temporal and spatial patterns are expected and should be modeled. Expanding the temporal scope of the models beyond 1 day will help capturing such aspect. On the other hand, though, the requirements mentioned in this paper, as well as other which may exist but have not been considered here, in a more distant future could be possibly relaxed, at least in some specific cases. Based on real-life experience rules of thumbs could emerge which would make some of them redundant. But now, as large SAV systems do not exist yet, the simple observations made here, the implied limitations of the current assessment approaches, and the modeling requirements which follows, as silly as they may seem, could be crucial to plan for a good transportation system, among the many possible SAV-based transportation systems which might appear in the future, and should be considered.

This research will be continued on two levels. On the one hand, other possible requirements implied by the widespread use of SAV fleets will be explored and the consequent modeling requirement discussed. These, together with those already discussed in this paper, will be formulated in a formal way and the discussion supported with more empirical examples. On the other hand, assessment of AV fleets for selected case studies according to the criteria proposed will be attempted. If the theoretical work and the concrete application will converge to further validate the qualitative discussion presented in this paper, the work in a slightly more distant future will focus on the further refinement of the modeling tools with the final goal of creating a modeling toolset to properly deal with the future that many imagine: a world where SAV fleets would be the backbone of transportation.

References

Are and BFS, 2017. Mikrozensus Mobilität und Verkehr. Neuchâtel, CH.

Bauer, C., Cox, B., Heck, T., Hirschberg, S., Hofer, J., Schenler, W., Simons, A., Del Duce, A., Althaus, H.-J., Georges, G., Krause, T., González Vayá, M., Ciari, F., Waraich, R.A., Jäggi, B., Stahel, A., Froemelt, A., Saner, D., 2016. Opportunities and Challenges for Electric Mobility: an Interdisciplinary Assessment of Passenger Vehicles. Final Report, THELMA (Technology-centered Electric Mobility Assessment), PSI, EMPA and ETH Zurich, Villigen, Dubendorf and Zurich.

Becker, H., Ciari, F., Axhausen, K.W., 2017. Measuring the travel behaviour impact of free-floating car-sharing. In: Paper Presented at 96th Annual Meeting of the Transportation Research Board, Washington, D.C. January 2017.

Bischoff, J., Maciejewski, M., 2016. Simulation of city-wide replacement of private cars with autonomous taxis in Berlin. Procedia Computer Science 83, 237–244.

Boesch, P.M., Ciari, F., Axhausen, K.W., 2016. Required autonomous vehicle fleet sizes to serve different levels of demand. Transportation Research Record 2542 (4), 111–119.

Boesch, P.M., Ciari, F., Axhausen, K.W., 2018. Transport policy optimization with autonomous vehicles. Transportation Research Record 2672 (8), 698–707.

Chen, T.D., 2015. Management of a Shared, Autonomous, Electric Vehicle Fleet: Vehicle Choice, Charging Infrastructure & Pricing Strategies (Ph.D. Dissertation). University of Texas at Austin.

Chen, T.D., Kockelman, K.M., 2016. Management of a shared, autonomous, electric vehicle fleet: implications of pricing schemes. In: Paper Presented at the 95th Annual Meeting of the Transportation Research Board, Washington DC, January 2016.

Ciari, F., Bock, B., Balmer, M., 2014. Modeling station-based and free-floating carsharing demand: a test case study for Berlin, Germany. Transportation Research Record 2416 (2), 37–47.

Ciari, F., Balac, M., Axhausen, K.W., 2016. Modeling carsharing with the agent-based simulation MATSim: state of the art, applications and future developments. Transportation Research Record 2564, 14–20.

Enoch, M.P., 2015. How a rapid modal convergence into a universal automated taxi service could be the future for local passenger transport. Technology Analysis and Strategic Management 27 (8), 910–924.

Fagnant, D.J., Kockelman, K.M., 2014. The travel and environmental implications of shared autonomous vehicles, using agent-based model scenarios. Transportation Research Part C: Emerging Technologies 40 (1–13). ISSN 0968090X.

Fagnant, D.J., Kockelman, K., 2015. Preparing a nation for autonomous vehicles: opportunities, barriers and policy recommendations. Transportation Research Part A: Policy and Practice 77, 167–181.

Fagnant, D.J., Kockelman, K.M., Bansal, P., 2015. Operations of shared autonomous vehicle fleet for Austin, Texas. Transportation Research Record: Journal of the Transportation Research Board 2536, 98–106.

Gruel, W., Stanford, J.M., 2016. Assessing the long-term effects of autonomous vehicles: a speculative approach. Transportation Research Procedia 13, 18–29.

Hörl, S., 2016. Implementation of an Autonomous Taxi Service in a Multi-Modal Traffic Simulation Using MATSim. Master thesis. Chalmers University of Technology.

Hörl, S., Ciari, F., Axhausen, K.W., 2016. Recent Perspectives on the Impact of Autonomous Vehicles, Arbeitsberichte Verkehrs- und Raumplanung, vol. 1216. IVT, ETH Zurich, Zurich.

Horni, A., Nagel, K., Axhausen, K.W. (Eds.), 2016. The Multi-Agent Transport Simulation MATSim. Ubiquity, London.

Janzen, M., Axhausen, K.W., 2017. Destination and mode choice in an agent-based simulation of long-distance travel demand. In: Paper Presented at the 17th Swiss Transport Research Conference, Ascona, May 2017.

Kang, N., Feinberg, F.M., Papalambros, P.Y., 2015. Autonomous electric vehicle sharing system design. In: Paper Presented at the ASME 2015 International Design Engineering Technical Conferences and Computers and Information in Engineering Conference, Boston, January 2015.

Litman, T., 2014. Autonomous Vehicle Implementation Predictions: Implications for Transport Planning. Victoria Transport Policy Institute.

Litman, T., 2016. Generated Traffic and Induced Travel. Victoria Transport Policy Institute.

Liu, J., Kockelman, K.M., Boesch, P.M., Ciari, F., 2017. Tracking a system of shared autonomous vehicles across the Austin, Texas network using agent-based simulation. Transportation 44 (6), 1261−1278.

Maunsell, D., Tanguturi, P., Hogarth, J., 2014. Realising the benefits of autonomous vehicles in Australia. Accenture. http://www.observationsociete.fr/structures-familiales/taille-des-menages-vers-une-stabilisation).html" \o. http://www.observationsociete.fr/structures-familiales/taille-des-menages-vers-une-stabilisation).html.

OECD/ITF, 2015. Urban Mobility System Upgrade: How Shared Self-Driving Cars Could Change City Traffic. OECD Publishing/ITF, Paris.

OECD/ITF, 2017. Shared Mobility Simulations for Helsinki. OECD Publishing/ITF, Paris.

Ordóñez Medina, S.A., 2016. Simulating Work-Leisure Cycles in Large Scale Scenarios: Models and Implementation. PhD Dissertation, ETH Zurich, Zurich.

SAE International, 2014. Taxonomy and Definitions for Terms Related to On-Road Motor Vehicle Automated Driving Systems, j3016 ed. Warrendale, PA. http://standards.sae.org/j3016_201401/.

Skinner, R., Bidwell, N., 2016. Making Better Places: Autonomous Vehicles and Future Opportunities. Parsons Brinckerhoff, WSP.

Spieser, K., Ballantyne, K., Treleaven, R.Z., Frazzoli, E., Morton, D., Pavone, M., 2014. Systematic approach to the design and evaluation of automated mobility-on-demand systems a case study in Singapore. In: Meyer, G., Beiker, S. (Eds.), Road Vehicle Automation (Lecture Notes in Mobility). Springer International Publishing, pp. 229−245. Available at. http://www.trafa.se/en/road-traffic/vehicle-statistics/.

Weikl, S., Bogenberger, K., 2015. A practice-ready relocation model for free-floating carsharing systems with electric vehicles−mesoscopic approach and field trial results. Transportation Research Part C: Emerging Technologies 57, 206−223.

Part D

Applications

Chapter 9

Public transport

Yannis Tyrinopoulos
University of West Attica, Department of Civil Engineering, Athens, Greece

Chapter outline

1. Introduction

Since many decades, public transport has been one of the most popular transportation sectors explored by many researchers. Its societal importance, the variety of public transport modes, and the rapid technological advancement encourage scientists to analyze a large variety of public transport topics. In order to examine public transport from different perspectives and derive results that could be proved useful to policy makers in order to improve public transport infrastructures and services, the researchers apply diverging analysis methods.

This chapter outlines applications of selected methods extensively used by many researchers and scientists to the public transport sector. More specifically, it provides examples of analysis methods, such as factor analysis, principal components analysis, discrete choice analysis, and structural equation modeling that have been used in studies and scientific analyses, aiming to uncover factors that affect the demand for public transport and determine users' satisfaction about quality of service. The chapter also includes

Demand for Emerging Transportation Systems. https://doi.org/10.1016/B978-0-12-815018-4.00009-7

guidelines that facilitate researchers to better use the methods in their analyses and to draw recommendations on how their results can help policy and decision makers to use them in an effective way so that public transport services can be improved.

The analysis of public transport demand, users' perception, and satisfaction is conducted using a large variety of methods; from simple descriptive statistical analysis to more complex and advanced methods, such as structural equation modeling. The application of these methods depends on several factors like the topic to be examined and the availability of data. Table 9.1 below outlines a list of indicative however representative public transport topics analyzed by scientists and researchers and the most common analysis methods used per topic.

2. Applications

2.1 Application A: The use of structural equation modeling to estimate factors affecting modal choice in urban mobility

Structural equation modeling (SEM) is a mathematical modeling technique and statistical method often used to estimate and evaluate unobservable variables, known as "*latent.*" The structural equation models contain a

TABLE 9.1 Common methods used to analyze selected public transport topics.

	Topics			
Methods	Demand	Customers satisfaction	Modal choice	Behavioral intentions
Descriptive statistics	√	√	√	√
Quadrant analysis		√		
Impact score analysis		√		
Factor analysis	√	√		
Principal components analysis	√	√		
Discrete choice analysis	√	√	√	√
Structural equation modeling	√		√	

measurement model that defines latent variables using one or more observed variables and a structural model that creates relationships between latent variables. SEM is commonly used in social sciences because of its ability to build relationships between unobserved variables (latent) from observable variables. In urban mobility, SEM is a good statistical method that, among others, demonstrates factors affecting modal choice. Public transport is a key determinant and policy measure that determines, to a major degree, the efficiency of urban mobility.

In their research, Tyrinopoulos and Antoniou (2013) estimated structural equation models to gain better insight of the factors effecting commuters' choice in the use of urban transport modes. The study area was the Municipality of Kalamaria (Thessaloniki, Greece) and their research was conducted in March 2008. A questionnaire survey was conducted aiming to acquire the mobility characteristics in the study area, the needs and requirements of the citizens, the factors that affect the choice of the mode to be used in their trips, their preferences on the services of a mobility center, and other mobility oriented attributes. Six hundred adult citizens responded to the survey.

The structural equation model developed by the authors is shown in graphical form in Fig. 9.1. The latent variable reflects the underlying mobility behavior of the respondents and is based on five indicators, i.e., the availability

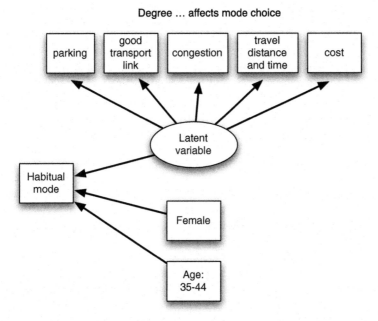

FIGURE 9.1 Path diagram of the structural equation model. *Reproduced from Tyrinopoulos, Y., Antoniou, C., 2013. Factors affecting modal choice in Urban Mobility. European Transport Research Review 5(1), 27–39.*

of parking places, the existence of good transport links, congestion, travel distance and time, and travel cost. Besides the latent variable, gender and age play a role.

The estimation results are presented in Table 9.2. The top part of the table shows the estimation results for the regression equation.

Female respondents show a higher tendency toward bus. Furthermore, respondents in the age group 36–44 years old show a higher tendency toward car. This is an intuitive finding, as these respondents are in the prime of their professional life and therefore can benefit from the increased mobility offered by the private automobile. Three summary measures of goodness of fit are reported: Standardized Root Mean Square Residual (SRMR), Root Mean Square Error of Approximation (RMSEA), and the Comparative Fit Index (CFI). Values of the SRMR range between zero and one, with well-fitting models having values less than 0.06, while values up to 0.08 can be considered acceptable. The obtained value of 0.06 for this model can therefore be reasonably accepted. The appropriate acceptable cut-off point for the RMSEA has been a topic of debate, but in general lies within 0.06 and 0.08, while 0.07 is often considered as having the general consensus. As such, the obtained value for this model (0.081) is marginally acceptable. The third goodness of fit measure, the Comparative Fit Index (CFI) is the one that provides worse performance (with a value of 0.811), as values larger of 0.90 or even 0.95 are advised.

This application of structural equation modeling and many others showed that it is an excellent method allowing to estimate the impacts of underlying mobility behavior of travelers, using their responses as indicators. When applying the structural equation modeling, the most critical decision is the selection of the latent variables and the development of the structural model.

2.2 Application B: The use of quadrant analysis to identify public transport characteristics that need improvement

Quadrant analysis is a simple method mainly used for the analysis of qualitative characteristics. The source data is collected through questionnaire surveys and its primary result is the identification of qualitative characteristics that require immediate improvement by the public transport organizations, according to the opinion of the respondents. The core of this analysis is the correlation of the mean scores of the importance and satisfaction attributed to each characteristic.

Quadrant analysis is widely used for the assessment of the quality of mobility and public transport services. One of the many applications of this analysis in the public transport business was implemented in 2005 and its results were published by Tyrinopoulos et al. (2006). It refers to a wide survey that was conducted in Thessaloniki, Greece, aiming at identifying the needs and priorities of the citizens, and at assessing the public transport services

TABLE 9.2 Structural equation model estimation results.

	Estimate	Standard error	z-value
Regressions			
Habitual mode	~		
Latent variable	−0.123	0.051	−2.408
Female	0.198	0.043	4.620
Age group 36−44 y.o.	−0.196	0.048	−4.129
Latent variables			
Latent variable	~		
Degree parking affects	1		
Degree good transport link affects	1.084	0.215	5.051
Degree congestion affects	1.569	0.276	5.679
Degree travel distance and time affects	1.768	0.311	5.683
Degree cost affects	0.936	0.196	4.775
Variances			
Degree parking affects	2.119	0.142	
Degree good transport link affects	1.543	0.108	
Degree congestion affects	1.047	0.104	
Degree travel distance and time affects	1.068	0.121	
Degree cost affects	1.536	0.105	
Habitual mode	0.209	0.013	
Latent variable	0.275	0.087	
Number of observations	511		
Log likelihood and information criteria			
Log likelihood user model (H_0)			−5304.78
Log likelihood unrestricted model (H_1)			−5263.70
Number of free parameters			14
Akaike (AIC)			10637.56
Bayesian (BIC)			10696.87
Sample-size adjusted bayesian (BIC)			10652.43
SRMR			0.060

Continued

TABLE 9.2 Structural equation model estimation results.—cont'd

RMSEA	0.081
Comparative fit index (CFI)	0.811

Reproduced from Tyrinopoulos, Y., Antoniou, C., 2013. Factors affecting modal choice in urban mobility. European Transport Research Review 5(1), 27–39.

provided by the local transit organization. For the needs of this survey, a questionnaire was developed, which was completed by 400 passengers. Among others, the questionnaire included 23 characteristics, which were rated by the passengers according to their importance and satisfaction using a scale from 1 (least importance and satisfaction) to 5 (highest importance and satisfaction). The Likert scale was used (Likert, 1932). The mean scores of importance and satisfaction calculated for all characteristics are presented in the following table (Table 9.3).

Based on the above table a scatter chart was created, as shown in Fig. 9.2.

The chart is divided into four quartiles. Based on the importance and satisfaction mean scores, the 23 qualitative characteristics are allocated to these quartiles. Special attention needs to be paid to the quartile D. This quartile includes characteristics, which received high score in importance and low score in satisfaction. So, this quartile contains transit characteristics, which are very important and for which the passengers are not satisfied. Thus, the transit organization should pay particular attention to these characteristics and improve them. In this survey, these characteristics are

- Onboard conditions
- Accessibility to busses for mobility impaired persons
- Buses cleanliness
- Onboard information provision
- Measures for the reduction of air pollution

Quadrant analysis reveals also qualitative characteristics, which are important and the passengers are satisfied (quartile C). This is another significant result, since these characteristics give a major competitive advantage for the local transit organization and they should be kept at high levels.

When applying quadrant analysis, researchers should pay special attention to the scale for importance and satisfaction, but also the points in the scale that separate the low importance/satisfaction from the high importance/satisfaction. In the case described above, the middle of the Likert scale was used, i.e., 3. For example, in case the public transport organization wants to be more strict with the satisfaction the respondents attributed to its services, it can decrease the separation point to 2. In this case, the results will be much

TABLE 9.3 Mean scores of importance and satisfaction for the characteristics examined.

	Qualitative characteristic	Importance	Satisfaction
1	Itineraries frequency	4.7	3.0
2	Schedules adherence	4.5	3.0
3	Transit operating hours	4.1	3.6
4	Transit lines coverage	4.6	3.5
5	General information provision related to itineraries, lines, tickets, and cards	3.6	3.2
6	Variety of tickets and cards	3.4	3.7
7	Cost of tickets and cards	4.4	3.3
8	Ticketing selling network	3.9	3.6
9	Drivers courtesy	4.2	3.2
10	Existence of bus lanes	4.5	3.4
11	Measures for the reduction of air pollution	4.3	2.8
12	Distance to bus stops	4.2	3.4
13	Information provision related to itineraries and lines at bus stops	3.8	3.3
14	Waiting conditions at bus stops	4.4	3.0
15	Safety during waiting at bus stops	4.3	3.0
16	Onboard conditions	4.7	2.6
17	Buses cleanliness	4.6	2.8
18	Driving behavior	4.4	3.3
19	Onboard information provision	3.4	2.7
20	Accessibility to busses for mobility impaired persons	4.6	2.2
21	Distance between interchange stops	3.8	3.5
22	Waiting time at interchange stops	4.2	3.0
23	Information provision facilitating interchanges	3.6	3.0

Reproduced from Tyrinopoulos, Y., Aifadopoulou, G., Papayannakis, A., Toscas, J., May 19–20, 2006. An Integrated Quality Control System for the Transit services of Thessaloniki. 3rd International Congress on Transportation Research. Thessaloniki, pp. 273–283.

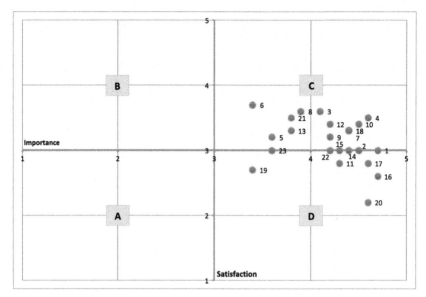

FIGURE 9.2 Quadrant analysis results. *Reproduced from Tyrinopoulos, Y., Aifadopoulou, G., Papayannakis, A., Toscas, J., May 19–20, 2006. An Integrated Quality Control System for the Transit services of Thessaloniki. 3rd International Congress on Transportation Research. Thessaloniki, pp. 273–283.*

different and the quality characteristics that need improvement will be much more.

Although quadrant analysis is a generally acceptable method for the correlation between importance and satisfaction of the qualitative characteristics, it cannot identify the impact of these characteristics to the overall satisfaction of the passengers to the transit service. The impact score analysis is the most suitable method for this purpose (TCRP, 1999).

2.3 Application C: The use of factor analysis to assess the public transport quality implications of users' perceived satisfaction

Factor analysis is a common statistical method that is extensively used in the analysis of transportation problems to uncover unobservable factors that describe the correlation among a set of variables. Factor analysis is based on a specific statistical model (Washington et al., 2003).

Tyrinopoulos and Antoniou (2008) analyzed a large number of data collected in the context of quality control programs applied to five different public transit systems in the two major cities of Greece: Athens and Thessaloniki. These systems are

- Attiko Metro Operation Company (AMEL)—Metro operator in Athens

- Company of Thermal Buses in Athens (ETHEL)—Bus operator in Athens
- Athens–Piraeus trolly busses (ILPAP)—Trolly bus operator in Athens
- Athens–Piraeus electric railways (ISAP)—Electric railway operator in Athens
- Organization of urban transport of Thessaloniki (OASTH)—Bus operator in Thessaloniki

In the part of the programs referring to the customers' satisfaction, the passengers were asked to assess certain attributes of these five systems both from the point of view of their importance and their level of satisfaction about the current transportation services. The customer satisfaction/dissatisfaction surveys involved 23 qualitative and operational service attributes.

The authors of this research applied the factor analysis method on the collected data to discern and recognize the underlying unobserved factors that the respondents perceive, and to assess the importance of each quality attribute according to the users. The factor analysis resulted in three main factors for each public transport operator, as depicted in the last line of Table 9.4. Each of these factors is interpreted as follows:

- Quality of service: comprising attributes related to price, information provision, behavior of personnel, waiting and in-vehicle conditions and accessibility;
- Transfer quality: comprising attributes related to transfer coordination (distance, waiting time, and information provision);
- Service production: reflecting service frequency and reliability;
- Information/courtesy: comprising attributes related to information provision and behavior of personnel.

Some of the most interesting results derived from the use of factor analysis are: for the transit companies operating bus and trolly bus services, quality of service, and transfer quality appear to hold a top priority for the customers. These are associated with quality attributes comprised prices, information provision, waiting and in-vehicle conditions, accessibility, and transfer coordination. On the other hand, for the only transit company operating a metro system, quality of service ranked third. There, the high quality services are taken for granted and, thus, customers emphasize on other quality attributes, such as the transfer coordination with other means and information provision. Overall and as expected, the customers expressed their strong preference to a well-coordinated and reliable transportation environment, since, currently, residents in the greater Athens area are serviced by many transport operators (currently six in total, as a tram service and a suburban railway service are in operation after the data was collected.). In Thessaloniki, the situation is different, since the passengers have no alternative to bus.

In conclusion, the factor analysis statistical method was proved to be quite useful and appropriate in the specific research as it effectively detected the

TABLE 9.4 Factor analysis results by operator—all respondents.

Loadings	OASTH			AMEL			ILPAP			ISAP			ETHEL		
	Factor1	Factor2	Factor3	Factor1	Factor2	Factor3	Factor1	Factor2	Factor3	Factor1	Factor2	Factor3	Factor1	Factor2	Factor3
Service frequency			**0.864**	**0.921**					**0.877**		**0.965**				**0.763**
On-time performance			**0.684**	**0.875**					**0.829**		**0.833**				**0.739**
Service hours			0.350	0.447					0.330		0.370				
Timetable information	**0.614**					0.361	**0.602**			**0.740**			**0.608**		
Price	0.491				0.467		0.567			0.375			0.444		
Behavior of personnel (excl. Driver)						0.542	**0.854**			**0.677**			**0.783**		
Existence of bus lanes			0.303		0.469		0.508			0.332					
Distance/time to access stop			0.325		0.412			0.426			0.419			0.354	
Timetable information at stop	**0.864**					**0.611**	**0.638**			0.471			0.569		
Waiting conditions at stop	0.553				**0.724**		**0.739**				0.422		0.468		
Condition in-vehicle	0.533				**0.990**		**0.661**				0.594		0.578		0.380
Driver behavior	0.472					0.426	**0.667**			**0.799**			**0.771**		

Information in-vehicle	0.828					1.065	0.574			0.880			0.454		
Accessibility (w.r.t. disabilities)	0.410			0.351			0.519			0.368			0.460		
Transfer distance		0.948		0.575				0.744				0.808		0.920	
Transfer waiting time		0.733		0.599				0.868				0.769		0.822	
Information regarding transfers	0.504	0.476				0.524		0.815				0.809		0.553	
Sum of square of loadings	3.504	1.863	1.778	2.861	2.336	2.630	4.236	2.418	1.805	3.373	2.794	2.186	3.357	2.298	1.597
Proportion variance	0.206	0.110	0.105	0.168	0.137	0.155	0.249	0.142	0.106	0.198	0.164	0.129	0.197	0.135	0.094
Factor interpretation	Quality of service	Transfer quality	Service production	Service production/ transfer quality	Quality of service	Information/ courtesy	Quality of service	Transfer quality	Service production	Quality of service	Service production	Transfer quality	Quality of service	Transfer quality	Service production

Reproduced from Tyrinopoulos, Y., Antoniou, C., 2008. Public transit user satisfaction: variability and policy implications. Transport Policy 15(4), 260–272.

underlying unobserved factors that the respondents perceive from the use of the five transit systems. As a general guideline, this analysis method should not be blindly applied to a dataset with several variables hoping that some underlying patterns would be uncovered; instead, a theoretical motivation should drive factor analysis applications.

2.4 Application D: The use of ordered regression modeling to predict transit passengers behavioral intentions

Since many decades, the scientific community recognizes that linear regression is inappropriate when the dependent variable is categorical, especially if it is qualitative. Ordered regression modeling is an appropriate method for analyzing the categorical variation of variables. Usually, these models are divided in ordered probit and ordered logit, according to the statistical errors distribution. Both models estimate parameter coefficients for the independent variables, as well as intercepts (or threshold values) between the choices given to the respondents that participate in surveys. The ordered probit model was originally developed by McKelvey and Zavoina (1975).

De Oña et al. (2016) proposed a methodology to analyze the influence of service quality factors on passengers' behavioral intentions toward the use of transit services. They used the light rail transit (LRT) of Seville (Spain). In particular, they collected the opinions of the passengers about the used LRT system, through an ad-hoc survey, and proposed an ordered probit model to explain how passengers' opinions influence their intentions to use the LRT.

The users had to express their opinions about 37 quality attributes of the LRT service, such as availability of the service, accessibility, information, timeliness, attention to client, comfort, safety and environmental pollution, as well as the overall service perception on an 11-numerical scale, from 0 to 10. They analyzed 3211 valid responses collected at LRT stations.

The ordered probit model developed by the authors of this research estimated the passengers' behavioral intentions to continue using LRT among three levels (low, medium, and high) by varying the level of satisfaction with any service quality factor considered in the model. The model results are presented in Table 9.5.

According to the model results, the key factor with the higher influence in the intentions of passengers to use LRT is "Speed of the trip". Looking at the table and taking into account the approach followed by the authors (three levels of satisfaction), if passengers reveal a low satisfaction level, the probability to have low level of intentions to use LRT system is equal to 8.93%, higher than the reference case (0.36%). On the other hand, the probability to have high satisfaction level decreases to the value of about 62.97%, lower than the reference case (95.12%). Concerning the rest of the factors, "Regularity of service" and "Updated, precise and reliable information in stations" demonstrate high levels of intentions to use LRT. Finally and concerning the medium

TABLE 9.5 Ordered probit model results.

Service quality factor	Variable	Estimated coefficient (β)	Wald	P-value	Estimated probability		
					0	1	2
Reference case					0.0036	0.0452	0.9512
Number of trains per day							
	[V1 = 0]	−0243	3.680	.055	0.0403	0.1836	0.7761
	[V2 = 1]	−0.260	8.500	.004	0.0281	0.1494	0.8225
	[V3 = 2]	0	–	–	0.0029	0.0412	0.9559
Regularity of the service							
	[V4 = 0]	−0.316	5.080	.024	0.0490	0.1939	0.7571
	[V5 = 1]	−0.339	14.082	.000	0.0339	0.1758	0.7903
	[V6 = 2]	0	–	–	0.0033	0.0441	0.9526
Easy access to stations and platforms from the street							
	[V7 = 0]	−0.246	1.225	.268	0.0645	0.2266	0.7060
	[V8 = 1]	−0.250	6.361	.012	0.0454	0.2035	0.7511
	[V9 = 2]	0	–	–	0.0044	0.0506	0.9450
Operation of elevators, escalators, etc.							
	[V10 = 0]	0.058	0.083	.773	0.0451	0.1841	0.7709

Continued

TABLE 9.5 Ordered probit model results.—cont'd

Service quality factor	Variable	Estimated coefficient (β)	Wald	P-value	Estimated probability		
					0	1	2
	[V11 = 1]	−0.177	3.092	.079	0.0436	0.1923	0.7641
	[V12 = 2]	0	—	—	0.0051	0.0537	0.9412
Updated, precise and reliable information in stations							
	[V13 = 0]	−0.302	3.653	.056	0.0610	0.2246	0.7145
	[V14 = 1]	−0.236	6.871	.009	0.0326	0.1679	0.7995
	[V15 = 2]	0	—	—	0.0037	0.0461	0.9503
Speed of the trip							
	[V16 = 0]	−0.721	20.913	.000	0.0893	0.2810	0.6297
	[V17 = 1]	−0.392	17.753	.000	0.0408	0.2014	0.7578
	[V18 = 2]	0	—	—	0.0038	0.0483	0.9479
Performance of the customer service							
	[V19 = 0]	−0.208	2.486	.115	0.0428	0.1779	0.7793
	[V20 = 1]	−0.177	4.536	.033	0.0206	0.1227	0.8567
	[V21 = 2]	0	—	—	0.0030	0.0410	0.9560

Level of comfort on vehicle

[V22 = 0]	−0.282	7.588	.006	0.0331	0.1556	0.8113
[V23 = 1]	−0.042	0.225	.635	0.0141	0.0962	0.8896
[V24 = 2]	0	–	–	0.0029	0.0394	0.9577

Sense of security against theft and aggression in stations and on vehicles

[V25 = 0]	−0.271	4.768	.029	0.0354	0.1648	0.7998
[V26 = 1]	−0.296	12.838	.000	0.0249	0.1377	0.8374
[V27 = 2]	0	–	–	0.0034	0.0427	0.9539

Number of observations	3211
k_1 (threshold)	−3.322
k_2 (threshold)	−2.129
ρ^2 (cox and snell)	0.126
ρ^2 (nagelkerke)	0.268
ρ^2 (McFadden)	0.212
Log likelihood	−547.609

Reproduced from De Oña, J., De Oña, R., Eboli, L., Forciniti, C., Mazzulla, G., 2016. An Ordered Regression Model to Predict Transit Passengers' Behavioural Intentions. CIT2016 – XII Congreso de Ingeniería del Transporte, Universitat Politècnica de València, València.

level of satisfaction, the factor "Easy access to stations and platforms from the street" presents the greatest impact on intention to use LRT.

Ordered probit is a very useful and popular method of ordinal regression analysis. Probit regression is used to model categorical response data. In the probit model, the inverse standard normal distribution of the probability is modeled as a linear combination of the predictors.

3. Conclusions

This chapter presented four applications of well-known and popular statistical methods to the analysis of public transport topics. These and other methods have been used by transportation researchers and scientists to uncover factors that affect the demand for public transport and determine users' satisfaction about quality of service. Especially the analysis of factors that determine the customers' satisfaction about quality of transit services has been one of the most popular topics.

Since the promotion of public transport is still a major challenge for many large urban agglomerations and metropolitan areas, it is also analyzed as part of many urban mobility studies and projects. In this context, many researchers use diverse analysis methods aiming at the deeper understanding of how public transport can play a greater role in urban environments. The applications review presented in this chapter revealed many factors that can give to public transport a strong competitive advantage against private cars, such as vehicles speed, accessibility to infrastructures for mobility impaired persons, regularity, transfer coordination, and many others.

The methods that can be used to analyze all these transit aspects are too many and quite different in terms of theoretical background and the way they are used. For the methods presented in the four examples, some hints were provided that may help researchers in future applications. Additionally, not all methods are suitable for the analysis of all transit topics; Table 9.1 provides a list of representative topics analyzed by scientists and researchers, and the most common analysis methods used per topic. Most importantly, there is a large variety of methods able to satisfy the analysis needs of researchers.

References

De Oña, J., De Oña, R., Ebolli, L., Forciniti, C., Mazzulla, G., 2016. An Ordered Regression Model to Predict Transit Passengers' Behavioural Intentions. CIT2016 — XII Congreso de Ingeniería del Transporte. Universitat Politècnica de València, València. https://doi.org/10.4995/CIT2016.2016.3199.

Likert, R., 1932. A technique for the measurement of attitudes. Arch. Psychol. (Frankf) 140, 55.

McKelvey, R.D., Zavoina, W., 1975. A statistical model for the analysis of ordinal level dependent variables. Journal of Mathematical Sociology 4, 103—120.

Transit Cooperative Research Program (TRCP), 1999. Report 47: A Handbook for Measuring Customer Satisfaction and Service Quality. US.

Tyrinopoulos, Y., Aifadopoulou, G., Papayannakis, A., Toscas, J., May 19—20, 2006. An Integrated Quality Control System for the Transit Services of Thessaloniki, 3rd International Congress on Transportation Research, pp. 273—283. Thessaloniki.

Tyrinopoulos, Y., Antoniou, C., 2008. Public transit user satisfaction: variability and policy implications. Transport Policy 15 (4), 260—272.

Tyrinopoulos, Y., Antoniou, C., 2013. Factors affecting modal choice in Urban Mobility. European Transport Research Review 5 (1), 27—39.

Washington, S.P., Karlaftis, M.G., Mannering, F.L., 2003. Statistical and Econometric Methods for Transportation Data Analysis. Chapman & Hall/CRC, London.

Chapter 10

Factors affecting the adoption of vehicle sharing systems

Dimitris Efthymiou[1], Emmanouil Chaniotakis[2], Constantinos Antoniou[1]

[1]*Chair of Transportation Systems Engineering, Department of Civil, Geo and Environmental Engineering, Technical University of Munich, Munich, Germany;* [2]*Bartlett School of Environment, Energy and Resources, University College London (UCL), London, United Kingdom*

Chapter outline

1. Introduction

Urban mobility preferences have been widely reconsidered during the last few years. The cost of purchasing and maintaining a car, the varying fuel prices, the restricted available parking space in urban areas, as well as the increase of personal and national environmental awareness through the establishment of environmental legislative frameworks, drive people to look for alternative ways of travel. When car ownership becomes a luxury and public transport restricts the freedom and quality of travel, vehicle-sharing schemes seem to be a middle viable solution (between individual car ownership and public transportation). In order to meet global environmental targets (greenhouse gases, GHG) (Walsh, 1990; EEA, 2010; EEA, 2014), governments resort to giving incentives for investment on alternative, sustainable, urban transport schemes, such as conventional or electrified carsharing and conventional or electrified bikesharing (Millard-Ball et al., 2005; Shaheen and Cohen, 2007; Barth and Shaheen, 2002; Shaheen et al., 2010a, 2010b, 2010c). These vehicle-sharing schemes are emerging, either supported by government funding, or promoted by ambitious entrepreneurs or established multinational corporations, that exploit these new opportunities. Relevant initiatives, like Getaround (www.getaround.com), offer peer-to-peer solutions, where car owners can rent their vehicles for the time they do not use them, while e.g., DriveNow (www.drive-now.com) and car2go (www.car2go.com), which recently merged into Share-Now (https://www.your-now.com/our-solutions/share-now), operate their own fleets. Shared mobility can be classified into seven categories: (i) Carsharing: Roundtrip, one way, peer to peer (P2P); (ii) Bikesharing: Public bikesharing, P2P, campus bikesharing; (iii) Scooter sharing; (iv) Ride sharing: Car pooling; (v) Other transit services; Shuttles; (vi) Courier Network services: P2P delivery services; and (vii) On-Demand ride services: Ride-sourcing, ride-splitting (Shaheen et al., 2015)

The objective of this chapter is to provide some insights into the factors that affect the adoption of vehicle-sharing systems, focusing on carsharing and bikesharing. These factors relate to the (a) system (e.g., distance between the stations, way of reservation, type of vehicles, restrictions of usage and cost), (b) user (e.g., age, income, current mode used for trips to different destinations, environmental consciousness), (c) environment (e.g., weather), or (d) geography (e.g., proximity to monuments, green areas). The structure of the chapter is as follows. The characteristics of vehicle-sharing systems are provided next. Then, the factors that affect the adoption of bikesharing and carsharing are analyzed. The chapter ends with discussion and conclusions.

2. Vehicle sharing systems

2.1 Carsharing

Carsharing constitutes an alternative transportation mode form, where users can enjoy the privacy of car, without the need for purchase. Users pay a combination of registration fee and cost per use, either per time used or distance traveled. Maintenance, insurance, parking, and usually congestion-charging costs are normally included in the price. The actual cost of the trip is miscalculated by the users, who underestimate the variable travel costs (Shaheen and Cohen, 2007; Walsh, 1990; Shaheen et al., 2009; Cohen et al., 2008; Morency et al., 2008).

The first carsharing system was introduced in Zurich back in 1948, but became more popular in the 1990s (Shaheen and Cohen, 2007). Among the first experimental projects in Europe were the Procotip (France, 1971), Witkar (Amsterdam, 1974), Green Cars (Giesel and Nobis, 2016), Bilpoolen, Vivallabil and Bilkooperativ (Sweden, 1979, 93, 85) and in the United States, the STAR (California, 1983 to 1985) and the Mobility Enterprise, a research project of Purdue University from 1983 to 1986 (Shaheen and Cohen, 2007). The first successful systems were in Zurich and Berlin in the late 1980s.

Nowadays, carsharing schemes operate in five continents and most major cities (Shaheen and Cohen, 2012). New technologies have enabled the development of new types, such as free-floating carsharing (FFCS). In contrast with Station-based carsharing, in FFCS users are allowed to return the cars in any location, within the borders of a "business district" predefined by the operator, usually referring to the city center, instead of fixed ones. Mobile phone applications allow users to check the vehicles' locations, type of vehicle, auto cleanliness and fuel level (Firnkorn and Mueller, 2011). The first free-floating system in the world was operated by car2go (Daimler's carsharing system) in Ulm, Germany in April 2009, and in the United States in May 2012 (Firnkorn, 2012).

The main trip purposes for carsharing users are leisure and shopping (Kopp et al., 2015). The origins of FFCS trips it is challenging to be estimated; however, areas with high number of trip destinations are consequently areas with many origins (Willing et al., 2017). The main disadvantage of the FFCS system is the unbalanced spatial deployment of cars. It is common to have areas with low concentration of vehicles, but high demand (hot spots) and areas with high availability, but with low demand (cold spots) (Weikl and Bogenberger, 2013).

2.2 Bikesharing

The unique characteristics of bikesharing, a combination of the most important advantages of bike usage, such as low cost, flexibility, autonomy, environmental and health benefits, and the benefits of renting, namely the zero purchase and maintenance cost, have led to the constant increase of their demand over the last few years. The first bikesharing initiative, called the "White Bike Plan", was introduced in Amsterdam in 1965. It was based on 53 bikes scattered around the city. It was soon abandoned, because the bicycles were damaged or stolen (Shaheen et al., 2010a). Since then, there has been gained significant experience regarding the key concerns of the service, namely security, insurance and liability, optimal allocation and redistribution of bicycles, information technology applications, system management and operations, pricing, as well as prelaunch considerations. Other revolutionary schemes that followed the "White Bike Plan" were the bikesharing operated in La Rochelle, France (1974) and in Cambridge, UK (1993). The second generation of bikesharing schemes was based on coin-deposit bikes, while Information Technology (IT) was introduced in the latest generations, bringing this promising mobility system closer to its current operating model. The system design is based on three main pillars: (1) bikes must be distinguishable; (2) bikes or docking stations, if they exist, must be scattered around the city; and (3) advanced information technology should be used for security (e.g., lock, GPS tracking), check-in and checkout. More recent and promising enhancements of bikesharing systems leading to the fourth generation include innovations such as e-bikes, independent operated bikes without docking stations, and integration with public transportation (Shaheen et al., 2012).

Free-floating bikesharing systems (FFBS), in contrast to station-based (SBBS) allow bikes to be locked to an ordinary bike-frame without the need for stations. The average walking distance to FFBS bike is shorter than SBBS, while users do not need to worry about returning the bikes to a docking station (Pal and Zhang, 2017). A drawback of the free-floating operation is that the spatial allocation of bicycles might be skewed during the peak-demand-hours, leading to bad customer experience. In order to minimize unbalanced distribution of FFBS, a rebalancing process is carried out, usually overnight, with financial and environmental cost, possibly higher than those of SBBS, where the reallocation logic is simpler (i.e., mode bikes from stations with surplus to others with deficit) (Pal and Zhang, 2017).

Bikesharing has now emerged in almost all major cities around the world, accounting to 800 programs with total fleet 900.000 bicycles, with the biggest being in Hangzhou, Paris, London and Washington D.C. (ITDP, 2013). Bikesharing systems have been growing worldwide with Europe and Asia leading the adoption (Meddin and DeMaio, 2015). In 2015, China had by far the biggest fleet in the world with 753.508 bicycles followed by France with 42.930 bikes and Spain with 25.084 (Meddin and DeMaio, 2015).

2.3 Impact of car and bikesharing to ownership benefits

Car- and bikesharing have social, economic, and environmental benefits. Carsharing reduces the private car ownership either by selling their cars after joining a scheme, or by avoiding the purchase (Shaheen and Cohen, 2012). Millard-Ball et al. (2006) found that each carsharing vehicle replaces between 4 and 23 cars depending on the characteristics of the city. Martin et al. (2010) stated that in North America, 60% of carsharing members do not own car; the system has removed between 75,000 and 94,000 vehicles from the road; and that the average reduction of vehicles per household is between 0.24 and 0.47. In Germany, Giesel and Nobis (2016) analyzed the car ownership patterns of the FFCC system users of DriveNow and Flinkster. They found that by 43% of DriveNow and 72% of Flinkster users do not own a car, mainly due to car ownership costs, with the principal argument to give away their car provided that carsharing is always available. The reduction of vehicle ownership implies a reduction in air pollution, traffic congestion, Vehicle Miles/Kilometers Traveled (VMT/VKT) and increases parking availability and use of public transportation (Rodier and Shaheen, 2004; Rodier, 2009; Shaheen and Cohen, 2012).

Carsharing leads to reduction of Vehicle Miles/Kilometers Traveled (VMT/VKT). Shaheen and Cohen (2012) estimated that on average, every carsharing user reduced his/her VMT by 44%. Carsharing system Communauto measured that every user makes 2900 km less (Shaheen et al., 2010c). Overall, carsharing leads to 23%–45% reduction of VMT per year (Shaheen and Chan, 2015). As stated by Lane (2005), users of carsharing denote increased environmental awareness after joining a scheme. Moreover, households save more money for their development (Ciari et al., 2009). Fishman et al. (2014) estimate that in 2012, bikesharing contributed to a reduction of 115K km in Melbourne, 243K km in Washington D.C. and 630K km in London.

A proxy to measure the environmental benefits of bikesharing is by the multiplication of the total bike kilometers made per year, with the average emissions of a motorized vehicle. For example, the bikes of Velib in Paris traveled in total 312,000 km per day. If these kms were made by a motorized vehicle, there would have been released 57,620 kg of CO_2. What is more, bikesharing systems are sometimes followed by infrastructure improvements. The total bicycle riding in Paris increased by 70% after the introduction of Velib (Shaheen et al., 2010a).

Carsharing leads to reduction of GHG between 109,000 and 155,000 t GHG per year (Martin and Shaheen et al., 2011). Shaheen and Chan (2015) found that these systems lead to reduction 0.58–0.83 metric tons per year, or 34%–41% GHG per year per household. Shaheen et al. (2012) found that in Hangzhou, carsharing has led to reduction of CO2 kilograms by 191,000 per day.

Car and bikesharing increase public transport usage. Kent (2014) found that users without cars have higher probability of choosing public transportation, bike, or walking in combination with carsharing. Shaheen et al. (2009) found that in North America, 95% of the respondents of a survey agreed that bikesharing leads to increase of public transport usage. Both systems lead to reduction of traffic congestion, mitigation of the parking shortage problem, and better urban design. The user is benefited by time and money savings, as well as health benefits in the case of bikesharing. With regards to infrastructure requirements, the last generation of both systems is more flexible, since stations are not mandatory for their operation. However, bikesharing's prerequisite is the existence of bike lanes, while the major requirement for carsharing schemes is the reservation of parking (Shaheen et al., 2010b, 2010c). Cheng (2016) recommend that vehicle-sharing systems support individuals to increase their financial savings. According to Shaheen and Chan (2015), in the United States, carsharing leads users to monthly household savings between 154 and 435 euros after becoming members.

3. Factors affecting the adoption of vehicle-sharing systems

The level of adoption of a vehicle-sharing system depends on the demographic characteristics of the population of the city that a system operates. Burkhardt and Millard-Ball (2006) found that in North America the carsharing members are usually between 25 and 35 years old, well educated, and environmentally aware. The number of users below the age of 21 is limited, which they attribute to insurance restrictions. Most of the users (72%) are members of households without other cars, their average household size is 2.02 person and half of them have income higher than 60K$. Shaheen and Cohen (2007) recommend that carsharing is a good option for students and low-income households, and people who drive maximum 10–16K per year (Shaheen and Cohen, 2007). Car owners and adults of high income are not willing to join the carsharing program in Austin (Zhou et al., 2011), while the education level does not determine the possibility of joining a scheme. Shaheen and Cohen (2007) found that in Germany, Switzerland, and United States the member-to-vehicle ratios are higher, because of many inactive members. Two of the most important barriers that carsharing providers face before expansion, are the insurance of the drivers and the on-street parking. Pay-as-you-drive (PAYD) insurance may be a potential solution to the insurance problem (Litman, 2011). Shaheen et al. (2010b) recommend that as the carsharing program in San Francisco Bay Area expands, the public entities need to consider formal policies to allocate dedicated spaces for it. In order to increase carsharing adoption and improve flexibility and competitiveness, carsharing companies invest on smart user interface technologies for reservation, check-in, and checkout, and the integration of electric vehicles in their fleets. Philipsen et al. (2019) found that punctuality in pickup time and arrival at the destination are important factors of the acceptance of shared autonomous vehicles, while the exact route of the journey and copassengers have lower impact.

Shaheen et al. (2011) examined the degree of adoption and behavioral response of the users of the largest bikesharing system in the world, in Hangzou (China). The authors found that the scheme, 1.5 years after its implementation, captured modal share from the bus transit, cars, taxis, and walk, while 30% of its members use it for most of their trips. The results showed that the acceptability of the program could be improved by providing bike/parking availability information, adding more stations, extending the hours of operation and offering better bike maintenance. The main trip purpose for bikesharing according to Fishman et al. (2013) is to work, on weekdays, and for leisure and social purposes.

Efthymiou et al. (2013) conducted a survey in Athens, Greece, to investigate the characteristics of the potential car- and bikesharing users. They developed three ordered logit models to model the willingness of people to join a program in three periods (short-, mid-, and long-term). The researchers examined the impact of environmental consciousness, demographic, household, and financial characteristics, as well as travel patterns. The results of their stated-preference survey show that the most environmentally conscious of the respondents are willing to join bikesharing the earliest possible, while carsharing in mid-term. Respondents with low annual income (15,000€ to 25,000€) are more likely to join both schemes. Concerning their travel patterns, on the one hand those who make most of their trips to social activities by taxi or drive 100–150 km per day, showed willingness to join carsharing. On the other hand, respondents who drive 15–100 km per day and go to work or school by bus, trolleybus or tram, are more likely to join bikesharing. Based on this, it is fair to consider bikesharing as a substitute of public transport. Furthermore, respondents with higher education and those between 26 and 35 years old are less willing to join bikesharing comparing with the less educated and younger, despite being less satisfied about their current travel patterns. Age and education level are not significant determinants of the potential to join carsharing.

Efthymiou and Antoniou (2016) used mixed data collected from electronic and paper surveys to measure the impact of factors that affect the propensity of young people to join carsharing. They developed a hybrid choice and latent variable model, retaining initially the consistency of the model similar to Efthymiou et al. (2013). They started by including all the available variables to the first specification and then gradually eliminated the statistically insignificant. The satisfaction of the respondents about their current travel patterns was included as latent variable into the model. The authors found that household size, high education (PhD) and people who use public transport for their trips to work or school, as well as age, are not significant determinants of the willingness of people to join. On the other hand, mid-income (15–25K€) and environmental consciousness increase the possibility to join. There is no evidence that low-income commuters will become members of a carsharing scheme, probably because public transportation remains the cheapest option for them. Moreover, the less satisfied the respondents are with their current travel patterns, the mode likely it is to join carsharing. Similar to Efthymiou et al. (2013), carsharing seems to be a good alternative for trips to social activity for those who currently choose taxi.

Both studies verify that environmentally conscious commuters have preference in joining carsharing, similar to Burkhardt and Millard-Ball (2006). With regard to income, carsharing forms a good choice for mid- to low-income households, as it combines the positive characteristics of the car without the need of purchase, a finding consistent with Burkhardt and Millard-Ball (2006) and Zhou et al. (2011). Burkhardt and Millard-Ball (2006) identify car-ownership as an important factor in joining a carsharing scheme, while in Efthymiou et al. (2013) and Efthymiou and Antoniou (2016) ownership is uncorrelated with potential to join the scheme.

4. Factors affecting the deployment of carsharing

The benefits of shared mobility and their adoption, depend on various endogenous and exogenous factors (Buettner and Petersen, 2011). Endogenous factors are those that can be adjusted depending on the external factors to the system and refer to either (a) physical design, such as hardware and technology and service design, or (b) institutional design, such as type of the operator, contract, ownership, financing and employment opportunities. Exogenous factors that are independent of the mobility system and correspond to specific characteristics of a city, and are the size of the city, climate, mobility behavior, population density, demographics, economics, geography, existing infrastructure, financial and political situation. Table 10.1 shows examples of factors from studies in selected literature.

Kang et al. (2016) explored the factors that affect the demand of station-based carsharing (SBCS) in Seoul and found that the coverage, share of population between 20 and 30 years old, the total number of registered cars and the entrances to the subway are important determinants. Celsor and Millard-Ball (2007) investigated the market potential of SBCS in 13 US regions developing a supply model. They found that on the one hand, there is significant correlation between supply and population density, number of single-person households, public transport, and walking market share, while on the other hand, income, education level and usage of bike are not significant. Kortum et al. (2016) researched the factors affecting the successful growth of FFCS from 34 cities of nine countries and identified as success factors the population density and household sizes. They attributed the deceleration of growth identified in some cities, such as Berlin and Munich, in saturation of the market. Willing et al. (2017) developed a gradient boosting machine (GBM) and generalized linear regression to identify the factors that affect the adoption of FFCS in Amsterdam. Their model revealed that the density of health services, restaurants (excluding 12:00–16:00) and banks have positive impact, while bus stations and book stores (excluding 4:00–8:00) have negative.

Schmoeller and Bogenberger (2014) visually analyzed the trips of FFCS and a hybrid carsharing solution (HCS) the users of which are allowed to park only in specific areas in the city of Munich. They found that degree of usage is related to the university areas, the old city border, and the distance to the Central Business District (CBD). Moreover, the utilization of FFCS is higher in zones with higher concentration of young inhabitants, while the analysis did not reveal correlation between weather and demand. Seign et al. (2015) developed a Pearson's correlation model to identify hot-spot areas of success factors, such as population density, distance to city center, rent prices, and density of restaurants and hotels, for FFCS. Their intention was to provide a model to support the successful design of FFCS areas, a key challenge in the implementation and expansion of carsharing. Schmoeller et al., (2015) analyzed the spatiotemporal relations of booking data of the FFCS in Berlin and Munich. They found that weather conditions have short-term impact, while sociodemographic factors have a strong long-term impact on carsharing demand.

TABLE 10.1 Exogenous factors in selected literature.

Factor	Chardon et al. (2017)	Schmoeller et al. (2015)	Kang et al. (2016)	Celsor and Millard-Ball (2007)	Comendador et al. (2014)	Faghih-Imani et al. (2014)	Caulfield et al. (2017)	Schmoeller and Bogenberger (2014)	Willing et al. (2017)
Population density	✓	✓	✓	✓	✓	✓		✓	
Job density		✓				✓			
Neighborhood age				✓					
Education level share	✓		✓	✓					
Vehicle ownership rate	✓			✓					
Inhabitants age share		✓	✓						✓
Household size share		✓	✓						
Rent prices		✓							
Land use type shares		✓	✓						

Continued

TABLE 10.1 Exogenous factors in selected literature.—cont'd

Factor	Chardon et al. (2017)	Schmoeller et al. (2015)	Kang et al. (2016)	Celsor and Millard-Ball (2007)	Comendador et al. (2014)	Faghih-Imani et al. (2014)	Caulfield et al. (2017)	Schmoeller and Bogenberger (2014)	Willing et al. (2017)
Registered vehicles			✓						
Bus lines serving the district			✓						
Mode to commute	✓								
Public transport station					✓				✓
Bikesharing station (distance)	✓				✓				
CBD (distance)					✓	✓			
Railways (distance)									
Services (distance)									✓

Factor											
Restaurants, coffee (distance)										✓	
Commercial enterprises (#)	✓				✓						
Roads length	✓										
Cycling ways length	✓										
Number of stations of BS	✓										
On-street parking capacity			✓								
Walkability			✓								
PT stations (#)	✓										
Frequency of use		✓					✓				
Use of the stations (daily)							✓				
Traveled distance							✓				
Vehicle availability (CS)					✓						

Continued

TABLE 10.1 Exogenous factors in selected literature.—cont'd

Factor	Chardon et al. (2017)	Schmoeller et al. (2015)	Kang et al. (2016)	Celsor and Millard-Ball (2007)	Comendador et al. (2014)	Faghih-Imani et al. (2014)	Caulfield et al. (2017)	Schmoeller and Bogenberger (2014)	Willing et al. (2017)
Docks per station (BS)	✓								
Frequency OD pair							✓		

5. Factors affecting the deployment of bikesharing

Table 10.2 summarizes recent studies that have investigated the adoption of bikesharing systems around the world. Most researchers model the demand with linear regression based on ordinary least squares (OLS). Chardon et al. (2017) analyzed the day-trips per bicycle (TBD) of 75 station-based bike-sharing systems (SBBS) in Europe, US, Canada, Australia, Brazil and Israel, and found average TBD values between 0.22 and 8.4. The response variable of their model is the TBD and independent the characteristics of the operator, the compactness, weather, geography and the existing transportation infrastructure. They concluded that the requirement for helmet, low temperature, high wind speed and the low number of docking stations decrease the demand for the system, while high population, high density of stations and cycling infrastructure have a positive impact.

Zhao et al. (2014) investigated the factors that affect daily ridership and turnover rate of 69 SSBS systems in China using OLS and partial least squares (PLS). They found that the ridership increases with population, government expenditure, number of registered users, and number of docking stations. Moreover, they suggest that personal credit cards (i.e., allowing members to pay with credit if they do not return bikes within the free hours limit) and universal cards (i.e., smart cards that integrate bikesharing with public transport systems) have a significantly positive impact on daily usage and turnover rate. Tran et al. (2015) developed a linear regression model aiming to identify the factors that affect the demand of the SBBS in Lyon, France, using data of the peak periods of a weekday. The results of their analysis indicate that the system is primary used for commuting by long-term members, while the non-systematic users prefer it for trips to leisure activities. Students are important users of bikesharing, proximity to railway stations, restaurants, cinemas and network density have positive impact, while altitude has negative. Higher population density has a positive impact in the morning, while the number of jobs has a positive impact in the afternoon.

Faghih-Imani and Eluru (2016) investigated the impact of spatial characteristics, such as population density at zip-level, transportation systems infrastructure, restaurants and park areas, temporal and weather attributes, on hourly arrivals and departures of the SBB CityBike in New York. They first segmented the customers into two groups, active members and daily users, and then developed four models for each group. Temperature is not correlated with arrivals or departures, while rain has a significant impact. Transportation infrastructure has either positive or negative, depending on the mode. On the one hand, the length of bicycle routes and the presence of subway stations increase the demand for the system, and on the other the length of railways in the areas decrease it. Moreover, the arrivals and departures of bikesharing stations located in areas with parks are higher on weekends. As expected, the

TABLE 10.2 Factors affecting the deployment of SBBS.

Category	Variable	Chardon et al. (2017)	Zhao et al. (2014)	Faghih-Imani and Eluru (2016)	Noland et al. (2016)	Wang et al. (2015)	El-Assi et al. (2017)	Faghih-Imani et al. (2014)	Tran et al. (2015)	Faghih-Imani et al. (2017)	Mattson and Godavarthy (2017)
Scheme design	Stations density	✓						✓	✓		
	Docks per station	✓	✓		✓		✓	✓	✓	✓	✓
City size	City population	✓	✓								
Demography	Population density			✓				✓	✓	✓	✓
	Jobs density			✓		✓		✓	✓	✓	
Topography	Altitude										
Existing infrastructure	Cycling infrastructure	✓		✓							
	Railways length			✓							
	Subway stations			✓	✓		✓		✓	✓	
	Rail stations								✓		

	Universities	Student residence	Restaurants	Cinema	Distance to CBD	Number of businesses	Parks	Residential land use	Parking land use	Distance to water body
	✓									
					✓					
		✓	✓	✓						
	✓		✓	✓	✓					
	✓									
		✓		✓	✓					✓
							✓	✓		
		✓				✓				

usage of CityBike stations with high number of restaurants around them is higher.

Caulfield et al. (2017) developed a logistic regression model to estimate the factors that affect the number of trips of the SBBS in Cork, Ireland. They found that in a small and compact city like Cork, the trip times are shorter. Regular users have habitual travel patterns, using the same SBBS stations and similar routes. Frequent users have incorporated bikesharing in their daily and weekly trips, mainly performing short and regular trips during the weekdays. Precipitation has a negative impact on the number and duration of the trips, while high temperatures and sunshine lead to a higher number of short trips. Moreover, the results of the model showed that the number of trips is higher during the morning peak. Reiss and Bogenberger (2017) examined the impact of exogenous factors on the demand of FFBS in Munich and found that major events, concerts, and sports games have high positive impact, while precipitation has negative.

Noland et al. (2016) developed Bayesian regression models to estimate the trip generation at bikesharing stations. They concluded that bikesharing stations near metro stations and bicycle infrastructure, as well as higher population and employment lead to higher utilization. Moreover, they found that in residential areas the number of trips is higher during the nonworking days. Wang et al. (2015) developed OLS regression models to measure the impact of the number of businesses on yearly total trips of the bikesharing system Nice Rides in Minneapolis—St. Paul. Their results show that the number of trips is positively correlated with restaurants and jobs accessibility near the stations, but not with general retail establishments. Demand is correlated with age, proximity to the CBD, water, accessibility to trails and distance to other bike stations. Faghih-Imani et al. (2017) built a mixed-linear model to measure the impact of sociodemographic, land-use and arrival/departures on bikesharing demand, using data from Sevilla and Barcelona. Moreover, they developed a bikesharing rebalancing framework, based on a binary logit model that identifies rebalancing periods, as well as a regression model that predicts the amount of rebalancing. They found that station density, capacity, share of POIs from businesses, restaurants and recreation have significant positive impact on the number of arrival and departures.

Chaniotakis et al. (2019) employed statistical and machine learning algorithms to measure the correlation between SBBS arrivals and departures and built environmental factors of six German and three European and North American cities. They developed 324 models in total for the number of arrivals and departures, workday, Saturday and Sunday, time of day (morning, afternoon), peak/off-peak, using three modeling methodologies [stepwise OLS, generalized linear models (GLM) and GBM] and three transformation techniques (logarithmic, Box Cox, and without transformation). The results of the models indicate that city population, distance to the CBD, bicycle parking, memorials, bakeries, residential areas and carsharing stations repetitively

TABLE 10.3 Distance of impact from rail stations.

Study	Buffer distance (m)
Schmoeller and Bogenberger (2014)	400
Noland et al. (2016)	400
Wang et al. (2015)	400
Tran et al. (2015)	300
Chardon et al. (2017)	300
Faghih-Imani et al. (2014)	250
El-Assi et al. (2017)	200

appear as significant and important in the statistical and machine learning models respectively. Table 10.3 shows the distance of impact to rail stations for bikesharing adoption.

6. Conclusion

Car- and bikesharing are forms of emerging transportation systems that combine the positive characteristics of public and private transport: economy, ecology, flexibility, coverage, and speed. In this chapter, the most recent literature focusing on the factors that affect the adoption and deployment of vehicle-sharing systems are reviewed. These factors are either endogenous (i.e., physical and institutional design) or exogenous to the system (e.g., population density, demographics, urban and spatial characteristics). The optimal deployment of car- and bikesharing vehicles and stations is a determining factor for their success.

The literature review shows that active car- and bikesharing users share similar demographic characteristics. More specifically, students, people up to 21 years old, those who belong to two-member households or have mid- to low-income, show greater preference. Moreover, people who drive between 100 and 150 km per day have higher potential to join carsharing, while environmentally conscious commuters, who mainly use public transport for their daily trips to work, show preference to bikesharing.

The successful implementation and development of vehicle-sharing systems is significantly dependent on the optimal deployment of the fleet. Age of the neighborhood inhabitants, density of population and jobs, household size share and land use share, are important determinants. The deployment of bikes and docking stations near public transportation infrastructure, such as subway and rail stations, as well as near restaurants, universities, cinemas, student residences, leads to higher demand for the system. Weather has a short-term impact on vehicle-sharing demand, with low temperature and high speed of wind to affect negatively. Previous studies have shown that carsharing replaces taxi for trips to social activities and entertainment, therefore the deployment of vehicles in areas with high number of commercial enterprises and short distance to restaurants and coffee shops, increases the potential of higher adoption. The use of smart interface technologies that facilitate check-in and checkout, parking flexibility, and high availability of vehicles have a positive impact.

References

Barth, M., Shaheen, S., 2002. Shared vehicle systems: framework for classifying carsharing, station cars, and combined approaches. Transportation Research Record: Journal of the Transportation Research Board 1791, 105–112. Transportation Research Board of the National Academies, Washington, DC.

Buettner, J., Petersen, T., 2011. Optimising Bike Sharing in European Cities: A Handbook. OBIS.

Burkhardt, J., Millard-Ball, A., 2006. Who's attracted to car-sharing? Transportation research record. Journal of the Transportation Research Board 1986, 98–105. Transportation Research Board of the National Academies, Washington, DC.

Caulfield, B., O'Mahony, M., Brazil, W., Weldon, P., 2017. Examining usage patterns of a bike-sharing scheme in a medium sized city. Transportation Research Part A: Policy and Practice 100, 152–161.

Celsor, C., Millard-Ball, A., 2007. Where does carsharing work?: using geographic information systems to assess market potential. Transportation Research Record: Journal of the Transportation Research Board 61–69.

Chaniotakis, E., Duran-Rodas, D., Antoniou, C., 2019. Built environment factors affecting bike sharing ridership: a data-driven approach for multiple cities. Transportation Research Record: Journal of the Transportation Research Board.

Chardon, C.M.D., Caruso, G., Thomas, I., 2017. Bicycle sharing system 'success' determinants. Transportation Research Part A: Policy and Practice 100, 202–214.

Cheng, M., 2016. Sharing economy: a review and agenda for future research. International Journal of Hospitality Management 57, 60–70.

Ciari, F., Balmer, M., Axhausen, K.W., 2009. Concepts for large scale car-sharing system: modelling and evaluation with an agent-based approach. In: Proceedings of the 88th Annual Meeting of the Transportation Research Board. Washington, DC, January.

Cohen, A., Shaheen, S., McKenzie, R., 2008. Carsharing: A Guide for Local Planners, Research Report UCD-ITS-RP-08-16. Institute of Transportation Studies. University of California, Davis.

Comendador, J., Lopez-Lambas, M.E., Monzon, A., 2014. Urban built environment analysis: evidence from a mobility survey in madrid. Procedia - Social and Behavioral Sciences 160, 362–371.

Efthymiou, D., Antoniou, C., 2016. Modeling the propensity to join carsharing using hybrid choice models and mixed survey data. Transport Policy 51, 143–149.

Efthymiou, D., Antoniou, C., Waddell, P., 2013. Factors affecting the adoption of vehicle sharing systems by young drivers. Transport Policy 29, 64–73.

El-Assi, W., Mahmoud, M., Habib, K., 2017. Effects of built environment and weather on bike sharing demand: a station level analysis of commercial bike sharing in toronto. Transportation 44 (3), 589−613.

European Environment Agency, 2010. Tracking Progress Towards Kyoto and 2020 Targets in Europe. EEA Report 7.

European Environment Agency, 2014. Tracking Progress Towards Kyoto and 2020 Targets in Europe. EEA Report 7.

Faghih-Imani, A., Eluru, N., 2016. Incorporating the impact of spatio-temporal interactions on bicycle sharing system demand: a case study of New York citibike system. Journal of Transport Geography 54, 218−227.

Faghih-Imani, A., Eluru, N., El-Geneidy, A.M., Rabbat, M., Haq, U., 2014. How land-use and urban form impact bicycle flows: evidence from the bicycle-sharing system (bixi) in Montreal. Journal of Transport Geography 41, 306−314.

Faghih-Imani, A., Hampshire, R., Marla, L., Eluru, N., 2017. An empirical analysis of bike sharing usage and rebalancing: evidence from Barcelona and Seville. Transportation Research Part A: Policy and Practice 97 (Suppl. C), 177−191.

Firnkorn, J., 2012. Triangulation of two methods measuring the impacts of a free-floating carsharing system in Germany. Transportation Research Part A: Policy and Practice 46 (10), 1654−1672.

Firnkorn, J., Mueller, M., 2011. What will be the environmental effects of new free-floating carsharing systems? The case of car2go in Ulm. Ecological Economics 70 (8), 1519−1528.

Fishman, E., Washington, S., Haworth, N., 2013. Bike share: a synthesis of the literature. Transport Reviews 33 (2), 148−165.

Fishman, E., Washington, S., Haworth, N., 2014. Bike share's impact on car use: evidence from the United States, great Britain, and Australia. Transportation Research Part D: Transport and Environment 31, 13−20.

Giesel, F., Nobis, C., 2016. The impact of carsharing on car ownership in German cities. Transportation Research Procedia 19, 215−224. Transforming Urban Mobility. mobil.TUM 2016. International Scientific Conference on Mobility and Transport. Conference Proceedings.

Institute for Transportation and Development Policy (ITDP), 2013. The Bike-Share Planning Guide. ITDP Report. Available online: https://itdpdotorg.wpengine.com/wp-content/uploads/2014/07/ITDP-Bike-Share-Planning-Guide-1.pdf.

Kang, J., Hwang, K., Park, S., 2016. Finding factors that influence carsharing usage: case study in seoul. Sustainability 8, 709.

Kent, J.L., 2014. Carsharing as active transport: what are the potential health benefits? Journal of Transport and Health 1 (1), 54−62.

Kopp, J., Gerike, R., Axhausen, K.W., 2015. Do sharing people behave differently? An empirical evaluation of the distinctive mobility patterns of free-floating car-sharing members. Transportation 42 (3), 449−469.

Kortum, K., Schoenduwe, R., Stolte, B., Bock, B., 2016. Free-floating carsharing: city-specific growth rates and success factors. Transportation Research Procedia 19, 328−340.

Lane, C., 2005. PhillyCarShare: first-year social and mobility impacts of carsharing in Philadelphia, Pennsylvania. Transportation Research Record: Journal of the Transportation Research Board 1927, 158−166. Transportation Research Board of the National Academies, Washington, DC.

Litman, T.A., June 8, 2011. Pay-As-You-Drive Pricing for Insurance Affordability. Victoria Transport Policy Institute Report. Available online. http://vtpi.org/payd_aff.pdf.

Martin, A.W., Shaheen, A., 2011. Greenhouse gas emission impacts of carsharing in North America. IEEE Transactions on Intelligent Transportation Systems 12 (4). Dec 2011.

Martin, E., Shaheen, S.A., Lidicker, J., 2010. Carsharings's impact on household vehicle holdings: results from a North American shared-use vehicle survey. Transportation Research Record: Journal of the Transportation Research Board 2143, 150–158. Transportation Research Board of the National Academies, Washington, DC.

Mattson, J., Godavarthy, R., 2017. Bike share in fargo, north dakota: keys to success and factors affecting ridership. Sustainable Cities and Society 34, 174–182.

Meddin, R., DeMaio, P., 2015. The Bike-Sharing World Map. http://www.metrobike.net.

Millard-Ball, A., Murray, G., ter Schure, J., Fox, C., Burkhardt, J., 2005. Car-sharing: where and how it succeeds. Transit Cooperative Research Program (TCRP) Report 108.

Millard-Ball, A., Murray, G., ter Schure, J., 2006. Car-sharing as a parking management strategy. In: Proceedings of the 85th Annual Meeting of the Transportation Research Board, Washington, DC.

Morency, C., Trépanier, M., Martin, B., 2008. Object-oriented analysis of a car sharing system. Transportation Research Record: Journal of the Transportation Research Board 2063, 105–112. Transportation Research Board of the National Academies, Washington, DC.

Noland, R.B., Smart, M.J., Guo, Z., 2016. Bikeshare trip generation in New York City. Transportation Research Part A: Policy and Practice 94, 164–181.

Pal, A., Zhang, Y., 2017. Free-floating bike sharing: solving real-life large-scale static rebalancing problems. Transportation Research Part C: Emerging Technologies 80, 92–116.

Philipsen, R., Brell, T., Ziefle, M., 2019. Carriage without a driver – user requirements for intelligent autonomous mobility services. In: Stanton, N.A. (Ed.), Advances in Human Aspects of Transportation [electronic Resource]. Springer, Cham, pp. 339–350. https://doi.org/10.1007/978-3-319-93885-1 vol. 786 of Advances in Intelligent Systems and Computing, 2194–5357.

Reiss, S., Bogenberger, K., 2017. A relocation strategy for munich's bike sharing system: combining an operator-based and a user-based scheme. Transportation Research Procedia 22, 105–114.

Rodier, C., 2009. Review of the international modelling literature: transit, land use, and auto pricing strategies to reduce vehicle miles traveled and greenhouse gas emissions. Transportation Research Record: Journal of the Transportation Research Board 2123, 1–12. Transportation Research Board of the National Academies, Washington, DC.

Rodier, C., Shaheen, S., January 2004. Carsharing and carfree housing: predicted travel, emission, and economic benefits. A case study of the Sacramento, California region. In: Proceedings of the 83th Annual Meeting of the Transportation Research Board, Washington, DC.

Schmoeller, S., Bogenberger, K., 2014. Analyzing external factors on the spatial and temporal demand of car sharing systems. Procedia - Social and Behavioral Sciences 111, 8–17.

Schmoeller, S., Weikl, S., Mueller, J., Bogenberger, K., 2015. Empirical analysis of free-floating carsharing usage: the munich and berlin case. Transportation Research Part C: Emerging Technologies 56, 34–51.

Seign, R., Schueßler, M., Bogenberger, K., 2015. Enabling sustainable transportation: tThe model-based determination of business/operating areas of free-floating carsharing systems. Research in Transportation Economics 51, 104–114. Austerity and Sustainable Transportation.

Shaheen, S., Chan, N., 2015. Mobility and the Sharing Economy: Impacts Synopsis. Transportation Sustainability Research Center, University of California, Berkeley. http://tsrc.berkeley.edu/sites/default/files/Innovative-Mobility-Industry-Outlook SM-Spring-2015.pdf.

Shaheen, S., Cohen, A., 2007. Growth in worldwide carsharing: an International comparison. Transportation Research Record: Journal of the Transportation Research Board vol. 1992, 81–89. Transportation Research Board of the National Academies, Washington, DC.

Shaheen, S.A., Cohen, A.P., 2012. Carsharing and personal vehicle services: worldwide market developments and emerging trends. International Journal of Sustainable Transportation 7 (1), 5–34.

Shaheen, S., Cohen, A., Chung, M., 2009. North American carsharing: a ten-year retrospective. Transportation Research Record: Journal of the Transportation Research Board 2110, 35–44. Transportation Research Board of the National Academies, Washington, DC.

Shaheen, S., Guzman, S., Zhang, H., 2010a. Bikesharing in Europe, the Americas and Asia: past, present and future. Transportation Research Record: Journal of the Transportation Research Board 2143, 159–167. Transportation Research Board of the National Academies, Washington, DC.

Shaheen, S., Cohen, A.P., Martin, E., 2010b. Carsharing parking policy: review of North American practices and San Francisco Bay area case study. Transportation Research Record: Journal of the Transportation Research Board 2187, 146–156. Transportation Research Board of the National Academies, Washington, DC.

Shaheen, S., Rodier, C., Murray, G., Cohen, G., Martin, E., 2010c. Carsharing and Public Parking Policies: Assessing Benefits, Costs, and Best Practices in North America. Report CA-MTI-10-2612. Mineta Transportation Institute.

Shaheen, S., Hua, Z., Elliot, M.G.S., 2011. Hangzhou public bicycle: understanding early adoption and behavioral response to bikesharing in Hangzhou, China. Transportation Research Record: Journal of the Transportation Research Board. Transportation Research Board of the National Academies, Washington, DC.

Shaheen, S., Martin, E., Cohen, A., Finson, R., 2012. Public Bikesharing in North America: Early Operator and User Understanding, MTI Report 11-19. Technical report, Mineta Transportation Institute.

Tran, T.D., Ovtracht, N., d'Arcier, B.F., 2015. Modeling bike sharing system using built environment factors. Procedia CIRP 30, 293–298, 7th Industrial Product-Service Systems Conference - PSS, Industry Transformation for Sustainability and Business.

Walsh, M., 1990. Global trends in motor vehicle use and emissions. Annual Review of Energy 15, 217–243.

Wang, X., Lindsey, G., Schoner, J., Harrison, A., 2015. Modeling bike share station activity: effects of nearby businesses and jobs on trips to and from stations. Journal of Urban Planning and Development 142 (1), 04015001.

Weikl, S., Bogenberger, K., 2013. Relocation strategies and algorithms for free-floating car sharing systems. IEEE Intelligent Transportation Systems Magazine 5 (4), 100–111.

Willing, C., Klemmer, K., Brandt, T., Neumann, D., 2017. Moving in time and space-location intelligence for carsharing decision support. Decision Support Systems 99, 75–85. Location Analytics and Decision Support.

Zhao, J., Deng, W., Song, Y., 2014. Ridership and effectiveness of bikesharing: the effects of urban features and system characteristics on daily use and turnover rate of public bikes in China. Transport Policy 35, 253–264.

Zhou, B., Kockelman, K., Gao, R., 2011. Opportunities for and impacts of carsharing: a survey of the Austin, Texas market. International Journal of Sustainable Transport 5 (3), 135–152.

Chapter 11

Carsharing: An overview on what we know

Stefan Schmöller, Klaus Bogenberger

Department of Civil Engineering and Environmental Sciences, Bundeswehr University Munich, Bavaria, Germany

Chapter outline

1. Introduction

Carsharing is a form of mobility that emerged within the last couple of decades. It is based on the idea that, in most cases, having access to a car is sufficient, while owning a car is not necessary. For this purpose, a carsharing organization (CSO) provides cars that can be used by each assigned member of (person that signs up) this organization. Therefore, users are given the opportunity to take a car whenever they need or want to use one. Although carsharing is not entirely new, it took until the late 1980s for it to finally start off. The very first known carsharing initiative was the Sefage ("Selbstfahrergenossenschaft") that was founded by a housing cooperative in Zürich in 1948 (Harms and Truffer, 1998) and operated until 1998. Further carsharing organizations started throughout the following decades, however, all of them had to close down after some time. The oldest CSO still operating today is the Mobility Cooperative in Switzerland that originated from the merger of the two carsharing initiatives Sharecom and ATG ("AutoTeilet-Genossenschaft"), both founded in 1987 (Harms and Truffer, 1998). In the following years, carsharing spread all over the world with many new CSOs emerging. Yet it

Demand for Emerging Transportation Systems. https://doi.org/10.1016/B978-0-12-815018-4.00011-5

took several more years until carsharing experienced its greatest boom in the late 2000s and especially the early 2010s. This boom was made possible by the emergence of mobile internet and smartphones and predominantly driven by new business models and the market entry of car manufacturers. As of 2016, there were CSOs in 46 countries with about 15 million members and more than 157,000 vehicles in operation (Shaheen et al., 2018a). Within this chapter, several results on different topics concerning carsharing are presented and linked with results of other studies. This aims to give a better understanding of how carsharing systems work and which problems still exist. The rest of this chapter is structured as follows: In the first part different forms of carsharing systems will be introduced. After that, some results on who uses carsharing and how carsharing is being used are presented. Finally, the vehicle relocation problem will be covered. In carsharing, this problem is one of the most researched topics and crucial for any CSO as relocations of vehicles are sometimes necessary to ensure availability.

2. The systems

There exist various types of carsharing services that are characterized by different policies e.g., for renting and returning vehicles or price structures. In this part, the main types of carsharing and some mixed forms will be introduced. The main characteristics are presented in order to easily distinguish the various types in the rest of this chapter. Apart from the very first carsharing initiatives like Sefage that operated on a private and cooperative basis, the oldest corporate CSOs like the Mobility Cooperative can be attributed to the so-called station-based carsharing. Other organizations using this form of carsharing are e.g., Zipcar, Cambio or Flinkster. In its original form (a more flexible one, allowing one-way trips, will be presented later in this part), this type of carsharing is very similar to traditional car rental services. The CSO owns or rents parking spaces, called stations, and distributes their vehicles among these. Users can then reserve available vehicles via internet and/or a smartphone application by stating the station at which they want to start their trip at as well as the expected start and end time. In this type of carsharing, users usually have to pay both for trip duration and mileage. All other costs like gasoline, insurance or cleaning are included in these fees. Many CSOs provide different car types (mostly at different prices) at each station, allowing a user to choose the one that is most suitable for the proposed usage. At the end of each trip, the vehicle has to be returned to the same station where the trip started. All the mentioned features are still very similar to car rental. Therefore, the differences between carsharing and car rental shall be pointed out by citing the explanation in (Millard-Ball et al., 2005): *"Three key differences distinguish car-sharing from traditional car rentals, its closest equivalent: short-term rentals; a decentralized, self-accessing network of vehicles; and the bundling of gasoline and insurance into rates. In addition, the primary purpose of car-sharing is often to provide an alternative to vehicle ownership. In contrast, most rental firms have centralized facilities, particularly in airports and downtowns, require a staff member to check the vehicle out, and offer minimum rental increments of 24 h. As a result, rental firms tend to cater far more to business travelers and other visitors, and people who need a replacement car, rather than occasional, short-duration trips by local residents — the core market for car-sharing operators."* The next and most important step in the development of the carsharing industry was taken when Daimler entered the market with its subsidiary car2go in the year 2009. car2go was the first CSO that offered free-floating carsharing. Apart from car2go, the best-known CSO offering free-floating carsharing is DriveNow, a subsidiary of BMW and Sixt. In this type of carsharing the organization usually does not acquire their own parking spaces but instead the public parking spaces available within the cities are used. The CSO defines an operating area wherein the vehicles are distributed freely. Users can then search for available vehicles on the internet and/or a smartphone application. In contrast to station-based carsharing, a reservation can be made in advance but is not obligatory. In most cases it is quite the contrary. A reservation can be made free of charge only for a short time (reflecting the time that is needed to reach a car, e.g., 15 min) but has to be paid if it exceeds this period. Instead, each car has a display showing its reservation status so that it can be taken on the spot if currently free. The user can then unlock the car using either a smartphone application or an ID-card they obtained from the CSO. Ending a reservation is very similar. The vehicle can be parked at any public parking space within the operating area and locked via the application or the ID-card. In free-floating carsharing, mileage usually is included in the fees as long as it does not exceed a predefined limit. The users only have to pay for the duration of the trip. As with station-based carsharing, all other costs are included as well. Between these two main types of carsharing several others emerged, mostly by combining single features of the two presented types. One of these hybrid-types is an area-based carsharing like e.g., Flinkster in Munich. Each car of their fleet is assigned to an area where it has to be returned to but within this area each public parking space can be used. Another type of system that is in operation today (e.g., by BlueSG in Singapore) is one-way station-based carsharing. As with traditional station-based carsharing, there are several stations throughout a city where a trip can be started. The difference is that cars can be returned at any station, so customers are allowed to make one-way trips. But with adopting the higher flexibility of one-way trips, also the drawback of possible vehicle imbalances is inherited in this case. Other mixed types could also be possible, e.g., combing a free-floating carsharing area in the center of the city with stations in the outer parts, but the majority of CSOs chooses one of the two main types. In the presented forms of carsharing, the vehicles are owned by the CSO, yet another alternative emerged in the past years with peer-to-peer carsharing. In this type of carsharing, users can offer their private cars for rental in times they don't need it themselves. They are even allowed to set the price for renting their vehicle themselves. The operator then obtains a fixed rate of the total price of each rental. Companies offering this type (e.g., Turo) are mainly responsible for two things: providing insurance for the private cars and matching people in need of a car with the ones offering one.

3. Characterization of carsharing users

For any CSO, it is very important to know, who is most likely to join (and use) their carsharing service. This way it is possible to identify cities and parts of cities where carsharing is most likely to be successful. For this purpose, several studies—some of which will be mentioned later—performed surveys with carsharing users. Most of these studies focused either on the demographics of the users or (changes in) their mobility behavior. These studies identified some key characteristics that seem to give a good idea of who carsharing customers are.

3.1 Demographics

Being a rather new form of mobility, it was challenging to predict who would become a carsharing user. In order to answer this question, several studies tried to identify demographic characteristics of users. The authors of this chapter participated in a research project called WiMobil, which tried to estimate the effects of carsharing on traffic and environment (BMUB Bundesministerium für Umwelt, Naturschutz, Bau und Reaktorsicherheit, 2016). One part of this project was a survey with users of the two CSOs Flinkster and DriveNow in the German cities of Munich and Berlin conducted by the German Aerospace Center (Deutsches Zentrum für Luft- und Raumfahrt; DLR). DriveNow offers a free-floating carsharing in both cities whereas Flinkster offers a traditional station-based service in Berlin and an area-based type in Munich. The results of this survey could be used to identify differences between users of the different carsharing systems. The most important questions that are posed in almost any survey among carsharing users concern the age structure, educational level, income, and household size of users. These are the key characteristics that can be used to identify new (parts of) cities where carsharing is most likely going to be successful. Fig. 11.1 is taken from the final report of the mentioned research project (BMUB Bundesministerium für Umwelt, Naturschutz, Bau und Reaktorsicherheit, 2016) and shows the age structure of the carsharing users of DriveNow and Flinkster.

It is apparent that there are substantial differences between the users of the free-floating system and the station/area-based system considering the age structure. The majority of DriveNow users are relatively young with more than 40% in the age group between 25 and 34 and an average age of 36. In contrast,

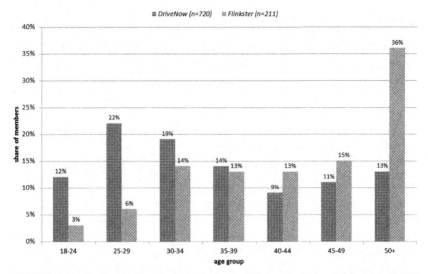

FIGURE 11.1   Distribution of carsharing members on different age groups. *Adapted from BMUB Bundesministerium für Umwelt, Naturschutz, Bau und Reaktorsicherheit, 2016. Wirkung von E-Car Sharing Systemen auf Mobilität und Umwelt in urbanen Räumen (WiMobil). Technical Report, Retrieved 07 April 2019: https://www.erneuerbar-mobil.de/sites/default/files/2016-10/Abschlussbericht_WiMobil.pdf.*

most Flinkster users are at least 50 years old and the average age is 45. Most of the other key characteristics show high similarities between the two systems. The majority of users are male, well educated (over 70% with a university degree), live in a small household (one or two persons), and have an above-average income (BMUB Bundesministerium für Umwelt, Naturschutz, Bau und Reaktorsicherheit, 2016; Giesel and Nobis, 2016). All of these key characteristics seem to be transferable as other user surveys obtain very similar results (Millard-Ball et al., 2005; Martin and Shaheen, 2011b; Wittwer and Hubrich, 2018; infas et al., 2018). It even seems that the demographic attributes of users are very common for all types of carsharing as a survey among users of peer-to-peer carsharing shows similar distributions (Shaheen et al., 2018b).

3.2 Mobility behavior

Until now, carsharing has become most successful in big cities. Although most of these cities also have a very good public transportation system, they often suffer from traffic problems like frequent traffic congestions or a lack of parking possibilities. It is obvious that carsharing reinforces these problems at the beginning as additional cars are brought into the city. Nevertheless, the more important question for researchers concerns what the long-term effects will be. On the one hand, some critics claim that carsharing incites people to use cars for trips they would have made by e.g., public transport or bike otherwise. On the other hand, carsharing can encourage people to discard cars that are rarely used. Due to these diverse opinions, several studies address the mobility behavior of carsharing users and the influence of carsharing on it. In the following, the focus will be on the modal split, trip purposes and car ownership of users.

3.3 Modal split of carsharing users

In order to describe the mobility behavior, several studies (BMUB Bundes-ministerium für Umwelt, Naturschutz, Bau und Reaktorsicherheit, 2016; Wittwer and Hubrich, 2018; Cervero et al., 2007) determine the modal split of carsharing users. At first glance, these studies seem to show that carsharing users use public transport and nonmotorized transport very often. Using the data from the German study MiD 2017 (infas et al., 2018), it is possible to take a closer look at the modal split. As the majority of carsharing users live in metropolitan areas (about 66% of registered members; the share of active members may be even higher), their modal split should be compared to the modal split of nonusers living in metropolitan areas. This comparison can be found in Fig. 11.2.

It is easy to see that the modal split of carsharing users strongly differs from the whole population of Germany, but it is fairly comparable to nonusers living in metropolitan areas. The main differences indeed show in a higher use of bike and public transport whereas cars are used less often. This suggests that the mobility behavior of carsharing users is more environmentally friendly.

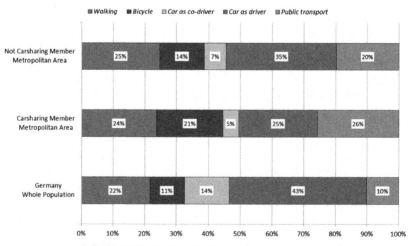

FIGURE 11.2 Modal split of selected groups of persons.

However, it is uncertain, if carsharing is the reason why their modal split is different. In order to find an answer to that question, researchers tried to find out how the mobility behavior of carsharing users changed compared to the time before their carsharing membership (Millard-Ball et al., 2005; Martin and Shaheen, 2011a). Even though the results in these papers are not entirely consistent, they indicate a modal shift from private cars toward nonmotorized modes or public transport. But even if these shifts may be caused by substantial changes in the mobility behavior of some individuals, they are far too small to affect the network of a whole city. Such an effect could potentially be prompted by a significant upscaling of carsharing fleet sizes but it is up to future research to work out whether the effects also scale up the same way.

3.4 Trip purposes

One of the most important arguments for usage of carsharing is that it can fill a mobility gap. Carsharing can enable people who cannot afford a privately owned vehicle (or do not want to have one e.g., because no private parking space is available) to use a car when they think they need one. This could be the case e.g., when heavy goods are to be transported. Yet, for the majority of carsharing users this might not be such a big problem given that they earn an above-average income as mentioned earlier. Therefore, the distribution of trip purposes could help to get an even better idea of why people use carsharing. Several studies dealt with this topic both for station-based (Millard-Ball et al., 2005; Cervero et al., 2007; Le Vine et al., 2013) and free-floating carsharing (Wittwer and Hubrich, 2018). In the already mentioned research project WiMobil, surveys were conducted with members of both types of carsharing. The resulting distribution of trip purposes (values add up to more than 100% since multiple answers were allowed) can be seen in Fig. 11.3.

As to be expected, some differences between the two types of carsharing are very apparent. The greatest differences occur with trips going home or to work. This is not surprising since both are typical one-way trips that are not allowed in the station-based carsharing system. The other trip types show similar frequencies except for social/recreational trips and shopping trips. As those two types can each be seen as a collective term for several underlying purposes, the survey also went more into depth at these points as illustrated in Figs. 11.4A and 11.4B.

These more detailed explanations show that the different types of carsharing are indeed used for different trip purposes. Station-based carsharing is used more often for sports, recreation, and especially weekend trips. All these trips usually are round-trips taking longer with extended parking periods of the vehicles. Due to the pricing structure, for the user, it is advantageous to use a station-based carsharing system for such trips. The same goes for the long-term needs. Shopping of long-term needs (like clothes or furniture) usually takes more time (especially longer parking periods) than the regular shopping

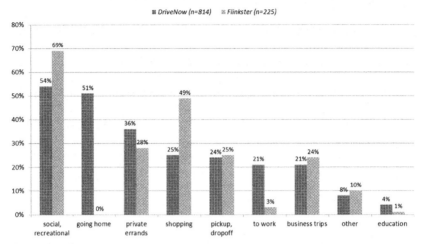

FIGURE 11.3 Trip purposes in carsharing. *Adapted from BMUB Bundesministerium für Umwelt, Naturschutz, Bau und Reaktorsicherheit, 2016. Wirkung von E-Car Sharing Systemen auf Mobilität und Umwelt in urbanen Räumen (WiMobil). Technical Report, Retrieved 07 April 2019: https:// www.erneuerbar-mobil.de/sites/default/files/2016-10/Abschlussbericht_WiMobil.pdf.*

trip e.g., for groceries. In contrast, free-floating carsharing favors typical evening activities like going to a bar, disco, restaurant or attending a cultural event. Even if there is a need to return home after these activities as well, a possible application could be to use carsharing for the way there, have something to drink and take public transport or taxi for the way home. The only purpose that shows a high ratio in both systems is to visit friends. This may be due to the fact that it usually is a round-trip but as visiting friends may

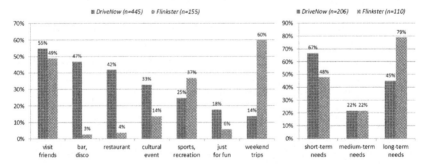

FIGURE 11.4 (A) Detailed usage of carsharing for social/recreational trips (left) and (B) Detailed usage of carsharing für shopping trips (right). *Both adapted from BMUB Bundesministerium für Umwelt, Naturschutz, Bau und Reaktorsicherheit, 2016. Wirkung von E-Car Sharing Systemen auf Mobilität und Umwelt in urbanen Räumen (WiMobil). Technical Report, Retrieved 07 April 2019: https://www.erneuerbar-mobil.de/sites/default/files/2016-10/Abschlussbericht_WiMobil.pdf.*

take some time, it would again be possible to use a free-floating car for the way there and another mode or a new carsharing vehicle for the return trip.

3.5 Influence on car ownership

One last topic that should be discussed here concerns the influence of carsharing on private car ownership. Using the data of the MiD 2017 (infas et al., 2018) again, it is safe to say that carsharing users own less cars than the rest of the population. While carsharing users own 0.6 cars per household, the average is 0.9 for people living in metropolitan areas. A similar ratio in car ownership is shown in several other studies (BMUB Bundesministerium für Umwelt, Naturschutz, Bau und Reaktorsicherheit, 2016; Wittwer and Hubrich, 2018; Cervero et al., 2007) as well. But again, it is hard to tell if carsharing was the reason for this difference. Carsharing may especially attract people without cars who get the opportunity to use a car when needed. If this is the case, carsharing would not be the reason for the low ratio of car ownership. But there also are people who change their car ownership because of carsharing. Some people could purposely shed cars they rarely used, or forego a planned purchase as they realize that carsharing is sufficient. But for others carsharing may also be the reason for buying a car as they realize that they would benefit from owning a private vehicle. A lot of studies tried to determine the balance between purchased and sold cars. This may be because a high number of discarded cars would be a very positive political message that could help in spreading carsharing even further. Three studies presenting very good literature reviews about this topic are (Millard-Ball et al., 2005) for literature before 2005 and (Shaheen et al., 2009; Chen and Kockelman, 2015) for more recent literature. Almost all references cited in these papers show a very high number of shed cars per user or carsharing vehicle, respectively. Yet, these values should be treated with caution. On the one hand, there is no consistent procedure for these surveys and the resulting values show a wide range. On the other hand, an exact elicitation is very hard as both purchased and sold cars should be incorporated into the balance. For an even better estimate, foregone purchases or sells should also be considered. Additionally, each car should be taken into account only with the share to which carsharing influenced the decision to purchase or sell, respectively. However, this is almost impossible as few people would be able to claim that the influence of carsharing could be put to a number of e.g., 10%. Therefore, these studies may give a reasonable estimate for the balance but even if the results are very positive, the drawbacks in their investigation methods should always be kept in mind.

4. Carsharing usage

With carsharing spreading more and more, researchers also had a higher interest on how carsharing is being used. Therefore, researchers had to find ways to obtain the usage data of CSOs. Some researchers (including the authors of this chapter) managed to agree to cooperate with CSOs whereas others acquired the data as well by repeatedly retrieving information from the web pages and reconstructing the data. With real usage data it is possible to identify usage patterns and interpret them in accordance with the results of the surveys. The patterns that are easiest to identify are the temporal ones. Grouping the trip data by means of weekdays or time of the day provides very characteristic trajectories. Figs. 11.5 and 11.6 are each generated by using the starting times of all trips and show how carsharing trips in Munich are distributed over time. Again, the figures are taken from the final report of the project WiMobil (BMUB Bundesministerium für Umwelt, Naturschutz, Bau und Reaktorsicherheit, 2016). As in this report it shows that the differences between the observed cities, Munich and Berlin, are only marginal, only the graphs for Munich are depicted here. For better comparability the axes of cohesive graphs are adapted even if another scaling would be preferable for a single graph.

The above figures reflect the trip purposes mentioned earlier. Free-floating carsharing is used more often for commuting trips and has its main trip purpose in recreational activities. Therefore, a lot of trips on workdays are taking place at times when most people start or finish working. Moreover, the recreational activities mentioned in the section about trip purposes are more often typical activities on (weekend) evenings, what explains that the highest share of trips is seen between 6 and 9 p.m. and that a substantial share of trips is done during night hours. The trajectories for station-based carsharing can be explained in a similar way. There is a very high number of trips starting on Saturday (especially before noon) that can be explained by the high ratio of weekend trips and shopping trips for long-term needs. As with the trip purposes, similar temporal patterns of carsharing trips were also detected in other

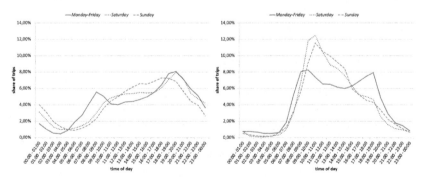

FIGURE 11.5 Carsharing usage in the course of a day differentiated between workday, Saturday and Sunday for DriveNow (left) and Flinkster (right). *Adapted from BMUB Bundesministerium für Umwelt, Naturschutz, Bau und Reaktorsicherheit, 2016. Wirkung von E-Car Sharing Systemen auf Mobilität und Umwelt in urbanen Räumen (WiMobil). Technical Report, Retrieved 07 April 2019: https://www.erneuerbar-mobil.de/sites/default/files/2016-10/Abschlussbericht_WiMobil.pdf.*

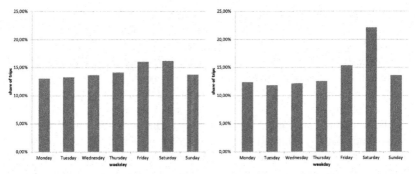

FIGURE 11.6   Carsharing usage in the course of a week for DriveNow (left) and Flinkster (right). *Adapted from BMUB Bundesministerium für Umwelt, Naturschutz, Bau und Reaktorsicherheit, 2016. Wirkung von E-Car Sharing Systemen auf Mobilität und Umwelt in urbanen Räumen (WiMobil). Technical Report, Retrieved 07 April 2019: https://www.erneuerbar-mobil.de/sites/default/files/2016-10/Abschlussbericht_WiMobil.pdf.*

studies throughout the world (see (Costain et al., 2012; Leclerc et al., 2013; Concas et al., 2013) for station-based carsharing and (Sprei, 2019) for free-floating carsharing). The different trip purposes for those two types of carsharing are also reflected in the distributions of trip durations and distances. Comparing Munich and Berlin again shows that the distributions are very similar except that Munich shows a small peak for trips going to the airport. As the rest of the trajectory is almost identical only the duration and distance distributions for Munich are shown in Figs. 11.7A and 11.7B taken from the final report of WiMobil (BMUB Bundesministerium für Umwelt, Naturschutz, Bau und Reaktorsicherheit, 2016).

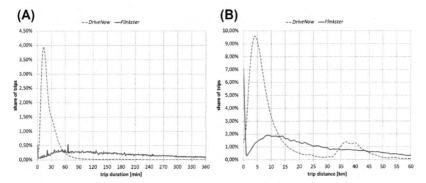

FIGURE 11.7   (A) Distribution of trip durations for DriveNow and Flinkster (left) and (B) Distribution of trip distances for DriveNow and Flinkster (right). *Both adapted from BMUB Bundesministerium für Umwelt, Naturschutz, Bau und Reaktorsicherheit, 2016. Wirkung von E-Car Sharing Systemen auf Mobilität und Umwelt in urbanen Räumen (WiMobil). Technical Report, Retrieved 07 April 2019: https://www.erneuerbar-mobil.de/sites/default/files/2016-10/Abschlussbericht_WiMobil.pdf.*

Again, these distributions show very distinct differences between free-floating carsharing and station-based carsharing. These differences can be affiliated to the different pricing models and associated trip purposes. In free-floating carsharing one-way trips are possible and every minute has to be paid for (with a higher price compared to the station-based carsharing system), so the trips tend to be rather short. This also matches the main trip purposes. Most of these (going home, going out, to work) are typical one-way trips where usually no detours are made. In case a return trip has to be made, it usually occurs much later so that an ongoing reservation would be too costly and therefore either another mode is used or another carsharing vehicle has to be found. In station-based carsharing, in contrast, the price per minute is much lower, so the price for a rented vehicle being parked is rather low. The distributions are widely spread with a substantially higher share of long trips. As customers are only allowed to do round-trips, longer-lasting shopping trips or recreational trips with long parking periods are favored by this type of carsharing. As with all the results presented before, these distributions also are in accord with the ones in other studies (Costain et al., 2012; Sprei, 2019; Wielinski et al., 2015). With all the usage data at hand, it is possible to complete the whole picture by taking a look at the spatial distribution of the trips. In a station-based system with round-trips and fixed reservations, this is not of high interest. Operators usually know in advance when and where their cars are going to be available. In free-floating carsharing, however, it is unclear how long a car is going to be rented and where it is going to be returned. The authors conducted a spatial analysis of trip data in (BMUB Bundesministerium für Umwelt, Naturschutz, Bau und Reaktorsicherheit, 2016; Schmöller et al., 2015) and were able to identify some trends in the vehicle movements. It was observed that within a city there are different area types of carsharing usage. In accordance with the trip purposes the most important areas are those with heavy use at any time (characterized by high population density and many shopping possibilities/workplaces), those with higher usage in the mornings (mostly residential) and those with higher usage in the evenings (many shopping possibilities and working places). While the destinations of spare time trips are hard to pinpoint as they can be spread all over the city, these distributions to some degree reflect commuting waves and therefore match a high percentage of the trip purposes of free-floating carsharing.

5. The relocation problem and solution approaches

The mentioned spatial analysis shows that there are opposing waves in vehicle movements. But not all the spatial vehicle movements in a free-floating carsharing system are balanced. From time to time vehicles accumulate at areas where they are not needed at that moment and cause a lack of availability elsewhere. Additionally, single vehicles are sometimes returned at far-off places where they might not be used again for several hours or days. In both cases, the operator may intervene by performing vehicle relocations. In this context, relocating a vehicle means that a car is taken from an area with expected low demand and brought to an area with expected high demand. While this is less of a problem in a station-based carsharing system with only round-trips, any system allowing one-way trips can suffer from this problem. However, the problem is hard to resolve as it has a lot of dimensions that have to be taken into account. At first it is necessary to know which cars are not needed at their current location and should therefore be relocated. Of course, the CSO should also know where the cars should be brought, i.e., the areas where they expect unsatisfied demand. Additionally, the operator has to balance the costs for performing relocations against the expected revenue. However, this task is very difficult as the revenue of a single relocation is very hard to quantify. One indicator may be the idle time of a vehicle after relocation, but it is almost impossible to determine to which extent a single relocation had influence on the following trips or even the whole system. And there are even more tasks to be considered in a relocation strategy, like scheduling of staff and route planning. With all these dimensions it is quite hard to find an optimal relocation strategy. It is even hard to specify a definition of optimal. It could be optimal to minimize costs, to maximize revenue or to satisfy customers i.e., have least possible unsatisfied demand. While finding an optimal or at least best possible relocation strategy is an unpleasant task for CSOs it also constitutes a very interesting research problem that has been addressed in a lot of studies. The most common way to approach this problem is to deploy a mathematical optimization problem (Jorge et al., 2014; Weikl and Bogenberger, 2015; Bruglieri et al., 2018). But even though the basic concept is the same, the exact formulation of the problem can differ a lot. This starts with the objective function, where again a definition of optimal is needed. In the mentioned references costs are offset against revenues to build a composite objective function. And the problem gets even more complex with the constraints as all the dimensions of the problem can be reflected. Therefore, the realizations of the optimization problem are quite different. No matter how the problem is addressed, it is additionally hard to evaluate the effects of relocations. In most cases (e.g., (Jorge et al., 2014; Bruglieri et al., 2018)), the presented relocation strategy was tested using a simulation framework where it could be tested against other strategies or a scenario with no relocations at all. In (Bruglieri et al., 2018) also a set of benchmark instances is used for better comparability between different algorithms. In one very special case also a field trial in cooperation with one CSO was conducted (Weikl and Bogenberger, 2015). All of these references claim that their relocation strategy led to higher revenue for the CSO. By now some CSOs use these or similar algorithms for their relocations but others (additionally) rely on local fleet managers who know their city and use their experience to decide which relocations are making sense.

6. Conclusion

Over the past years, researchers gathered a lot of information about users and usage of carsharing. But even if carsharing is assumed to help reduce traffic problems as well as emissions, it still is more of a side note. The cities with the highest number of carsharing vehicles are mostly very large cities where they only account for a small margin compared to the total number of cars there. And by now these cities are the ones where most CSOs focused on. In rural areas or even small to medium-size cities, the most one can expect to find are few station-based vehicles. But when talking about emissions, rural areas are very important as well. Usually people living there hold more cars and use them more often for longer trips. Yet it is not surprising that carsharing did hardly find its way out of large cities. Even there, despite all the knowledge research has collected, there is no guarantee that carsharing will be profitable in a particular city. So, it is no surprise that in history of carsharing a lot of organizations had to close down or at least withdraw from particular cities. And it falls into line that two of the biggest free-floating CSOs, car2go and DriveNow, just recently decided to build a joint venture. The true reasons for merging are not communicated, but both organizations were said to be unprofitable and this way they should at least be able to cut costs. But yet the market for carsharing is still growing. New organizations and new types of carsharing are introduced all over the world. And some of the older organizations try to keep up with the times and evolve. The Mobility Cooperative now also offers one-way trips between specific stations for one car type, a free-floating scootersharing in Zürich and a platform for carpooling. And with more carsharing vehicles entering the streets, the positive effects of carsharing will hopefully also become more apparent. Additionally, new forms like peer-to-peer carsharing may have further potential to carry carsharing to areas where it was not yet successful. And few years from now the biggest change may be lying ahead. Autonomous vehicles have the potential to substantially change our mobility behavior. With shared autonomous vehicles, private car ownership could become completely obsolete. Whenever a car is needed, it can approach the user and after they finished their trip the car either serves the next customer or relocates itself by driving to where it is most likely going to be needed. This way, an even higher utilization of cars can be achieved. In (Dandl and Bogenberger, 2018) a case study of Munich was conducted and showed that one-shared autonomous vehicle can replace between 2.8 and 3.7 free-floating carsharing vehicles. Assuming this factor could be scaled up to the traffic of a whole city, autonomous vehicles have the potential to resolve traffic problems as well as environmental problems, especially when powered by an electric engine. But as this is still a long way to go, carsharing can at least initiate first small changes on the way to a new mobility.

References

BMUB Bundesministerium für Umwelt, Naturschutz, Bau und Reaktorsicherheit, 2016. Wirkung von E-Car Sharing Systemen auf Mobilität und Umwelt in urbanen Räumen (WiMobil). Technical Report. Retrieved 07 April 2019. https://www.erneuerbar-mobil.de/sites/default/files/2016-10/Abschlussbericht_WiMobil.pdf.

Bruglieri, M., Pezzella, F., Pisacane, O., 2018. A two-phase optimization method for a multi-objective vehicle relocation problem in electric carsharing systems. Journal of Combinatorial Optimization 36 (1), 162–193. https://doi.org/10.1007/s10878-018-0295-5.

Cervero, R., Golub, A., Nee, B., 2007. City Carshare: longer-term travel demand and car ownership impacts. Transportation Research Record 1992 (1), 70–80. https://doi.org/10.3141/1992-09.

Chen, T., Kockelman, K., 2015. Carsharing's Life-cycle impacts on energy use and greenhouse gas emissions. In: Paper Presented at the 94th Annual Meeting of the Transportation Research Board, Washington, D.C.

Concas, S., Barbeau, S., Winters, P., Georggi, N., Bond, J., 2013. Using Mobile Apps to Measure Spatial Travel-Behavior Changes of Carsharing Users. In: Paper Presented at the 92nd Annual Meeting of the Transportation Research Board, Washington, D.C.

Costain, C., Ardron, C., Habib, K., 2012. Synopsis of users' behaviour of a carsharing program: a case study in Toronto. Transportation Research Part A: Policy and Practice 46 (3), 421–434. https://doi.org/10.1016/j.tra.2011.11.005. ISSN 0965-8564.

Dandl, F., Bogenberger, K., 2018. Comparing future autonomous electric taxis with an existing free-floating carsharing system. IEEE Transactions on Intelligent Transportation Systems. https://doi.org/10.1109/TITS.2018.2857208.

Giesel, F., Nobis, C., 2016. The impact of carsharing on car ownership in German cities. Transportation Research Procedia 19, 215–224. https://doi.org/10.1016/j.trpro.2016.12.082. ISSN 2352-1465.

Harms, S., Truffer, B., 1998. The Emergence of a Nation-wide Carsharing Co-operative in Switzerland. Prepared for EAWAG – Eidgenössische Anstalt für Wasserversorgung, Abwasserreinigung und Gewässerschutz, Switzerland.

infas, DLR, IVT, infas 360, 2018. Mobilität in Deutschland (On Behalf of the BMVI).

Jorge, D., Correia, G., Barnhart, C., 2014. Comparing optimal relocation operations with simulated relocation policies in one-way carsharing systems. IEEE Transactions on Intelligent Transportation Systems 15 (4), 1667–1675. https://doi.org/10.1109/TITS.2014.2304358.

Le Vine, S., Sivakumar, A., Polak, J., Lee-Gosselin, M., 2013. The market and impacts of new types of carsharing systems: case study of greater London. In: Paper Presented at the 92nd Annual Meeting of the Transportation Research Board, Washington, D.C.

Leclerc, B., Trépanier, M., Morency, C., 2013. Unraveling the travel behavior of carsharing members from global positioning system traces. In: Paper Presented at the 92nd Annual Meeting of the Transportation Research Board, Washington, D.C.

Martin, E., Shaheen, S., 2011a. The impact of carsharing on public transit and non-motorized travel: an exploration of North American carsharing survey data. Energies 4 (11), 2094–2114. https://doi.org/10.3390/en4112094.

Martin, E., Shaheen, S., 2011b. Greenhouse gas emission impacts of carsharing in North America. IEEE Transactions on Intelligent Transportation Systems 12 (4), 1074–1086. https://doi.org/10.1109/TITS.2011.2158539.

Millard-Ball, M., Murray, G., Ter Schure, J., Fox, C., Burkhardt, J., 2005. Car-Sharing: Where and How it Succeeds. Transit Cooperative Research Program (TCRP) Report 108. Transportation Research Board, Washington.

Schmöller, S., Weikl, S., Müller, J., Bogenberger, K., 2015. Empirical analysis of free-floating carsharing usage: the Munich and Berlin case. Transportation Research Part C: Emerging Technologies 56, 34–51. https://doi.org/10.1016/j.trc.2015.03.008.

Shaheen, S., Cohen, A., Chung, M., 2009. North American carsharing: 10-year retrospective. Transportation Research Record 2110 (1), 35–44. https://doi.org/10.3141/2110-05.

Shaheen, S., Cohen, A., Jaffee, M., 2018a. Innovative Mobility: Carsharing Outlook. Transportation Sustainability Research Center, UC Berkeley.

Shaheen, S., Martin, E., Bansal, A., 2018b. Peer-to-Peer (P2P) Carsharing: Understanding Early Markets, Social Dynamics, and Behavioral Impacts. Retrieved from. https://escholarship.org/uc/item/7s8207tb.

Sprei, F., Habibi, S., Englund, C., Pettersson, S., Voronov, A., Wedlin, J., 2019. Free-floating carsharing electrification and mode displacement: Travel time and usage patterns from 12 cities in Europe and the United States. Transportation Research Part D: Transport and Environment 71, 127–140. https://doi.org/10.1016/j.trd.2018.12.018.

Weikl, S., Bogenberger, K., 2015. A practice-ready relocation model for free-floating carsharing systems with electric vehicles – mesoscopic approach and field trial results. Transportation Research Part C: Emerging Technologies 57, 206–223. https://doi.org/10.1016/j.trc.2015.06.024.

Wielinski, G., Trépanier, M., Morency, C., 2015. What About Free-Floating Carsharing?. In: Paper Presented at the 94th Annual Meeting of the Transportation Research Board, Washington, D.C.

Wittwer, R., Hubrich, S., 2018. Free-floating carsharing experiences in German metropolitan areas. Transportation Research Procedia 33, 323–330. https://doi.org/10.1016/j.trpro.2018.10.109.

Chapter 12

SMART mobility via prediction, optimization and personalization

Bilge Atasoy[1], Carlos Lima de Azevedo[2], Arun Prakash Akkinepally[3], Ravi Seshadri[4], Fang Zhao[4], Maya Abou-Zeid[5], Moshe Ben-Akiva[3]

[1]*Department of Maritime and Transport Technology, Delft University of Technology, Delft, the Netherlands;* [2]*Department of Management Engineering, Technical University of Denmark. Lyngby, Denmark;* [3]*Department of Civil and Environmental Engineering, Massachusetts Institute of Technology, Cambridge, MA, United States;* [4]*Singapore-MIT Alliance for Research and Technology (SMART), Singapore;* [5]*Department of Civil and Environmental Engineering, American University of Beirut, Lebanon*

Chapter outline

Demand for Emerging Transportation Systems. https://doi.org/10.1016/B978-0-12-815018-4.00012-7
227

1. Introduction

Technological advancements are altering the paradigm of transportation in various aspects. Information and communication technology is the key for this change providing new forms of travel platforms. Given the widespread availability of smartphones and ubiquitous connectivity, users are now planning their transportation activities through smartphone apps which enable them to reach various services easily. They also receive real-time information regarding their trips as advanced sensors are widely available. Therefore, they can reconsider their choices based on the latest updates. Furthermore, vehicle technology is advancing with electrification, automation, and connectivity. Technological advancements, taken together with a growing demand for mobility under environmental and energy constraints, have been key drivers of emerging mobility options that are on-demand, shared, integrated, real-time, energy efficient, and flexible. Ridesourcing, provided by transportation network companies (TNCs) such as Uber and Lyft, is one prominent example of a disruptive mobility alternative that matches passengers and drivers via location-enabled smartphone apps in real-time. Another emerging example is Mobility as a Service (MaaS) whereby consumers "buy mobility services (from participating providers) based on consumer needs instead of buying the means of mobility" using a single intermodal platform and payment (Kamargianni et al., 2016). In addition to increased passenger convenience and service efficiency, these new modes and services have the potential to reduce car ownership in the long term (e.g., Iacobucci et al., 2017; Schechtner and Hanson, 2017) and to complement mass transit as a first-/last-mile access mode (e.g., Jiao et al., 2017; Lyft, 2015). Automated vehicles will make these trends even more likely and will further enable new forms of mobility supply (Mahmassani, 2016).

Smart Mobility is broadly defined as the family of mobility solutions that use appropriate technologies and methodologies and that may leverage the availability of big data for the sustainability of transportation systems (e.g., Benevolo et al., 2016). Smart Mobility is acclaimed to bring about benefits including gains in safety, reduction in individual travel costs due to increased efficiency of operation, greater consumer choice, and more sustainable travel (Docherty et al., 2018).

We present in this chapter a Smart Mobility approach that consists of three key features: (1) *prediction*, (2) *optimization,* and (3) *personalization*. Firstly, *prediction* is the key for adapting the system to changing conditions on the network. Real-time data therefore needs to be incorporated to predict network conditions, e.g., congestion, in order to have proactive decision-making mechanisms. Secondly, *optimization* is the key to have decision-making mechanisms that achieve system-level objectives, e.g., minimizing network-wide travel times and maximizing revenue and/or consumer surplus. Appropriate optimization models need to be formulated (based on predicted network conditions) and solution methodologies need to be developed to ensure real-time efficiency. Finally, *personalization* is the key to safeguard users' benefits and attract various types of travelers through understanding their preferences. Methodologies need to be developed for estimating and updating individual-level preferences (e.g., willingness to pay) and optimizing the travel option to match those preferences while maintaining the system-level objectives. Furthermore, Smart Mobility solutions need to be assessed in terms of their user-level and system-level impacts. Multilevel simulation is a core of our approach for assessing the impacts of Smart Mobility before real-life implementation.

As an example of a Smart Mobility service that embeds the above features, Tripod (Lima Azevedo et al., 2018) is a smartphone-based system to influence individual real-time travel decisions by offering information and incentives to optimize system-wide energy performance. A system-wide incentive strategy is optimized using predictions for the multimodal transportation network in real-time, while its app menu is personalized for each user based on her/his travel preferences on an on-demand basis. Bringing together these methodologies in an appropriate and efficient way is the key distinction we bring for Smart Mobility. Yet, today's Smart Mobility solutions are characterized by just one or two of these features with similar principles and goals. For example, the MaaS concept may allow for personalization of mobility plans and accommodate for demand optimization given real-time supply conditions observed through participating mobility providers.

The remainder of the chapter is organized as follows. Section 2 presents the proposed Smart Mobility approach with the formulation of specific prediction, optimization and personalization methodologies, as well as the simulation-based evaluation. For each of them, we also introduce the platforms that have been developed to facilitate those methodologies and present example applications to show their added values. Section 3 provides examples of Smart Mobility together with their implications on the transportation network. Finally, Section 4 concludes the chapter and discusses future developments.

2. Smart mobility methodology

This section presents the three key methodologies and the simulation-based evaluation that constitute the proposed Smart Mobility approach.

2.1 Smart mobility: prediction

Effective smart mobility solutions need accurate and reliable traffic state estimates and predictions. This involves explicitly considering demand and supply-side characteristics and their interactions. The traffic state prediction approaches in the literature can be divided into two categories: data driven and model-driven. The data-driven approaches rely on the availability of big data

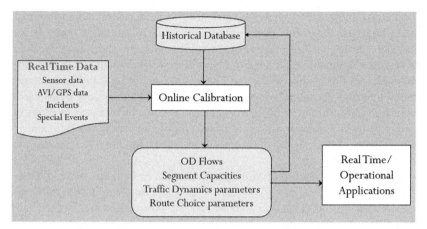

FIGURE 12.1 Online calibration framework.

(e.g., from sensors and other equipment) and filtering or machine learning algorithms. On the other hand, there are model-driven approaches that rely purely on traffic flow models. We propose a hybrid approach that combines the empirical nature of data-driven approaches with theoretically sound traffic flow models: we term the approach as *online calibration*. Thus, the hybrid approach has the advantage of using data to model recurring congestion and using models to predict the traffic evolution under nonrecurring congestion, especially when the data on rare events is sparse. Online calibration entails calibrating a dynamic traffic assignment (DTA) system in real-time, which involves adjusting the demand and supply parameters of the DTA system, using the most recent observed traffic measurements (see Fig. 12.1). Note that for the methodology presented below, the DTA system can be either analytical or simulation based.

2.1.1 State space formulation

The online calibration problem can be formulated either as an optimization problem or as a state-space problem. We present the state-space formulation as it is more general, i.e., it can be adapted to different parameters and measurements. The reader is referred to Ashok and Ben-Akiva (2002) and Antoniou et al. (2007) for a more detailed discussion.

Consider an analysis period which is divided into equal intervals $h = 1, 2, ..., T$ of size t. The transportation network is represented by $G(N, L, S)$, where N represents the set of nodes, L represents the set of links, and S represents the set of segments. The network has n_N nodes, n_L links, and n_S segments. The segments are sections of road with homogeneous geometry; a link comprises one or more segments. The set of OD pairs are represented by R

and are n_R in number. Further, n_s of the n_S segments are assumed to be equipped with surveillance sensors.

The state-space formulation consists of three main components: (i) a state vector that succinctly characterizes the system, (ii) a transition equation that captures the evolution of the system, through the state-vector, in time, and (iii) a measurement equation that captures the relationship between the state-vector and the measurements or observations of the system. Following the proposal in Ashok and Ben-Akiva (2002) and Antoniou et al. (2007), it is better to express the state-space formulation in terms of the *deviations* of the relevant variables from their historical values. By modeling in terms of the deviations in parameters, we can capture the critical structural information of the trip and network patterns present in the historical values.

In the current context, let π_h represent a vector containing the parameters of the DTA system in the time interval h; it can contain the OD flow variables along with behavioral and supply parameters. Let π_h^H represent the historical values of the parameters in interval h. The historical values π_h^H are generally obtained through offline calibration (Balakrishna, 2006). The state-vector is then denoted by $\Delta\pi_h = \pi_h - \pi_h^H$, whose evolution can be represented through the following generic transition equation:

$$\Delta\pi_h = f(\Delta\pi_{h-1}, ..., \Delta\pi_{h-q}) + \eta_h \qquad (12.1)$$

where q denotes the number of previous interval states that influence the current interval state; and η_h is a vector random of errors in the transition equation in interval h.

Further, let $\mathbf{m}_h$ denote the vector of measurements in interval h; these can be both point-based measurements (like flows and speeds) or spatial measurements (like GPS or AVI). As before, let $\mathbf{m}_h^H$ represent the historical values of the measurements in interval h. The historical values of measurements are generally obtained by running the DTA system with the historical parameters or they can also be actual measurements used for offline calibration. The measurement-vector in deviations is then denoted by $\Delta\mathbf{m}_h = \mathbf{m}_h - \mathbf{m}_h^H$, which is related to the state-vector through the following generic measurement equation:

$$\Delta\mathbf{m}_h = g(\Delta\pi_h, ..., \Delta\pi_{h-p}) + \zeta_h \qquad (12.2)$$

where p denotes the number of previous interval's states that influence the current interval's measurements; and ζ_h is a vector of random errors in the measurement equation in interval h.

Eqs. (12.1) and (12.2) together form the state-space formulation of the generic online calibration problem. In practice, two assumptions are made on the generic formulation: (i) the transition equation is approximated through a linear autoregressive process and (ii) the measurement equation uses a DTA simulator to relate the parameters and measurements. After applying the above assumptions, the resulting transition and measurement equations are as follows:

$$\Delta\pi_h = \sum_{i=h-q}^{h-1} \mathcal{F}_i^h \Delta\pi_i + \eta_h \tag{12.3a}$$

$$\Delta m_h = \mathcal{S}(\pi_h, \ldots, \pi_{h-p}) - \mathcal{S}\left(\pi_h^H, \ldots, \pi_{h-p}^H\right) + \zeta_h \tag{12.3b}$$

In Eq. (12.3a), $\mathcal{F}_i^h$ represents a matrix relating the parameter estimates of interval i to the estimates of interval h, and q denotes the degree of the autoregressive process in the deviations. In Eq. (12.3b), $\mathcal{S}$ represents a DTA model, that can be either analytical or simulation-based, whose inputs are the parameters and outputs are the simulated measurements in the current interval, and p represents the maximum number of previous intervals whose parameters influence the measurements in the current interval.

Finally, to predict the parameters in the subsequent intervals $h + 1$, $h + 2$, ..., the estimates calculated using equation in (3a) are used. For example, the prediction for the time interval $h + 1$, if the current interval is h, is calculated as

$$\pi_{h+1} = \pi_h^H + \sum_{i=h-q}^{h-1} \mathcal{F}_i^h \Delta\widehat{\pi}_i + \eta_h \tag{12.4}$$

where $\Delta\widehat{\pi}_i$ represent the a posteriori estimates of OD-flow deviations in interval i.

In the context of online systems, as presented in this chapter, the problem in Eq. (12.3) is solved to obtain an estimate of only the parameters in interval h, π_h. The parameter estimates of the earlier intervals $h - 1, h - 2, \ldots$ are not reestimated. In effect, the parameter estimates of the previous intervals are treated as constants in the current interval.

However, the observations in the current time interval might contain information about parameters from the previous time intervals. For example, sensor flow counts in the current intervals can be a result of OD flows from previous intervals. Therefore, ideally, the parameter estimates from the previous time intervals need to be corrected based on the measurements in the current interval. In the context of state space formulation, this correction of the parameters estimated in previous time intervals is formulated using state augmentation approach (Ashok, 1996). Although state augmentation results in better estimates of the parameters, it can be computationally intensive as it requires "rolling back" the simulator in real-time. In other words, the simulator needs to rerun with the new parameter estimates (from the previous time intervals) to update the simulated measurements. Ashok and Ben-Akiva (2002) found that the state augmentation can be reasonably approximated using the sequential estimation procedure we described in the chapter.

2.1.2 Solution procedure

The Kalman filter—based approaches are a natural and efficient way to recursively solve the system of equations in (3). The Kalman filter efficiently determines the estimate of the current interval using the estimate from the previous interval and the measurements in the current interval. The classical Kalman filter, which is a minimum mean square estimator, is applicable to linear state-space models. For the nonlinear state-space models, as in the problem in Eq. (12.3), the extended Kalman filter (EKF) was introduced. The EKF linearizes the nonlinear transition or measurement equations around the a priori estimates and adopts the procedure for linear state-space models to estimate the state-vector. The main conceptual drawback of the EKF is that it is not an optimal estimator; however, its practical application has been demonstrated in various studies (Antoniou, 2004). Note that for the application of the Kalman filter—based methods, we impose an assumption that the error terms η_h and ζ_h, from Eqs. (12.3a) and (12.3b), are zero mean Gaussian variables and that they are independent over time.

There are three main steps in the EKF algorithm: (i) time-update, (ii) linearization, and (iii) measurement update. In the time-update step, the prediction for parameter deviation vector $\Delta\pi_{(h|h-1)}$ is made using the transition equation and the optimal estimates from the previous interval $h-1$, $\Delta\pi_{(h-1|h-1)}$. These estimates, $\Delta\pi_{(h|h-1)}$, are termed *a priori* estimates as they use data only until the previous time interval $h-1$. In the second step, the measurement equation is linearized around the a priori estimates of the current interval, $\Delta\pi_{(h|h-1)}$. In the third step, the a priori estimates are updated using the linearized measurement equation to obtain the a posteriori estimates for parameter deviation vector $\Delta\pi_{(h|h)}$. Please refer to Antoniou (2004) and Prakash et al. (2018) for a more detailed discussion of the procedure.

The main bottleneck to apply the EKF algorithm to the online calibration problem is the linearization of the measurement equation, which involves calculating the Jacobian of the measurement equation. As the measurement equation represents the simulator, it has no closed-form expression. Therefore, the Jacobian is calculated through the numerical derivatives of $\mathcal{S}(\pi_h, \dots \pi_{h-p})$. Determining the centered numerical derivative involves perturbing each of the parameters and running the simulator $2n_K$ times, which can be computationally intractable. To overcome the computational intractability under nonlinear measurement equation, two approaches have been proposed in the literature: (i) limiting extended Kalman filter (LimEKF) and (ii) dimensionality reduction. The LimEKF entails using a constant "gain" matrix, thus eliminating the need to estimate the Jacobian at every time-interval (Antoniou et al., 2007). The gain matrix is then estimated offline periodically and an updated matrix is used whenever available. The second approach, involves reducing the dimensions of the parameter vector so that the computation requirements of the Jacobian are mitigated. Prakash et al. (2018) formulate the problem using principal components of the parameters resulting in the reduction of state vector by 50 times.

2.1.3 Example application

As an example of the prediction methodology, we present a case study conducted on the Singapore Expressway Network. The road network is depicted in Fig. 12.5, which has 939 nodes, 1157 links, and 3906 segments. The network specification also contains information about segment lengths, segment curvatures, speed limits, lanes specifications, lane-connections, and dynamic tolling gantries which are replicated from the real-world.

The network has 4121 OD pairs, whose locations and historical values were determined by an earlier work through offline calibration. The network has 357 sensors, each of which is associated with a segment; these video camera−based sensors count the vehicular flow for a period of 5 min. For the current case study, the simulation time-period was taken from 06:00−12:00, which includes the morning peak period and also the peak to off-peak transition. The estimation interval was 5 min and the prediction interval, to estimate future traffic states and provide guidance, was 15 min. Thus, we have 72 estimation intervals with a total of $72 \times 4121 = 102,312$ variables.

For this study, sensor count data of 30 weekdays in August−September 2015 was used. The 30-day data was divided into a training set of the first 25 days and the calibration procedures were tested on the last 5 days. As a real-time DTA system, DynaMIT (see Section 2.2.1 for a description of DynaMIT) was employed. For more details, please see Prakash et al. (2017) and Prakash et al. (2018).

The performance measures adopted were the normalized root mean squared (RMSN) errors and mean absolute percentage errors (MAPEs) which are defined as

$$\mathbf{RMSN} = \frac{\sqrt{n \sum_{i=1}^{n} \left(y_i - \widehat{y}_i \right)^2}}{\sum_{i=1}^{n} y_i} \tag{12.5a}$$

$$\mathbf{MAPE} = \frac{100}{n} \sum_{i=1}^{n} \frac{\left| y_i - \widehat{y}_i \right|}{y_i} \tag{12.5b}$$

where y_i represents actual measurement and $\widehat{y}_i$ represents simulated measurement. Note that as MAPE is not normalized to consider the size of measurement, it can be high when the sensor-flows are small even though the deviation from the observations is acceptable.

The aggregate RMSNs and MAPEs of the procedures for estimation and prediction across the five test days are presented in Table 12.1. In the context of estimation, the OD-EKF on average exhibits an RMSN of 0.287 and MAPE of 28.21%. It improves over historical by 32% in RMSN and 30% in MAPE. The results from the predictions are represented in three steps, which represent the three 5-minute intervals in the complete 15-minute prediction interval. From Table 12.1, the EKF on average exhibits an RMSN of 0.290, 0.295, and 0.3 for the three steps and MAPE of 24.60%, 26.44%, and 27.71% for the three steps. By comparing the RMSNs and MAPEs after calibration with those of the historical values, we see that RMSNs after calibration are significantly better than those of the historical, but the MAPEs after calibration are only marginally better than those of the historical. It implies that calibration improves on the predictions of sensor-flow counts of the sensors with higher flows than those with the lower flows.

Fig. 12.2 depicts the scatter plots of estimated and predicted sensor counts across the five test days. The complete 5 days' sensor-flow count values are represented in a single plot as a heat map. A line was fit between the estimated/predicted and the actual values in each of the plots and its equation is presented. From the plot, we see that the fits are closer to 45-degree line with no significant systemic bias or variance; however, for longer prediction intervals there seems to be some evidence of bias.

Some of future research directions in predicting short-term traffic states include (i) incorporating disaggregate data, at individual level including trajectories, into online calibration, (ii) fusing DTA and machine learning techniques, specially to predict the advent and impacts of incidents, and (iii) exploring adaptive dimensionality reduction techniques that are specific to the situation.

2.2 Smart mobility: optimization

The design and operation of efficient and sustainable smart mobility solutions require the application of "online" optimization models that drive the system toward desirable system-level objectives. These models are of relevance in various contexts to make real-time operational decisions such as ride-sharing pricing policies and operational strategies including matching of vehicles to requests and rebalancing, incentive allocation schemes, tolls, signal timings, and so on.

The literature on optimization in the context of smart mobility is vast and includes both emerging on-demand services (ride-hailing, car sharing, bike sharing) and network control strategies (tolls, ramp metering, signals, etc.). The optimization of on-demand services has traditionally focused on vehicle routing and scheduling and falls under a broad class of dial-a-Ride problem or DARP (refer to Cordeau and Laporte (2007) for a review). More recently, studies have focused on incorporating the ride-sharing component of on-

TABLE 12.1 Aggregate values of RMSNs and MAPEs of sensor-flow counts (5 min) for historical and EKF.

Method	RMSN estimation	RMSN prediction			MAPE estimation	MAPE prediction		
		step1	step2	step3		step1	step2	step3
Hist	0.423	0.422	0.42	0.419	28.21	28.18	28.19	28.1
OD-EKF	0.287	0.290	0.295	0.305	19.77	24.60	26.44	27.71
% diff	32.15	31.28	29.76	27.21	29.92	12.70	6.21	1.39

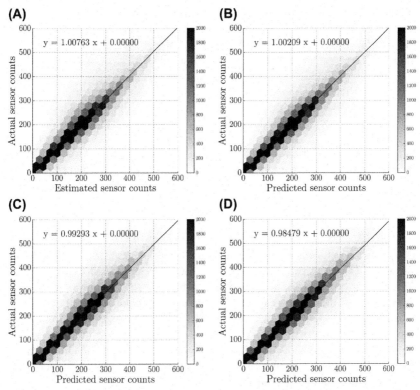

FIGURE 12.2 Comparison estimations and predictions of EKF procedures through the scatter plots of 5 min predicted versus actual sensor counts across all the five test days. The darker the cell, higher the number of points in it. (A) Estimations, (B) 1-step predictions, (C) 2-step predictions, (D) 3-step predictions.

demand services to estimate minimum fleet sizes required to service existing taxi demands in different urban contexts (Santi et al., 2014; Vazifeh et al., 2018; Alonso-Mora et al., 2017). The aforementioned studies typically employ graph theoretic and operations research techniques and do not explicitly model the complex demand and supply interactions within the transportation system. Extensive literature also exists on the optimization of network control strategies and the most commonly used approaches include feedback control (Zhang et al., 2008; Lou et al., 2011) and simulation-based optimization (Hassan et al., 2013; Hashemi and Abdelghany, 2016; Gupta et al., 2016). Typically, the approaches (with a few exceptions) tend to ignore system-level interactions and are reactive in that they are based on only current network states and not predicted network states.

Given that the optimization framework for Smart Mobility needs to be adaptive and computationally efficient, responding in real-time to recurrent/

nonrecurrent transportation supply and demand fluctuations, the approach we propose utilizes short-term predictions of the multimodal transportation system within a rolling horizon framework. More specifically, within this framework, a simulation-based optimization problem is solved periodically (e.g., every 5 minutes) wherein different candidate strategies of the smart mobility service operation are evaluated using predictions of the transportation system over a short-term future horizon period (e.g., 1 hour). The predictions are generated by a real-time dynamic traffic assignment (DTA) model system and involve detailed behavioral and supply models, explicitly taking into account the responses of users to the strategies. Examples of such real-time DTA systems include DYNASMART-X (Mahmassani, 2001), DynaMIT2.0 (Ben-Akiva et al., 2010; Lu et al., 2015b), and DIRECT (Hashemi and Abdelghany, 2016).

2.2.1 Real-time DTA and rolling horizon framework

The proposed optimization approach is built upon the prediction methodology (Section 2.1) and therefore utilizes traffic state predictions from a real-time DTA system operating in a rolling horizon mode. Although in principle, any simulation-based or analytical DTA system could be applied, in the following description, we make use of DynaMIT2.0 (Lu et al., 2015b). Some distinguishing features of DynaMIT2.0 include the modeling of multiple modes (e.g., car, transit, on-demand services) and generation of guidance information that is consistent with actual network conditions that users will encounter when responding to the guidance.

DynaMIT2.0 is composed of two core modules, state estimation and state prediction, and operates within a rolling horizon mode. In the example shown in Fig. 12.3, at 8:00 a.m., an execution cycle begins with DynaMIT2.0 receiving real time data from various sources including surveillance sensors, traffic information feeds, special event websites, weather forecasts, social networks, etc. This data is used in conjunction with historical information to first calibrate or "tune" the demand and supply parameters of the simulator so as to replicate prevailing traffic conditions as closely as possible (termed online calibration or state estimation; refer Section 2.1 for more details) for the time interval from 7:55—8:00. Based on this estimate of the current network state, the state prediction module predicts future traffic conditions for a prediction horizon (8:00—9:00 a.m.) taking into account the response of the drivers to the provided travel time (or other) guidance information. The outputs of the prediction module are forecasts of network conditions that are consistent with the expectation of users when responding to the guidance. Within our approach, the optimization of smart mobility services utilizes the state prediction module iteratively to evaluate potential candidate strategies based on the multimodal network predictions from 8:00 to 9:00 a.m. These are then applied to the system for the time interval from 8:00—8:05 a.m. At 8:05

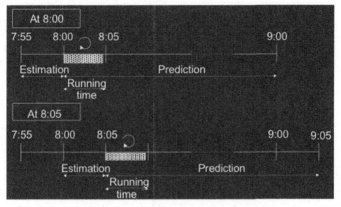

FIGURE 12.3   Rolling horizon framework.

a.m., the next execution cycle or "roll period" begins and the process repeats. The multimodal network predictions are based on behavioral models that incorporate the response of travelers to the smart mobility services.

2.2.2 Optimization formulation and solution approaches

In this section, we formally define the generic optimization problem applicable to the design/operation of any of the previously discussed "smart mobility" solutions. Consider a network $G(N, A)$, where N represents the set of n network nodes and A represents the set of m directed links and assume that the simulation period consists of $h = 1, \ldots, T$ estimation intervals of length t. Further, let the prediction horizon be K intervals, i.e., length to Kt, where each subinterval of length t within the prediction horizon is termed a prediction interval. Let $\theta_h = \left(\theta_h^1, \theta_h^2, \ldots, \theta_h^K\right)$ denote a vector of decision variables for the prediction horizon corresponding to estimation interval h that are to be optimized based on desired system or operator level objectives. The decision variables could involve pricing policies for smart mobility services, incentive allocation schemes, network tolls, etc. and are revised every estimation interval. For example, in Fig. 12.4, we have $K = 3$ prediction intervals and $\theta_h^1, \theta_h^2, \theta_h^3$ represent the values of the decision variables for the three prediction subintervals in roll period h.

The state of the multimodal network over the prediction horizon associated with estimation interval h is denoted by a vector $\mathbf{x}$ which could include link flows, speeds, densities, bus/train dwell times, and so on. With this background, the optimization problem to be solved in roll period (i.e., estimation interval) h is formulated as follows:

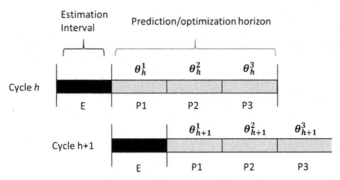

FIGURE 12.4 Notation for the rolling horizon approach.

$$Min_{\theta_h} Z = f(\theta_h, \mathbf{x})$$

$$s.t \ \ S(\eta, \theta_h) = \mathbf{x}$$

where, η represents the forecasted demand and supply parameters for the prediction horizon, $S(.)$ represents the complex coupled demand and supply simulators of the DTA system and $f(.)$ represents the objective function of interest. The objective function could include the maximization of social welfare, minimization of energy, maximization of operator profits, fleet utilization, and so on. The objective function of optimization problem does not have a closed form and is the output of a complex simulator. Therefore, it is typically nonlinear and nonconvex. Solution approaches to solve this problem include meta-heuristics (Gupta et al., 2016; Hashemi and Abdelghany, 2016) which are amenable to the use of parallel and distributed computing and can achieve real-time performance. In the example application presented in the next section, we use a genetic algorithm approach that enables such parallelization. Nevertheless, the framework is flexible and already implemented with other solution algorithms including search heuristics.

2.2.3 Example application

In this section, we discuss the application of the framework to a dynamic toll optimization problem using a case study on the Singapore Expressway Network shown in Fig. 12.5 where there are 16 gantries. The decision vector θ_h in this case is a vector of toll rates on those gantries to be determined for the prediction horizon. Note that, Singapore already has toll optimization in place through Electronic Road Pricing (ERP) in the form of time-of-day tolling (Seik, 2000).

The impact of the predictive optimization of network congestion is evaluated using a closed-loop setup wherein the DynaMIT2.0 system is interfaced with a traffic microsimulator MITSIM (Yang et al., 2000). MITSIM is run concurrently with DynaMIT2.0 and mimics the real network, providing sensor

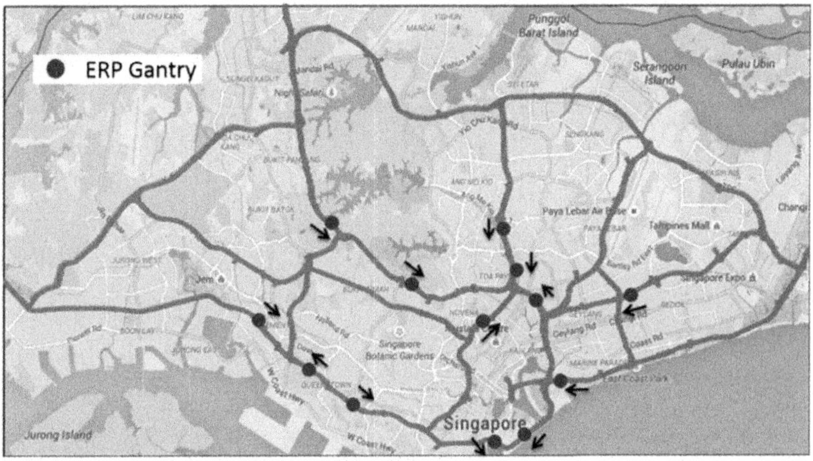

FIGURE 12.5   Singapore Expressway Network (map data: Google Maps, 2018).

counts (surveillance data) to DynaMIT2.0, which in turn provides predictive guidance and optimized tolls to MITSIM. The impact of the guidance and optimized tolls is then examined by obtaining relevant performance measures from MITSIM. For the experiments, in order to obtain a realistic representation of demand and supply on the Singapore expressway network, an offline calibration is performed in two stages. In the first stage, MITSIM is calibrated against real-world sensor count data (for details see Prakash et al., 2017) and in the second stage, the demand and supply parameters of DynaMIT2.0 are calibrated against simulated outputs from the calibrated MITSIM system.

In the numerical experiments, the performance of the predictive optimization is examined against two benchmarks, a *no-toll* scenario and a *static-optimum*, where tolls are time-invariant and optimized offline using historical demands. Two demand scenarios are considered, a base demand (calibrated MITSIM demand) and a high demand scenario (base demand increased systematically by 20%). In both cases, the MITSIM demand is also randomly perturbed to represent recurrent demand fluctuations. The simulation period is 6:30 a.m. to 12:00 p.m., which includes the morning peak in Singapore, and the estimation interval and prediction horizon are 5 and 15 min, respectively. For each demand scenario, the closed-loop simulation is performed 20 times (to account for simulator stochasticity) and the performance measures (trip travel times) are averaged.

The average trip travel times (aggregated in 5-minute departure time windows) in the two demand scenarios are shown in Figs. 12.6 and 12.7 (the bands represent the standard deviation in the travel time estimates based on the 20 replications). The results show that predictive optimization can yield

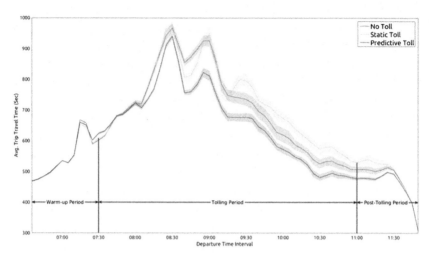

FIGURE 12.6   Average Travel Times (Base demand).

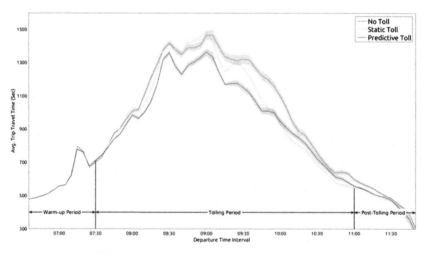

FIGURE 12.7   Average Travel Times (High demand).

statistically significant (at a 95% confidence level) travel time savings at the network level. The average trip travel times (across the entire tolling period from 7:30 to 11:00) in the case of the predictive optimized tolls are lower than the static-optimum and no-toll cases by 9.12% and 6.74% in the base demand case, and 4.00% and 8.38% in the high demand case.

There are several future promising directions related to real-time predictive optimization for improving transportation network conditions. An immediate direction is including more advanced demand models in the optimization framework in order to personalize the transport policies such as tolls, incentives, etc., and personalization methodology will be discussed in the next section.

2.3 Smart mobility: personalization

Travelers' needs are different and the preferences are heterogeneous across the population and across time. Smart Mobility solutions therefore need to present alternatives that are personalized in order to achieve long-term performance while ensuring that system-level objectives are met. For this purpose, we identify two main methodologies that make personalization possible: behavioral modeling and personalized menu optimization. First, behavioral modeling is the key to understand the heterogeneity across observations, and for Smart Mobility, the behavior of interest could be mode choice, route choice, departure time choice, etc. Second, user-specific optimization uses the behavioral information in order to optimize the Smart Mobility offer to be presented to the user. This optimization is represented by a menu optimization model that selects the optimal set of alternatives to be presented and this set of offered alternatives is referred as *menu*.

2.3.1 Behavioral modeling

Discrete choice methodology is well accepted to model behavior in various contexts (Ben-Akiva and Lerman, 1985). Different types of models have been developed and used in understanding behavior with various applications to travel behavior. Heterogeneity in behavior is particularly important to model and most of the literature focuses on heterogeneity across the population (inter-consumer heterogeneity). It is typically modeled as logit mixture (or mixed logit), and depending on the specification, simulation techniques are developed and used for the estimation (Train, 2009). More recently, researchers have investigated the heterogeneity across the choice situations (or menus) of the same individual (intraconsumer heterogeneity), especially when the data is collected over a long time with multiple observations for each individual (Cherchi et al., 2009; Hess and Rose, 2009; Ben-Akiva et al., 2019). This is especially relevant for Smart Mobility—based apps, where user data is likely to be available for multiple time periods.

Logit mixtures that account for both inter- and intraconsumer heterogeneity are estimated with maximum simulated likelihood (MSL) estimators (Hess and Rose, 2009). Building on the Allenby-Train procedure (Train, 2001), a Bayesian estimator is developed by Becker et al. (2018) for Logit mixtures with both levels of heterogeneity by extending the 3-step Allenby-Train procedure as a 5-step procedure. Population level, individual level, and menu level parameters are obtained with the proposed 5-step estimator. They compare the estimator to MSL and show that the proposed estimator retains the MSL estimates and is computationally 5 times less costly. Furthermore, based on the mentioned Bayesian methodology, the authors developed an offline—online update mechanism in order to continuously update the parameters as individuals make choices in the system (Danaf et al., 2019a). Therefore, our proposed approach is to use the Bayesian estimator and the update mechanism for Smart Mobility in order to estimate parameters that represent the heterogeneity across population and across choice situations accurately and also to keep the estimates up-to-date based on the recent observations.

We will now illustrate a typical logit mixture model with inter- and intraconsumer heterogeneity. We have population-level parameters given by μ, individual-level parameters represented by ζ_n for each individual n and menu-level parameters given by η_{mn} for menu m and individual n. Furthermore, we have the interconsumer covariance matrix Ω_b and the intraconsumer covariance matrix Ω_w. We assume that ζ_n and η_{mn} are normally distributed as follows:

$$\eta_{mn} \sim \mathcal{N}(\zeta_n, \Omega_w) \tag{12.6}$$

$$\zeta_n \sim \mathcal{N}(\mu, \Omega_b) \tag{12.7}$$

Consider the following utility function for individual n alternative j in menu m:

$$U_{jmn} = V_{jmn} + \varepsilon_{jmn} = X_{jmn}\eta_{mn} + \varepsilon_{jmn} \tag{12.8}$$

where V_{jmn} is the systematic utility and X_{jmn} represents alternative attributes. In the context of Smart Mobility, those attributes are typically travel time, cost, frequency, reliability, level of service, etc. Assuming that the error term ε_{jmn} follows the Gumbel distribution and the choice set for individual n for menu m is represented by J_{mn}, the choice probability of alternative j is given as:

$$P_j(\eta_{mn}) = \frac{\exp(V_{jmn}(\eta_{mn}))}{\sum_{j'=0}^{J_{mn}} \exp(V_{j'mn}(\eta_{mn}))} \qquad \forall j \in J_{mn} \tag{12.9}$$

Such models with advanced level of heterogeneity needs appropriate datasets with multiple observations for individuals together with the contextual information. For achieving the data needs, we utilize the Future Mobility Sensing (FMS) platform that was developed by the intelligent transportation system (ITS) Lab at MIT and SMART (Cottrill et al., 2013; Zhao et al., 2015). FMS is mainly used to collect high-resolution mobility data in the form of activity diaries through a smartphone app, where users can validate their entire set of trips and activities during a day. As users are typically asked to use the app for a few weeks, multiple choices of mode, route, departure time, etc., are observed. The users also provide socioeconomic information when installing

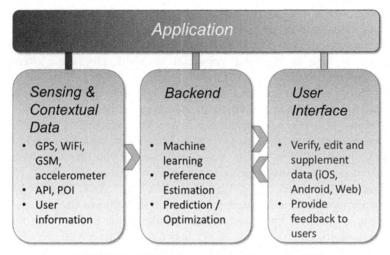

FIGURE 12.8 FMS platform overview (Zhao et al., 2018).

the app. Therefore, FMS enables the collection of rich datasets and the development of individual-level choice models.

Fig. 12.8 provides an overview of the FMS platform. FMS collects location, accelerometer, and contextual data continuously making use of the available sensors on smartphones. The FMS backend system processes the collected data through machine learning algorithms. The web and app interfaces allow the users to access the information about their trips and activities and also to validate them. The machine learning techniques are continuously being improved in order to reduce the burden on the user, i.e., minimize the need for the user to correct trip and activity information on their diaries. Note that, FMS is extended with stated preferences capability for understanding the behavior toward new mobility services (Atasoy et al., 2018; Danaf et al., 2019b) and it can be used for obtaining reasonable parameter values in the early phases of the Smart Mobility solution (in a simulation environment or real-life) before any estimation is possible based on observed choices.

2.3.2 Personalized menu optimization

In order to provide a personalized menu of travel options for Smart Mobility, differentiation of individuals and choice situations need to be taken care of with an appropriate behavioral model. Therefore, a logit mixture model with inter- and intraconsumer heterogeneity described above is the building block for personalized menu optimization. Given the logit mixture model, the personalized menu optimization will choose an M-size menu out of C many available alternatives for individual n in order to maximize an objective function of interest. It can be maximization of revenue, consumer surplus, a combination of the two, etc. In recommender systems for mobile apps, it is common to have a menu-size constraint to avoid information overload (Zhuang et al., 2011).

Personalized menu optimization is closely related to the assortment optimization, where the goal is similarly to select a subset of items to offer to the user from a universe of substitutable items. The objective is typically to maximize the revenue under random choice behavior of users. To represent the user behavior, different choice models are used in the literature such as multinomial logit, nested logit, and logit mixture (Davis et al., 2013, 2014; Feldman and Topaloglu, 2015). We refer to Kök et al. (2008) for a review of assortment optimization literature together with industry practice.

Here, we present a personalized menu optimization with revenue maximization, where p_j is the revenue of alternative $j \in C$. This revenue may be the monetary value or energy savings or any other benefit brought by the Smart Mobility system. The model for each individual n, with binary decision variables x_j that decide whether alternative j will be in the menu or not, is then provided as follows:

$$\max_{x_{j'} j=1,\ldots,C} \sum_{j=1}^{C} p_j \frac{x_j \exp(V_{jmn}(\eta_{mn}))}{\sum_{j'=1}^{C} x_{j'} \exp(V_{j'mn}(\eta_{mn})) + \exp(V_n^{opt})} \tag{12.10}$$

subject to

$$\sum_{j=1}^{C} x_j \leq M_n \tag{12.11}$$

$$x_j \in \{0, 1\}, \forall j \in \{1, \ldots, C\} \tag{12.12}$$

where the objective function (10) is a function of binary decision variables through the choice probability that is given by the behavioral model introduced in the previous section. V_n^{opt} denotes the utility of opt-out alternative (not choosing anything on the menu) for individual n. We include the opt-out alternative in order to represent the fact that the user is not captive and may leave the Smart Mobility system and this utility may be different across individuals. Constraint (11) is the menu-size constraint and it is given by M_n, as in principle the size of the menu could also be personalized.

The above-presented model (10–12) represents a complex problem as it has a nonlinear objective function and binary decision variables. There are ways to simplify the problem under different assumptions. We refer to Song (2018) for a discussion of those cases and also for different versions of the model with an objective function of consumer surplus.

2.3.3 Example application

We applied the personalization approach with a real data set from Massachusetts Travel Survey (MTS) which includes travel diaries for 33,000 individuals from 15,000 households collected between June 2010 and November 2011. The individuals reported travel diaries for a preassigned weekday and provided transport mode, arrival/departure times, activity location, etc. We used a sample of 5154 individuals who made at least one trip during the specified day. The choice set for those trips was constructed by using Google Maps API based on the origin, destination, and departure time information from MTS data. Considered modes are walk, bike, car, car-pool, and transit, and with different route options the choice set may include 4 to 16 alternatives. Note that more than 80% of the trips in the MTS data were performed by car/ car-pool. For more details we refer to Song (2018) and Song et al. (2018) also used a smaller sample from this dataset for an earlier version of this work.

A logit mixture model is specified and the utility for individual n of alternative j for a given choice situation (menu) m is given by

$$U_{jmn} = \frac{\left(ASC_{mode} - \exp\left(\eta_{mn,Time}\right)Time_{jmn} - Cost_{jmn}\right)}{\exp\left(\eta_{mn,Cost}\right)}$$

where ASC_{mode} denotes the alternative specific constant for each of the five modes that are considered and it is set to zero for the walk mode. The utility is in willingness-to-pay specification (i.e., in monetary units) as it is normalized by the cost coefficient. ASCs are normally distributed; travel time and cost coefficients are introduced as exponential terms in order to have them lognormally distributed and to control their signs.

For the example application here, we consider 1733 individuals who performed at least nine trips during the specified day. The parameters are estimated based on the first eight trips with the previously mentioned Bayesian estimator and the menu is optimized for the ninth trip. In order to assess the benefits of personalization, we compare it to its *nonpersonalized* counterpart, which does not capture individual-level preferences. The comparison is done in terms of the *hit rate*, which is the proportion of the cases the optimized menu for trip nine includes the "true" choice. This analysis is carried out under two settings of the assumed consumer heterogeneity, first assumes inter-only heterogeneity and the second considers both inter- and intraconsumer heterogeneity.

Figs. 12.9 and 12.10 provide the comparison under inter-only and inter- and intraconsumer heterogeneity, respectively. For the analysis, different menu sizes are considered between 2 and 10 and as mentioned previously the choice set may be of size 4 to 16 across different observations. As expected, when menu size gets closer to the size of the choice set, the hit rate approaches 1 and the difference between personalized versus nonpersonalized menu optimization gets smaller. Fig. 12.9 shows that, for menu sizes of until 6,

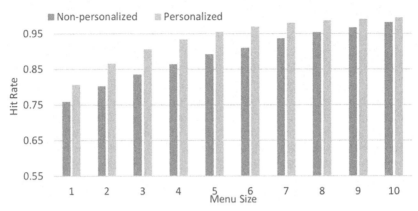

FIGURE 12.9 Comparison under inter-only heterogeneity.

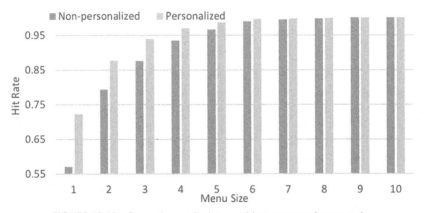

FIGURE 12.10 Comparison under inter- and intraconsumer heterogeneity.

personalization increases the hit rate by more than 5% under inter-only heterogeneity. When we look at the case under inter- and intraconsumer heterogeneity in Fig. 12.10, it is observed that the hit rate of both methods increased significantly in general which shows that the behavior can be captured much better with a more accurate representation of heterogeneity. The difference between personalized versus nonpersonalized menu optimization becomes very small as of menu size 6. Nevertheless, with smaller menu sizes, there is a significant benefit of personalization, e.g., for menu sizes of 1 and 2, personalization brings around 15% and 8% increase in hit rate, respectively, which are bigger differences compared to the inter-only case.

The presented results show the added value of more advanced behavioral models with detailed representation of consumer heterogeneity as well as the personalized menu optimization. It shows the potential for Smart Mobility solutions and will definitely be more powerful when the user history is tracked over a time horizon and several choices from the same individual is observed.

2.4 Simulation-based evaluation of smart mobility

Similar to other mobility solutions, Smart Mobility can be assessed by means of surveys, laboratory or field experiments, and simulations. When such solutions are not yet deployed in the field, analysts tend to resort to stated preference surveys for the assessment of demand impacts. Yet, insights from these are known to be unreliable in scenarios, where the context is too far from situations familiar to the subjects (see, for example, Choudhury et al., 2018 for the assessment of the willingness to pay for different smart mobility options). Laboratory experiments are usually useful for cognitive and other human factors issues associated with the interaction of a certain technology, thus providing even further insights into demand aspects. Field experiments on the other hand, allow for coupling insights on such demand impacts with reduced context bias together with limited supply characteristics of the Smart Mobility solution at stake. Such experiments are at the forefront of Smart Mobility assessment but are still constrained to a limited range of potential operational settings, either due to technology limitations or the associated experimental costs, thus limiting supply related insights. Harb et al. (2018), for example, collected pioneer insights on travel behavior patterns shifts for automated mobility by mimicking a privately owned self-driving vehicle with 60 h in 7 days of free chauffeur service for each of the study participants.

While the above methods are extremely useful for demand specific insights, system-level impact assessment, effects from demand-supply interactions or freedom of scenario testing have been recently tackled by means of simulation. With advances in computational power, the research community has been tackling the assessment of Smart Mobility impacts in large urban areas with integrated demand-supply complex simulators. These simulators are typically composed of several interconnected models for each of the dimensions of the transportation system: land-use, demographic, and economic model; travel (often activity-based) demand model; and a multimodal network supply assignment model. An example of current state-of-the art platforms targeting this aim are Polaris (Auld et al., 2016), CEMDAP + MATSim (Ziemke et al., 2015) or SimMobility (Adnan et al., 2016). For assessing the impacts of different operational settings for *prediction, optimization,* and *personalization,* simulation platforms require a set of features. We summarize in this section SimMobility's features for assessing Smart Mobility.

SimMobility is an integrated agent-based simulation platform used to evaluate a wide range of future mobility related scenarios (See Fig. 12.11). It is comprised of three integrated modules differentiated by the time-frame in which we consider the traveler behavior and operations of an urban system:

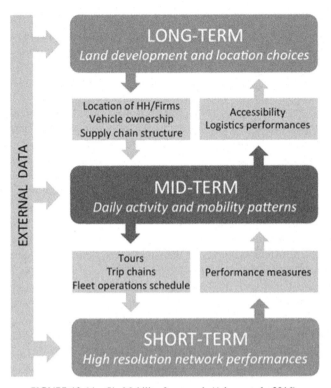

FIGURE 12.11 SimMobility framework (Adnan et al., 2016).

short-term (a microscopic mobility simulation, few hours simulated at 0.1-second time resolution), *mid-term* (an activity-based model integrated with a dynamic multimodal assignment simulator, daily simulation at 5-second resolution), and *long-term* (a land use and long-term behavioral model, at 6-month to 1 year resolution) (Adnan et al., 2016). The integrated nature of SimMobility enables consistency between the levels through a single database model which is used by all three levels. Thus, an agent's travel behavior and characteristics will be consistent across all levels. For example, the short-term uses trip chains generated by the mid-term model, which are also generated by using land use information from long-term. Demand in mid-term, vehicle ownership and the geographic distribution of the population in long-term rely on supply performance through a feedback loop. Introducing new mobility solutions in the simulation affects the aforementioned agents' choices, including mode choice. In this context, Smart Mobility is expected to directly influence an agent's preferences of mode choice due to the presentation of personalized and shared alternatives which have different characteristics such as travel time, schedule delay, and privacy.

SimMobility long-term is designed to simulate the interrelations between the transportation system and land-use mainly capturing the decision-making related to the household location choices, school and workplace choices, and vehicle ownership choices (Zhu et al., 2018). The main model is a housing market module simulating daily dynamics in the residential housing market and affecting the remaining long-term choices (e.g., vehicle ownership) together with overall transportation performance coming from the mid-term model in the form of utility-based accessibility measures. While the impact of different smart mobility scenario performances is already taken care of in long-term decision-making by means of accessibility changes, direct extensions to the current formulation of individual behavior are being implemented to reflect cost of vehicle ownership, such as subscription services (e.g., to new smart mobility services) and new modes such as personal mobility devices (Zhu et al., 2018).

It is at the level of the travel demand and network simulation, where critical smart mobility simulation features are required. In SimMobility, the travel behavior models are present in the mid-term simulator, which comprises two groups of behavioral models: preday and within-day (Lu et al., 2015a). The preday models follow an econometric day activity schedule approach, detailed in Hemerly Viegas de Lima et al. (2018), to decide on the initial overall daily activity schedule of the agent, particularly its activity sequence (including tours and sub-tours), with preferred modes, departure times by half-hour slots, and destinations. As the day unfolds, the within-day models are applied to the agents to transform the activity schedule (plans) into effective decisions, revise the preday patterns as needed, and decide on the routes for their trips (actions).

For a particular scenario and to accommodate the effects of Smart Mobility in the preday models, individuals from the synthetic population have access to the available Smart Mobility modes at stake in their choice set while constructing their activity schedules. The systematic utility of each mode in the combined mode and destination choice model of preday considers the key attributes of the Smart Mobility mode, individual, and context characteristics (such as *travel times, costs, trip purpose, vehicle ownership, smart mobility and other mode subscription, age, gender,* etc.). General assumptions on the generalized travel attributes of the Smart Mobility mode at stake need to be made usually based on related past literature, experiments, stated preferences, and/or proxy modes. Under this approach, the formulation of the remaining choices in preday's day activity schedule approach (e.g., activity participation, number of tours, etc.) would still rely on estimations from existing datasets and, if existing, additional calibrations using the Smart Mobility related data sets.

At the within-day level, user interactions with the daily operations of the Smart Mobility service at stake are simulated. Using SimMobility's event publish/subscribe mechanism (Adnan et al., 2016), travelers subscribe to the Smart Mobility service. For a planned trip under the Smart Mobility mode from the preday model, simulated travelers first have to choose if they access the actual Smart Mobility interface first during the simulation. This intermediate decision allows for changes in decision-making due to dynamic characteristics of the transportation system. When accessing the service, a second model decides on the service product within the Smart Mobility service to select (or rejection of all offers). Finally, if selecting a certain product, one may need to consider a potential rescheduling of the remaining day activity schedule, namely if the alternatives offered by the Smart Mobility service rely on drastic changes to the planned activities (e.g., significant trip delay, much longer travel times, etc.). Such feature is not yet available in SimMobility; currently, if travelers chose not to use the Smart Mobility service or reject all product offers, they act as nonusers and follow preday plans; if they select a product, they follow the choice for that particular trip and follow the remaining preday plans (for a detailed description, data for estimation and actual estimation procedure see Xie et al., 2019).

Finally, to allow the simulation of operations of Smart Mobility services, SimMobility introduced two new relevant agents at the supply level, both in mid-term and short-term: the service-driver and the Smart Mobility controller. Such current implementation is flexible to allow for the simulation of diverse Smart Mobility scenarios: (i) multiple service providers, (ii) service-drivers/vehicles subscribing to multiple service-providers, and (iii) flexible exchange of information between the service-providers and service-drivers/vehicles. First, as multiple service-providers can be simulated in tandem, we can replicate currently available services like Uber and Lyft and also test the impact of new competitors on the network. Second, as a service-driver/vehicle can subscribe to multiple service-providers, we are able to simulate the effect on the system of doing so. Third, the exchange of information between service-provider and service-driver/vehicle may channel travel information or control from the service-provider to service driver/vehicle and, vice-versa, transfer dynamic driver/vehicle specific data (e.g., location) to the service provider.

The Smart Mobility controller consists of three main components: i) initializer, ii) fleet/driver manager, and iii) service monitor. The initializer initializes any existing service fleet or drivers and their attributes. The manager deals with servicing the traveler after receiving his/her travel request. It processes the request, selects and offers the service products to the traveler, and services accordingly. For example, in an Uber-like scenario, vehicle-driver matching, pricing, dispatching, routing, and rebalancing algorithms are part of the manager. The service monitor component monitors the servicing, the dynamic attributes of service vehicle and driver assets and the spatial and temporal distribution of demand. The simulation of a wide range of Smart Mobility services in SimMobility can be found in the literature, such as (i) regular taxis (ii) ride on-demand (iii) ride-sharing, and (iv) information provision within SimMobility (Lima Azevedo et al., 2016; Adnan et al., 2017; Basu et al., 2018).

3. Smart mobility examples

In this section, we provide examples of Smart Mobility solutions that are designed based on the methodologies we presented above.

3.1 Flexible Mobility on Demand (FMOD)

FMOD is an app-based service that provides an optimized menu of travel options including taxi, shared-taxi, and minibus in real-time (Atasoy et al., 2015a). The traveler can select one option in the menu for their trip or reject all options. It is illustrated in Fig. 12.12 a user accessing the system through a smartphone app and receiving a menu including the three services with different attributes. FMOD taxi provides door-to-door service in a private vehicle, which is typically the highest priced service. FMOD shared-taxi serves multiple passengers in the same vicinity, and travel time may increase due to the pick-up and drop-off of other passengers. FMOD minibus runs along fixed stops but adapts to passengers' schedule and typically has the lowest fare. These different modes give a spectrum of services ranging from private to public transportation.

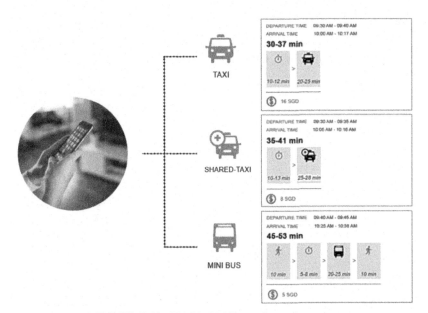

FIGURE 12.12   Flexible Mobility on Demand system.

The modeling framework for FMOD includes a behavioral model, a dial-a-ride problem, and a personalized menu optimization model. The behavioral model is a mode choice model that defines the utilities of the FMOD alternatives as well as the opt-out alternative. Considered attributes include travel time, cost, access/egress times (if any), and schedule delay.

When a user request is received, a dial-a-ride problem (refer to Cordeau and Laporte, 2007 for a review) is solved in order to generate a set of feasible transport alternatives that fit the request of the user (i.e., origin, destination and preferred departure/arrival time) and the capacity and existing schedules of the vehicles. Finally, a personalized menu optimization model is solved in order to get the optimal (e.g., maximum revenue and/or maximum consumer surplus) menu among the full set of feasible solutions. As described in Section 2.3, this personalized menu optimization model embeds the behavioral model that represents the choice probability toward FMOD alternatives and the opt-out alternative. For more details on the models and solution approach, we refer the reader to Atasoy et al. (2015a).

FMOD is evaluated in Singapore with the SimMobility platform introduced in Section 2.4. Fig. 12.13 indicates the simulated network and the shaded area is assumed to be the service area for FMOD. It is assumed that 10% of all the road users in the shaded area have access to FMOD (i.e., access FMOD app to make a travel request). For this experiment, the behavioral model is a rather simple logit mixture model that considers only interconsumer heterogeneity, i.e., the willingness-to-pay varies across the population but not across different choice situations of the same individual. Dial-a-ride problem is solved with insertion heuristics such that when a user request is received, the existing schedules of the potential vehicles are evaluated to see whether the requested trip can be inserted or not. For the personalized menu optimization model,

FIGURE 12.13 Singapore network, pink shaded area represents the central business district area, where FMOD is assumed to operate.

three versions are considered with the objectives of profit maximization, consumer surplus maximization, and both. The trade-off between operator's profit versus user benefit is analyzed under the different versions.

A base case is considered where there is no FMOD in the provided network. It is observed that when FMOD is introduced, 5% system-wide travel time reduction is obtained compared to the base case. Moreover, around 10% −20% reduction is obtained in volume-to-capacity ratio. Furthermore, the comparison of the three objective functions is provided in Table 12.2, where the base scenario is considered to be the consumer surplus maximization. The relative profit and consumer surplus of the two other scenarios are provided with respect to the base scenario. It is observed that when we maximize profit, we end up reducing the consumer surplus significantly which may in the long run mean that the users will not revisit the FMOD system and the envisioned profit may not be reached. When we optimize both profit and consumer surplus, it is observed that consumer surplus is regained without significant reduction in profit. Therefore, it is important to consider the benefit to both users and operators and FMOD framework enables that as a behavioral model is embedded in the menu optimization. FMOD is also evaluated for a network in Tokyo under different objective functions and scenarios (Atasoy et al., 2015a, 2015b).

Note that the presented application of FMOD focuses on the personalization aspect and it is evaluated by SimMobility. In principle and similarly to the case study presented in the next section, this Smart Mobility solution could also be developed in a predictive framework where the travel time in the network is predicted in real-time and the operation of the system is carried out based on the predicted traffic conditions. Furthermore, the prediction framework could be extended for the arrival of user requests such that, the number of requests that will be received in the near future is predicted and the resources are allocated more efficiently.

TABLE 12.2 Results for FMOD under different objective functions.

Scenario objective	Relative profit	Relative consumer surplus
Maximize consumer surplus	Base case	Base case
Maximize profit	+45%	−140%
Maximize total welfare	+40%	−31%

3.2 Tripod: sustainable travel incentives with prediction, optimization and personalization

Tripod is a smartphone-based system to influence individuals' real-time travel decisions by offering information and incentives with the objective of optimizing system-wide energy savings (Lima Azevedo et al., 2018). When starting a trip, travelers can choose to access Tripod's *personalized* menu via a smartphone app and are offered incentives in the form of tokens for a variety of *optimized* energy-reducing travel options (i.e., mode, route, departure time, driving style alternatives as well as the option of canceling the trip) (see Fig. 12.14). Options are presented with *predictive* information to help travelers understand the energy and emissions consequences of their choices. By accepting and executing a specific travel option, a traveler earns tokens that depend on the system-wide energy savings she or he creates, encouraging them to consider not only their own energy cost but also the impact of their choice on the system. Tokens can then be redeemed for services and goods from participating vendors and transportation agencies.

The Tripod system relies on the simulation-based multimodal network prediction system described in Section 2.2. As Tripod aims at maximizing system-wide energy savings, the prediction simulation framework was extended with (1) individual specific preferences toward different alternatives and incentives, (2) a simulated personalization which simulates the generation of the menu of alternatives shown by the Tripod app, and (3) TripEnergy (Needell and Trancik, 2018), a detailed model that estimates the energy impacts of multimodal travel.

Tripod's overall system-wide maximization of energy efficiency is achieved through a bilevel optimization approach with the system *optimization* as strategy (top level) and the app menu generation as the *personalization* (lower

FIGURE 12.14 Tripod interface (Lima Azevedo et al., 2018).

level). The link between these two loosely coupled problems is achieved through the real-time computation of the token energy efficiency (TEE), defined as the amount of energy a traveler must save to earn one token (Araldo et al., 2019). The TEE is the key decision variable of the system optimization and is used in every menu personalization, then triggered by each trip request from a control point traveler, i.e., Tripod user. In this framework, there are two optimization cycles: the system optimization is triggered at every roll period and each individual menu for a trip request is personalized on an individual on-demand basis. The Tripod app also keeps track of Tripod users' preferences from their menu selections and informs the system optimization for better predictions. As previously mentioned, the response to different TEE and overall predicted demand is embedded in the prediction framework (for more information the reader is referred to Araldo et al., 2019).

Similar to the FMOD service presented in the previous section, Tripod's menu personalization in real-time maximizes a user-specific objective function based on the guidance from the obtained network predicted conditions as well as the TEE. The tokens associated with each option are determined before running the personalization based on the formula provided in Section 2.3.1., the optimal TEE and the estimated energy consumption for each potential menu alternative using TripEnergy (Needell and Trancik, 2018). The savings are the key variables to be maximized in Tripod. A reference energy value is computed for each trip request based on the expected energy consumption without tokens. The reader is referred to Lima Azevedo et al. (2018) and Araldo et al. (2019) for details on the formulation, implementation, and configuration of Tripod.

In preliminary assessments of different Tripod designs, a simulation-based evaluation, as in Section 2.4, was used. Results were obtained by implementing Smart Mobility features and the controls generated by Tripod in SimMobility, in an interactive manner. During each roll period, the following sequence of interactions occur: (1) Tripod *prediction* module obtains sensing information (e.g., counts and speed measurements) from SimMobility for the latest roll period, conducts online calibration of DynaMIT supply and demand simulators, performs the system optimization loop based on state prediction for the duration of the rolling horizon to find the optimal TEE for the current roll period, and passes the TEE and predictive traffic and energy information to the personalization module. (2) The latter receives Tripod requests from simulated users in SimMobility and generates personalized menu with tokens potentially assigned for each request using the latest TEE and predictive information. (3) SimMobility then simulates each Tripod user's responses to the personalized menu as well as all other travelers' choices and loads all travelers to the network. This closed-loop framework reflects how Tripod would work in real life where SimMobility is replaced by the real world.

The preliminary experiments on the route and departure time choice dimensions of Tripod were conducted on a simulation model of the Boston

FIGURE 12.15 Map of Boston CBD (Lima Azevedo et al., 2018).

Central Business District (CBD), in Massachusetts, United States (Fig. 12.15) with a network of 843 nodes, 1879 links, 3075 segments and 5034 lanes including both highways and arterials. The simulation period was from 6:00 a.m. to 9:00 a.m. with a roll period of 5 min and a rolling horizon of 15 min. The total number of travelers was 47,588.

The effectiveness of Tripod was evaluated by performing two simulations: with and without Tripod. In both simulations, all travelers receive real-time predicted information on network conditions and thus the difference in performance is only due to tokens. The performance measures were the average travel time and energy consumption per vehicle and the distribution of travel time and energy consumption.

In the preliminary tests, a budget of 2000 tokens per 5 min was used (a total of 72,000 over a 3-hour period and a monetary value of a token of $0.50). Since the models are not calibrated, our discussion focuses more on the relative magnitude of savings, instead of the absolute values.

As seen in Table 12.3, as the penetration rate of Tripod increases, the energy savings increase. The rate of increase, however, is not a monotonic function of the penetration rate, suggesting a highly nonlinear underlying

TABLE 12.3 Preliminary results with route and departure time choice in Boston CBD.

Penetration rate	Average energy consumption per Trip (MJ)	Energy savings per Trip	Average Travel time (seconds)	Travel time savings per Trip
0 (base case)	9.2	N/A	458	N/A
25%	9.0	2.1%	442	3.5%
40%	8.7	5.4%	409	10.7%
50%	8.7	5.4%	417	9.0%
60%	8.7	5.4%	413	9.8%
75%	8.6	6.5%	420	8.3%
80%	8.6	6.5%	420	8.3%

system, and specifically, an effect of saturation as the penetration rate gets close to 80%.

4. Discussion and conclusions

In this chapter, we provided an overview of three methodological components of smart mobility systems analysis: prediction, optimization, and personalization. These methodologies are designed to interact with each other during the operations of Smart Mobility. Predictions are critical so that the optimization of several policies (e.g., tolls, incentives) is done taking into account the real-time data in a predictive manner. Prediction and optimization both guide personalization such that the attributes of alternatives reflect the real-time conditions and the optimal policies when offering menus to individuals.

Those methodologies can be enhanced in several dimensions. First of all, the demand representation in prediction and optimization methods is typically at an aggregate level. Extending them with disaggregate models is a promising direction. This naturally may come at the expense of computational burden and efficient methodologies for prediction and predictive optimization need to be developed. The prediction is considered with a focus of predicting traffic conditions. Nevertheless, predicting user requests in the future is very important during the operation of Smart Mobility solutions in order to better allocate the resources across received requests. Furthermore, the presented methodologies have more of a model-driven nature even though high-resolution data is exploited from the behavioral perspective. Ways of effectively and efficiently combining model-driven and data-driven methodologies across prediction, optimization, and personalization need to be further investigated.

While this chapter illustrated the methodologies on two case studies, the approach is suitable for any type of Smart Mobility solution. Mobility as a Service (MaaS) is one example of an emerging integrated mobility platform that is amenable to this type of analysis. MaaS offers mobility bundles to users that combine urban public transport, taxi and on-demand services, shared bikes and personal mobility devices (e.g., e-scooters), and carshare and rental services. Ongoing research on MaaS demonstrates its benefits. For example, a stated preferences survey conducted by Matyas and Kamargianni (2017) deployed in Greater London found higher preference for flexible, mass-transited oriented plans. And field experiments with MaaS subscribers in Helsinki, where users can choose monthly subscription packages or pay-as-you-go schemes, indicate a significant increase in mass transit share and taxi trips per person as well as monthly public transport spending. Simulation of FMOD, as a special case of MaaS, also indicates the potential benefits of flexibility and personalization in MaaS: potential reduction of system-wide travel time by 5% and about 10%−20% reduction in volume-to-capacity ratio in Singapore network simulated through SimMobility. Such MaaS systems would be working more efficiently when integrated with prediction and optimization methodologies presented in this chapter.

Two issues not addressed in this chapter will likely influence the long-term impacts and the adoption of Smart Mobility solutions. The first is the interplay between on-demand mobility options and public transit. For example, a study by UC Davis indicated that ride hailing resulted in a decline in mass transit usage by 6% in the United States from 2014 to 2016. On the other hand, few cities have partnered with ridesourcing services to provide first-/last-mile connectivity to public transit (Shen et al., 2017; Lyft, 2015). If shared on-demand mobility is to replace mass transit, large fleet sizes will be required to meet demand resulting in additional congestion. For example, Basu et al. (2018) found that a scenario of automated mobility on demand (AMOD) substituting mass transit in Singapore would result in 50% higher in-vehicle travel times compared to a scenario where AMOD complements mass transit. Future research should study various integration scenarios of on-demand mobility with mass transit to assess their impacts on mass transit ridership and network performance.

Another factor that has helped in the quick adoption of on-demand mobility is shifting societal mobility preferences of millennials, i.e., those who were born between 1981 and 2000. Millennials are less likely to own cars and more likely to adopt a lifestyle of city living, environmental sustainability, and walking and cycling (Circella et al., 2015). They are also comfortable with information technology and services of the sharing economy including on-demand ride hailing services such as Uber and Lyft shared mobility (Mah-massani, 2016). It is unclear, however, whether these preferences are stable or whether millennials would revert to car-based modality styles as they enter the (delayed) child-rearing phase of their life. At any rate, the evolution of these preferences is likely to have an impact on the speed of uptake of on-demand shared mobility services of the future.

Acknowledgments

The data for the Singapore and Boston networks was provided by the Singapore Land Transport Authority (LTA) ITS division and the Boston Region Metropolitan Planning Organization (Boston MPO), respectively. Research related to Tripod was carried out under the U.S. DoE's Advanced Research Projects Agency-Energy (ARPA-E) TRANSNET Program, Award Number DE-AR0000611. FMOD concept was developed in collaboration with Fujitsu Laboratories, Ltd., Japan, in the earlier phases of the research. Singapore related prediction and optimization work was supported by the National Research Foundation of Singapore (SMART program). The research presented in this chapter is a collaborative effort of the Intelligent Transportation Systems (ITS) Laboratory at MIT and at SMART covering various research projects over the last few years. Therefore, this chapter is a result of the interactions with students and colleagues: Andrea Araldo, Kakali Basak, Simon Oh, Muhammad Adnan, Mazen Danaf, Xiang Song, Samarth Gupta, Isabel Hemerly Viegas de Lima, Haizheng Zhang, and others.

References

Adnan, M., Pereira, F.C., Azevedo, C.M.L., Basak, K., Lovric, M., Raveau, S., Zhu, Y., Ferreira, J., Zegras, C., Ben-Akiva, M., 2016. SimMobility: a multi-scale integrated agent-based simulation platform. In: Proceedings of the 95th Annual Meeting of the Transportation Research Board, Washington, D.C.

Adnan, M., Pereira, F.C., Lima Azevedo, C., Basak, K., Koh, K., Loganathan, H., Peng, Z.H., Ben-Akiva, M., 2017. Evaluating disruption management strategies in rail transit using SimMobility mid-term simulator: a study of Singapore MRT North-East line. In: Proceedings of the Transportation Research Board 96th Annual Meeting, Washington, D.C.

Alonso-Mora, J., Samaranayake, S., Wallar, A., Frazzoli, E., Rus, D., 2017. On-demand high-capacity ride-sharing via dynamic trip-vehicle assignment. Proceedings of the National Academy of Sciences 114 (3), 462–467.

Antoniou, C., 2004. On-Line Calibration for Dynamic Traffic Assignment. PhD thesis. Massachusetts Institute of Technology, Cambridge, MA.

Antoniou, C., Ben-Akiva, M., Koutsopoulos, H.N., 2007. Nonlinear Kalman filtering algorithms for on-line calibration of dynamic traffic assignment models. IEEE Transactions on Intelligent Transportation Systems 8 (4), 661–670.

Araldo, A., Gao, S., Seshadri, R., Lima Azevedo, C., Ghafourian, H., Sui, Y., Ayaz, S., Sukhin, D., Ben-Akiva, M., 2019. System-level optimization of multi-modal transportation networks for energy efficiency using personalized incentives: formulation, implementation and performance. In: Proceedings of the Transportation Research Board 98th Annual Meeting, Washington, D.C.

Ashok, K., 1996. Estimation and Prediction of Time-dependent Origin-Destination Flows. Ph.D. thesis. Massachusetts Institute of Technology, Cambridge, MA.

Ashok, K., Ben-Akiva, M.E., 2002. Estimation and prediction of time-dependent origin-destination flows with a stochastic mapping to path flows and link flows. Transportation Science 36 (2), 184–198.

Atasoy, B., Ikeda, T., Song, X., Ben-Akiva, M., 2015a. The concept and impact analysis of a flexible mobility on demand system. Transportation Research Part C: Emerging Technologies 56, 373–392.

Atasoy, B., Ikeda, T., Ben-Akiva, M., 2015b. Optimizing a flexible mobility on demand system. Transportation Research Record: Journal of the Transportation Research Board 2536 (1), 76–85.

Atasoy, B., Lima de Azevedo, C., Danaf, M., Ding-Mastera, J., Abou-Zeid, M., Cox, N., Zhao, F., Ben-Akiva, M., 2018. In: Context-aware Stated Preferences Surveys for Smart Mobility, 15th International Conference on Travel Behavior Research (IATBR), July 15–20, Santa Barbara, California.

Auld, J., Hope, M., Ley, H., Sokolov, V., Xu, B., Zhang, K., 2016. POLARIS: agent-based modeling framework development and implementation for integrated travel demand and network and operations simulations. Transportation Research Part C: Emerging Technologies 64, 101–116.

Balakrishna, R., 2006. Off-line Calibration for Dynamic Traffic Assignment Models. Ph.D. thesis. Massachusetts Institute of Technology.

Basu, R., Araldo, A., Akkinepally, A.P., Nahmias Biran, B.H., Basak, K., Seshadri, R., Deshmukh, N., Kumar, N., Azevedo, C.L., Ben-Akiva, M., 2018. Automated mobility-on-demand vs. Mass transit: a multi-modal activity-driven agent-based simulation approach. Transportation Research Record: Journal of the Transportation Research Board 2672 (8), 608–618.

Becker, F., Danaf, M., Song, X., Atasoy, B., Ben-Akiva, M., 2018. Bayesian estimator for Logit Mixtures with inter- and intra-consumer heterogeneity. Transportation Research Part B: Methodological 117 (A), 1–17.

Ben-Akiva, M.E., Lerman, S.R., 1985. Discrete Choice Analysis: Theory and Application to Travel Demand. MIT Press, Cambridge.

Ben-Akiva, M., Koutsopoulos, H.N., Antoniou, C., Balakrishna, R., 2010. Traffic simulation with dynamit. In: Fundamentals of Traffic Simulation. Springer, New York, NY, pp. 363–398.

Ben-Akiva, M., McFadden, D., Train, K., 2019. Foundations of stated preference elicitation consumer behavior and choice-based conjoint analysis. Foundations and Trends in Econometrics 10 (1–2), 1–144.

Benevolo, C., Dameri, R.P., D'Auria, B., 2016. Smart mobility in smart city. In: Torre, T., Braccini, A., Spinelli, R. (Eds.), Empowering Organizations. Lecture Notes in Information Systems and Organisation, vol. 11. Springer, Cham.

Cherchi, E., Cirillo, C., de Dios Ortuzar, J., 2009. A mixed logit mode choice model for panel data: accounting for different correlation over time periods. Presented at International Choice Modelling Conference (ICMC).

Choudhury, C.F., Yang, L., e Silva, J.D.A., Ben-Akiva, M., 2018. Modelling preferences for smart modes and services: a case study in Lisbon. Transportation Research Part A: Policy and Practice 115, 15–31.

Circella, G., Tiedeman, K., Handy, S., Mokhtarian, P., 2015. Factors Affecting Passenger Travel Demand in the United States. National Center for Sustainable Transportation, UC Davis.

Cordeau, J.F., Laporte, G., 2007. The dial-a-ride problem: models and algorithms. Annals of Operations Research 153 (1), 29–46.

Cottrill, C., Pereira, F., Zhao, F., Dias, I., Lim, H., Ben-Akiva, M., Zegras, P., 2013. Future mobility survey: Experience in developing a smartphone-based travel survey in Singapore. Transportation Research Record: Journal of the Transportation Research Board 2354 (1), 59–67.

Danaf, M., Becker, F., Song, X., Atasoy, B., Ben-Akiva, M., 2019a. Online Discrete choice models: applications in personalized recommendations. Decision Support Systems 119, 35–45.

Danaf, M., Atasoy, B., Lima de Azevedo, C., Ding-Mastera, J., Abou-Zeid, M., Cox, N., Zhao, F., Ben-Akiva, M.E., 2019b. Context-aware stated preferences with smartphone-based travel surveys. Journal of Choice Modelling 31, 35–50.

Davis, J., Gallego, G., Topaloglu, H., 2013. Assortment Planning under the Multinomial Logit Model with Totally Unimodular Constraint Structures. Department of IEOR, Columbia University. Available at: http://www.columbia.edu/~gmg2/logit_const.pdf.

Davis, J.M., Gallego, G., Topaloglu, H., 2014. Assortment optimization under variants of the nested logit model. Operations Research 62 (2), 250–273.

Docherty, I., Marsden, G., Anable, J., 2018. The governance of smart mobility. Transportation Research Part A 115, 114–125.

Feldman, J., Topaloglu, H., 2015. Bounding optimal expected revenues for assortment optimization under mixtures of multinomial logits. Production and Operations Management 24 (10), 1598–1620.

Google Maps, 2018. Singapore Expressway Network.

Gupta, S., Seshadri, R., Atasoy, B., Pereira, F.C., Wang, S., Vu, V.A., Ben-Akiva, M., 2016. Real time optimization of network control strategies in DYNAMIT 2.0. In: Proceedings of the 95th Annual Meeting of the Transportation Research Board, Washington, D.C.

Harb, M., Xiao, Y., Circella, G., Mokhtarian, P.L., Walker, J., 2018. Projecting Travelers into a World of Self-Driving Vehicles: Estimating Travel Behavior Implications via a Naturalistic Experiment. Working paper, July 2018.

Hashemi, H., Abdelghany, K.F., 2016. Real-time traffic network state estimation and prediction with decision support capabilities: application to integrated corridor management. Transportation Research Part C: Emerging Technologies 73, 128–146.

Hassan, A., Abdelghany, K., Semple, J., 2013. Dynamic road pricing for revenue maximization: modeling framework and solution methodology. Transportation Research Record: Journal of the Transportation Research Board 2345, 100–108.

Hemerly Viegas de Lima, I., Danaf, M., Akkinepally, A., De Azevedo, C.L., Ben-Akiva, M., 2018. Modelling framework and implementation of activity- and agent-based simulation: an application to the greater Boston area. Transportation Research Record: Journal of the Transportation Research Board 2672 (49), 146–157.

Hess, S., Rose, J.M., 2009. Allowing for intra-respondent variations in coefficients estimated on repeated choice data. Transportation Research Part B: Methodological 43 (6), 708–719.

Iacobucci, J., Hovenkotter, K., Anbinder, J., 2017. Transit systems and the impacts of shared mobility. In: Meyer, G., Shaheen, S. (Eds.), Disrupting Mobility: Impacts of Sharing Economy and Innovative Transportation on Cities (Lecture Notes in Mobility). Springer International Publishing AG 2017, pp. 65–76.

Jiao, J., Miro, J., McGrath, N., 2017. What Public Transit Can Learn from Uber and Lyft. https://theconversation.com/what-public-transit-can-learn-from-uber-and-lyft-85145.

Kamargianni, M., Li, W., Matyas, M., Schäfer, A., 2016. A critical review of new mobility services for urban transport. Transportation Research Procedia 14, 3294–3303.

Kök, A.G., Fisher, M.L., Vaidyanathan, R., 2008. Assortment planning: review of literature and industry practice. In: Retail Supply Chain Management, pp. 99—153 (Springer US. Chicago).

Lima Azevedo, C.L., Marczuk, K., Raveau, S., Soh, H., Adnan, M., Basak, K., Loganathan, H., Deshmunkh, N., Lee, D.H., Frazzoli, E., Ben-Akiva, M., 2016. Microsimulation of demand and supply of autonomous mobility on demand. Transportation Research Record: Journal of the Transportation Research Board 2564, 21—30.

Lima Azevedo, C., Seshadri, R., Gao, S., Atasoy, B., Akkinepally, A.P., Christofa, E., Zhao, F., Trancik, J., Ben-Akiva, M., 2018. Tripod: sustainable travel incentives with prediction, optimization, and personalization. In: Proceedings of the Transportation Research Board 97th Annual Meeting, Washington, DC (No. 18-06769).

Lou, Y., Yin, Y., Laval, J.A., 2011. Optimal dynamic pricing strategies for high-occupancy/toll lanes. Transportation Research Part C: Emerging Technologies 19 (1), 64—74.

Lu, Y., Adnan, M., Basak, K., Pereira, F.C., Carrion, C., Saber, V.H., Loganathan, H., Ben-Akiva, M.E., 2015a. SimMobility mid-term simulator: a state of the art integrated agent based demand and supply model. In: Proceedings of the Transportation Research Board 94th Annual Meeting, Washington, DC.

Lu, Y., Seshadri, R., Pereira, F., OSullivan, A., Antoniou, C., Ben-Akiva, M., 2015b. DynaMIT2. 0: architecture design and preliminary results on real-time data fusion for traffic prediction and crisis management. In: Intelligent Transportation Systems (ITSC), 2015 IEEE 18th International Conference on. IEEE, pp. 2250—2255.

Lyft, 2015. Friends with Transit: Exploring the Intersection of Lyft and Public Transportation. https://take.lyft.com/friendswithtransit/.

Mahmassani, H.S., 2001. Dynamic network traffic assignment and simulation methodology for advanced system management applications. Networks and Spatial Economics 1 (3—4) 267—292. https://doi.org/10.1023/A:1012831808926.

Mahmassani, H.S., 2016. Technological innovation and the future of urban personal travel. In: Schofer, J.L., Mahmassani, H.S. (Eds.), Mobility 2050: A Vision for Transportation Infrastructure. The Transportation Center, Northwestern University.

Matyas, M., Kamargianni, M., 2017. Stated preference design for exploring demand for "mobility as a service" plans. In: Proceedings of the International Choice Modeling Conference (ICMC), Cape Town, South Africa.

Needell, Z.A., Trancik, J.E., 2018. Efficiently simulating personal vehicle energy consumption in mesoscopic transport models. In: Proceedings of the 97th Annual Meeting of the Transportation Research Board.

Prakash, A.A., Seshadri, R., Antoniou, C., Pereira, F.C., Ben-Akiva, M., 2017. Reducing the dimension of online calibration in dynamic traffic assignment systems. Transportation Research Record: Journal of the Transportation Research Board 2667, 96—107.

Prakash, A.A., Seshadri, R., Antoniou, C., Pereira, F.C., Ben-Akiva, M., 2018. Improving scalability of generic online calibration for real-time dynamic traffic assignment systems. Transportation Research Record: Journal of the Transportation Research Board 2672 (48), 79—92.

Santi, P., Resta, G., Szell, M., Sobolevsky, S., Strogatz, S.H., Ratti, C., 2014. Quantifying the benefits of vehicle pooling with shareability networks. Proceedings of the National Academy of Sciences 111 (37), 13290—13294.

Schechtner, K., Hanson, M., 2017. Shared mobility in asian megacities: the rise of the apps. In: Meyer, G., Shaheen, S. (Eds.), Disrupting Mobility: Impacts of Sharing Economy and Innovative Transportation on Cities (Lecture Notes in Mobility). Springer International Publishing AG 2017, pp. 77—88.

Seik, F.T., 2000. An advanced demand management instrument in urban transport: Electronic road pricing in Singapore. Cities 17, 33–45.

Shen, Y., Zhang, H., Zhao, J., 2017. Embedding autonomous vehicle sharing in public transit system: example of last-mile problem. In: Proceedings of the 96th Annual Meeting of the Transportation Research Board, Washington, D.C.

Song, X., 2018. Personalization of Future Urban Mobility. PhD dissertation. Department of Civil and Environmental Engineering, MIT.

Song, X., Danaf, M., Atasoy, B., Ben-Akiva, M., 2018. Personalized menu optimization with preference updater: a Boston case study. Transportation Research Record: Journal of the Transportation Research Board 2672 (8), 599–607.

Train, K.E., 2001. A Comparison of Hierarchical Bayes and Maximum Simulated Likelihood for Mixed Logit (Working paper).

Train, K.E., 2009. Discrete Choice Methods with Simulation, second ed. Cambridge University Press, New York.

Vazifeh, M.M., Santi, P., Resta, G., Strogatz, S.H., Ratti, C., 2018. Addressing the minimum fleet problem in on-demand urban mobility. Nature 557 (7706), 534.

Xie, Y., Danaf, M., Lima De Azevedo, C., Prakash, A., Atasoy, B., Jeong, K., Seshadri, R., Ben-Akiva, M., 2019. Behavioral modeling of on-demand mobility services: general framework and application to sustainable travel incentives. Forthcoming in Transportation.

Yang, Q., Koutsopoulos, H., Ben-Akiva, M., 2000. Simulation laboratory for evaluating dynamic traffic management systems. Transportation Research Record: Journal of the Transportation Research Board 1710, 122–130.

Zhang, G., Wang, Y., Wei, H., Yi, P., 2008. A feedback-based dynamic tolling algorithm for high-occupancy toll lane operations. Transportation Research Record: Journal of the Transportation Research Board (2065), 54–63.

Ziemke, D., Nagel, K., Bhat, C., 2015. Integrating CEMDAP and MATSim to increase the transferability of transport demand models. Transportation Research Record: Journal of the Transportation Research Board 2493, 117–125.

Zhao, F., Ghorpade, A., Pereira, F.C., Zegras, C., Ben-Akiva, M., 2015. Quantifying mobility: pervasive technologies for transport modeling. In: Adjunct Proceedings of the 2015 ACM International Joint Conference on Pervasive and Ubiquitous Computing and Proceedings of the 2015 ACM International Symposium on Wearable Computers. ACM, pp. 1039–1044.

Zhao, F., Seshadri, R., Gershenfeld, S., Lima Azevedo, C., Kumarga, L., Xie, Y., Ben-Akiva, M., 2018. The Modes They Are A-Changin': A New Framework for Passenger Travel Modes (Working paper).

Zhu, Y., Diao, M., Ferreira, J., Zegras, C., 2018. An integrated microsimulation approach to land-use and mobility modeling. Journal of Transport and Land Use 11 (1), 633–659.

Zhuang, J., Mei, T., Hoi, S.C., Xu, Y.Q., Li, S., 2011. When recommendation meets mobile: contextual and personalized recommendation on the go. In: Proceedings of the 13th International Conference on Ubiquitous Computing. ACM, pp. 153–162.

Chapter 13

Urban air mobility

Raoul Rothfeld[1,2], Anna Straubinger[1], Mengying Fu[1], Christelle Al Haddad[2], Constantinos Antoniou[2]
[1]*Bauhaus Luftfahrt e.V., Taufkirchen, Germany;* [2]*Chair of Transportation Systems Engineering, Department of Civil, Geo and Environmental Engineering, Technical University of Munich, Munich, Germany*

Chapter outline

1. Introduction

Current technological advances in energy storage densities, as well as in electric and distributed propulsion, facilitate the development of passenger-carrying, short-haul air vehicles—so-called personal air vehicles (PAVs) or next-generation vertical takeoff and landing (VTOL) vehicles. These vehicle concepts, which promise to be quieter, safer, and cheaper to produce and operate than conventional helicopters, revitalize the idea of using urban airspace for intracity passenger transport, i.e., urban air mobility (UAM).

The concept of using urban aerial transportation is not novel, however, and had—at one time—been well established in, most notably, New York with New York Airways, which operated commercial helicopter-based passenger transport services from 1953 to 1979. After a series of fatal accidents and crashes, however, New York Airways ceased its operation and filed for bankruptcy shortly after. While this chapter of urban aerial mobility came to an abrupt end, today, various helicopter transport services have reemerged in traffic-stricken metropolises such as São Paulo, Mexico City, and, yet again, New York.

Companies like Fly Blade Inc. and Voom offer helicopter passenger transport services on an on-demand basis by making use of mobile applications for ad hoc ridehailing. For those helicopter services, flight schedules have, thus, been made obsolete by Internet-connected technologies. Now, with

Demand for Emerging Transportation Systems. https://doi.org/10.1016/B978-0-12-815018-4.00013-9

the advent of novel vehicle concepts for VTOL, an additional driver of UAM could be emerging.

Recently, a multitude of companies can be observed that race each other to advance VTOL technologies and to prototype and mass-produce the first next-generation VTOL vehicle, as illustrated by Shamiyeh et al., 2017). Besides the vehicles themselves, however, it is necessary to understand a vast array of research, as UAM requires the coordination and interaction of various fields, such as air traffic management, infrastructure development, integration with ground-based transport systems, public safety and acceptance, and regulations. The remainder of this chapter provides a literature overview of three key aspects for understanding potential demand, supply, and external effects of UAM by discussing its passenger adoption, transport modeling, and spatial as well as welfare effects.

2. Passenger adoption

By making use of aerial transport capacity, UAM is aimed at reducing problems facing the growing demand for mobility in an increasingly crowded environment, such as congestion, pollution, and scarcity of urban space. Advances in automation technology, notably for ground vehicles, could potentially also be applied for air mobility, leading to autonomous flying vehicles. The underlying assumption, feeding into the idea of widespread UAM usage, is that UAM vehicles will be fully autonomous in order to provide affordable on-demand aerial mobility for everyone.

The time frame for its potential implementation, however, remains unknown as it is subject to many challenges. These are mostly related to regulations, technology, safety, but also public and the potential passengers' acceptance; with social acceptance being one of the key components to UAM's implementation (c.f. Liu et al., 2017). As technological solutions are constantly evolving and regulations being negotiated, social acceptance remains one of the less predictable components and, therefore, a main challenge to UAM's introduction to the market.

Adoption and usage are the result of complex decision processes and depend on many unobserved variables. Therefore, many surveys focus on improving the understanding of people's perception toward new technologies, thereby identifying the most influential factors in their acceptance and adoption. Still, in the case of UAM, research lacks studies focusing on user perception and most existing surveys have been focusing on autonomous ground-based vehicles.

Only recently, research institutions have begun to take interest in UAM's social acceptance. A study by Garrow et al. (2018a) from the Georgia Institute of Technology, collected responses from about 2500 high-income workers in different areas of the United States, to more accurately predict demand for VTOL trips. NASA commissioned two comprehensive market studies (see

Cohen et al., 2018; Berger, 2018) looking at UAM from market, regulatory, societal barrier, and weather impact perspectives. In Germany, research on UAM has been facilitated by the city of Ingolstadt as part of the so-called Urban Air Mobility Initiative, supported by the European Commission. The Technical University of Munich has also taken interest in this topic, with first research into establishing mode choice models including autonomous ground- and air-based transport modes by Fu et al. (2019) and a factor study for passenger adoption among Munich residents by Al Haddad et al. (2019). Lately, several consulting groups including Berger (2018) and HorvathPartners (2019) focused on defining UAM success factors and assessing the UAM market potential, respectively.

Al Haddad et al. (2019) conducted an online survey and collected 221 responses, among which 97 were Munich residents, to extract the factors influencing the potential adoption and use of UAM. The initial findings confirmed that most of the respondents ranked safety as the most important factor affecting their adoption of UAM. By using exploratory factor analysis, the following factors were extracted and had a relatively high explanatory power: value of time savings, affinity to automation, safety concerns, data concerns, environmental awareness, and affinity to online services, social media, and sharing. Discrete choice models, i.e., ordered logit models, allowed to identify patterns for adoption, where uncertain adopters (uncertain about their time of UAM adoption) had similar attitudes to late adopters. Trust was found to be a key factor in the intention to adopt UAM and was positively influenced by the perceived reliability of automation, perceived vehicle's safety, perceived locus of control, previous automation experience, and the service provider's reputation.

Understanding passenger perception of UAM is a must to understand the technology as it allows the relevant stakeholders, such as governments or manufacturers, to take the corresponding measures to best address social acceptance. In this perspective, research should also focus on mode choice in an environment comprising both conventional modes of transport, which might be autonomous in the future, and UAM.

Current research concerning VTOL and UAM often focuses on techno-logical and operational aspects (see e.g., Holden and Goel, 2016; Parker, 2017; Schuchardt et al., 2015). Only very little mode choice research can be found that analyzes the potential user preference among conventional transport modes and novel transport service, such as UAM. Though, based on a general review of factors affecting transport mode choice, as well as existing studies using choice theory to model various aspects of autonomous vehicles (AVs) and shared autonomous vehicles (SAVs), mode choice factors can be categorized into three groups when applied to UAM: (1) transportation service variables, (2) individual-specific variables, and (3) attitudinal/psychological variables.

With regard to transportation service variables, cost- and time-related attributes have been most commonly considered in transportation mode choice studies (c.f. Fu et al., 2019). Several other factors have been found relevant as well, particularly regarding the adoption of AVs and UAM. For instance, Winter et al. (2017) conducted a stated preference experiment and developed logit models to study mode choice among car-sharing, private car, public transportation (PT), and SAV in the Netherlands. Among the travel time-related attributes, waiting time for SAVs has been found to be insignificant. Nevertheless, other studies (e.g., Fagnant and Kockelman, 2018; Krueger et al., 2016) estimated the value of time (VOT) and willingness to pay of AVs and SAVs, showing an opposing view that waiting time is a critical service attribute of SAV operations. Similar to the findings of Krueger et al. (2016) on travel time and travel cost of SAVs, the recent mode choice study of Fu et al. (2019) concluded that travel time and travel cost might also be significant determinants of UAM adoption, although further research is expected to provide insights into the impact of waiting time and first- and last-mile services.

To understand individuals' willingness to pay for travel time savings, VOT measures have been commonly conducted for transportation mode choice studies in different countries or regions. For example, Atasoy et al. (2011) and Axhausen et al. (2006) have conducted studies in Switzerland regarding private car and public transportation usage. A Europe-wide meta-analysis (Wardman and Chintakayala, 2012) concerning VOT of conventional transportation modes has also been conducted with regard to different trip purposes, e.g., leisure or business purpose. Although rare, a few recent studies, which present VOT findings of autonomous transportation services, have been found as well. For instance, Correia et al. (2019) published VOT study results regarding SAVs in the Netherlands, while Fu et al. (2019) presented preliminary VOT estimations on SAVs and UAM. Nevertheless, it is worth noting that the measures of VOT differ greatly in-between studies and study areas, as the value of time can be affected by many, highly diverse factors, such as income level or quality and performance of existing transportation systems—all of which may vary greatly by study area and time.

The result of a general mode choice literature review indicates that socioeconomic variables, such as gender, age, and income have impact on mode choice behavior (see e.g., Fu et al., 2019; Atasoy et al., 2011; Vrtic et al., 2009). However, concerning the influence of personal and household characteristics on the choice to travel by AVs or SAVs, the before-mentioned research does not provide consistent findings (Fu et al., 2019). Assessing age as a factor, some studies state that younger individuals are more willing to adopt AVs (Bansal et al., 2016), while others found that SAVs could constitute an attractive mobility option especially for the elderly (Fagnant and Kockelman, 2018). Moreover, Bansal et al. (2016) and Kyriakidis et al. (2015) observed a positive relationship between willingness to pay for autonomous features and income. In addition, a few studies also revealed a significant impact of education level and presence of children in the household (c.f Haboucha et al., 2017; Zmud et al., 2016). Similar aspects have been mentioned in recent research regarding flying vehicles and UAM: Castle et al. (2017) presented survey results which indicate that younger and more educated respondents are more willing to accept pilotless aircraft. Cohen et al. (2018) revealed greater excitement regarding UAM among middle- and upper-income households and younger and middle-aged respondents, as well as among respondents with higher level of educational attainment. Fu et al. (2019) mode choice study concerning UAM suggested that market penetration rate for UAM may be greater among younger respondents and older individuals with high income, who also have a relatively high propensity to use ground-based AVs.

Besides socioeconomic variables, other factors, such as current modality patterns, have also been found relevant to the adoption of AVs and UAM. For example, car users (drivers) are more likely to switch to SAVs than PT users (Krueger et al., 2016). Similar findings have been stated by Fu et al. (2019) that switching to either autonomous taxi or UAM is less likely if the individuals currently use PT or soft modes, i.e., walking and cycling, most often. Trip purpose may be another influencing factor. Similar to the results of the mode choice study including UAM (Fu et al., 2019) (as illustrated in Fig. 13.1), an Airbus study (Thompson, 2018), Garrow et al. (2018b), and Cohen et al. (2018) found that individuals may be particularly interested in using a flying taxi service for performing business and recreational trips.

Attitudinal factors, such as the preference for convenience, comfort, and flexibility have attracted increasing attention and found to be relevant to transportation mode choice behavior (Vredin Johansson et al., 2006). Existing literature highlights the impact of safety on AVs adoptions (e.g., Haboucha et al., 2017; Fu et al., 2019). Individuals who tend to use AVs or SAVs also express greater concern for the environment (Haboucha et al., 2017; Howard and Dai, 2014) and stronger technological awareness (Bansal et al., 2016;

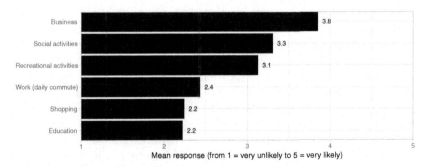

FIGURE 13.1 Survey results of likelihood to use UAM based on various trip purposes, own depiction based on Fu et al. (2019).

Schoettle and Sivak, 2014; KPMG, 2013). Amenities and vehicle automation have also been identified as being influential (Winter et al., 2017; Howard and Dai, 2014). Similarly, safety is regarded as one of the main psychological barriers to adopting flying vehicles (Cohen et al., 2018; Lineberger et al., 2018; Yedavalli and Mooberry, 2019). Interestingly with regard to automation, piloted aircraft are still generally preferred over fully autonomous flying vehicles (Cohen et al., 2018).

The impacts of other potential psychological factors, affecting UAM-related mode choice, have not been thoroughly studied yet. However, the survey results of Fu et al. (2019) regarding attitudes of different demographic groups indirectly reflect the potential technological and environmental concerns, which may affect choice behavior. Similar to the previously mentioned findings related to AV adoption (see Haboucha et al., 2017), Fu et al. (2019) survey results also indicate that younger individuals are more open toward new technologies (see top-left illustration in Fig. 13.2) and, thus, are more likely to adopt novel transport modes. Meanwhile, another group of potential adopters who are older and with high income may be more willing to pay for new technological and environmental-friendly transportation services. However, the low-income group with lower education level is likely to have less technological and environmental concerns and, therefore, may be less willing to accept novel transportation concepts, such as UAM.

Various findings have been presented by different UAM-related studies with focus on passenger adoption perspectives. Not all studies provide consistent conclusions regarding the factors affecting UAM adoption. However, several highly relevant demand drivers of UAM adoption, such as travel time, costs, value of time savings, safety concerns, income, environmental awareness, and affinity to sharing have been commonly highlighted in most of the mentioned studies.

3. Modeling urban air mobility

To provide a general picture of the operational UAM environment, current research focuses on investigating concept of operations by identifying various vehicle types, infrastructure requirements, environmental impact, and other potential constraints (c.f Holden and Goel, 2016; Antcliff et al., 2016; Kleinbekman et al., 2018; Vascik and Hansman, 2017a). In another study, Vascik and Hansman (2017b) provide specific operational suggestions regarding the identification of locations for VTOL infrastructure, so-called vertiports, and the capacity of air traffic control; while Balakrishnan et al. (2018) present an overview of routing strategies for UAM operation. General guidance in transportation network design and its various influencing factors is given by Rodrigue et al. (2017), with first studies confirming the importance of the number and distribution of UAM vertiport within a study area, as, e.g., shown by Rothfeld et al. (2018a) in the use case of Sioux Falls.

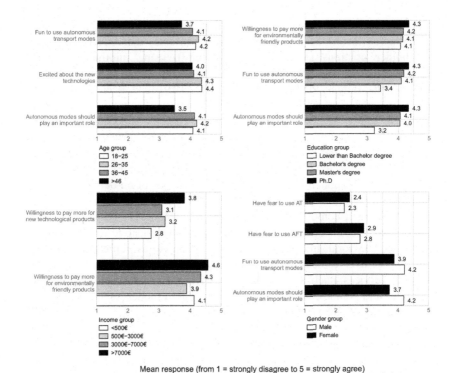

FIGURE 13.2 Survey result of technological and environmental concerns of different demographic groups, own depiction based on Fu et al. (2019).

Several studies analyze the UAM supply side based on modeling and simulation approaches. The object-oriented model developed by Kohlman and Patterson (2018) showed that a vehicle's recharging/refuelling rates can affect its ability to meet potential demand. Kohlman and Patterson (2018) also highlighted the importance of having a sufficient number of vertiports. Another simulation evaluation of Bosson and Lauderdale (2018) applied the so-called Autoresolver algorithm, which focused on the seamless integration of a new transport mode into an existing system by identifying valid vertiports locations. The Autoresolver algorithm has been proposed as a service with the potential to manage an entire UAM network with both strategic and tactical scheduling capabilities.

Meanwhile, estimating the demand and evaluating the demand drivers is a prerequisite for introducing UAM to the market (Straubinger and Rothfeld, 2018). A few studies address demand estimation of UAM-based on logit model for mode choice (e.g., Fu et al., 2019; Syed, 2017). The preliminary results of Syed (2017) show that the cost of on-demand VTOL must be kept rather low for UAM, for it to become a significant competitor to other modes.

Although not directly linked to UAM, Reddy and DeLaurentis (2016) explored demographic factors as well as stakeholder variables that affect public and stakeholder opinions about unmanned aircraft, using multinomial probit models. To identify a market niche, which can be filled by UAM, a few market studies (e.g., Berger, 2018; HorvathPartners, 2019) have been implemented based on analyzing market models. The UAM market potential has been projected, following a two-fold modeling approach, comparing the demand with and without considering current technological restrictions, economic constrains, and social barriers. One study (HorvathPartners, 2019) stated that UAM will play an important part in future multimodal mobility concepts.

Having been applied to modeling non-UAM types of on-demand aviation, the so-called strategic modeling method estimates future demand using socioeconomic and demographic information (see Moore and Goodrich, 2013; Smith et al., 2012). Strategic models are currently sensitive to many of the required behavioral impacts and can be adapted to represent changing behavior (Travel forecasting resource, 2018). The implementation of new mobility services, such as AVs or UAM, allows for and might require new strategies and policies. As the traditional trip-based models (such as four-step transport model) are not sufficiently sensitive to emerging policy and policy questions, many transport modelers now apply activity-based approaches which take, e.g., individual's budget, their time for activities, and travel patterns throughout a day into account (Travel forecasting resource, 2014).

Currently, the majority of studies modeling and simulating AV operations use MATSim (Horni et al., 2016), an open-source framework, to implement large-scale agent-based transport simulations. Bischoff and Maciejewski (2016a, 2016b) as well as Hörl (2016) estimated SAV demand using MATSim's agent-based model by utilizing the DVPR (Dynamic Vehicle Routing Problem) extension, in order to simulate a wide range of vehicle routing and scheduling processes. Moreno (2017) implemented another approach by modeling SAV services, while considering the feedback between land-use and changes in transportation systems, by coupling the land-use model SILO, the travel demand model MITO, and the transport model MATSim. Thus, providing a comprehensive modeling framework to account for the effects of AVs on transportation as well as land-use. Recently, this agent-based simulation approach using MATSim is also considered as a valid approach to analyze UAM performance.

First studies (e.g., Rothfeld et al., 2018a; Rothfeld et al., 2018b; Balac et al., 2018) regarding UAM infrastructure, vehicles' characteristics, network, and operational fleet capabilities; provide an initial basis for further UAM transport research. The modeling results indicate that the potential travel time reduction perceived by potential passengers, as well as UAM infrastructure and ground-based UAM processes, have an elemental influence on UAM adoption. For smaller study areas, such as Sioux Falls (Rothfeld et al., 2018b) and Zurich (Balac et al., 2018), the importance of short times for accessing

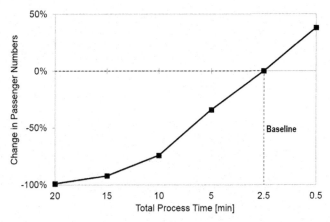

FIGURE 13.3 Impact of UAM process time variations on passenger numbers within a MATSim simulation of Sioux Falls, US (Rothfeld et al., 2018b).

vertiports and boarding UAM vehicles has been repeatedly highlighted. Compare, for example, Figs. 13.3 and 13.4, which show the greater effect of UAM process time increases versus faster UAM cruise speeds on passenger numbers. The travel time savings, gained by UAM's expected high travel speeds, when compared to, e.g., cars, could be negated by potentially long UAM processes before and/or after a UAM flight.

Initial research on UAM ground infrastructure has been presented by, e.g., Vascik and Hansmann (Vascik, 2019) or Fadhil (Fadhil, 2018), who take existing helicopter infrastructure as an approximation for future vertiports from a sizing and throughput perspective. Especially for the envisioned short-

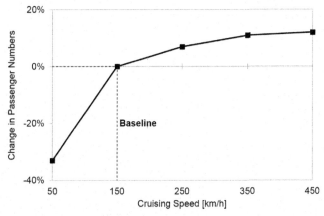

FIGURE 13.4 Impact of UAM cruise speed variations on passenger numbers within a MATSim simulation of Sioux Falls, US (Rothfeld et al., 2018b).

distance, i.e., intracity, usage of UAM, Wölfel (2019) identified the importance of infrastructure placement as a potential bottleneck for the implementation of UAM in Germany. Thus, space requirements and placement options for vertiports, in combination with the high impact of short access times, renders UAM infrastructure positioning as being a major factor in any potential UAM implementation and, thus, should receive even more attention in future UAM modeling research.

A well-functioning transportation system should allow the transport supply to meet transport demand. According to the results of a general literature review, current studies mainly focus on modeling UAM networks and operations. Further research is expected to consider both demand and supply sides of UAM as a whole, in order to enhance the understandings of the overall UAM environment and its impacts. Future studies on modeling UAM should, therefore, combine extended supply- and demand-side approaches to enable comprehensive analyses that fully encompass the various aspects of introducing UAM as a novel transport mode into existing transport systems.

With regard to existing UAM transport modeling approaches using MATSim, further improvements are required to reflect this merging of supply- and demand-side attributes, such as vehicle energy storage capacities, vertiport vehicle capacities, and ensuring vertical and horizontal separation of UAM vehicles during flight. Further, vehicle dispatching algorithms and fleet distribution optimization, as presented by, e.g., Hörl et al. (2019) for autonomous ridehailing services in Zurich, will be aspects relevant to UAM services and might be transferable in their approach to modeling of UAM.

4. Spatial and welfare effects

Besides the impact on the overall transport system, it is essential to understand the influence of UAM on the inhabitants' welfare and the implications for the city. Welfare changes should hereby not only consider shifts directly related to the transport market but also adjustments on other markets due to the introduction of UAM.

Transferring Milakis et al. (2017) methodology, who applied the ripple effect approach to the introduction of automated vehicles, one can differentiate between first-, second-, and third-order implications:

- First-order implications: travel costs, travel time, value of time, travel comfort, mode choice and modal shift, vehicle miles traveled, additional infrastructure
- Second-order implications: impact on other modes (road congestion, existing transport infrastructure, public transport usage), shifts in the location choice of companies and households, changes of the prices on

other markets (e.g., land market, commodity market, labor market), changes in the accessibility of different parts of the urban area

- Third-order implications: urban sprawl, negative environmental aspects: noise, visual annoyance, emissions, safety, social equity, economic impact, public health, energy consumption

While most of the first-order implications have been described in the previous chapters, the following discusses the resulting changes on related markets. Some discussions have already taken place in the literature (see, e.g., UBER, 2016; Holmes et al., 2017; Straubinger and Rothfeld, 2018) Yet, especially in contrast to the literature on the technology of VTOL vehicles, a lot of open questions remain in the field of wider economic impacts of UAM. Nevertheless, some of the findings from autonomous ground vehicle research (c.f Fagnant and Kockelman, 2013; Gruel and Stanford, 2016) can be transferred to UAM as both concepts are rather similar from an end-user perspective.

One decisive question is whether UAM will take car-based transport demand and shift it to the air, or whether additional transport demand will be induced by the introduction of UAM. Potentially, both effects might occur simultaneously. This is an effect that has already been identified in the field of autonomous ground-based vehicles. Duarte and Ratti (2018), for example, discuss the question of whether autonomous vehicles lead to more or less traffic on roads. Large parts of their reasoning can be transferred to UAM.

Additionally, potential modal shifts from public transport or soft modes to UAM are relevant, as this might result in increasing externalities. It is, therefore, essential to ensure a close linkage of any potential UAM introduction with existing transport systems, to reduce the probability of UAM drawing from the demand for PT or soft modes. According to Otte et al. (2018), an efficient integration of UAM and public transport is inevitable, not only from a physical perspective as in developing joint mobility hubs, but also from an organizational point of view with regard to ticketing and distribution platforms.

Besides mode choice, location choice of households and companies within cities can significantly influence the vehicle miles traveled. Thakur et al. (2016) and Duarte and Ratti (2018) already discussed these developments for autonomous ground-based vehicles and indicate that an influence on land rents and location choice is to be expected. Existing literature qualitatively proves that transport investments and, by that, positive changes in accessibility provoke rising land rents and increasing attractiveness of certain housing locations (see Cervero and Kang, 2011).

In the case of UAM, Straubinger and Verhoef (2018) expect two effects to occur: 1) the additional land demand for vertiport infrastructure will decrease the land supply for housing and company locations and 2) the land demand from households and companies will increase due to higher accessibility. These effects and their correlations are depicted in Fig. 13.5.

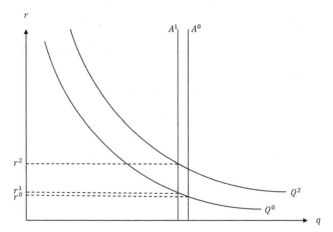

FIGURE 13.5 Changes in land rents in the suburbs due to additional demand and decreasing supply (Straubinger and Verhoef, 2018).

As described by Straubinger and Verhoef (2018), the x-axis denotes the quantity of land q, and the y-axis denotes the land rent per measurement unit r. The land supply for housing and company locations is fixed. A^0 hereby depicts the land supply in the suburb in a scenario without UAM. The introduction of UAM and the arising need for infrastructure result in a decreased land supply (A^1).

With the original demand for land from companies and households (Q^0), an initial price (r^0) is identified. The introduction of UAM is assumed to lead to increased connectivity of the suburb to the city and employment centers. High travel speeds, which UAM might offer, enable massive decreases in travel time. Together with the above-mentioned increasing attractiveness of suburban locations, due to transport service enhancements, the constancy of travel times (see Levinson and Kumar, 1997) allows to assume an increase in land demand by households and companies in the suburb (Q^2). In line with this increase of demand, the land rents in the suburb are expected to increase as well (r^2).

Straubinger and Verhoef (2018) reasoning shows that changes in land rents can arise based on the introduction of new mobility services. The decrease in travel time will also enable households to locate farther away from cities, where they can afford more land for housing. This effect could be reinforced with the advent of autonomous transport technology. Thakur et al. (2016) assume that, in the case of autonomous ground vehicles, people will relocate further away from the city. Additionally, the value of travel time savings decreases, since travel time could be used more productively with automated controls. Transferring this assumption to UAM strengthens the above-made assumption on the relocation of households. Yet, this might not only have positive effects. Longer distances to the city center are likely to result in more vehicle miles traveled. Besides that, most cities do not favor their residents moving away from the city centers, as this leads to urban sprawl. Urban sprawl, i.e., the undesired relocation of people toward the suburbs, leads to lower population densities in city centers, which can result in massive inefficiencies in public services, such as with public infrastructure and public transport provisions (Squires, 2002).

Following Straubinger and Verhoef (2018) approach for UAM and transferring the findings of Thakur et al. (2016) and Duarte and Ratti (2018) for autonomous ground vehicles, relocation of households, due to a potential introduction of UAM, appears to be very likely. Thus, UAM involves the potential for causing undesired urban sprawl.

UAM's ecological impact strongly depends on all different aspects that have been mentioned so far. Only after estimating the vehicle miles traveled and modal splits of holistic transport system analyses, an assessment of UAM's ecological impact can be performed. Even when assuming UAM operators to exclusively use fully electric, shared, and on-demand vehicle services—by that trying to minimize the environmental effect of UAM with regard to, e.g., CO_2 and NOx emissions—noise and visual disturbance are externalities that cannot be avoided. Additionally, UAM also faces similar risks to those of autonomous cars (c.f Goodall et al., 2014; Hubaux et al., 2004; Maurer et al., 2015), in that loss of jobs due to automation, data privacy concerns, and ethical problems with regard to vehicle's automated decision making remain challenges yet to be tackled.

The externalities and other risks should be minimized and/or internalized by an adequate service design. The service design and interests of the service provider strongly relate to the market structure and business model. UAM has different submarkets and players: the vertiport infrastructure provider, the communication infrastructure provider, the air traffic management provider, the vehicle manufacturer, the vehicle owner, the service provider, and the platform provider. The various levels will face different intensities of competition within one level and vertical integration with players on other business levels (Cohen et al., 2018).

As multiple of the submarkets are likely to be dominated by a few market players, in combination with the above-discussed externalities, a potential UAM market is expected to be regulated like most of the other transport modes (see e.g., Baake and von Schlippenbach, 2014; Cairns and Liston-Heyes, 1996; Cantos and Maudos, 2001; de Palma and Lindsey, 2004; Haucap et al., 2015; Weiß, 2003). Thus, regulation strategies, e.g., price regulation, quantity regulation, and quality regulation can be expected to be implemented for UAM services.

As indicated above, there is little to no research in the fields of urban economics and market regulation in the context of UAM. Thus, changes in location choice of households and companies, as well as changes in land rents and urban form, often remain unconsidered. To improve the assessment of overall changes in vehicle miles traveled this is a necessary step. Besides that, households locating farther from the city center might lead to urban sprawl and, by that, to massive inefficiencies especially regarding infrastructure and traveling patterns. To minimize the negative effects of UAM, e.g., externalities (emissions, noise, congestion) and urban sprawl, it also is essential to address regulatory options in future research. The effects of different market regulating policies could be assessed together with UAM's impact on urban structures in an urban spatial computable general equilibrium (CGE) model as proposed by Straubinger and Verhoef (2018).

5. Conclusion

While research surrounding UAM steadily emerges with all its facets from vehicle performance, vehicle design, air traffic management, as well as its adoption, transport system modeling, and spatial and welfare effects; further understanding must be inspired. Only combining findings from the various disciplines of research into one coherent picture—while a formidable task—will facilitate in-depth analyses of the interdependencies of a potential UAM implementation within current transport systems and mobility patterns.

For UAM to become the reality that is currently being envisioned, a vast number of requirements must be fulfilled, from minimal noise levels, to trust building safety standards, and public accessibility that fosters public acceptance. It remains yet to be seen, however, whether manufacturers, transport planners, and researchers can live up to such promises.

The presented overview of research regarding UAM as a novel transport mode illustrates the uptake in UAM-related publications and research from other novel ground-based mobility concepts, such as autonomous ridehailing, that seems applicable to aerial mobility. Throughout the various discussed topics it became obvious that UAM research requires more in-depth analyses and, especially, conjoint studies that bridge multiple subject areas in order to gain a more widely applicable understanding of UAM, its acceptance, modeling, and further-reaching effects.

References

Al Haddad, C., Chaniotakis, E., Straubinger, A., Ploetner, K., Antoniou, C., 2019. User acceptance and adoption of urban air mobility. In: Transport Research: Part A (submitted).

Antcliff, K.R., Moore, M.D., Goodrich, K.H., 2016. Silicon Valley as an Early Adopter for On-Demand Civil VTOL Operations, pp. 1—17.

Atasoy, B., Glerum, A., Bierlaire, M., 2011. Mode choice with attitudinal latent class: a Swiss case-study. In: Second International Choice Modeling Conference, pp. 1—16.

Axhausen, K., Hess, S., König, A., Agay, G., Bates, J., Bierlaire, M., 2006. State of the Art Estimates of the Swiss Value of Travel Time Savings.

Baake, P., von Schlippenbach, V., 2014. Taximarkt: kein markt für eine vollständige liberalisier-ung. DIW-Wochenbericht 81 (31/32), 751−755.

Balac, M., Vetrella, A.R., Rothfeld, R., Schmid, B., 2018. Demand estimation for aerial vehicles in urban settings. IEEE Intelligent Transportation Systems Magazine.

Balakrishnan, K., Polastre, J., Mooberry, J., Golding, R., Sachs, P., 2018. BluePrint For The Sky - The Roadmap for the Safe Integration of Autonomous Aircraft.

Bansal, P., Kockelman, K.M., Singh, A., 2016. Assessing public opinions of and interest in new vehicle technologies: an Austin perspective. Transportation Research Part C: Emerging Technologies 67, 1−14.

Berger, R., 2018. Urban Air Mobility, the rise of a new mode of transportation. Technical Reports.

Bischoff, J., Maciejewski, M., 2016. Autonomous taxicabs in berlin−a spatiotemporal analysis of service performance. Transportation Research Procedia 19, 176−186.

Bischoff, J., Maciejewski, M., 2016. Simulation of city-wide Replacement of private cars with autonomous taxis in berlin. Procedia Computer Science 83 (Ant 2016), 237−244.

Bosson, C., Lauderdale, T.A., 2018. Simulation evaluations of an autonomous urban air mobility network management and separation service. In: 2018 Aviation Technology, Integration, and Operations Conference, p. 3365.

Cairns, R.D., Liston-Heyes, C., 1996. Competition and regulation in the taxi industry. Journal of Public Economics 59 (1), 1−15.

Cantos, P., Maudos, J., 2001. Regulation and efficiency: the case of European railways. Trans-portation Research Part A: Policy and Practice 35 (5), 459−472.

Castle, J., Fornaro, C., Genovesi, D., Lin, E., Strauss, D.E., Waldewitz, T., Edridge, D., 2017. Flying solo − How Far are We Down the Path Towards Pilotless Planes?, p. 53.

Cervero, R., Kang, C.D., 2011. Bus rapid transit impacts on land uses and land values in Seoul, Korea. Transport Policy 18 (1), 102−116.

Cohen, A., Susan, S., Emily, F., 2018. The potential societal barriers of urban air mobility, Ex-ecutive Briefing urban air mobility (UAM) market study. Tech. Rep. Booz Allen Hamilton.

Correia, G.H.d.A., Looff, E., van Cranenburgh, S., Snelder, M., van Arem, B., 2019. On the impact of vehicle automation on the value of travel time while performing work and leisure activities in a car: theoretical insights and results from a stated preference survey. Transportation Research Part A: Policy and Practice 119 (November 2018), 359−382.

de Palma, A., Lindsey, R., June 2004. Congestion pricing with heterogeneous travelers: a general-equilibriumwelfare analysis. Networks and Spatial Economics 4, 135−160.

Duarte, F., Ratti, C., October 2018. The impact of autonomous vehicles on cities: a review. Journal of Urban Technology 25, 3−18.

Fadhil, D.N., 2018. A GIS-Based Analysis for Selecting Ground Infrastructure Locations for Urban Air Mobility. Master's Thesis. Technical University of Munich, Munich.

Fagnant, D., Kockelman, K., 2013. Preparing a nation for autonomous vehicles. Tech. Rep. Eno Center for Transportation.

Fagnant, D.J., Kockelman, K.M., 2018. Dynamic ride-sharing and fleet sizing for a system of shared autonomous vehicles in Austin, Texas. Transportation 45 (1).

Fu, M., Rothfeld, R., Antoniou, C., 2019. Exploring preferences for transportation modes in an urban air mobility environment: munich case study. In: Transportation Research Record. https://doi.org/10.1177/0361198119843858.

Garrow, L.A., German, B., Mokhtarian, P., Daskilewicz, M., Douthat, T.H., Binder, R., June 2018. If you fly it, will commuters come? A Survey to Model Demand for eVTOL Urban Air Trips (Atlanta).

Garrow, L.A., German, B.J., Ilbeigi, M., 2018. Conceptual models of demand for electric propulsion aircraft in intra-urban and Thin-haul markets. In: Transportation Research Board 97th Annual Meeting, Washington DC, United States.

Goodall, N.J., 2014. Machine ethics and automated vehicles. In: Meyer, G., Beiker, S. (Eds.), Road Vehicle Automation. Springer International Publishing, Cham, pp. 93−102.

Gruel, W., Stanford, J.M., January 2016. Assessing the long-term effects of autonomous vehicles: a speculative approach. Transportation Research Procedia 13, 18−29.

Haboucha, C.J., Ishaq, R., Shiftan, Y., 2017. User preferences regarding autonomous vehicles. Transportation Research Part C: Emerging Technologies 78, 37−49.

Haucap, J., Pavel, F., Aigner, R., Arnold, M., Hottenrott, M., Kehder, C., 2015. Chancen der Digitalisierung auf Märkten für urbane Mobilität: Das Beispiel Uber. In: DICE Ordnungspolitische Perspektiven 73. University of Düsseldorf, Düsseldorf Institute for Competition Economics (DICE).

Holden, J., Goel, N., 2016. Fast-forwarding to a Future of On-demand Urban Air Transportation. Tech. rep..

Holmes, B.J., Parker, R.A., Stanley, D., McHugh, P., Garrow, L., Masson, P.M., Olcott, J., Jan. 2017. NASA Strategic Framework for On-Demand Air Mobility - A Report for NASA Headquarters Aeronautics Research Mission Directorate.

Hörl, S., 2016. Implementation of an Autonomous Taxi Service in a Multi-Modal Traffic simulation Using MATSim. Department of Energy and Environment Chalmers University of Technology, p. 82. June.

Hörl, S., Ruch, C., Becker, F., Frazzoli, E., Axhausen, K., 2019. Fleet operational policies for automated mobility: a simulation assessment for zurich. Transportation Research Part C: Emerging Technologies 102, 20−31.

Horni, A., Nagel, K., Axhausen, K.W. (Eds.), 2016. The Multi-Agent Transport Simulation MATSim. Ubiquity Press.

Horvath, Partners, 2019. Business between Sky and Earth, Assessing the Market Potential of Mobility in the 3rd Dimension. Tech rep..

Howard, D., Dai, D., 2014. Public perceptions of self-driving cars: the case of Berkeley, California. MS Transportation Engineering 2014 (1), 21.

Hubaux, J.P., Capkun, S., Luo, J., May 2004. The security and privacy of smart vehicles. IEEE Security Privacy 2, 49−55.

Kleinbekman, I.C., Mitici, M.A., Wei, P., September, 2018. eVTOL arrival sequencing and scheduling for on-demand urban air mobility. In: AIAA/IEEE Digital Avionics Systems Conference - Proceedings, 2018.

Kohlman, L.W., Patterson, M.D., 2018. System-level urban air mobility transportation modeling and determination of energy-related constraints. In: 2018 Aviation Technology, Integration, and Operations Conference, p. 3677.

KPMG, 2013. Self-Driving Cars: Are We Ready? Retrieved from. https://home.kpmg/content/dam/kpmg/pdf/2013/10/self-driving-cars-are-we-ready.pdf/.

Krueger, R., Rashidi, T.H., Rose, J.M., 2016. Preferences for shared autonomous vehicles. Transportation Research Part C: Emerging Technologies 69, 343−355.

Kyriakidis, M., Happee, R., De Winter, J.C., 2015. Public opinion on automated driving: results of an international questionnaire among 5000 respondents. Transportation Research Part F: Traffic Psychology and Behaviour 32, 127−140.

Levinson, D.M., Kumar, A., 1997. Density and the journey to work. Growth and Change 28 (2), 147−172.

Lineberger, R., Hussain, A., Mehra, S., Pankratz, D., 2018. Passenger Drones and Flying Cars. Retrieved from. https://www2.deloitte.com/insights/us/en/focus/future-of-mobility/passenger-drones-flying-cars.html/.

Liu, Y., Kreimeier, M., Stumpf, E., Zhou, Y., Liu, H., May 2017. Overview of recent endeavors on personal aerial vehicles: a focus on the US and Europe led research activities. Progress in Aerospace Sciences 91, 53—66.

Maurer, M., Gerdes, J.C., Lenz, B., Winner, H., 2015. Autonomes Fahren: Technische, Rechtliche Und Gesellschaftliche Aspekte. Springer.

Milakis, D., van Arem, B., van Wee, B., 2017. Policy and society related implications of automated driving: a review of literature and directions for future research. Journal of Intelligent Transportation Systems 21 (4), 324—348.

Moore, M.D., Goodrich, K.H., 2013. High speed mobility through on-demand aviation. In: 2013 Aviation Technology, Integration, and Operations Conference, p. 4373.

Moreno, A.T., 2017. Autonomous Vehicles: Implications on an Integrated Landuse and Transport Modelling Suite, pp. 10—13.

Otte, T., Metzner, N., Lipp, J., Schwienhorst, M.S., Solvay, A.F., Meisen, T., September 2018. User-centered integration of automated air mobility into urban transportation networks. In: 2018 IEEE/AIAA 37th Digital Avionics Systems Conference (DASC). IEEE, pp. 1—10.

Parker, R.A., 2017. NASA Strategic Framework for On-Demand Air Mobility A Report for NASA Headquarters.

Reddy, L., DeLaurentis, D.A., 06 2016. Multivariate probit models and qualitative analysis of survey on public and stakeholder perception of unmanned aircraft. In: 16th AIAA Aviation Technology, Integration, and Operations Conference.

Rodrigue, J.-P., Comtois, C., Slack, B., 2017. The Geography of Transport Systems, fourth ed. Routledge.

Rothfeld, R., Balac, M., Ploetner, K.O., Antoniou, C., 2018. Initial analysis of urban air mobility's transport performance in sioux falls. In: 2018 Aviation Technology, Integration, and Operations Conference, p. 2886.

Rothfeld, R., Balac, M., Ploetner, K.O., Antoniou, C., 2018. Agent-based simulation of urban air mobility. In: 2018 Modeling and Simulation Technologies Conference, p. 3891.

Schoettle, B., Sivak, M., 2014. A survey of public opinion about connected vehicles in the U.S., the U.K., and Australia. In: 2014 International Conference on Connected Vehicles and Expo, ICCVE 2014 - Proceedings, No. July, pp. 687—692.

Schuchardt, B.I., Lehmann, P., Nieuwenhuizen, F., Perfect, P., 2015. Final List of Desirable Features/Options for the PAV and Supporting Systems.

Shamiyeh, M., Bijewitz, J., Hornung, M., 2017. A review of recent personal air vehicle concepts. In: Aerospace 6th CEAS Conference. Council of European Aerospace Societies, Bucharest, pp. 1—16 no. 913.

Smith, J.C., Viken, J.K., Guerreiro, N.M., Dollyhigh, S.M., Fenbert, J.W., Hartman, C.L., Kwa, T.-S., Moore, M.D., 2012. Projected demand and potential impacts to the national airspace system of autonomous, electric, on-demand small aircraft. In: 12th AIAA Aviation Technology, Integration, and Operations (ATIO) Conference and 14th AIAA/ISSM, vol. 5595. AIAA.

Squires, G.D., 2002. Urban Sprawl: Causes, Consequences, & Policy Responses. The Urban Institute.

Straubinger, A., Rothfeld, R., 2018. Identification of relevant aspects for personal air transport system integration in urban mobility modelling. In: Proceedings of 7th Transport Research Arena TRA 2018, (Vienna).

Straubinger, A., Verhoef, E.T., 2018. (Working Paper) Options for a Welfare Analysis of Urban Air Mobility (Hong Kong).

Syed, N., 2017. On Demand Mobility Commuter Aircraft Demand Estimation. Master Thesis. Faculty of the Virginia Polytechnic Institute and State University.

Thakur, P., Kinghorn, R., Grace, R., 2016. Urban form and function in the autonomous era. In: Australasian Transport Research Forum 2016 Proceedings.

Thompson, M., 2018. Panel: perspectives on prospective markets. In: Proceedings of the 5th Annual AHS Transformative VTOL Workshop, San Francisco, CA.

Travel forecasting resource, 2014. Benefits of Activity Based Models. http://tfresource.org/Benefits_of_Activity_Based_Models.

Travel forecasting resource, 2018. Autonomous Vehicles: Modeling Frameworks. http://tfresource.org/Autonomous_vehicles: _Modeling_frameworks.

UBER, Oct. 2016. Fast-Forwarding to a Future of On-Demand Urban Air Transportation.

Vascik, P., 2019. Development of vertiport capacity envelopes and analysis of their sensitivity to topological and operational factors. In: AIAA Scitech 2019 Forum, (San Diego, California, United States).

Vascik, P.D., Hansman, R.J., June 2017. Constraint Identification in On-Demand Mobility for Aviation through an Exploratory Case Study of Los Angeles. MIT International Center for Air Transportation (ICAT).

Vascik, P.D., Hansman, R.J., 2017. Evaluation of Key Operational Constraints Affecting On-Demand Mobility for Aviation in the Los Angeles Basin: Ground Infrastructure, Air Traffic Control and Noise, pp. 1–20.

Vredin Johansson, M., Heldt, T., Johansson, P., 2006. The effects of attitudes and personality traits on mode choice. Transportation Research Part A: Policy and Practice 40 (6), 507–525.

Vrtic, M., Schuessler, N., Erath, A., Axhausen, K.W., 2009. The impacts of road pricing on route and mode choice behaviour. Journal of Choice Modelling 3 (1), 109–126.

Wardman, M., Chintakayala, P., May 2012. European wide meta-analysis of values of travel time. Final Report.

Weiß, H.-J., 2003. Die Doppelrolle der Kommunen im ÖPNV. Tech. Rep. Diskussionsbeitr äge// Institut für Verkehrswissenschaft und Regionalpolitik.

Winter, K., Oded, C., Martens, K., van Arem, B., 2017. "Stated choice experiment on mode choice in an era of free-floating carsharing and shared autonomous vehicles: raw data. In: Transportation Research Board, 96th Annual Meeting, vol. 1, pp. 1–17.

Wölfel, P., 2019. An Analysis for an Imminent Implementation of Urban Air Mobility in Germany. Seminar paper. WHU - Otto Beisheim School of Management, Vallendar.

Yedavalli, P., Mooberry, J., 2019. An Assessment of Public Perception of Urban Air Mobility (UAM). Retrieved from. https://www.airbus.com/newsroom/news/en/2019/02/urban-air-mobility-on-the-path-to-public-acceptance.html.

Zmud, J., Sener, I.N., Wagner, J., 2016. Consumer Acceptance and Travel Behavior Impacts of Automated Vehicles Final Report PRC 15-49 F, p. 65.

Part E

Outlook

Chapter 14

Conclusions

Constantinos Antoniou[1], Emmanouil Chaniotakis[2], Dimitrios Efthymiou[1]

[1]*Chair of Transportation Systems Engineering, Department of Civil, Geo and Environmental Engineering, Technical University of Munich, Munich, Germany;* [2]*Bartlett School of Environment, Energy and Resources, University College London (UCL), London, United Kingdom*

A key premise of this book is that mobility is a very active field that keeps changing at a very fast pace. Thus, the primary focus of this book has been placed on the necessary actions that should be taken to transform mobility planning toward agile planning for rapid innovation reality and increased data availability.

To achieve this, efforts have been directed toward the compilation of a number of contributions from researchers of high caliper and relevance in the field. The objective is to provide a reference that will be useful to researchers, policymakers, and practitioners active in the field of human mobility, also when the exact parameters of the prevailing modes evolve. The various contributions have been directed toward first establishing the ground with a critical review of relevant pertinent literature, followed by the exploration of methods that guide expected future work. These have been presented with the use of examples and real data to illustrate their capabilities. The final part of this book includes the presentation of various case studies on the exploration of demand for emerging transportation systems.

Naturally, there have been aspects related to emerging transportation concepts that have been left out. We have tried to resist the temptation to focus on buzzwords and modes of uncertain longevity that currently seem to receive a lot of attention (such as e-scooters). What we chose to do was to provide the background on the examination of such concepts based on established emerging systems. We also refrained from including solely methodological chapters, aiming at conveying knowledge through applications.

This book aims to advance the discussion on the factors that affect the way that humans engage with well-established and emerging mobility services.

Modern consumers make modal choices based on cost, time, service quality, and other attributes contributing to Mobility on Demand (MOD) and Mobility as a Service (MaaS) growth. An overview of MOD and MaaS

Demand for Emerging Transportation Systems. **https://doi.org/10.1016/B978-0-12-815018-4.00014-0**

mobility concepts is presented (see Chapter 3). MOD services are bikesharing, carsharing, microtransit, ridesharing, Transportation Network Companies (TNCs), scootersharing, shuttle services, UAM, public transportation, and app-based delivery services. Although closely related to MaaS, MOD encompasses human and goods transportation, while MaaS constitutes mobility service aggregation into a pricing package. In this mobility environment, public transportation agencies are increasingly being challenged with opportunities to establish partnerships with private-sector mobility providers.

The implications of vehicle automation on the accessibility of vulnerable social groups and their transport-related social exclusion are presented (see Chapter 4). On the one hand, the positive implications for accessibility increase with the level of automation; on the other hand, the requirement for digital access and payment could compromise the potential gains on social inclusion.

Conventional and emerging transportation data sources are classified based on the component of the transportation system that they represent and their orientation into space (e.g., maps, environmental data, POIs), network (e.g., stationary traffic, travel times), concept (e.g., carsharing, bikesharing, AVs, ridehailing), and user (e.g., attitudes, user traces, preferences). An overview of the data quality criteria is presented, consolidating the definitions for completeness, consistency, accuracy, timeliness, accessibility, and interpretability (see Chapter 5).

The benefits of the advances in urban mobility sensing technologies are presented (see Chapter 7). As it allows the collection of individual traveler traces at a large scale and over extended periods of time, individual mobility has become an emerging field for extracting patterns that describe spatio-temporal individual movements.

The adoption of car- and bikesharing depends on local cultural and operational characteristics of the areas they cover, demographic, environmental, and economic factors, and the current travel patterns of potential future users. Policymakers and public transport operators, who plan strategically the end-to-end passenger journey, should consider vehicle-sharing systems both as competitors and collaborators of public transportation (see Chapter 6). The most important exogenous factors that affect the launch and demand of vehicle-sharing systems are population density, age, household size, education level, proximity to public transport stations, land-use, distance to the central business district (CBD), distance to services, number of businesses near the stations, and vehicle availability (see Chapter 10). The acceptance of shared autonomous vehicles mainly depends on punctuality of pickup at the origin and arrival at the destination.

The promotion of public transport remains a major challenge for cities and metropolitan areas. Transportation researchers and scientists have extensively analyzed the role of public transport using diverse analytical methods, aiming at the deeper understanding of how public transport can hold a leading position in urban transportation. Public transport maintains and can extend its competitive advantage against private car in terms of vehicles speed, accessibility to infrastructures for mobility impaired persons, regularity, transfer coordination, and many others (see Chapter 9).

Free-floating carsharing systems are mainly established is large urban areas, while in small urban and rural areas, where car ownership is higher and the impact from emissions is equally significant, such systems are absent. The long-term perspective of shared autonomous vehicles is expected to substantially change human mobility behaviors (see Chapter 11). Strategic planning of transportation systems, based on shared autonomous vehicles, is coming with new modeling requirements (see Chapter 8). Solutions are proposed to deal with these issues.

A Smart Mobility methodological approach based on prediction, optimization, and personalization is presented. These three features are integrated in a way that predictions of real-time data are being used for the optimization of policies. When the attributes of the alternatives reflect the real-time conditions, the optimization of the policies can be personalized (see Chapter 12).

Finally, an overview of urban air mobility (UAM) is presented. Initial research aiming to identify the main factors of passenger acceptance and potential passengers' value of time is outlined. Furthermore, first UAM modeling approaches are presented, along with potential spatial and welfare effects of UAM implementations (see Chapter 13).

References

[1] Atasoy, Bilge, Lima de Azevedo, Carlos, Akkinepally, Arun Prakash, Seshadri, Ravi, Zhao, Fang, Abou-Zeid, Maya, Ben-Akiva, Moshe, 2020. Smart mobility via prediction, optimization and personalization. In: Constantinos Antoniou, Dimitrios Efthymiou, and Emmanouil Chaniotakis. Demand for Emerging Transportation Systems: Modeling Adoption, Satisfaction, and Mobility Patterns. Elsevier.

[2] Chaniotakis, Emmanouil, Efthymiou, Dimitrios, Antoniou, Constantinos, 2020. Data Aspects of the Evaluation of Demand for Emerging Transportation Systems. In: Constantinos Antoniou, Dimitrios Efthymiou, and Emmanouil Chaniotakis. Demand for Emerging Transportation Systems: Modeling Adoption, Satisfaction, and Mobility Patterns. Elsevier.

[3] Ciari, Francesco, Janzen, Maxim, Ziemlicki, Cezary, 2020. Planning shared automated fleets: Specific modeling requirements and concepts to address them. In: Constantinos Antoniou, Dimitrios Efthymiou, and Emmanouil Chaniotakis. Demand for Emerging Transportation Systems: Modeling Adoption, Satisfaction, and Mobility Patterns. Elsevier.

[4] Efthymiou, Dimitris, Chaniotakis, Emmanouil, Antoniou, Constantinos, 2020. Factors Affecting the Adoption of Vehicle Sharing Systems. In: Constantinos Antoniou, Dimitrios Efthymiou, and Emmanouil Chaniotakis. Demand for Emerging Transportation Systems: Modeling Adoption, Satisfaction, and Mobility Patterns. Elsevier.

[5] Milakis, Dimitris, Bert van Wee, 2020. Implications of vehicle automation for accessibility and social inclusion of people on low income, people with physical and sensory disabilities and older people. In: Constantinos Antoniou, Dimitrios Efthymiou, and Emmanouil Chaniotakis. Demand for Emerging Transportation Systems: Modeling Adoption, Satisfaction, and Mobility Patterns. Elsevier.

[6] Rothfeld, Raoul, Anna, Straubinger, Fu, Mengying, Al Haddad, Christelle, Antoniou, Constantinos, 2020. Factors Affecting Emerging Transportation Systems: Modelling Adoption, Satisfaction and Mobility Patterns. In: Constantinos Antoniou, Dimitrios Efthymiou, and Emmanouil Chaniotakis. Demand for Emerging Transportation Systems: Modeling Adoption, Satisfaction, and Mobility Patterns. Elsevier.

[7] Schmöller, Stefan, Bogenberger, Klaus, 2020. Carsharing — an overview on what we know. In: Constantinos Antoniou, Dimitrios Efthymiou, and Emmanouil Chaniotakis. Demand for Emerging Transportation Systems: Modeling Adoption, Satisfaction, and Mobility Patterns. Elsevier.

[8] Shaheen, Susan, Cohen, Adam, 2020. Mobility on Demand (MOD) and Mobility as a Service (MaaS): Early Understanding of Shared Mobility Impacts and Public Transit Partnerships. In: Constantinos Antoniou, Dimitrios Efthymiou, and Emmanouil Chaniotakis. Demand for Emerging Transportation Systems: Modeling Adoption, Satisfaction, and Mobility Patterns. Elsevier.

[9] Nakamura, Toshiyuki, Uno, Nobuhiro, Kuwahara, Masahiro, Yoshioka, Akira, Nishigaki, Tomoki, Schmöcker1, Jan-Dirk, 2020. Location Planning for One-way Carsharing Systems Considering Accessibility Improvements: The Case of Super-Compact Electric Cars. In: Constantinos Antoniou, Dimitrios Efthymiou, and Emmanouil Chaniotakis. Demand for Emerging Transportation Systems: Modeling Adoption, Satisfaction, and Mobility Patterns. Elsevier.

[10] Tyrinopoulos, Yannis, 2020. Public Transport. In: Constantinos Antoniou, Dimitrios Efthymiou, and Emmanouil Chaniotakis. Demand for Emerging Transportation Systems: Modeling Adoption, Satisfaction, and Mobility Patterns. Elsevier.

[11] Zhao, Zhan, Koutsopoulos, Haris N., Zhao, Jinhua, 2020. Uncovering Spatiotemporal Structures from Transit Smart Card Data for Individual Mobility Modeling. In: Constantinos Antoniou, Dimitrios Efthymiou, and Emmanouil Chaniotakis. Demand for Emerging Transportation Systems: Modeling Adoption, Satisfaction, and Mobility Patterns. Elsevier.

Index

Printed in the United States
By Bookmasters